# Dear Munificent Friends

Henry James's Letters to Four Women

*Edited by Susan E. Gunter*

Ann Arbor

THE UNIVERSITY OF MICHIGAN PRESS

2002   2001   2000   1999      4   3   2   1

*A CIP catalog record for this book is available from the British Library.*

Library of Congress Cataloging-in-Publication Data

James, Henry, 1843–1916.
    Dear munificent friends : Henry James's letters to four women /
edited by Susan E. Gunter.
        p.      cm.
    Includes bibliographical references and index.
    ISBN 0-472-11010-1 (cloth : alk. paper)
    1. James, Henry, 1843–1916 Correspondence.   2. Authors,
American—19th century Correspondence.   3. Authors, American—20th
century Correspondence.   4. James, Alice Howe Gibbens
Correspondence.   5. Jones, Mary Cadwalader Correspondence.
6. Prothero, Margaret Frances Correspondence.   7. Wolseley, Louisa,
Viscountess, 1843–1920 Correspondence.   I. Gunter, Susan E., 1947–  .
II. Title.
PS2123.A4   1999
813'.4—dc21
[B]                                                                          99-29474
                                                                                  CIP

Page i: Sample from a letter from Henry James to Alice Howe
Gibbens James, Houghton bMS Am 1094 (1649). (Courtesy of the
Houghton Library, Harvard University, and Bay James.)

*To the memory of*
*Esther Anna Ropp Dowling*
*(1918–1982)*

# *Contents*

# *Preface*

When invited to speak to a group of Western romance novelists on the topic of "setting the scene" a few years ago, I agreed. I know little about romance novels, but I couldn't refuse my good friend, Jean Case, herself an accomplished writer. The romancers turned out to be congenial and versatile, most of them ardent researchers and serious writers. I had a pleasant time, and thanks to Jean, I stumbled onto a literary find. I told Jean that I had written a dissertation on Henry James, and she remembered that her former English professor at South Dakota State, Jeannette Kenyon, knew a woman, Emma Warner, who owned letters James had written to her great-grandmother. Shortly thereafter, thanks to the wisdom of Westminster College's academic vice president, Steve Baar, I was flying over the snow-capped Wasatch Mountains east of Salt Lake City, Utah, on my way to Omaha, Nebraska. The next day at eleven P.M. I stood over a Xerox machine on the upper floor of the Omaha Opera House, copying twelve letters from Henry James to his friend, Boston socialite Sarah Train Winslow. I was eager to share these letters at the James sesquicentennial meeting the following spring in New York.

Twelve letters, that is, of the ten thousand or more James dispatched over a fifty-year span. I assumed that most of this important writer's letters had been published, so I knew that the literary world would be interested in this new material. But the next spring, when I read my paper to the James community, I learned that the Anglo-American writer had in fact written thousands and thousands of letters whose existence was known only to relatively few scholars. And of all those letters, only three thousand had been published, three thousand letters not always indicative of the man he was. In fact, the many wonderful letters written to his best friends, powerful women and younger men, are only sparsely represented in the published collections. These witty, erudite, and poetic records have remained for decades in Harvard's Houghton Library, in the Hove Library in

Sussex, England, and in over a hundred other repositories around the world. They hold the key to understanding Henry James the person because in them he wrote most freely.

Publication of the letters in this edition is by permission of the Houghton Library, Harvard University, and by permission of the Hove Reference Library, Sussex, England. I am grateful for the help of the staff at the Houghton Library (Leslie Morris, Melanie Wisner, Susan Halpert, and others), at Westminster College's Giovale Library (Dick Wunder, Oresta Esquibel, Tanya Stastny, David Hales, Hilde Benham, and Diane Raines), and at Radcliffe College's Arthur Schlesinger History of Women Library. Zoë Lubowiecka at the Hove Reference Library checked my transcripts of the Wolseley letters and was an invaluable help, both in establishing authoritative texts and in annotating the letters.

I have many individuals to thank for helping make this edition possible. First, my unending gratitude goes to Professor Steven Jobe of Hanover College, Indiana, for allowing me to help him with his "Calendar of Henry James's Correspondence." For years Professor Jobe has worked diligently to catalog the extant letters, which are scattered in over 130 libraries, archives, and private collections around the world. Using a draft of his work, I was able to locate the letters included here. His meticulously assembled "Calendar" will spawn important projects in both British and American studies for decades to come.

Sheldon M. Novick, author of *Henry James: The Young Master* (New York: Random House, 1996), shared his substantial knowledge of James and the James papers with me; my conversations and correspondence with him shaped this edition. He provided constant encouragement and excellent advice. His unique conception of James will affect the next generation of scholars. Conversations with David Lehman, acclaimed poet and public intellectual, at Cambridge in 1994 gave me the initial idea for two editions of James letters: this volume and the subsequent one, *Dearly Beloved Friends: Henry James's Letters to Younger Men.* He patiently worked through the text's format with me and later provided invaluable advice as I revised my introduction.

Robert Gale, Professor Emeritus at the University of Pittsburgh, critiqued my introduction and generously shared with me his encyclopedic knowledge of James's world. R. A. Sheehan, Ph.D., of the Boston Athenaeum, gave me invaluable information about the James family as well as a whirlwind tour of Jamesian landmarks in the Boston area. I am also indebted to the enormous contributions Adeline Tintner and the late Leon

Edel have made to James studies. While they bear no responsibility for either the success or failure of this edition, their work has informed mine.

Generous grants from the Gore Fund at Westminster College of Salt Lake City, endowed by Genevieve Gore and Ginger Gore Giovale, supported my work. In an age of declining public commitment, their support of private colleges deserves recognition. Thanks to Westminster College for awarding me merit leave to complete this project. Dr. Stephen Baar, Academic Vice President, and Dr. Ray Ownbey, Dean of Arts and Sciences, consistently supported my efforts.

Elizabeth Archuleta, Nicole Carrera, Jennifer McLing, Natalie Martinez, and Cory Updyke, my able research assistants, patiently searched for obscure people and facts and gave me ideas that enriched my work. John Kimmey, Professor of English at the University of South Carolina, first introduced me to James's texts. He is a master teacher and a superb scholar. Michael Anesko, of the Pennsylvania State University, helped me transcribe several difficult phrases. His edition of the James-Howells letters sets standards in editing for decades to come. Daniel Fogel accepted my paper on the letters to Sarah Train Winslow to read at the N.Y.U. James Sesquicentennial Conference in 1993, thus allowing me to meet other James scholars.

Thanks go to those who critiqued drafts of the introduction, giving me invaluable advice: Millicent Bell, Susan Cottler, Cheryl Fox, Susan Gardner, Ray Ownbey, and R. A. Sheehan. Professor Steve Haslam, of Westminster's French department, along with Paula Collmar, provided translations of James's French phrases. Millicent Bell's fine scholarship on James and Edith Wharton helped me establish an overall context for the section on Mary Cadwalader Jones. The Eliot House at Harvard University kindly provided accommodations for me in the F. O. Matthiessen Room during my visits to Cambridge. Elizabeth Kaplan and Marissa Walsh of the Ellen Levine Agency encouraged me when I feared this edition would never see print.

I thank LeAnn Fields, Shelly Emmett, Alja Kooistra, Richard Isomaki, Mary Meade, and the entire publishing team at the University of Michigan Press, who deserve praise for their hard work and expertise in publishing this manuscript. The late Alexander R. James, former executor of the James papers, and the new executor, Bay James, granted me permission for this edition. She graciously shared her knowledge of the James family with me and granted permission for me to use quotes in introductory material. I appreciate her support and friendship, as well as her dedication to preserving the James family papers for future family members. Rayburn and Margaret Moore generously provided helpful information on editing James letters and on identifying various correspondents. I am grateful for their support.

Finally, I want to thank my family, Bill, Colin, Ben, and Dan Gunter, who encouraged me during all the months I spent preparing this edition. They even read parts of the book.

# Editor's Note

The text for this edition is based on the original holographs and typescripts (in instances when James dictated a letter to a scribe). All the letters to Alice H. G. James, Mary Cadwalader Jones, and Margaret Frances Prothero are housed in the Houghton Library and are quoted by permission of the Houghton Library, Harvard University; those to Lady Louisa Wolseley are in the Hove Reference Library, Sussex, England, and are quoted by permission of the Hove Library. At the end of each letter I have placed the Houghton or Hove catalog number, for scholars who wish to consult the original texts. Letters are arranged chronologically within each of the four sections, to help readers see the unfolding of James's complex relationships. Two undated letters to Lady Wolseley are placed approximately when they must have been written, given the letters' context, so that they fit with the overall narrative flow of the correspondence. Steve Jobe's "Calendar of Henry James's Correspondence" provided cross-checking on ambiguous dates, in instances where letters were dated by librarians, William James, or people other than James himself. In these cases I have placed the dates within brackets.

Before selecting the letters for this edition, I transcribed all extant letters to the four women and then chose those that seemed most indicative of his overall relationships with them. Some themes are repeated from one section to the next, but in general his relationship with each woman was different, and my selection reflects those differences. I hope that this edition will be accessible to general readers, as well as useful to scholars. The brief headnotes that precede each letter are not meant as abstracts or annotations, but rather as guides to each letter's tone and as invitations to the reader. I have provided notes to names and facts as aids to understanding James's complex world. While the letters speak for themselves, an understanding of their context will make them more comprehensible. I have identified personal names whenever possible, but since most of his letters have not been published, I could not always establish a context for names and relationships. If my annotations occasionally differ from those in previous collections of James letters, it is because work on my nearly completed "Biographical Register of Henry James's Correspondents" (based on Steven Jobe's "Calendar") has yielded new information not yet assimilated in James studies. Further work will inevitably correct mine, but I hope that my present notes will aid scholars who prepare subsequent editions. Eventually, through the hard work and commitment of Greg Zacharias and Pierre Walker, we will have available a complete, definitive edition of James letters, a project long awaited and sorely needed.

My transcriptions aim to preserve the original flavor of James's correspondence as closely as possible. His letters, while informal modes of discourse that sometimes ignore conventional rules, have their own internal coherence and logic. During my multiple checkings of transcripts against originals, I learned that if mistakes in flow and syntax had been made, they were mine. James had such an incredible vocabulary, original style, and sense of rhythm that his letters approach the condition of lengthy narrative poems. He used dashes, underlinings, double underlinings, parentheses, commas, and exclamation points to achieve an unparalleled sense of immediacy. Scholars who wish to reproduce these letters should in all cases consult the holographs, as no single editor can guarantee complete accuracy when the texts themselves are so informal.

I kept James's punctuation as closely as possible. Reading holographs of his letters (I read many more than are included in this edition) helped me gain a sense of his practices, but sometimes it is difficult to ascertain, for example, whether a comma is within or without quotation marks. Attempting to preserve his own internal logic, I followed his typical practices, which were themselves sometimes erratic. He frequently used a period at the end of a salutation rather than a comma. He also often put a period after his name in the final closing. He sometimes used a colon between the month and day, and the day and year (e.g., Dec: 27: 1909), particularly when he placed the date at the end of a letter. Periods frequently follow various parts of a letter's provenance. Some Lamb House stationery, for example, has commas after *Lamb House* and *Rye,* and then a period after *Sussex,* while other Lamb House stationery has no punctuation marks whatsoever. I have rendered all commas and periods within provenances, salutations, and closings as he did, although I did not include the telephone numbers that appeared on stationery toward the end of his life. He usually placed short dashes within sentences (which I have indicated by using an em dash) and longer dashes between sentences (which I have rather arbitrarily rendered by using a two-em dash), marks of punctuation that again give rhythm and urgency to his prose. Sometimes James used a long line of dashes between sentences that seemed to indicate a pause in his train of thought, and I have kept this usage. Infrequently James used a double hyphen within a word rather than a single hyphen and I have retained them. Occasionally I could not tell whether he had used a colon or a semicolon, but I again tried to follow his own habits. James sprinkled his sentences with commas, in part as a way of adding rhythm. He usually placed them within parenthetical expressions, so I have followed suit.

I have italicized all words that James underlined. I do not indicate the number of underlinings beneath a word or phrase, due to my own typographical constraints. Foreign phrases are italicized only if James underlined them; translations of those phrases are provided in brackets directly after the phrase. James occasionally capitalized words other than proper names within sentences, and I have retained those capitals. If I was not sure whether or not he intended a word to be capitalized (*c*s, for example, are hard to differentiate from *C*s), I followed today's standard American usage. Very often he used an ampersand rather than writing out the word *and*. I have also honored this practice. (In dictated letters, the word *and* appears.) I have kept his abbreviations, including his use of "&c" for *etc.* I have retained his own spelling in his holographs in all instances.

While James had too many idiosyncratic writing habits to name them all, I might also note that he seldom used paragraphs. His letters were one long note; perhaps paragraphing distracted him from rapidly recording his ideas. Occasionally I was not able to decipher a word, and in these cases, I placed the word or words within angled brackets, with a question mark following the word. In a few other instances, when he dictated letters to one of his scribes, I have corrected what must surely be the scribe's errors. For example, a word that appears in the dictated holograph as "Continong" is transcribed as "Continent." James's distinctive handwriting is usually readable, given time, but often he ended letters by turning them sideways and writing along the left and upper margins. In such cases it is difficult to transcribe those words and punctuation marks that are written over other words. In a few places I have inserted a word that seems necessary given the context, using brackets to show my editorial emendation. ("H. J. wants me [to] spend this May with him in Venice.")

I have regularized the placement of letter headings (including provenance and date), as well as the placement of James's final signature, primarily as an aid to typesetting this manuscript. A letterhead imprinted on James's stationery, hotel stationery, and the like, is designated in print by use of small capitals. I have placed dates and/or provenances within brackets in cases where this information has been provided by sources other than James's own handwriting.

# Biographical Register

**Walter Van Rensselaer Berry
(1859–1927)**

Lawyer and diplomat with many important friends, including James and Edith Wharton. He and Wharton first met and flirted in 1883; they renewed their friendship fourteen years later.

**John Lambert Cadwalader**

Lawyer and Princeton graduate, son of a former assistant secretary of state. He was Mary Cadwalader Jones's cousin, and she and her daughter Beatrix went with him each August to Scotland, where he had a hunting camp, to act as his hostesses.

**Beatrix Jones Farrand
(1872–1959)**

Daughter of Mary Cadwalader Jones, she became a famous landscape gardener. At age eleven she helped lay out the grounds of Reef Point, her parents' home in Bar Harbor. She studied with Professor Charles Sargent and his wife in Brookline, Massachusetts, and later designed Dumbarton Oaks outside of Washington, D.C. In 1913 she married Max Farrand, head of Yale's history department.

**Julia Constance Fletcher
(1858–1938)**

Minor American writer and playwright who lived in Venice with her mother and stepfather, Eugene Benson. She was friends with both Fanny Prothero and James and visited them in Rye. James frequently satirized her in his letters to Fanny.

**Ellen Temple Emmet Hunter
(1850–1920)**

Elly Hunter was James's first cousin and the sister of HJ's beloved Minny Temple. She first married Christopher Emmet; after his death in 1884 she married George Hunter. She lived in England when James

**Mary Smyth Hunter**
(1857–1933)

was at Lamb House in Rye. He saw her frequently, often expressing exasperation at her behavior.

Socialite and friend of James, Edith Wharton, and many other writers and artists. She had an estate at Essex just north of London and entertained her friends there.

**Alexander Robertson James**
(1890–1946)

The fourth son and last child of William and Alice James, "Aleck" had trouble deciding on an occupation. He visited James, who at one point thought his nephew should attend Harvard. Alex became an artist instead.

**Alice James**
(1848–92)

Henry James's sister. Suffering from varied illnesses throughout her life, she belonged to the Boston "Bee" and taught in Miss Ticknor's Society to Encourage Studies at Home, a women's correspondence school. She died in England in 1892, with James at her bedside. Katherine Loring had *The Diary of Alice James* privately printed in 1894.

**Alice Howe Gibbens James**
(1849–1922)

Wife of William James and dear friend to Henry James. She was a teacher as a young woman; she and William James had five children. James spent time in America with her and her children after William's death in 1910, and Alice came to England to be with him in his last weeks and months. James wrote her at least 142 letters, from 1878 to 1915.

**Alice Runnells James**
(d. 1957)

Wife of James's nephew William James III and daughter of an affluent railroad family. Both James and his sister-in-law Alice thought her a fine young woman. She suffered from various illnesses throughout her life.

**Caroline (Carrie) Cary James**
(1851–1931)

Wife of Garth Wilkinson James, Henry James's younger brother. James deplored her "imbecility."

**Garth Wilkinson James**
(1845–83)

Younger brother of Henry James. He was wounded in the Civil War and suffered from rheumatism from those wounds later. He also had kidney disease, which affected

| | |
|---|---|
| | his heart, and he died at the age of thirty-eight. |
| Henry (Harry) James III (1879–1947) | Oldest son of Alice and William James. He was first a lawyer and then director for the Rockefeller Institute for Medical Research. He visited James in England fairly often and through his mother later inherited Lamb House. |
| Mary Lucinda Holton James (1847–1922) | She was the wife of Robertson James, Henry's youngest brother, and was from Prairie du Chien, Wisconsin. James sympathized with the trials she endured from Bob James's drinking, philandering, and quarreling. |
| Margaret Mary (Peggy) James (1887–1950) | Daughter of Alice and William James. In 1899 they sent her to school in England, where she stayed with the Clarke family and became friends with her uncle Henry. As a young woman she suffered from depression, much like her aunt, Alice James. After James's death she married Bruce Porter, twenty-two years her senior. |
| Robertson (Bob, Rob) James (1846–1910) | Youngest brother of Henry James. He served in the Civil War, worked for the railroad and the newspaper, and wrote occasionally. He became an alcoholic and separated from his wife and children, later living in a sanitorium. |
| William James (1842–1910) | Older brother of Henry James and renowned psychologist and philosopher. For years he taught at Harvard and wrote numerous articles and books. He often criticized James's fiction for its length and ambiguity, while James in turn satirized his brother's achievements and seriousness in letters to William's wife Alice. Both brothers, though, remained close until William's death, which led to a spell of depression for Henry. |
| William (Billy) James III (1882–1961) | Second son of Alice and William James. He studied and taught painting, and then was with the United States Air Service for years. |

Mary (Minnie) Cadwalader Rawle Jones (1850–1935)

Socialite and wife of Frederic Rhinelander Jones (Edith Wharton's brother). James stayed with her in New York on visits to America, and she in turn saw him in England. He wrote her many letters.

Sir George Walter Prothero (1848–1922)

Writer, editor, and professor. He was James's neighbor in Rye and sponsored him when he applied for his British citizenship in 1915.

Lady Margaret (Fanny) Prothero (1854–1934)

Wife of George Prothero and close friend to James. They gossiped together about Rye friends, and Mrs. Prothero helped him manage his household both in Rye and in London, dealing with finances and servants. He wrote over 150 letters to both Protheros, most of them to her.

Ellen Gertrude (Bay) Emmet Rand (1876–1941)

Daughter of James's cousin, Ellen Temple Hunter. An artist, she painted James's portrait at Lamb House in 1900. He was fond of her.

Edith Newbold Jones Wharton (1862–1937)

Well-known writer and close friend of James. They criticized one another's work and socialized both in America and abroad. In 1910 she unsuccessfully sponsored James for the Nobel Prize. James frequently expressed his concerns about Edith in his letters to Minnie Jones.

Edward Robbins (Teddy) Wharton (1850–1928)

Husband of Edith Wharton and Boston socialite. He suffered various ailments, most of them psychological, and the marriage was troubled. James feared disaster for the Whartons, who finally divorced in 1913.

Field Marshal Viscount Garnet Joseph Wolseley (1833–1913)

British military hero and writer who met James in 1877 in Warwickshire. James socialized frequently with the Wolseleys and called him a "charmer."

Lady Louisa Erskine Wolseley (1843–1920)

Wife of General Wolseley and close social friend of James's. He wrote her more than one hundred letters over three decades.

# Chronology

(1878), *French Poets and Novelists* (1878), *Confidence* (1879), *Haw-thorne* (1879), *Washington Square* (1880), and a new volume of stories. James's novella "Daisy Miller," appearing in *Cornhill Magazine*, tells the story of a young American girl whose innocence before jaded European society undoes her. It is his first commercial success. He writes to his future sister-in-law, Alice Howe Gibbens, to welcome her to the James family, a family he claims is "not without . . . its intrinsic resources."

1881 *Portrait of a Lady*, one of the great books of his career, appears first in serial form. Its heroine, Isabel Archer, embodies all the independent women James loved. Although she seems destined for failure, betrayed by that very independence and by the evil manipulations of others, James suggests that she will turn her ill fortune into an eventual triumph of will.

1881–83 James visits America twice, the first visit preceding his mother's death and the second just after his father's demise. During these trips he reacquaints himself with family and friends and collects material for subsequent fiction. He has no desire to return permanently to his native land. On the second trip he meets Mary Cadwalader Jones at a dinner in New York, and later that year visits her at Mount Desert Island in Maine.

1884–86 James begins his great comic realistic novel, *The Bostonians*. Satirizing doctrinaire feminists, journalists, and proper Bostonians alike, the novel receives mixed reviews. It concludes with the heroine's unhappy marriage to a conservative southerner. James writes *The Princess Casamassima*, a compelling tale of an artistic but poor London bookbinder, Hyacinth Robinson, who falls in love with the beautiful princess, a proud and fiery political revolutionary. Hyacinth's devotion to her leads him to a tragic end. In late 1884 sister Alice James moves to England with Katherine Loring; Alice and HJ are close friends until her death in 1892.

1889 James begins the next of his novels featuring brilliant heroines, this time selecting the worlds of theater, politics, and art as a setting. *The Tragic Muse* presents Miriam Rooth, a talented actress who must choose between romance and her beloved stage career.

1890 In an attempt to find a more lucrative form of writing, James begins to write plays, first adapting his early novel *The American* for the stage. While he never achieves success in the theater, the lessons he learns enrich his later work.

1892 Alice James, Henry's loved younger sister, dies of breast cancer in England. Her intimate friend and companion Katherine Loring helps James make the funeral arrangements.

1896 Abandoning the theater, James writes another novella, *The Spoils of Poynton*, which draws on both his empathy for some women and his

|         | fascination with the outward trappings of the wealthy English: their great estates and their complicated social relationships. |
|---------|---|
| 1897    | *What Maisie Knew,* another novella, also reveals James's extensive acquaintance with upper-class British society. Here he condemns that group for their amoral, self-centered lifestyles, as his young heroine Maisie must grow up alone amid a nasty tangle of parents and step-parents. |
| 1898    | James moves from London to rural Rye, where he leases (and later buys) Lamb House. Here he can write in peace as well as entertain friends and a series of loved younger men, including Hendrik Andersen, Morton Fullerton, Jocelyn Persse, Jonathan Sturges, Howard Sturgis, and Hugh Walpole. |
| 1900    | James makes an initial payment on Lamb House and writes *The Sacred Fount,* a satiric novel that draws heavily on the innumerable country weekends he spent observing British manners and morals. |
| 1902    | With the publication of *Wings of the Dove* James inaugurates his major phase, a brief but glorious period when he writes the greatest of his novels and tales. The novel's heroine, Milly Theale, eulogizes the many women he had loved and admired for almost half a century, as well as embodying his own passionate feelings for both men and women. |
| 1904    | *The Golden Bowl,* the last and one of the greatest of James's novels, appears first in America, followed by British publication early the next year. Maggie Verver surpasses even Milly Theale as a great dramatic heroine. Her courage and determination allow her to both salvage her marriage (broken like the golden bowl) and retain her own self-worth. |
| 1905    | After an absence of more than two decades, James revisits America and writes *The American Scene,* an incisive commentary on American commercial life. He lauds American women, who uphold his own cultural ideals despite their husbands' materialism. |
| 1906    | Back at Lamb House, James begins his extensive revisions of all his written work for a twenty-four-volume definitive edition, the New York Edition. Fanny Prothero, wife of important British academic Sir George Prothero, becomes a treasured friend and helps him cope with domestic life in a small town. |
| 1906–15 | James writes his autobiographies: *A Small Boy and Others* (1913), *Notes of a Son and Brother* (1914), and the unfinished *Middle Years* (1917). He continues his lifelong habit of letter writing. Letters, in fact, become his last artistic triumph, as he composes long and moving epistles to his myriad friends of both sexes. Plagued by depression and ill health, he burns most of the letters written to him in 1910, yet many of the letters he wrote survive to proclaim him one of the greatest correspondents in all history. |

1916      Alice Howe Gibbens James comes to Rye to nurse her beloved brother-in-law during his final illness. Just before his death, James receives the Order of Merit from King George V. After he dies, on February 28, Alice has him cremated and smuggles his ashes back to Cambridge for burial in the James family plot.

# Introduction

Henry James slowly and carefully climbed the four stone steps from the dark cobbled street.[1] He pulled a long metal key from his pocket and, opening the massive door, stepped into Lamb House's wide entrance hall. Long shadows from the brass octagonal lantern overhead radiated to all corners of the square room. He walked across the geometrically patterned red carpet and placed his gray felt hat near the Chinese bowl atop a perfectly polished mahogany table, chosen by his antiquing companion Lady Louisa Wolseley, then set his gold-headed cane inside the umbrella stand near the solid grandfather clock. As he stood glancing toward the stairs, it chimed eleven times, a deep melodious sound. He was at home.

Tonight had been a success, he mused. Fanny and Sir George Prothero had arrived at nearby Dial Cottage for the summer, the summer of 1906, and had held an intimate dinner party for him. The academic Sir Sydney Waterlow and his wife Alice, the socialites Dacre and Margaret Vincent, mystical Alice Dew-Smith, and the kindly Protheros had all listened to him as he slowly and deliberately described his revisions for the New York Edition of his writing. They appreciated him and his work, and he in turn welcomed such a genial audience. They knew him for the literary giant that he was, yet they also treasured him as friend and neighbor. James no longer needed to impress anyone: his very presence commanded attention, and all acknowledged his genius, both in rural Rye and in jaded fin de siècle London.

But now fatigue overtook him as he climbed the stairs with their white spindle railing to the Green Room. He sank into the stuffed velvet chair next to the marble fireplace, loosening his yellow-checked blue waistcoat and unbuttoning his green trouser band. He rubbed his hands slowly together as he stared into the flickering fire. The paneled walls around him bore tintypes and lithographs of dear friends and family: sister Alice; his brothers William, Robertson, and the long-departed Wilky; sister-in-law

Alice Howe Gibbens James; and the writers and dear friends who had nourished his life's work. He dozed, lulled by the fire's warmth and Fanny's rich food. His stomach bothered him a bit, even though he had slowly chewed each mouthful of food, as was his practice, and it grumbled in time to his low-keyed snoring.

The grandfather clock in the hall below struck midnight. Its deep tones wakened him, and he pulled himself up from the warm corner by the fire and walked to the desk on the near wall. Pulling the desk door down, he selected a pen from a cubbyhole. He removed his cuff links, shaped like miniature cannons, and pushed back his sleeves from his massive wrists. Then he slid a sheet of vellum paper, with the words LAMB HOUSE, RYE, SUSSEX embossed at the top, from a drawer on the lower left, and he began to write, hastily and almost illegibly. "Dear munificent friend," he saluted his first correspondent. By the time the clock chimed one, he had finished three letters.

> Dearest Mary C.
>
> Let this convey you Célimare's very eagerest, tenderest & most devoted welcome. He awaits you & greets you, & proposes to embrace you *here*—as nothing wd. have induced him not to. And oh how he hopes you will have arrived soothed (by a peaceful interlude;) rather than strained (by an agitated one.) At all events he so yearns for the sight & sound of you that he is going to turn up at a decent after dinner hour tonight just to see whether, fatigued though you may be, you can't stand 1/2 an hour of him. There is so much to tell & to be told! That will be about *9*, & I count the weary hours before. So you see I am more than ever your ownest old Célimare. (15 June 1912, Houghton bMS Am 1094 [805]²)

Imagine you have received a letter like the one above: you are a woman with few means, you are divorced from your husband (who happens to be Edith Wharton's brother), and you help support yourself and your daughter by working part of the year as a housekeeper for a demanding male cousin. Unlike thousands of other Edwardian women in similar circumstances, however, you have an emotional resource. That resource is a loving and solicitous friend who comforts you throughout all your troubles, and this letter is just one of the many warm, affectionate letters he has written you over the past three decades. That friend is Henry James. While some commentators on James's life and work have found him reticent, withdrawn, and almost asexual, these letters show him to be a vital, loving, and witty individual.

Mary Cadwalader Jones was just one of James's myriad friends. Along with younger men and a few treasured relatives, women indeed became his best friends. But most of James's wonderful letters to them have never been published. These letters have gathered dust for almost a century now, some in Harvard's Houghton Library, some in the Hove Reference Library near Brighton, England, and others scattered in more than 115 other archives around the world. While James wrote over ten thousand letters during his lifetime, only three thousand have been published. And those three thousand, while representative of the literary James, are not always representative of the man he was. James himself said of Rupert Brooke, in an introduction to an edition of Brooke's letters, "The chances and changes, the personal history of any absolute genius, draw us to watch his adventure with curiosity and inquiry, lead us on to win more of his secret and borrow more of his experience."[3] But James's own "secrets," such as they may be, cannot be fully won while so many primary documents remain unavailable.

James was born into an eccentric family, which may have allowed him to wander from the traditional Victorian male's path. His father, Henry James Sr., was an unorthodox religious thinker and writer, and his mother, Mary Robertson James, was a housewife who tolerated her husband's idiosyncrasies while raising five children. Henry Sr. was a nonconformist, a contentious man who advocated Swedenborgianism, communal living, and open sexual practices. Living on inherited funds, he devoted his life to promoting his radical ideas. He wanted his children to be independent, so he moved them from school to school and from country to country, always striving for the best way to educate them. His oldest son, William James, became one of America's foremost philosophers and first psychologists. His second son, Henry Jr., became one of our most eminent writers, while his only daughter, Alice, taught in a correspondence school for women and left a journal recording her remarkable thoughts.

James Jr. followed and then surpassed his father. Writing about provincial Americans encountering a sophisticated Europe, about young women who resisted social pressures to conform, about complex families, and about inherent human evil, he left an enormous body of work. He wrote short stories, novels, essays, biographies, autobiographies, reviews, literary criticism, travel guides, and obituaries. And he wrote letters, thousands of them. Starting at midnight, after a day filled with work and social activities, he usually wrote three to four letters a night.

Close to 450 of James's over 950 correspondents were women, many of them wives, daughters, or sisters of powerful men. James sensed what all primitive people knew: that women should be admired for their mysterious, life-giving powers. Because he intuitively understood this, he sought women out and befriended them. His friends, who claimed relatively little public recognition during their lives, may have seemed inconsequential, but James knew better.

All four of the correspondents in this edition were married to powerful men: Alice Howe Gibbens James to William James, one of America's greatest philosophers and psychologists; Mary Cadwalader Jones to Frederic Rhinelander Jones, wealthy New York socialite and Edith Wharton's brother; Margaret Frances Butcher Prothero to Sir George Prothero, Cambridge historian and head of the Royal Society of Literature; and Lady Louisa Wolseley to Viscount General Garnet Wolseley, commander in chief of Her Majesty's forces. These women shared their husband's influence; they too were powerful figures, directing events from the sidelines but directing them forcefully and decisively.

Like the chameleon he delighted in finding in his Lamb House garden, James could adapt to a wide variety of circumstances, changing colors at will. Thus, he became all things to these women: father, brother, bosom friend, and household familiar. He attended their social functions and advised them during family crises. He shopped, decorated, gossiped, and traveled with them. He nursed sister Alice through her final illness, with the help of her intimate companion Katherine Loring, and he became Alice Howe Gibbens James's surest emotional support when William James died in 1910. He championed many women writers, befriending sentimental novelists like Rhoda Broughton and Mary Elizabeth Braddon. What he learned from these women enriched his writing. In his own fictional texts, his most powerful and interesting characters are women. Isabel Archer in *Portrait of a Lady*, Fleda Vetch in *The Spoils of Poynton*, Milly Theale in *Wings of the Dove*, and Maggie Verver in *The Golden Bowl* are all heroic and independent, like the four women in this edition. Without his participation in his friends' daily lives, he might not have been able to portray his literary heroines so vividly.

James's own sexual preferences and his decision not to choose one lifelong partner perhaps freed him to indulge in warm friendships with the opposite sex. Unencumbered by the demands of marriage and child rearing, he freely participated in women's lives with no fear of draining entanglement. They in turn confided in him and relied on him during emotional crises. Given the nineteenth century's more rigid construction of gender, James's friendships with women allowed him to cross gender boundaries without endangering himself. Viewing their lives from a close but protected vantage point may have made him a voyeur, yet it also made him an astute chronicler of life. Thus, the letters collected in this volume exhibit a delightful picture of late Victorian and early Edwardian culture, including health cures (Fletcherizing—chewing one's food hundreds of times—and visiting health spas), social scandals (he feared that Teddy Wharton would destroy Edith), historical events (Queen Victoria's funeral, the Dreyfus trial, strikes, war policies, and wars), the difficulties of the marriage market (James maintained a bachelor's interest in the institution), childbearing and rearing (he satirically debated the right name for one of much-maligned brother William's children), domestic arrangements, and the weather.

The nineteenth and early twentieth centuries defined James's friends as wives, daughters, and sisters. In 1910 Cora Castle undertook a statistical study of eminent women in history on the basis of names appearing in any three out of six major European encyclopedias. She found 868 women, given all of human history on which to draw. Her list included queens, politicians (mostly French salon women of the 1600s), mothers, mistresses, beauties, religious women, women of tragic fate, and women important only through marriage.[4] While encyclopedias of his day may have ignored women, James did not. Instead, he valorized their lives in their private spheres, viewing his friends as powerful and interesting.

Those friends were of the upper middle or upper classes, and the social, intellectual, and cultural world they inhabited during the Victorian and Edwardian eras was a rich one, but a world in the process of cataclysmic change. James's friends were among the last women in history who could satisfactorily, and without guilt, claim their own rank from their husbands' position. Unashamed of their marital status and powerful figures in their own right, these women dominated both their families and a good deal of intercontinental society. They wielded power carefully, guiding events from secure positions. To call them "marginalized" negates their achievements. Although they may not have been physical presences in parliament, businesses, or universities, they were still significant players in their day. "Women's involvement in teaching, social work, and the shared family career makes utter nonsense of the idea that women's sphere was the private sphere and only men operated in public."[5] These women enjoyed companionate marriages, where their contributions were essential to the maintenance of their family's social position. To think of them as victims denies their humanity and their strength as individuals. In fact, their power extended far beyond the confines of their parlors. Twentieth-century marriages may be less egalitarian than earlier Victorian marriages, in a time when the boundaries between home and the business world were more fluid.

Just how did Victorian and Edwardian women alternate between public and private spheres almost seamlessly? While not surrendering the traditional power assigned to them by virtue of their gender, they used this prototypically feminine power to influence their world. One age-old source of their power was the marriage market: "Marriage was the most important social institution for the great majority of women in Victorian and Edwardian Britain."[6] Money was crucial in arranging marriages, and both partners brought as much capital to the marriage as the parents could or would provide.[7] Complex negotiations protected the woman's interests; the bride's family took great precautions to ensure she would be an equal partner in this lifelong arrangement. Victorian women waited longer to marry than in previous centuries, and parents were less likely to sell their daughters to the highest bidder.[8] In 1872 the mean age for marriage was 25.7 years for women, 27.9 years for men.[9] This was a society that was pragmatic about marriage: Victorians realized that while brokered marriages might not bring total bliss, they would secure women a central place in society. A Victorian marriage, at least in the upper middle and upper classes, was a vocation for women, a shared partnership they took seriously: "Marriage and a husband, far from putting women outside the realm of decision making, often widened their realm of financial power."[10] Mothers prepared their daughters carefully for this undertaking, aware that a good marriage would ensure them privilege and power. They helped them with their "coming out" parties (usually in London during the "Season") and took them to country house weekends, all social activities carefully contrived to introduce young women to acceptable suitors. These activities in themselves were expensive and exhausting undertakings, yet they were an important part of Victorian women's work.

James frequently commented on marriageable daughters, analyzing and satirizing this economically driven activity in his fiction and in his letters. His comments were often ironic. When Lord and Lady Wolseley's only daughter Frances was presented in London in 1887, James told her mother, "I take refuge in hoping that Miss Frances will not marry young" ([20]

6

January 1887, Hove 14).[11] In a letter to sister Alice dated 5 January 1880 he commented,

> I don't know what news to give you, save the sad intelligence that Lord Wentworth has at the last moment overthrown Miss Fletcher . . . whom he was to have married on the 29*th*. It is a brutal blow to the poor girl, who expected to have been lifted into a respectability of position which, thanks to her mother's irregularities she has never enjoyed, & I hear from Rome that she has fallen very ill. But she is well rid of her half-mad & physically untidy suitor. (He is supposed to be, in person, the *dirtiest* man in England.) (5 January 1880, Houghton bMS Am 1094 [1592])

Here James's sympathies were clearly with Constance Fletcher, a minor writer and playwright who never married, and whom James constantly ridiculed in later letters to Fanny Prothero. He realized the economic necessity of such a marriage for poor Miss Fletcher, but he also empathized with the price these convoluted marital arrangements exacted. While a good marriage ensured women power in their society, they paid a price for their social status.

Childbearing and rearing constituted another source of real power. Here again, though, it is a reductionist view to say that child rearing was a duty only for women. Victorians agreed that successful marriages produced children, but once produced, a variety of caretakers took responsibility for them. Husbands were involved from the beginning. Even with complicated pregnancies, most births took place at home with husbands present.[12] Contrary to prevalent myths of nineteenth-century motherhood, Victorian women had no stronger attachments to their children than the women of any other era. Some were intimately involved with their children's day-to-day activities, while others abandoned them to a series of caretakers. Children represented family continuity as a whole, a carrying on of traditional power. "If there was no mystique of motherhood in the nineteenth-century upper-middle-class home, there was surely one way in which many Victorians saw their offspring: they were the bearers of family traditions, they brought earthly continuity, immortality in the world to their parents and their forebears."[13]

Fathers, mothers, members of the extended family, nannies, governesses, and even gardeners all worked together in the work of child rearing. In his letters James empathized with his friends' complex and difficult task, realizing that producing children gave women added status. While he undoubtedly often relished his own childless state, he always admired others' children. In his last extant letter to his cousin Ellen Temple (Mrs. George) Hunter, the mother of painter Bay Emmet Rand, James praised her grandson:

> However the bewildered old bachelor does *like* being the centre of a photographic nursery & but desires to keep the account as straight & clear as he may. Therefore I miss the new sweet picture that you tell me you send over—& which yet hasn't come. Please don't let me fail of it—each fresh apparition helps my vision of your own so peopled (little=peopled) existence. Close to where I am writing on the wall here hangs a beautiful photog. of Blanchard with little hypnotized and hypnotizing Christopher [her son-in-law and grandson] on his lap, & it's hard to say whether father or son is the lovelier. (3 September 1915, Houghton bMS Am 1094 [743])

Many of his warm letters to Alice Howe Gibbens James concerned her children's health, education, and welfare. In a letter dated 23 March 1891 he debated the right name for her fourth son. William insisted the child be called Francis Tweedy, while Henry preferred Robertson: "Just a word to thank you for your last kind and indulgent letter—written after the receipt of mine about the little nursling's name." After mulling over various reasons not to call the child Temple or Tweedy but to choose instead the family name of Robertson, he ended, "Give my love to William and to all—especially to the unspeakable or unnamable babe. I hope he is of a flourishing form" (Houghton bMS Am 1094 [1614]). Mourning when an acquaintance, Mabel Sinclair, died after childbirth, he wrote a moving account of her end to Katherine Sands Godkin:

> Little Mabel's case was apparently bad from the third day after the birth of her boy—being, so far as I understand, complicated with some taint of blood-poisoning (accursed universal blight, as it seems to be nowadays!) supposed to have been contracted last winter in Sicily. At all events her four doctors—the last to be called was Sir Oscar Clayton, the great surgeon &c—were rapidly beaten, & I believe she was conscious of her situation— poor little lady (infinitely pathetic it is to write it!) *knew* herself to be going. Mrs. Sands told me on Wednesday that Mabel that day asked her—or rather it was Tuesday 28*th*—whether she *thought* there was hope for her. . . . I saw her [Mabel] less than a month ago—met her driving in a low Victoria, stopped by a block of carriages, in Knightsbridge, & walked along beside her for some moments, talking with her & struck by her remarkably *well* & happy look. She was full of brightness & asked me to come & see her soon &c. Dear little lady—I shall always think of her so. (30 October 1892, Houghton bMS Am 1083 [1365])

Rather than confining women to a world of childbearing and rearing, James exalted the richness of life these occupations lent them. He always acknowledged the importance of their children, but treated his friends as individuals with many other interests. They led healthy, vigorous lives, exercising frequently (walking, bicycling, riding), and enjoying life, transcending the limits placed upon them by society.

James's four friends were intelligent, as well as vigorous and healthy. James's letters themselves suggest the breadth and depth of his correspondents' education. Although denied a formal education (as was James himself), their intellectual concerns transcended the reading of sentimental novels, texts on household management, and religious material. Many Victorian women were voracious readers and accomplished writers. Men, fathers and others, helped educate girls. Women attended lectures through the nineteenth century; and in general, women (at least in the social circles that James frequented) were expected to be well informed.[14] They learned languages, read complex texts, and followed contemporary politics. Alice Howe Gibbens James provided her brother-in-law Henry with astute responses to many of his texts. When she finished reading his *Notes of a Son and Brother* (1914), her warm and loving response must have made James feel that he had at least one perceptive reader:

> Dear Henry,
> I fairly clutch at the lonely evening and the vacant library to tell you, if I can, something of all I feel about your "Notes". It seems to me surpassingly beautiful, even more perfect a creature than its predecessor [*A Small Boy and Others*]. This volume is so *abounding*,—rich in characterization both in what it gives and in what it so beautifully, so elusively tells without saying it! And the tone of the book is so benignant. As I told Harry last night I felt as if I had seen a great potentate, a prince of the blood, dismiss his followers one by one, giving to each a gracious word of farewell. (14 March 1914, Houghton bMS Am 1092.11 [54])

James also commented on his own and others' books to his women friends, especially in the letters to Alice James and Minnie Jones. His rebuttals to William's frequent attacks on his novels were usually conveyed through Alice. In one letter he told her what he thought of William's comments on the villain Gilbert Osmond in *The Portrait of a Lady*. The novel appeared in monthly installments in the *Atlantic Monthly,* and William had criticized Osmond's characterization in the first chapters:

Tell William I thank him kindly for his remarks on my novel—especially on the character of the depraved Osmond. I am afraid it won't be in my power, however, to change him much at this late day. As however he was more intended than W*m* appears to have perceived, to be disagreeable & disappointing, it may be that the later numbers of the story have already justified my first portrait of him. I think on the whole he [Gilbert Osmond] will be pronounced good—i.e. horrid. (6 August 1881, Houghton bMS Am 1094 [1610])

James's letters contained such difficult syntax, complex vocabulary, and sophisticated literary references that uneducated women could not have understood him.

James became for these women an important confidante, sharing their daily pursuits, realizing that, then as now, the fabric of our daily lives best defines us. He knew that housekeeping, shopping, and social life—and all their many daily activities—*were* Victorian and Edwardian life. To Mary Cadwalader Jones he waxed eloquent on a bowl she had sent him. (His gifts from these friends were often decorative household objects.)

The admirable little exotic bowl, with its harmonious adjuncts, that you have been so good as to drop upon me out of the blue—a deeper, diviner blue than bends over us here, from which (here) nothing so good as an unpurchased parcel ever drops—is, in truth, a lovely thing in itself; but what is lovelier still to me is the thought and remembrance, the sign of the generously reverting *mind,* that pushed it forth on its way. (9 June 1903, Houghton bMS Am 1094 [788])

With Lady Wolseley he discussed interior decorating, clothes, and food. In one letter he related his admiration for Lord Rosebery's country home: "It is a most dear & delightful old red brick house of the early Georges, full of white paint & red carpet, & *old* racing pictures & long sunny corridors filled with blue china & delicious books—the very nicest kind of house in all the wide world" (11 December 1887, Hove 18). He also talked about food: "Your figs are as beautiful as your character—though, alas, less permanent. They have melted lusciously away—though kept as long as I *could* keep them, to be the pride of my breakfast table" (8 September 1900, Hove 59). And he included clothing: "London is very pretty & spring-like—one scarcely knows 'what to wear'" (23 January 1888, Hove 20).

Besides household matters, James gossiped about mutual friends. And he was a very funny gossip. In a letter to Lady Anne Thackeray Ritchie, William Makepeace Thackeray's daughter and a writer, James assassinated the character of a mutual acquaintance, possibly a minor writer named

McCabe or MacKaye. He began by telling Lady Ritchie what he thought of their mutual acquaintance; she had evidently asked James if he liked the individual better after spending time with him:

> No, dearest Anne Ritchie, I can't say that "I liked him any better"—I liked him, I'm afraid, considerably *worse!* He is really too awful to be borne, & I sit in stupefaction at yours, & at Richmond's [her husband's], long patience. I could bear, too, to hear him say every five—every 2—minutes that you are lovely & that he adores *you,* but where I break down is on his perpetual proclamation that you find *him* lovely and adore *him.* . . . He is the scourge of God—the Attila of his age. And he got so *very,* so uncontrollably, as it were, drunk—Ouf!—It has really added 10 years to my life. . . . That he was so soon to *be* with you—that you were so eagerly expecting him—this, as he poured it out, made me think of you with a positive sinking of the heart & a *sickness* of compassion—wanted to warn & to save you—to wire . . . to you, *hiss* to you, "*fly!*" But he is as fate—we must submit to him. There is no help but in the grave. We must therefore cling to each other. It's a reason the more. (2 September 1899, Houghton bMS Am 1094.1 [5])

James must have relished his close friendships with women, as he wrote to them so openly. In a letter to Mary (Mrs. Charles) Hunter he laughed at himself as he informed her he was coming to London to see her on Monday:

> And I book then the 24th all joyously for the greatest pleasure. I'm putting all my best goods—tuppenny matters though they be—into my shop window, my poor old shopwindow! in advance; and trying to make such a muster there as may make you pull up and look smilingly, charitably in for the sum of minutes required! Yes, I'm quite feverishly *studying* the art of window-dressing, & only fear to perhaps present the appearance of selling-out for close of business. (10 January 1912, Houghton bMS Am 1237.16)

In all, his letters to these women are warmly human. These are not the letters of a withdrawn, asexual, neurotic individual.

Letters, in fact, were a natural way for James to create such rhetorical (and, by extension, personal) intimacy. The nineteenth century viewed the epistolary genre as a feminine genre. Letter writing was a private form of discourse with a very narrow and intimate audience; this, in effect, reinforced the idea that women were most comfortable in private spaces. While they were not always confined at home, nonetheless the idea that domesticity was natural for women and letter writing an acceptable activity (confined as that discourse was to sender and receiver) remained a cultural fiction in the Victorian era.[15] Maintaining strong friendships with women through letters, therefore, allowed James to experiment with intimacy in a culturally sanctioned fashion. Such fluid relationships were crucially important to him, bachelor that he was. Intimacy occurred only with certain family members, his close women friends, and with the younger men he loved. And as he never formed a permanent relationship with any of his lovers (and today it is virtually impossible to discern the reasons for this), it was with these women instead that he achieved long-lasting ties.

The letters in this volume are often brilliantly metaphorical, sometimes denser in metaphors than the fiction. To Alice James he compared the progress of William's health to taking a pig to market:

> You speak of William's "morning of gloom," through bad weather, discomfort, &c—&of his seeing Dr. Sigard & what Sigard says. As to this last, I rejoice in it heartily. Alas, for the interruption of benefit—but that is the way *all* improvements go! It is like driving a pig to the fair: sometimes he gets round & behind you & you have to bring him back. But at last to the fair you *do* get him—& meanwhile, all the time, you are on the road to it. Ask William to forgive my homely simile, but that is his natural progress. (14 February 1900, Houghton bMS Am 1094 [1635])

Writing to Lady Wolseley from his country home in Rye, he used an elaborate conceit to describe the act of letter writing itself:

> Here it is—late, very late in the evening, while the little town sleeps roundabout Lamb House as a large flourishing nursery of little cribs sleeps around the spectacled old nurse who sits up by the lamp economically darning stockings. I darn *this* stocking for you, dear Lady Wolseley—the good old stocking in which I have hoarded for long years the precious savings of our friendship. It is in capital condition still, thank goodness, & my needle would be capable of making good a much bigger hole than will ever yet be worn in it. (3 August 1906, Hove 76)

He told his neighbor Fanny Prothero a late supper at the literary Edmund Gosses resembled a fruit compote: "The Gosses' banquet was a cold, sandwichy, compote of mixed-fruity (mainly *bananine*)—you taste it from here—midnight supper" (1 January 1907, Houghton bMS Am 1094.3 [11]). To his bosom companion Mary Cadwalader Jones, James personified the egg caps sent him as a Christmas gift: "The little red caps of the boiled eggs cocked themselves, of their own motion, quite consciously and *crânement* [pluckily], as from the pride of their connection with you" (31 December

1903, Houghton bMS Am 1094 [794]). James extolled the weather, his travels, his garden, and his home.

While the four women were from different backgrounds and had disparate interests, they shared their love for their friend Henry James, partially because he affirmed and acknowledged their central roles in their society. And all four accepted him as he was, his idiosyncrasies only making them love him more. Like Jane Austen in her early epistolary text *Lady Susan,* James conceived of his correspondence with all these women as a creative, fictional voice capable of manipulating and undermining social convention. Through this voice James both appropriated women's power and asserted his own authorial mastery, even after his fiction-writing days ended. James's own warmth and love, sometimes unnoted, permeates this previously unpublished correspondence. Part of women's power over him lay in the fact that they allowed him to love them unconditionally.

In an age of rapid electronic communication, when we can send messages around the globe in an instant, we have lost the art of composing letters. Writing them late at night in his quiet Green Room, Henry James captured the essence of a brilliant Victorian/Edwardian world, a world that has vanished. Although James burned most of the letters written to him, it might give him pleasure to know that a new generation of readers would find and enjoy his correspondence. The extraordinary letters in this edition will enable us to recapture his lost world, a world of Machiavellian politics, eccentric geniuses, and manifest eroticism.

NOTES

1. The following description of James is an imaginative reconstruction of a scene based on photographs of Lamb House and on his own description of his life as detailed in unpublished letters too numerous to list here.

2. This and subsequent citations marked "Houghton," with the corresponding catalog number, refer to holographs in the James Family Correspondence in the Houghton Library, Harvard University. Citations are by permission of the Houghton Library and by permission of Bay James, literary executor of the James papers.

3. Henry James, intro. to Rupert Brooke, *Letters from America* (London: Sidgwick and Jackson, 1916), ix.

4. Cora Castle, "A Statistical Study of Eminent Women," *Archives of Psychology* 7 (1913): 167.

5. Jeanne M. Peterson, *Family, Love, and Work in the Lives of Victorian Gentlewomen* (Bloomington: Indiana University Press, 1989), 188.

6. Pat Jalland, *Women, Marriage, and Politics: 1860–1914* (Oxford: Clarendon Press, 1986), 4.

7. Jalland, *Women, Marriage, and Politics,* 68, 71.

8. Georgiana Hill, *Women in English Life: From Medieval to Modern Times,* vol. 2 (London: R. Bentley and Son, 1906), 97.

9. This average comes from the records of all registered marriages where age was recorded (Jalland, *Women, Marriage, and Politics,* 79).

10. Peterson, *Family, Love, and Work,* 123. She goes on to add that marriage settlements gave upper middle-class women financial freedom.

11. This and subsequent citations marked "Hove," with the corresponding catalog numbers, refer to holographs in the Wolseley Papers in the Hove Reference Library, Sussex, England. Citations are by permission of the Hove Library and by permission of Bay James.

12. Jalland, *Women, Marriage, and Politics,* 144.

13. Peterson, *Family, Love, and Work,* 104.

14. Peterson, *Family, Love, and Work,* 33–40.

15. Elizabeth C. Goldsmith quotes a member of the French Academy who in 1849 explained women's affinity for the epistolary genre as an outcome of gender: "Nature gave them [women] a more mobile imagination, a more delicate organization. . . . Their sensibility is quicker, more lively, and touches a wider variety of objects. . . . from this [comes] that suppleness and continual variety in everything, that we so often see in their letters; that facility for jumping from one subject to other completely diverse ones, without effort and with unexpected but natural transitions." Quoted from "Authority, Authenticity, and the Publication of Letters by Women," in *Writing the Female Voice: Essays on Epistolary Literature,* ed. Elizabeth C. Goldsmith (Boston: Northeastern United Press, 1989), 53.

*Letters to Alice Howe Gibbens James*
*1878–1915*

## Time Line

1843    Henry James is born.

1849    Alice Howe Gibbens is born.

1878    Alice Gibbens marries William James, becoming Henry's sister-in-law.

1893    Alice James and her family visit Europe and Henry.

1905    Henry visits America and Alice's summer home in Chocorua, New Hampshire.

1910    After years of ill health, William James dies, with Alice and Henry at his side.

1916    Henry dies in England, Alice and her daughter Peggy with him.

1922    Alone with her memories, Alice James dies in Cambridge, Massachusetts.

Alice Howe Gibbens James as a young woman. (Reprinted by permission of the Houghton Library, Harvard University.)

# Introduction

I hear from mother that you are enjoying life and leisure in the Adirondacks, & that the infant Harry is in danger from the Cows. Remember that I haven't seen him yet, & rescue him at any price: I will make it up to you. I hope your rustication is doing you all good, & that when I come home I shall find you fat and brown & lusty. I am beginning to feel the nearness of that event, & to anticipate both social & vegetable delights. The breeze from the lawn is fluttering my paper, & the big lawn-tennis net (which occupies half the small garden) is shaking amain. I have promised myself to write two other letters before lunch, so I send you all my blessing & remain ever affectionately yours   —*H. James jr.* (6 August [1881?], Houghton bMS Am 1094 [1610])

Alice carefully buried her small china dog in a shallow hole beneath the oak trees.[1] The warm California sun shone down upon her as she turned and walked toward the ranch house. The next day her family left to return to New England. Dr. Gibbens's western venture had come to an end.

Alice Howe Gibbens was born in Massachusetts on 5 February 1849, to a country physician and a genteel New Englander. In 1856 the Gibbens family moved to California, where Dr. Gibbens tried ranching, a venture that eventually failed. Perhaps her sociable father's personal weaknesses made Alice serious. A tintype of her taken at age seven or eight shows her a solemn child with a round face, regular features, and large dark eyes.

Battling alcoholism and financial problems, Dr. Gibbens joined the

---

1. Part of the material in this introduction to her life is based on the account her son Henry James III (1879–1947) wrote of her life (mimeograph in the Houghton, MS Am 1095.1).

Union army at the outbreak of the Civil War. At the war's end, en route to Boston, he committed suicide. Sixteen-year-old Alice, now wearing simple white dresses and sweeping her dark hair behind her oval head in a tight bun, took charge of the family. Three years later Mrs. Gibbens and her three daughters set sail for Germany, where Alice studied voice with Clara Schumann. And five years later, once again beset with financial difficulties, the Gibbens women returned to America, where Alice taught school to support her mother and sisters. By now she possessed great fortitude and serene self-control, qualities that would endear her to two James brothers.

In 1876 Henry James Sr. met young Alice at Boston's Radical Club. He returned home and announced to William that he had found his eldest son a bride. Both William and Alice were serious and cautious. When they announced their engagement, Henry Jr. wrote a remarkable letter welcoming her to the James family, the first of many warm letters that would sustain her emotionally the rest of her life. Alice and William married on 10 July 1878, and their first child was born the next year. William James built an international reputation as a philosopher and psychologist, while Alice smoothed his way and that of their four surviving children. At first she was intimidated by her brilliant brother-in-law Henry, fearing he would find her wanting. On New Year's Day, 1883, just after James Sr.'s death, she wrote to William:

> I think your brother Harry makes one miserable in a fine, inexplicable fashion. He is trying all the time to do his whole duty by me, but I know it is adverse fortune which thrusts me upon him, and though I try to temper myself to him and be as slight a shock as possible, I am constantly diverted by want of success. (Houghton bMS Am 1092.9 [285])

Their friendship grew over the years, however, and a decade later she wrote her husband, "And I shall always love Harry for his kindness to me and to everybody. And the 'Brothers' could hardly have given him a serener face" (17 July [1893], Houghton bMS Am 1092.9 [302]). Alice was indeed a strong figure in the James family throughout her life, both for William and Henry and for all the others. When the Jameses traveled to Europe on the ship *Friesland* in 1892, Alice nursed sick children and went nights without sleep. After William's younger brother, Bob, developed drinking problems, Alice sheltered him at her Quincy Street home. While she applauded her husband's success, she had pangs of regret at her own less public role. When William lectured at Radcliffe in 1907 she told Henry, by then one of her dearest friends and most trustworthy confidants,

He gave a most exquisite little address to the Association of College Alumnae at Radcliffe on the test of the higher education, "The power to know a good man when you see him." It was wise, impressive & exquisitely formed.

I thought as I listened to him that it was the only test which I have ever successfully passed—but perhaps I flatter myself and I was just born with a vocation for Jameses! (11 November 1907, Houghton bMS Am 1092.11 [47])

Henry James helped provide her the intellectual life she had denied herself.

Her sincere thoughts and spiritual insights sustained William's life and work. Many nights Alice sat in the library of their Quincy Street home, listening to William read drafts of his lectures and often supplying the quote he needed. It was Alice who found the ending quotation for the speech William gave at the dedication of the Saint-Gaudens monument to Civil War hero Colonel Robert Shaw; it was Henry James who wrote and applauded Alice for her role in that great day's events.

James empathized with Alice's demanding tasks of rearing children, assisting her husband, and entertaining the family's many friends. He was her steady and trustworthy confidant, her secret champion. On 21 May 1899, she told him of William's heart troubles and her burdens:

But was ever man born of woman harder to take care of than William! Do you wonder that I want to get him away from all the frustration which wearies him more than work, and establish if possible a well-ordered plan of life? (Houghton bMS Am 1092.11 [40])

She spent her vacation summers laboring on the family farm at Chocorua, New Hampshire, running a large household, entertaining visitors, caring for the children, and always ensuring that William relaxed. Henry finally warned Alice that she must rest: "*you need an Easier Life,*" he proclaimed in one long letter (Houghton bMS Am 1094 [1681]).

Henry came to treasure his close relationship with his sister-in-law as much as his blood ties with William. Hearing Henry joke about her husband must have let Alice vent the frustrations inevitable in a marriage to such a brilliant and loving but erratic husband. James's letters mix love and gentle cynicism on the subject of William, but he always approved of Alice. He invited her to leave her family in Switzerland and visit him in 1892, and although his invitation tempted her, she stuck fast to her duties:

I thank you very much dear Harry, for your kind invitation to me and only wish I could accept it. But I shall not leave the children to the care of strangers. And I am not likely to have any other guardian for them. This may strike you as weak-hearted but if my existence is to justify itself it must be through other lives, and the children need me now, every one of them. (11 April 1892, Houghton bMS Am 1092.11 [29])

Unlike William, who frequently criticized his brother's writing style, Alice was warmly appreciative of Henry's books. His novel *The Tragic Muse* moved her deeply:

I finished, two days ago, *The Tragic Muse,* and rest there's none for me till I tell you how very beautiful I think it. You seem to me to have crossed the border into the kingdom of the great, into the land where the few, the Masters live and create by laws and immensities of their own. The book is so new, so unlike any other—so that perhaps people won't take it in today or tomorrow, but its own day is waiting for it. (22 June 1890, Houghton bMS Am 1092.11 [27])

As their friendship deepened, his letters lengthened. He showed interest in all facets of her life. When William developed serious health problems, Henry's letters contained brotherly advice and encouragement. After William's death in 1910, Henry stayed with Alice in New England to help settle the estate and mourn their loss. And he followed her children's lives closely: Harry's burgeoning career, Peggy's depression and her matriculation at Bryn Mawr, Bill's marriage to wealthy socialite Alice Runnells, and the youngest Aleck's struggles to find himself, first in western travel and then in art. Alice still appreciated James's writing, especially the autobiographies he wrote at the end of his life. After reading *A Small Boy and Others* she said, "I cannot begin to tell you how beautiful it seems to me. I suspect you have made there an imperishable record of a child—an immortal child. And the grace,—and the tenderness—and the charm!" (1 April 1913, Houghton MS Am 1092.11 [51]).

As William was dying in 1910 he asked Alice to go to Henry during his final days. So when Henry James drew his last breath on 28 February 1916, Alice was there. To Bostonian Elizabeth Glendower Evans she confided, "I am grateful too that I could come to Henry and be with him to the end. Through the physical ravage and mental bewilderment came a revelation of the spirit, so erect, so untouched, so *immortal* that the going over seemed but an episode. It was easy to think of him in that other country" (11 March 1916, Schlesinger Library, Radcliffe College, Elizabeth Glendower Evans Papers, folder 88).

After Henry's death Alice smuggled his ashes back to the United States for burial in the James family plot in Cambridge. Now she sat alone at the tremendous table in the darkened library, reading over her dear brother-in-law's funny and moving letters. By then her hair was white, her face wrinkled and gaunt, and her clothes black. Alice died in 1922 in her home at 95 Quincy Street, surrounded by her memories and the ghosts of the Jameses.

*James welcomes Alice Howe Gibbens to the James family, telling her "you are engaged, more or less, to the whole family."*

[The Reform Club]

My dear Miss Gibbens. June *7th* '78.

Ever since my brother wrote to me, the other day, of his engagement, I have wanted very much to tell you, as well as him, as nearly face to face as we may be at this distance, how happy the news has made me & how heartily & tenderly I congratulate you both. I sent you a message which I trust he gave you literally, but I must repeat it and do the little that may belong to me in bidding you welcome into a family which—though perhaps not without a dim appreciation of its intrinsic resources—will feel greatly honored by your touching it so nearly. Of course, by the time this reaches you, you will have been deluged with compliments & congratulations & you will listen, with a deadened sense, to my poor prayers for your welfare. But you will perhaps believe this—that there is no one just now so extremely desirous as I to see you & know you & learn to discharge toward you the natural offices of a brother. This may not come to pass for some time yet; but I can assure you that you will lose nothing by waiting. I shall come home or you & William will come out here; wherever we meet it will be equally agreeable. Meanwhile, however, as a beginning of an acquaintance, I very much hope you will write me a line—if only to tell me this has safely reached you. I suppose you have had a good many reassuring things said to you about W*m,* & feel fairly justified by public opinion. But there is no harm in my saying that I, who have known him longer than any one save his parents, regard him as an altogether good creature. I have an idea, too, that since I left America he has sensibly improved. So I congratulate you not only in form, but in spirit. I hope you are seeing a good deal of the rest of them—for I hold it to be part of the bargain that you are engaged, more or less, to the whole family. You will have discerned in this case that we are all good creatures, & thoroughly safe & sensible. On the other hand both my mother & my father have written to me in terms which leave no manner of doubt as to what they think of you. But I didn't mean to write so many pages—I only wanted to give you, personally, what my brother asked for—my blessing. I send you all possible, & impossible, good wishes—& I venture to add my very kind regards to your mother & sisters. Believe me, my dear Miss Gibbens, very faithfully yours—

*H. James jr.*

ALS: Houghton bMS Am 1094 (1609)[2]

*James informs sister-in-law Alice of his sister Alice's visit to England. He also sends a message to William that the villain Gilbert Osmond in* The Portrait of a Lady *was meant to be disagreeable. James feels that Alice should rescue her baby Harry from the cows in the Adirondacks, because he has not seen him yet.*

Holme Lodge, Walton-on-Thames

Dear Alice. Aug 6*th* [1881?]

I received about a fortnight ago a co=operative note from William & you. He had supplied the sentiments, & you the penmanship; so it seems to me that to you this effort of my own pen should be addressed. I should have answered you before, but since my return from the continent I have had an accumulation of duties of every kind which has made me postpone familiar letters. I have been occupied for instance a good deal in seeing Alice, who has been in the country near London, & with whom I have, naturally had much conversation. She is doing very well in spite of one or two drawbacks, & seems to be both enjoying her life here and gaining strength from it. It is of course very quiet, but she and Miss Loring[3] do whatever they like & see a good deal of the picturesque. I am sorry she doesn't see more people; but that, for the present, seems impossible. She will at any rate, I think, go home much refreshed & encouraged. I am glad to find myself in England again, after a four months' absence, especially as we are having a remarkably beautiful summer. It is what we call in America a "real" summer—so real that the poor Britons don't know what to make of it & suffer anguish from the visibility of the sun. The heat, indeed, during much of July was intense; but now the heavens only smile, without scorching. I am spending a couple of days about 15 miles from London, in a little cottage occupied for the summer by Fred. Macmillan & his pretty little American wife,[4] whom William encountered here. It is very rustic and bowery, very quiet and very "restful"—close to the river, near Hampton Court &c. Tell William I thank him kindly for his remarks on my

---

2. All transcriptions of the letters marked *Houghton* in this edition are used by permission of the Houghton Library, Harvard University, and by permission of Bay James, literary executor of the James papers. The prefix *ALS* means "autograph letter signed." *TLS* stands for "typed letter signed."

3. Katherine Peabody Loring (1849–1943), Alice James's intimate companion. They had been friends since 1873, and they taught together in Miss Ticknor's Society to Encourage Studies at Home in Boston. She lived with Alice in England and was with her when she died. Loring later published four private copies of Alice James's diary.

4. Lady Georgiana Elizabeth Warrin Macmillan (d. 1943) and Sir Frederick Orridge Macmillan (1851–1936). He was with Macmillan and Company, which published some of James's work. They were social as well as business friends.

novel—especially on the character of the depraved Osmond. I am afraid it won't be in my power, however, to change him much at this late day. As however he was more intended than W*m* appears to have perceived, to be disagreeable & disappointing, it may be that the later numbers of the story have already justified my first portrait of him. I think on the whole he will be pronounced good—i.e. horrid.——I hear from mother that you are enjoying life and leisure in the Adirondacks, & that the infant Harry is in danger from the Cows. Remember that I haven't seen him yet, & rescue him at any price: I will make it up to you. I hope your rustication is doing you all good, & that when I come home I shall find you fat and brown & lusty. I am beginning to feel the nearness of that event, & to anticipate both social & vegetable delights. The breeze from the lawn is fluttering my paper, & the big lawn-tennis net (which occupies half the small garden) is shaking amain. I have promised myself to write two other letters before lunch, so I send you all my blessing & remain ever affectionately yours

*H. James jr.*

ALS: Houghton bMS Am 1094 (1610)

*James laments Aunt Kate's final illness. He has been in the courtroom watching the Pigott trial, which he finds thrilling, but is disgusted with the "imbecility of the Times." (Richard Pigott had been instrumental in engineering Irish hero Charles Stewart Parnell's downfall.)*

34 D[e]. V[ere]. G[ardens]., W. [London]

My dear Alice.                                    March 1*st* [1889]

Your beautiful letter of January 12*th* has had to wait longer for an answer than I have at any time intended. Dear old Aunt Kate's[5] condition has been the cause of my writing with unwonted frequence to New York—to Lila Walsh,[6] Helen Ripley[7] &c—as well as of a quantity of correspondence with Leamington—so that although this very situation has quickened my desire to be in relation with William & you the time has more than ever

---

5. Catherine Walsh (Aunt Kate) (ca. 1812–1889) was Mary Walsh James's sister. For many years she lived with the James household, traveling with them to Europe and helping Mrs. James raise her five children. In 1853 she married Captain Charles H. Marshall, a rich New York widower aged sixty. After two years they separated and she moved back in with the Jameses.

6. Elizabeth (Lila, Lilla) Robertson Walsh was HJ's aunt on his mother's side. She took care of Aunt Kate during her final illness.

7. Helen Ripley was the daughter of Catharine Walsh Andrews Ripley and Joseph Ripley of Connecticut and was related to the Walshes.

failed me for a talk with the pen. I am afraid that even now it must be brief—a few snatched words. I happen to be in a *press* of literary production[8] & rather nervous till a certain crisis of "creation" is over: which will be by the middle of this month. Please therefore regard these hurried words as rudely provisional. You shall have better ones with the 1st better occasion.——I think of nothing in these days but Aunt Kate—lying there in her last, helpless weakness—& I do nothing but pray, each day, that we may hear she has passed painlessly away. Not to have seen her for so long is an immense regret to me—she passed so quickly & strangely beyond call or touch. Moreover, to be so far from her, in all these weeks seems unnatural & ungrateful—& not really to have known she was vanishing until she had almost vanished. It has seemed to Alice and me a drama so swift as to take one's breath away—the rapidity of her decline after the 1st vague signs of it that we noticed in a letter or two immediately following on her visit to you at Chocorua.[9] By the time these signs had become distinct she ceased to write at all. I envy William his day with her in New York just before she utterly collapsed—I mean when she was already bad—it would have seemed the end of so many things in the past—things reaching back to our earliest memories. But thank heavens for the brave & lucid Lila Walsh—who has taken, throughout, a weight off my mind.——When we don't—Alice & I—think of 44*th* St. I suspect we think, just now, like every one else here, almost only of the high Irish imbroglio & the wonderful abyss into which the tiresome *Times* has fallen, with its abominable Pigott[10] & its abominable malignity. Seen so near as this, (& I have spent two quite thrilling days in the court-room,) it is all a very palpitating drama, the successive vivid scenes of which give—or have given—a zest to each day's rising. The imbecility of the *Times* has been colossal, and unless there is some secret history in it to come out, it will always remain an unexplained mystery why & how people with 1/2 a century of "shrewdness" behind them came to embark upon so dangerous an enterprise with the naïveté of greedy little boys.——When I think neither of Aunt Kate nor of the injured Parnell, I think of your new house & wish it every sort of

---

8. He was working on his novel *The Tragic Muse* at this time.

9. Alice and William James's country home in New Hampshire.

10. Richard Pigott (1828?–1889), Irish journalist and forger. He forged papers incriminating Irish nationalist hero Parnell in the Phoenix Park murders in Dublin, then published articles on Parnell's role in that tragedy in a series of *Times* articles entitled "Parnellism and Crime." He later confessed the papers were forged and fled to Madrid, where he shot himself.

good omen & firm support. It will be a rare pleasure to think of you permanently & capaciously housed. I long to see the plans. Your anecdote of Charles Norton[11] lights up unexplored abysses of human self-complacency—c'est trop fort [it's too much]! I hope William is carrying his various loads with forthcoming strength. I feel, somehow, very selfish & isolated & as if I were not pulling the waggon, over here, at all. But it wouldn't improve the situation much for me to invest in a "family" & a building site of my own, & perhaps I contribute as much to your welfare by letting you alone as by an attempt at sympathetic interference. How dreadfully sad the picture of the poor dear old Tweedies[12]—they too go so far back—& I feel as if I ought to hold out an arm to them somehow. At least some benevolent younger relation ought to come to the rescue—for Tweedy. Alice appears to be recovering steadily from her serious cataclysm of 2 months ago. I saw her a fortnight since. She vibrates powerfully on the Irish question. Excuse, dear Alice, this very uninspired scrawl—to tell the truth I have been feeling *sick* since I sat down to write it—in consequence of some abnormal element my cook must have inadvertently dropped into my lunch: probably the rich rosy colouring=matter of some cooked pears! It only leaves me coherency to bliss and embrace you all round. Ever giddily yours

*Henry James*

ALS: Houghton bMS Am 1094 (1612)

*HJ thanks Alice for her praise of* The Tragic Muse, *and he hopes William is enjoying the fat volume between naps under a tree. He himself enjoys Italy's artistic charms.*

Siena

My dear Alice, July 9*th* 1890

How can I sufficiently thank you for your delightful & most touching letter of June 22*d* which reached me a few days ago in Florence. It gave me immense pleasure & brought the tears to my eyes. Nothing indeed could gratify me more—or ever does—than to know that some "work" of mine is valued by an exquisite & distinguished mind. It was very sweet of you to

---

11. Charles Eliot Norton (1827–1908), American professor, scholar, critic, editor, and cofounder of the *Nation*. Norton promoted James's career from its start, publishing his early works and introducing him to important writers.

12. Mary Temple Tweedy (d. 1891) and Edmund Tweedy (d. 1901), the guardians of HJ's Temple cousins (including HJ's beloved Minny Temple). They lived in Pelham, New York, and in Newport.

express so liberally such interest as you have extracted from the present one. This refreshes my own interest in it—that interest that always fades & fails giving place to the vision & project of something further & better—as soon as one of my productions is fairly finished. So I can't "take up" what may be said, either in praise or blame: the thing is done—or not; the attempt at any rate is over—& I can't talk about it. But I can, thank heaven, enjoy some of its fruits—such, dear Alice, as your charming & generous words. By the time the book is finished I feel as if I were quite indifferent about it—the concern in it only having lasted long enough to finish it. But I am *not* indifferent to such responses as yours. I almost groan a little at the idea that poor weary William has had to begin *my* fat volume as soon as he has finished his own. But I hope he is taking it between naps, under a tree, on the grass—feeling a summery indulgence in anything I may be supposed to expect of him. I wrote to him some 3 weeks ago from a charming little valley in the Bavarian Highlands—from which just after- wards I took my way back to this irrepressible, or rather, irresistible, Italy *via* Innsbrück, the ⟨Torensur?⟩ & Verona. I came back even to Florence, where I have just been (for a *2d* time since the middle of May,) spending a week made sweet by the absence of the Tourist horde & the presence of delightfully cool weather. I find this summer aspect of Italy delightful indeed—a kind of family party, with strangers away, hotels & railway trains empty & the country a "dream of beauty". I am spending 4 or 5 days here, where every charm of artistic antiquity surrounds me—& am going to start on the 12th for a little circuit (4 or 5 days) of a few other picturesque & unfrequented place—Volterra, Monte Pulciano, the Etruscan Chiusi. Would that you & William & the children were along!—this is perfectly sincere. I think afterwards of going for 10 days up to the divine Val- lombrosa (where I lately spent a day & woods & hills & views & air produce together the finest essence of the romantic:) as a prelude to a final return, after three months of pure restful holiday, to the empty London of the late summer and autumn where I shall get back to work. I am sorry the summers both late & early roll by so without my sniffing of the primitive earth at Chocorua. We are perhaps likely to meet in some such place as this before I plough across the Atlantic—for, somehow, for better for worse, my ligatures to my native land seem individually & collectively cut. But when our meeting befalls—heaven send it be as soon as William plans—I shan't quarrel with the place. I will lend you De Vere Gardens all to yourselves—& sleep (to give you room) at a neighboring inn. I wish, dear Alice, that you were tasting as I much as I, this summer, of the irresponsible. I feel too gross & grasping. I wish I could spirit you all to Vallombrosa—such places *there*—to be upon the grass, under the chestnuts—or the pines—with all the violet world of Italy, seen through such delicate air, at one's feet. I embrace you all—especially the *bambina,* & am ever affectionately your

*Henry James*

ALS: Houghton bMS Am 1094 (1613)

*Alice's baby should* not *be called Francis Tweedy. James prefers Robertson, his mother's family name. (William and Alice named the baby Francis Tweedy, but several years later changed the child's name to Alexander Robertson.) Meanwhile James is very busy working on his plays.*

Hotel Westminster   Paris.

My dear Alice.

Mch. 23*d* [1891]

Just a word to thank you for your last kind & indulgent letter—written after the receipt of mine about the little nursling's name. I am very sorry my suggestions raised a gust—they were intended only to still the breezes—& I thought the matter still open for discussion as the child had not, as I suppose, been Christianly baptized & registered. There are probably elements & complexities in it that I don't understand—I mean that your letter seems to point to engagements with *Tweedy,* on the subject, that I don't divine. (You say that you *will* write to him that you withdraw *Temple.* But *what* has he to do with that?—& why need you formally notify him?) Don't answer these mystified questions—for I of course believe in your thought out reasons for everything—& I only want to minimise my own perturbing power. Spilt milk—if the milk *is* spilt—is worth no tears; still I can't help clinging to 2 hopes—one that the *Temple* will be practically & utterly eradicated & the other that the name the child is to be *called by* (in daily intercourse) will *not* be "Tweedy"—especially all his life! I utterly detest it—I find it ugly & ridiculous (unless indeed E. T. is going to leave him money on it—where I reluctantly retract.) Haven't you & W*m,* in your frequent humane visitations to Newport, peopling its solitude and brightening its dullness, shown, for years, enough good will to our good old friend without this supreme tribute?—I mean of the ugly surname, for I should have *hailed* "Edmund"—which I like—"Francis Edmund." I venture still to put in a plea for something that is of our *own* people or of *yours*—before going to *other* families. I stick to my Robertson, all the more that of mother's 7 other grandchildren not *one* has bethought

28

itself of having it, though it was her own christened name. But I pause—
for you will regard this note perhaps—or it may seem to William only an
aggravation. Even if you are annoyed & bothered & have to re=think &
re=delay, that is *little*—when the child's case may be for a long lifetime—in
a world of which we are our reasons are shall *not* be.[13] I have been for this
last month in this place—working very hard—of course at the Drama—
& *never* getting out till 4 or 5 p.m. I have never been, on the spot, so little
*in* Paris. But I return to London 10 days hence. I came over because it
happened to be a moment when I *could* take the only absence (& an
absence from London is always a simplification,) that seemed possible for
me for indefinite months to come—including the period from this April
to October next. I go back for the rest of the spring & the whole summer.
You will have heard of Alice's having taken a furnished house for a year—
41 Argyle Road, Campden Hill, W. It is 10 minutes from DeVere Gardens;
& Katherine has, in my absence, miraculously moved her into it. I of
course don't know "how" she is—but I surmise rather favourably, for the
hour, affected by the change—till the steady tide of her weakness rises
again. It was (the house in London,) by far the best & the *only* thing to do.
Give my love to William & to all—especially to the unspeakable or
unnamable babe. I hope he is of a flourishing form. I should have written
sooner about his denomination were it not that at the right time a preoccupation of work more imperious than I have ever had *in my life,* &
absolutely *exclusive* & absorbing, veiled & muffled my sense of responsibility in the matter.———I hear the American (now in Ireland) goes on from
marked to still more marked success. The Belfast papers of last Saturday
calls the applause the night before an "unparalleled" demonstration. Ever
your scene-shifting

Henry

ALS: Houghton bMS Am 1094 (1614)


*James discusses where William and Alice should "plant" their children while traveling
in Europe. He suffers with his sister Alice's "infinite Protean dying."*


34, DE VERE GARDENS. W.

My dear Alice,                                                    Feb. 15*th* [1892]
    Many thanks both to you & William for your explanation about the
January remittance. None was needed; because no inconvenience was

---

13. Michael Anesko helps explain this last confusing phrase as follows: "in a world of
which we [and] our reasons shall not be." I am indebted to him for this suggestion.

caused. I wrote to William a week ago. It is delightful to hear from you—but how much more will it be to see you! Would that we didn't have to wait for the scheme (of your migration) to be so difficultly worked out. I hope indeed William *will* go to Dublin, for the sake of all the impressionism of it. I have just been invited there by the Wolseleys (Lord W. is commander-in-chief of the forces in Ireland,) to stay with them a week, but haven't been able to accept the invitation. Any way in which I can help you to solve the plan of what to do, on coming abroad, and how to do it, will be a way delightful to me. But I don't foresee, as yet, what you wish to do with the infants—plant them abroad or *here.* Abroad, somehow, seems to be getting more for your money; yet I greatly desire that you and William, naturally, should be here. London isn't the thing for *them*—at least the ideal thing, in the summer—and yet one shrinks from recommending the dreary British seaside resort. But we must think it out.——There *is* nothing to tell, nowadays, of a condition so monotonous & so intensely simplified as Alice's. She is very ill for 10 days in every way—having at once most of the forms of illness she does have—& then she is easier for a few days, & can see one & talk: that is all that is to be said about her—except that she lives & lives & lives through all her infinite Protean dying. The sense of it all is like some dreadful endless nightmare. The influenza is leaving us & has been a short visitation & less severe than its two foreyears. I peg away at my usual occupations—& have rejoiced in a particularly bland & brilliant winter. Now the days grow longer & there are smells of spring. Alice had a sublime letter from Bob[14] the other day—but I never hear from him. I ache with all of William's aches—I deplore all his fatigues. But I hail the months of rest & I embrace you all, dear Alice, & am ever affectionately yours

*Henry James*

P.S. Please say to W. that I *have* sent to B. Temple 10 dollars.

ALS: Houghton bMS Am 1094 (1615)


*The death of sister Alice ends one chapter in James's life, and he shares what her death meant to him. He expresses a renewed interest in Alice and William's children, for whom he developed a constantly deepening affection.*

My dear Alice. 34, DE VERE GARDENS, W.

    I must ask you to forgive me for the brevity with which I shall have to

---

14. Robertson James (1846–1910), the fourth James brother.

thank you for your letter of the 22*d,* & the 3 most rejoicing photographs. I am still rather exhausted with the innumerable letters I have had lately to write, & the end of which is even not yet. I wrote you very briefly ten days ago or so, & a few days since wrote again to William. Your letter partly answers the petition I then put forth—for information as exact as possible about your general plan. It tells me that you sail on May 25*th* & go straight to Switzerland—& these facts are enough for me to "go by." I shall probably be abroad at the time you arrive—& if I am not I shall certainly come to you. I shall either meet you at Antwerp or, if you like the latter more, will prepare a receptacle for you in Switzerland. With so large a party it will not be amiss to have someone doing something for you on the spot. My wish is to be absent from *London,* in one way or another, from about the 20*th* (or 25*th*) of April to the 1*st* of August. I *may* go to Italy for 5 weeks—or I may go only to the south of England—it will depend on circumstances that will clear up during the next few days. But in either case I will be on the continent & looking out for you in the 1*st* days of June. I rejoice in your universal advent & shall be infinitely disappointed if anything happens to delay it. I hope therefore the great push will be found possible & every circumstance will favour. I go to Liverpool 2 days hence to see Katherine L. "off" on the *Etruria* (9*th.*) Alice's little friendly, but now oh, so haunted, house is closed—everything terminated & wound up, & Katherine is spending this last week with Annie Richards,[15] & in a short pilgrimage to some of Alice's Leamington pieties. When she departs I shall feel that the chapter is closed indeed, & it seems strange enough now, the intense & in spite of all that weakness powerful, life it represents is mere silence & memory. So few people knew Alice here that the silence is all the stranger substitute for the place she filled so full while she did fill it. I wish you could have seen her once more; & I wish the children could. Their photographs take away my breath—they are all 5 years older than my thought of them. But they look delightful, & I expect to become great friends with them. M.[argaret] M.[ary][16] looks to me a little like the infant Alice. I'm sorry Billy[17] is omitted—& sorrier still that you are. Please let

---

15. Annie Ashburner Richards was a close friend of HJ's sister Alice from the days the James family spent in Cambridge in the mid-1860s. She was one of the four people that Alice James asked to attend her funeral in England; the others were Henry, Katherine Loring, and her nurse.

16. Margaret Mary (Peggy) James (1887–1950) was Alice and William James's only daughter. She and James later became very close friends and companions.

17. William James (1882–1961), Alice and William James's second son.

me have another definite word, & your ideas about a Swiss whereabouts. Don't select a *cold* one. Ever, dear Alice, yours affectionately & W*m*'s

*Henry James*

April 6*th* 1892

ALS: Houghton bMS Am 1094 (1616)

*James extends pungent congratulations on William's speech at the dedication of the Saint-Gaudens monument to Colonel Shaw and his Civil War brigade, noting his own emotional response to the Civil War. He comments on Queen Victoria's Diamond Jubilee and describes a typical marriageable American girl.*

[*Dictated*][18]

34, DE VERE GARDENS, W.

Dearest Alice,                                                  15th June, 1897.

Your delightful letter of the 31st, with its enclosure and accompaniments, has been a deep joy to me. I thought of you both with extraordinary emotion at the time, and the text of the business, in the two Boston newspapers, only made me feel what solid ground I had for it.[19] Tell William I jubilate with him, and over him, and under him, and round about him in every manner, even more than I promised myself. I think his address most wisely and admirably conceived, and if it was uttered—as it evidently was—in a way to give it the right value, it must have held the multitude with all the intensity even you and I could have desired for it. There are just a few little things of detail which give me a kind of sense that I should have liked to have thrown my weight—at points of preparation, I mean—into the scale another way. But these are nothing, of no significance at all, in the mass of the success. Grace Norton[20] has written me briefly—wrote me the next day—that he covered himself with glory; and I have just spent two days with the Godkins[21] (who, with the reinforcement

---

18. Letters that bear the heading *Dictated* were dictated by James to one of his scribes.

19. Here HJ refers to the speech William James gave at the dedication of Saint-Gaudens's memorial sculpture to Robert Gould Shaw and the Fifty-fourth Massachusetts Regiment. During the Civil War this was the first black regiment recruited in a free state, and Garth Wilkinson James, the third of the four James brothers, served in it. Shaw was killed in the attack on Fort Wagner, South Carolina, on July 18, 1863. As HJ indicates, William's speech was a great success.

20. Grace Norton (1834–1926) was Charles Eliot Norton's sister and one of HJ's closest friends.

21. Edwin Lawrence Godkin (1831–1902), author and editor of the *Nation,* and his second wife Katherine Buckley Sands Godkin (1846–1907).

of Mrs. Sands, Mrs. G's mother, have taken, down in Surrey, for two months, a rather big, ugly house, in a beautiful "place" and position) where I had the reading of a letter from Arthur Sedgwick[22] to G., to just the same purport. I congratulate you both therefore, tenderly, on the beauty and majesty and poetry of the whole occasion and achievement. I should think that to have done it would make William feel he could do anything. Alas that I am so out of it!—not getting any anecdotes or side-winds or souvenirs, or indeed any kind of "consequence" from it. I think his whole manner about Shaw himself everything one could have wished and the peroration truly inspired. I trust he rose to it and, in delivery and audibility, thoroughly let himself go. Once he had got it, that was all it wanted. But how it will expose him—to solicitations and importunities. He will have much more news of it; but before that I trust his fill of rustication and repose. You say *when* you go to Chocorua, but I rejoice that you do go. May you then, may you there, see the whole episode as a big fixed, framed and detached picture—a great permanent history-piece. Even to me here, too utterly isolated and out of communication, it gives the last sensible vibration of the old emotion of the War—buried under all the accumulated other emotions and years, estrangements and effacements that have supervened, but with a deep-down tremor of life and memory, a dim residuum and phantasm of youth and imagination, playing up, through all, into secret parts of one's being, and indeed into one's overcharged eyes. What it would have brought back to me—what *wouldn't* it have brought back!—to have seen what your mere mention of moves me to see—the last "grizzled remnant" of the 54th! What a day for them—if especially there were officers in proportion to men, coming after such years, so many, probably, for most, of the hardest battle of life and of the romance (for all its Blood) of that brief time built out as if for ever. Shall you not sooner or later (best sooner) be able to send me a photograph—I mean a really big and fine one, if such exist? They must, surely—they will; will they not? A copy of Harper's Weekly has come to me with a big double-page print of the group, which I have found of a beauty extraordinarily impressive and moving. But I want something I can possess and suspend. How glad I am that William could bring in those passages of

22. Arthur George Sedgwick (1844–1915) was an American lawyer, journalist, and editor who knew HJ socially and professionally.

letters of the brother![23]—so relevant, so absolutely to his purpose and yet having the effect of not leaving wholly out of it that most relegated and pathetic of ghosts. I hope poor W[ilky]. was present in some demonstrated form (I mean that you and William could catch) to not a few remembrances and sympathies. Carrie[24] and her offspring are somewhere on the Continent—but I have never got abroad at all, you see, and of the matter of the 31st [William's speech] I have had no sound of any sort (any more than any other for months) from her. I hope that since you wrote some of the Shaws have given some sign. Basta [Spanish for "enough"]—though I long for more from you, still more of echo and reference. What a funk indeed—over the voice-question—you must have been in the night before! But now it all adds to the romance and the drama. To all your great doings I feel as if my meagre non-doing had nothing at all to contribute. I am still in London—up to the very edge of the portentous saturnalia of the 22nd.[25] I have practically—at any rate for this month—given up going abroad. It was too late, before I could at all really manage it, for Italy; and once Italy drops out I find myself not solicited in any other way (so far as leaving England is concerned) that I can't pretty easily resist. I go, at any rate, within this week down to the seaside somewhere, to get out of the crowd, the dust, the Babylonian barricades, and turn round and take breath from a good deal of continuous work. I have meanwhile, for the Jubilee, lent the Godkins these rooms. They come up to a magnificent Rothschild position to see the show, but are otherwise unable to find in the whole place, for two or three nights, a pillow to lay their heads. It will be the biggest crowd ever, since the beginning of time, collected together in one place. I have had—that is I had a month ago—a couple of very good invitations to seats, but I declined them (still expecting then to go abroad) and have now lost them and don't in the least regret them. But enough of this. I hope it will find you in act of departure or on the eve of it. I embrace you both afresh, and if my brow wore any laurels to speak of would pluck

---

23. Here HJ refers to excerpts from their brother Garth Wilkinson (Wilky) James's letters. Wilky suffered from war injuries and chronic kidney disease, as well as numerous financial reverses. HJ hoped in some way his spirit was present at this occasion. William James himself would later dabble with the idea that the dead could be summoned back for communion with the living, and HJ himself believed this in the early 1900s.

24. Caroline Eames Cary James (1851–1931), Wilky's wife. HJ said in 1883, after visiting Carrie and Wilky in Milwaukee, "Carrie's imbecility is especially deplorable."

25. Celebrating Queen Victoria's Diamond Jubilee.

them all thence to place them on William's. But his own are too thick to miss anything. Yours, dearest Alice, more than ever,

*Henry James*

P.S.—Sara Norton[26] was with the Godkins, and very charming and interesting and communicative about you all; so that it was a positive comfort to have her there to foregather with. She seems to me completely changed from the girl she first grew up to be—with a certain hardness and bitterness and pessimism, a certain Anglophobia even—begotten not unnaturally by some of her contacts; but still very attractive and even clever; so much so, at any rate, that I wish with all my heart, for the general good and for hers in particular, that some proper person would only lead her to the altar. But she is in the modern young female cosmopolitan fix—having, fatally, seen more men and nicer ones than the individual potentially offering!

TLS: Houghton bMS Am 1094 (1621)


*James questions his brother's views on school for Peggy and comments on the Dreyfus case.*


LAMB HOUSE, RYE.

Beloved Alice, Aug. 19*th* 1899.

More days than I meant have gone by without my thanking you for your last beautiful letter—the one enclosing the long & interesting one from the brave Billy. But everything is so utterly all right that there is no hurry. Even my woe at having *shown* you any woe has subsided—& when you come here it will only have led up—our little correspondence—to such appreciation on your & W*m's* part as will make you wish to snatch the place from me for yourselves. I'm sorry you're in for so many weeks but they will pass faster, much, after these 1*st*. Everything *flashes* by, now—to my sense. I have a card from W*m* this a.m. about the little mediaeval Friedberg, on which I congratulate you. His case of books has gone these 3 days; as well as I could send it, please tell him, from *here*. There is no forwarding *agent* in this little place, & I had to commit it to the South Eastern railway—which, however, deals largely—directly—with the continent &c. It was perceptibly the smallest of the boxes, but it hadn't been opened anywhere, & seemed wholly strong & needing no clamping. An-

---

26. Sara (Sally) Norton (1864–1922), elder daughter of Charles Eliot Norton.

other box—a very old & battered black trunk, marked C. W. (strange ghost of Aunt Kate!) came *after* the four boxes & is small, but I don't suppose W*m* meant that.——I should like to write you much about the school-question for Peggy; but we must *talk* it well out. I am both mystified & appalled at what you make me gather of W*m*'s derision of your wish for a "gentle" school for her. What kind of a one—just heaven—would he advocate? Tell him that any second-rate girls school in the British Island would be a *horror*—she must have the "best people" or nothing. Strange would be such views. The *one* shade of objection to Mlle. S's[27] house is that it is definitely "middle-class." But *all* schools here are that—it's thought very awful, at best, to send girls to them. We will flood the subject with light. I keep Billy's letter for you—how intelligent & happy! I live in the shadow of the dark Dreyfus[28] misery. He is a condemned man—to assassination certain if he is acquitted. But the C.M. [court-martial] will perish rather than acquit him—& with a *guilty* verdict there will be fresh convulsions in the country & execration (at the absence of evidence) all over the world. It darkens our days & poisons the gentle summer, which is lovely here. Wondrous weather. I wish I could help you more to pass the time. But I am whirled along in work. Much love to Baldwin.[29] Ever your affectionate

*Henry.*

ALS: Houghton bMS Am 1094 (1625)

*James compares the progress of William's health to driving a pig to the fair. He complains of Rye's unpleasant weather but looks forward to spring.*

27. Mlle. Marie Souvestre (born approximately 1834) had a French school in Wimbledon Park, London. She taught the children of many distinguished families, including the Stracheys and Eleanor Roosevelt.

28. Alfred Dreyfus (1859–1935) was a French army officer of Jewish descent who was convicted of treason in 1894 and imprisoned on Devil's Island. A retrial in 1898, forced by Émile Zola, proved that the papers used to convict Dreyfus had been forged. The case generated waves of anti-Semitic feelings and countering pro-Semitic groups. Dreyfus was finally cleared of all charges in 1906 and restored to his former military rank; he was also awarded the Legion of Honor.

29. Dr. William Wilberforce Baldwin (1850–1910), noted American physician who befriended and counseled William, Henry, and Alice James. James toured Italy with Baldwin in 1890. The doctor diagnosed Alice's breast cancer in 1890 and William's heart disease in 1899.

Dearest Alice,

I got your letter of Friday last only yesterday, Tuesday, & meant to answer it last evening. But some pressing printer proofs that I had to spend time over prevented, & I'm afraid this will seem long in coming to you. You speak of William's "morning of gloom," through bad weather, discomfort &c—& of his seeing Dr. Sigard & what Sigard says. As to this last, I rejoice in it heartily. Alas, for the interruption of benefit—but that is the way *all* improvements go! It is like driving a pig to the fair: sometimes he gets round & behind you & you have to bring him back. But at last to the fair you *do* get him—& meanwhile, all the time, you are on the road to it. Ask William to forgive my homely simile, but that is his natural progress. Things will come *up* again, & the brightening spring will more & more keep them together. I'm awfully glad he had Sigard's examination.——— You sound rather surrounded & overwhelmed with people, & Richet's[30] visit will crown the edifice—to say nothing of Mrs. Thompson's, &c; which I regret (for the addition to your household &c;) but it will all *pass*—& peace will again be with you before too long. I am delighted to hear that you think of coming back to England for the summer—after the 1st go at Nauheim,[31] I suppose you mean: but I hope you'll hug Carqueiranne[32] & stick fast to it so long as it can do you any good whatever.— —I have as little news as usual. *Nothing* happens here but weather—sleet & snow & howling gales & frost & days occasionally beginning well recently only to spoil utterly just as one hopes to get out. This and the black monotony of military misery—heart-breaking & sinister[33] (one sometimes, to excess, feels it,) are our only diet. Yet I bear it all well, & the brave little house is loyal & cheerful & warm.——I have opened at last Miss Wiess's packet & fish out the documents that seem most to concern you & to be most transmissible. Her *bill* appears to be among them. Her package is labelled "School-Reports" &c, & so heavy that the foreign postage would be (I learned,) several shillings. So I ignorantly detained it. Goodnight—& forgive my dull letter. The imprisonment here (want of air

---

30. Charles Robert Richet (1850–1935), professor at the Sorbonne. He let the Jameses use his chateau on the Mediterranean near Hyères for the winter.

31. German watering resort of Bad Nauheim, where William James took painful cold-water baths. The then-popular treatment evidently made his health worse.

32. Richet's French chateau.

33. Probably a reference to the Boer (South African) War, where military operations escalated to a critical point in January and February 1900.

& walks, &c) stupefies me a little. Yet spring distinctly, with it all, begins—in the distance, to hover, & the worst is over. Next week it will be daylight until 6 o'clock—& exercise will recommence. It is taking it alone that is tasteless. Tender love to William. Courage, courage! Ever your affectionate

Henry.

ALS: Houghton bMS Am 1094 (1635)

*HJ has met George B. McClellan, the new Napoleon of Harpers. Peggy is adjusting to her new school and to the Clarke family, with whom she boards, but he wishes he had room for her and a governess at Lamb House.*

LAMB HOUSE, RYE.

Dearest Alice, April 4*th* 1900.

I just have your letter of Sunday & I respond to it while I wait to take the 1.8 train to go up to town *again* for one night! You will think me "irreclaimable"—but I go alas, partly, for the dentist having suddenly had an uncomfortable, very, but fortunately arrangeable, au plus tôt [quickly], dental accident. Also—the other 1/2—to meet at dinner "George B. Mc-Clellan Harvey"[34] the extraordinary young Napoleonic taker=over of the so-compromised Harper business, proprietor of the N. A. Review &c—to whom the London parties to the situation are giving a small rather intime [intimate] banquet this p.m. As they have asked me I've thought it more encouraging to them, as employers of labour, as well as to myself, not to decline. Fortunately they work in with the restorative Goldsmith [his dentist]. I wrote you 2 days ago, after a postcard from W*m* which seemed to *imply* that, to the Albion; but your things—for I send some periodicals too—will of course be extractable thence. If P. Lowell, e.g., is there, he may, mayn't he? rescue them for you. May fortune & nature combine to smile on you at the new quarters. I am of course not a little concerned at what you tell me of Peggy's news[35]—all the more that I feel myself so terribly useless a wheel to that particular coach (that of her education:) or rather no wheel at all. Except that she looked remarkably *well*—stout,

34. Colonel George Brinton McClellan Harvey (1864–1928) was the owner and editor of the *North American Review* from 1899 to 1926 and the president of the publishing house of Harper and Bros. from 1900 to 1915.

35. Peggy James was attending school in England and living with the Emily (b. 1859) and Joseph Thatcher Clarke (d. 1920) family. Mr. Clarke was a historian of ancient architecture; Mrs. Clarke helped him with his work. They had a number of children. Alice had met Clarke in 1868 when she lived in Dresden.

sound & fresh-coloured—she gave me no impression, in town, the other day, of positive high spirits. On the contrary, I thought her rather perceptibly incommunicative—though communication, in the presence of the Clarke children, theatricals, publicity & junketing, was of course at the best difficult. But she *hesitated* just perceptibly (only,) when, on the top of a bus, I got her beside me long enough to ask if she were "happy." She said "Yes," but without emphasis. And she gave no sign of positive congruity with her companions. I shouldn't, frankly, have expected a great deal of that *for* her—though of course my vision was too limited to help me much to judge of more than the immediate evidence. I don't believe she is morbid—but I believe she is essentially *older* than 19 out of 20 of the children she may be with—much more sensitive & reflective & without high animal spirits. These things would quite account for her disparity with the young C.'s (whose personal conditions, shabbiness &c, may also have ended by depressing her;) I mean without the hypothesis of her having brooded on her wrongs. Luckily, I say, she struck me as really *well*. I tried to "draw" her on her school—but she said little about it. Of course, on the other hand, at all times she says little about many things. If I could only take her, house her, down here with a nice governess! But so much of the house would have to go to them! Don't at any rate be nervous about her—or about anything. I shall cover you all in, if you only give me time. Forgive this headlong confusion—I shall miss my train. It's balmy, sun-showery, Aprilish, today, & the garden & place so amiable that I regret leaving them even for the few hours. Mrs. McKaye's[36] letter is a pure "documentary" gem: only making me, as a novelist, wish so I had written it *for*, or *as*, her. Thank W*m* for the tip about Santayana[37]—not lost on me. I sent Harry an excellent letter to *Mrs. Hays*—she being in charge of all their hospitalities &c; but *wrote*, independently, both to Harry & to her *about* him—they will be very benevolent & interested. Ever your

*Henry*

ALS: Houghton bMS Am 1094 (1637)

---

36. She may have been the wife of famous actor James Steele Morrison MacKaye (1842–94), who had been a close boyhood friend of WJ's from a Newport summer in 1858. Or she may have been the wife of his son, dramatist Percy MacKaye (1875–1956). There was also an American writer named Maria Ellery MacKaye (b. 1830).

37. George Santayana (1863–1952), Spanish-born philosopher who taught at Harvard with William James.

*James advises Alice on dressmakers, warning her that she will find only "trashy" dressmakers in Rome. He is exasperated with his cousin Elly Hunter, who is endlessly unreasonable.*

Dearest Alice.                                                     Oct. 14*th.* 1900

I had a dear little letter from you the other day—the day, I gather, before you were leaving Nauheim, which I've never thanked you for. May its good account of your phase & situation have only been confirmed by later developments, & may your migration to Lucerne have been prosperously effected—I hope you & William are having these autumn days of equivalent beauty to these admirable ones of ours. But if that is indeed the case, how wonderful they must be! The season continues, with insignificant breaks, *invraisemblable* [unbelievably] here. It *is* a climate, too, after all.——When I speak of your good account of your phase, I except, alas, the sad bearing on it of the fulmination of your dressmaker, foudroyée par les dieux [stricken by the gods], who evidently prefer your beauty unadorned. Don't, however, let me beseech you, be discouraged by it—I mean to the degree of not trying to get the clothes, elsewhere, at Geneva. *You will want clothes in Rome*—& won't find it, I fear, convenient or easy to get them properly there. I shld. suppose the dressmakers there trashy & cheaty—& the AngloSaxons *all* to get their clothes north of the Alps. But don't let me add to your difficulties by preaching the non-feasible or exaggerating the inconvenient. It may be that *Florence* would have help for you. But I recommend you to get, on that point, the best advice you can. I *doubt* of Florence. I rejoice to say tranquillity reigns here—though Elly & Leslie[38] still linger. The latter, however, definitely goes back to Paris on Tuesday, & Elly & Grenville[39] also depart; but for *where* I quite don't know. E's *non-sequiturs* & unreasonablenesses are endless, & if one had any real dealings with her would be maddening. They make me at moments think almost indulgently of Hunter,[40] for whom she seems to be in a mood, just now, of compassion—based on nothing that I can discover. She at any rate talks of Hayward's Heath (1/2 way between London & Brighton) for the winter, there being there a small boys' preparatory school

---

38. Ellen Gertrude Emmet (Mrs. George) Hunter (1850–1920), Minny Temple's sister and HJ's first cousin. Leslie was her daughter, Edith Leslie Emmet (b. 1877).

39. Eleanor James Temple Emmet (b. 1880) and Grenville Temple Emmet (1877–1937), brother and sister, were HJ's cousins. Their parents were Katharine (Kitty) Temple (Minny Temple's sister) and Richard Stockton Emmet.

40. George Hunter (1847–1914), Scotch, second husband of Ellen James Temple Emmet.

that she has suddenly, without the least knowledge, begun to think—or to talk—of putting Grenville at. "She makes me tired"—& it will not be pure depression, sorry as I am for her, to see her depart. I've become extremely fond of Leslie, who has much sense & judgment as well as absolute amiability. She has lost all faith in her mother's reason. She thinks she has in view two good French ladies, takers of pensionnaires, ladies &c, to be with this winter, & she has a cheque to change tomorrow at the Rye Bank! John Bancroft[41] & his daughter were here to lunch—down from town, wondrously—2 days ago: he very old & ill & shaky, so that I was afraid of his really remaining on my hands. It was a drearyish, dullish episode. They passed almost no remarks. I learned from him that Baldwin [Dr. William] was still—then,—in London; only going down to Sandringham to see the Duchess of York! Also that Mrs. John is to spend the winter in Rome wholly under his care. Borrow some clothes of *her!* As usual it's the midnight hour. I enclose you both with my affectionate solicitude. I wrote an hour ago to Peggy—& am going to write to Harry (not tonight.) I hold McA.'s second copy of W*m's* lecture all this time for him—afraid to send it till he gives me the word. He had better have it while still in Schweiz. The registered, in Italy, is a bore to receive. The peace of possession here, deepens & fructifies. I hope *your* portents & auspices all keep up & I am your ever affectionate

*Henry.*

P.S. I will tell you when I next write what the interminable delay is over the Flournoy books: the good edition wholly out of print & Bain[42] looking for 2*d* hand copies, to be bound.

ALS: Houghton bMS Am 1094 (1644)

---

*Alice and William should not go to Italy, because of William's health and the weather. He has just taken Peggy James and her friends to Madame Tussaud's wax museum to see the murderers.*

REFORM CLUB, PALL MALL, S.W.

Dearest Alice. Jan. 7*th 1901*

Your two letters of very recent date—W*m's* & yours, are both to hand, & on the whole very consoling. William's rally from his recent drop greatly moves me—such faith have I in what it must mean; but almost better still,

---

41. John Bancroft, American painter and son of George Bancroft (1800–1891), U.S. historian and diplomat.

42. James Stoddart Bain (b. 1872), a London bookseller James frequented.

best of all, is your *sane* decision not—in these midwinter days—to take the road. You lately struck a chill to my heart by speaking of the possibility of your going to "the country"—the country, in Italy, in January, being so dark a dream! It is madness to move till March—don't, *don't, don't!* Very sad your acct. of poor Myers[43]—& much, I shld. suppose, like the beginning of the end. I am deeply sorry for him. But his presence must be depleting, I fear, to all your sensibilities. May he bear as lightly as you can manage. I've had an afternoon of Peg last week—last Friday: meeting the 4 children at Baker St. at 1.30 & taking them to the Hippodrome, a wonderful show. Then I took them & tea'd them; & wound up with M*me* Tussaud's & all the murderers; seeing them off again in the 7 train. I think they really enjoyed; but I want an afternoon soon with Peg alone, & shall get it. I am so pressed with work, letters, London &c—after my long absence, that I shall ask you to excuse brevity. This place works *beautiful.*[44] But a snowstorm more or less rages, & we have strange stories, in the prints, of *your* temperature. May it already have passed. I will write you better the next time. Cling to Rome—don't think you've wasted—it *sinks.* Poor John Bancroft! I thought that was just what he was last spoiling for— when he came to me at Rye in the autumn. She oughtn't to go [to] him— he doesn't desire her. Sturgis Bigelow[45] dines with me tonight. À bientôt [see you soon] again. Great thanks to W. for his last. Ever yr

Henry.

P.S. Too enchanted with what you tell me of W.'s feeling for his work, in spite of his own so true remarks about work slowly done. Ah me! Elly Hunter at Salisbury, Conn.!

ALS: Houghton bMS Am 1094 (1648)

*He congratulates William on his "cerebral boom." James's poor health makes him compare his doctors to "mere blind bulls in a china-shop" and himself to "a long-suffering, patient cow."*

43. Frederick William Henry Myers (1843–1901), English writer and leader in psychical research in England. He helped found the Society for Psychical Research in 1882; William James was also involved with this group at various times.

44. Michael Anesko indicates James may have underscored this word to indicate his awareness of the solecism.

45. William Sturgis Bigelow (1850–1926), cousin of Mrs. Henry Adams. He became a Buddhist.

*Monday*

Dearest Alice. [ Jan. 14. 1901.—William James's hand]

Your blessed letter of the 11*th* just comes in & brings me refreshment of soul. W*m*'s cerebral boom—advancing lectures & ever crowded life—all give me a taste of the shining web & flashing shuttle on the loom of Existence, or even of Providence, & of peace & plenty still in store for us. The close-pressing world around you must indeed be a trial & a test; but you can count the days off, against it, & the sands will run more & more quickly. Poor Myers must indeed be a drain on William's nerves—but the sense of helping him along his dark passage does I suppose also help resistance & revival (I mean yours & William's,) & you are after all—generally—paying the penalty of your distinction & your halo.——Don't meanwhile add to your tension, for heaven's sake, by worrying about me. I *haven't* been well, all the autumn, & for long, with the continuance of the obstinate eczema—for that was it—that broke out upon me last summer & that has been the final deviltry of other bad conditions horribly fixed & aggravated all these last 3 years—ever since (though it's but a coincidence) 1st settling at Rye. But I am *better*—& shall be so. I've been in a damnable black hole, but am emerging & know how & why: & the torment of my poor skin is abating—& all without doctors & drugs—at least without *theirs.* They (Doctors) are with *me* mere blind bulls in a china-shop; & though doubtless myself but a long-suffering, patient cow, I smash *less* of the establishment itself, & can still carry on business. By the time you come back I shall be really better; & I now cutaneously suffer much less. There have been times when it was maddening. London is better for me at present—*much*—than Rye; & *this* place works admirably. I am really *using* these 2 clubs for the 1st time in all the years I've had them & paid dues; & the resource is, in all ways of comfort & convenience immense. This, only, for tonight—more in a day or two. The Aïdé-Stanley-Tennant[46] combination *sounds* a dose; but don't get scared—they will percolate *other* channels & you will be limpets on your rock. Besides, the convictions they will fortify—always a comfort! Much love. I *shall* soon have a p.m. with Peg alone. I long for it. Ever your
*Henry.*

ALS: Houghton bMS Am 1094 (1649)

---

46. Charles Hamilton Aïdé (1826–1906), prolific poet, musical composer, artist, play-wright, and writer, socialized with HJ frequently. Dorothy "Dolly" Tennant Stanley was the wife of explorer Sir Henry Morton Stanley (1841–1904). Gertrude Collier Tennant was the daughter of a naval attaché at the British embassy in France and a friend of Flaubert's.

*James gives a poignant view of Queen Victoria's funeral and an account of his niece Peggy's school progress.*

THE ATHENAEUM, PALL MALL, S.W.

Dearest Alice. *January 30th 1901*

To hand your interesting letter of the 25*th,* with William's conclusion. Your news of him & his of himself is, alas, what I but too acutely feared from the moment of hearing from you that that stricken family [the Frederick Myers family] were due. I felt that he had come to Rome to die & that you wd. be stricken by their stroke. I wonder, only, that W*m* has held out as he has—& you must remember what stiff & peculiar *cause* he has had for a collapse. Truly a quite too utterly efficient one. He will rebound, with a little *time* to do it in, & meanwhile the 8 lectures[47] are a magnificent achievement—very wonderful thing. Great glory & profit do I feel that they represent. I cling to the image of your staying quiet there a while longer—with the blessing of the opening spring on you—under the good & gallant Baldwin, to whom I send much love & thanks. I'm glad you see & like the excellent & charming young Andersen,[48] "artist" & sincere & intelligent being (though handicapped by a strange "self-made" illiteracy & ignorance of many things,) as he seems to me through & through. But see if he has any specimens near him—his portrait-busts. They seem to me to be really—given his age—masterly.——I went out on Sunday to see Peggy, & had a couple of hours with her—a little empty through bad weather (so that we couldn't walk;) the absence of Clarke, (who goes only to *Milan* & Berlin;) &c., &c. She looked extremely well & seemed serene, but I doubt if the *normal* in her can really assert itself so long as she is on her present basis of "entourage." One has to allow too much for her reaction against it (which I'm bound to say I don't wonder at,) in judging of her state. But don't in the least worry about her—she is in a very good moment, & now that the end of her time there is more in sight I think she is, & everything is, very easy. She comes in to go with me, alone, to some afternoon play on Saturday week next.—— *This* Saturday is given up to the Queen's funeral—a great military procession across London, on the way from Osborne to Windsor; with foreign Kings & Emperors (Germany, Russia, Portugal, Greece, &c) in the van. We are still

---

47. This refers to the Gifford Lectures on Natural Religion William was to give in Scotland.

48. Hendrik Christian Andersen (1872–1940), Norwegian-born American sculptor and relation of writer Hans Christian Andersen. After they met in 1899, James and Andersen were temporarily quite intimate.

much under the shadow of the old lady's death, & it seems to be generally felt that she was really, for 60 years, a very politically & beneficently operative person. The country, in short, feels quite *motherless*—& I to some extent have my part in the feeling. If you had lived here long you wd. know what I mean. It makes one think of her very kindly. But the gush is being very fearfully overdone—even about the new King. But why do I write to you about these baubles?———I am sorry you, dear Alice, feel so *dépaysée* [disoriented or homesick] in Rome—but glad you have Theodora,[49] to whom I send much love, to be dépaysée with. I hope the oncoming relenting of winter will initiate you both, more.———When you write again do kindly mention to me what I spoke of in my last—how the $1000 laid up for me can be got at? I only want for the present to *know* that: how I could, if needful, draw them. I may not be needful—on the whole probably not. I've just paid my income tax; which the war has made fearful—just a shilling in the pound. That is what has made me think of the $1000. My blessing on the new course of lymph, & on the well-earned rest, for W*m*, which is to accompany it. Think of me as singularly well-placed here—at 105—& as working very straight. I dined the other day, with the S. B.'s [Stopford Brookes],[50] in my flat. I find I painfully love it still! Ever your affectionate

Henry

ALS: Houghton bMS Am 1094 (1650)

*James wishes William luck with his Gifford lectures, encouraging William and Alice to visit Stratford during their forthcoming visit to England.*

LAMB HOUSE, RYE.

Dearest Alice.                                        [June 3, 1901]

Your letter is a blessed boon to me—followed by a fresh & almost as welcome *Scotsman*. You tell me just what I wanted to know—about the attitude of William's public, "Edinburgh Society" &c, & they seem all one could desire & "do with." The lectures indeed, even as shining dimly through the newspaper reports, must be different & more succulent fare than any the Gifford audiences have known the like of. And with this top

---

49. Maria Theodora Sedgwick (1851–1916) knew the Jameses first in Newport in 1860 and was friendly with them in Cambridge after that, remaining a family friend throughout her life.

50. Clergyman and writer Stopford Augustus Brooke (1832–1916) rented HJ's London flat for a time. They had met in 1878 at a Reform Club dinner.

of the hill reached William *will,* surely, slide gently & securely down to the bottom of the hither side. Let him figure *me* with open arms to receive him there. I got back last night from Welcombe, very gratefully—in spite of the inordinate loveliness of all that Warwickshire land in this splendour of blossom & colour & early summer generally. It was a very pleasant little visit, & mercifully quiet, with only one other person (Sidney Lee, of the D. N. B. & the Shakespeare,[51]) & 2 or 3 exquisite drives. *He* indicated to me your probably best place if you go to Stratford, as I greatly hope you will, & I will let you know it as soon as you shall have the need in sight.— —I hope you are thoroughly making up your minds to stay to your *latest* summer date—hope it most intensely. Don't for one instant lose sight of the fact that this house, with its peace & ease, stands open to you for the whole time, beguiling, assisting, beseeching. That *ought* to weigh heavily in the scale of Aug. 31*st*—as also it being, for perhaps so long, *my* last sight of you. How I understand your wonder at having been able so to forfeit Harry—the blessing that one feels him. But I hope he'll see his Scotland. Mille tendresses [much love] to *William.*——*How* does Peggy come? I wish I could assist at one lecture! But I seem in that respect doomed. Ever, dearest Alice, your affectionate

*Henry.*
Sunday *night*

ALS: Houghton bMS Am 1094 (1652)

*To relieve his gout, James bathes his left foot in thick bran and hot water. He has been asked to give eight Lowell Lectures on English authors when he visits America next year but feels unqualified to lecture. He is finishing* The Golden Bowl *and may start another novel to be serialized in the* North American Review.

[*Dictated*]

Lamb House, Rye, Sussex.

Dearest A.                                                           Jan. 19th, 1904.

I am in receipt of great bounty from you all—in the shape, first, of poor dear W's so beautifully typed letter of New Year's day (oh what's his exquisite *machine?* that I may acquire the like of it and simulate a beautiful

---

51. Sir Sidney Lee (1859–1926), English editor and scholar. He replaced Sir Leslie Stephen as the editor of the *Dictionary of National Biography* after Stephen's death in 1891. He also wrote several books on Shakespeare and a biography of Queen Victoria (1902).

hand;) and then your own two, the second immediately following the first, and the first enclosing such interesting ones from Peg and from Bob. I put all this, as you see, into one basket to answer it, and make no apology for answering thus. I grieve to say that, like W, I am just emerging from an access of very tiresome gout, which lasted long enough to leave me rather sickeningly in arrears with all letters; especially with the tail of the Christmas and New Year's superabundance. So I make up as I can. My gout is better and I have been able to walk, in spite of lameness and pain, several times; also to get to Hastings and take four Turkish baths. Before this, and during the worst (which kept me in bed but three days, however,) I found relief for my stricken left foot in baths (for the foot itself of course only) of thick *bran* and hot water; the bran into the density of a pudding and kept as hot as one could bear it—by adding fresh hot water; and also kept as thick by equivalent additions. It doesn't cure, but it soothes and soothes, and takes down the inflammation. But enough of this goodwife's remedy—which, however, no other doctor till Skinner[52] had ever put me up to. You probably know all about it. And I trust that W, meanwhile, has long since quite completed *his* convalescence, and been restored to his eminent usefulness. Auch dear Billy, with his influenza, and fainting in the snow—so pathetic, tell him, that I have wept over it: I pray *his* upset may be a thing of the past. These cares and ministrations must tell on *you,* dearest A; and I only hope you haven't been paying for them. W's letter was interesting to me in every way, and not least in its mention of a call on you from Eliot,[53] while he was ill, about his mitigated retirement; but what demands my most immediate attention is your having written me that Laurence Lowell[54] was also writing me, and in what sense. His letter in fact arrived with yours, and I am answering it to-night. But how shall I without feeling I perhaps *afflict* you (but only till I've explained!) tell you, disconcertingly, in what sense I am absolutely obliged to answer it? I say "afflict" you because I see that ever since the few light and vague words we exchanged here on the matter two or three years ago, the idea (of what L. L. proposes) must have sunk into you more than I supposed. I infer this because you appear quite to take for granted my acceptance of his overture. Had I known you were doing this, all the while, I would have returned to

52. Dr. Ernest Skinner, Rye's general practitioner.
53. Charles William Eliot (1834–1926), president of Harvard.
54. A. Lawrence Lowell (1856–1943), Charles Eliot's successor as president of Harvard in 1909.

the subject, specifically, and warned you of considerations that must at present govern me, and that make my promising a course of eight Lowell Lectures for his designated time, next winter and spring, an impracticable dream. I have promised so much other work, for many, many months to come, that my hands are completely tied as against preparing Lectures; and even if they were not I shouldn't see my way, either economically or otherwise speaking, to crowd such a feat into my American visit. William and you so breathe, and flourish upon, the air of Lectures, which has been your daily bread, both material and intellectual, for years, that you impute to me, alas, a facility that I'm far from possessing, and that my possession of in a miraculous degree would alone make thinkable that I might close with Lowell. I am sixty years old, and have never written a lecture in my life— besides being utterly unprepared for any course present to Lowell's mind. This would mean that I should fall to immediately and give myself up to them, working as hard as possible on them, and on nothing else, till the beginning of the Course; and as I have no "literary subject" (which is what he names) in any readiness without a long period of reading-up, my preparation wouldn't at all land me in port by Lowell's date, but would also involve my settling down to the job as soon as I should arrive among you, and my shutting myself up with it until the latest possible day. And all this for a pecuniary reward which, though respectable, would, at the end of so much lavished time, leave me comparatively bankrupt. I can only *think* of my pilgrimage on condition of my doing something as lucrative as possible in the interval—which, fortunately, as against Lowell, is provided for by such engagements, of a different sort, as are already almost pressing upon me. I am just about to terminate a long novel [*The Golden Bowl*], which, as I think I have told you, is, like another, to follow its issue at about eight months' distance, contracted for with Methuen and Co here and the Scribners in N. Y. It will take me, however, another month or two; after which I must immediately begin on the second, somewhat shorter, and which I shall spare no effort to have finished before I sail. On top of this the Harpers (only please speak no word whatever of it) have asked me to give them another thing, of the length of the Ambassadors, to be serialised in the N. A. R. [*North American Review*], and if I close with them on this, as I with high probability shall, it must be the next ensuing thing I give my attention to *except* one other (an overture from McClure,[55] in anticipation

---

55. This is probably Samuel Sidney McClure (1857–1949), dynamic editorial, publishing, and commercial genius who founded *McClure's Magazine* (1893–1929), which became famous for publishing work by muckrakers, notably Ida Tarbell and Lincoln Steffens.

of my pilgrimage, on the subject of something I won't speak of yet, and my decision as to which ought, cannily, to await my arrival, but in which there may be much profit, and no small interest, for me.) I mention these things to exonerate myself, in your minds, from any levity in not committing myself to the Lectures. *Some* day, some year, if I am spared, the idea of delivering eight on The English Novelists will appeal to me; but I must before that have made myself able to afford the time and the deliberation which my complete and aged unacquaintance with the mystery (of the process) would render indispensable. The levity would be for me now to say Yes; as you will easily recognise when I tell you that Lowell's total fee represents a very minor part, not more than a third, of what I should get for the mere serialisation of an N. A. R. novel, quite apart from the royalties on the book. The same with the McClure matter that I allude to—and as to which please also be dumb: if it is worth anything at all to me, it will be worth a great deal, (more easily too, and more promptly, realised;) and it can't *not* be worth something. Even if these two last engagements did *not* so loom, moreover, I should feel I ought to think twice before giving a pledge that would necessarily clap me into a shut-up state of reading and writing hard from the moment of my disembarkment. With my second (present) novel finished, I shall want to draw a long breath for several weeks, and above all, both then and after, to get, *outside,* as many impressions as possible. The McClure job absolutely makes them, and in as great a variety as possible, imperative; whereby I (privately) quite rise, in prospect & in imagination, to the McClure job. But I've said enough, & more than enough to give you, better than you have, naturally, been having them, my necessary bearings; & I only add, now, that I beg you earnestly to consider the matter in the light of all this (perhaps too profuse & too explicit explanation) when you hear from Lowell that I have, with intense civility, declined, so that I may seem to you perhaps a little to have given you away. I catch, at any rate, the post, and will write you soon less sordidly. I bless you all and am ever

*Henry James*

TLS: Houghton bMS Am 1094 (1659)

*James proclaims himself anxious to experience family life as he prepares for his trip to America. He compares his "Fletcherizing" (chewing his food many times before swallowing) to Wordsworth's attachment to his Lucy.*

Dearest A.                                         Aug. 2nd, 1904.

I have two highly-valued letters from you; one, of the 22nd, this morning received from you, and one the other day accompanying beautifully a scarcely less beautiful letter of Harry's, which I immediately answered with a message to you. It is fairly looking now as if I should see you so soon that these forerunners may be brief—therefore I put in tonight but these few and meagre lines. I haven't, for many reasons, really *seen* myself launched till within these few past days; but now the phenomenon takes on a certain objectivity—which seems certain, at last, to augment from day to day. I thank you with all my heart for your welcome and your words about your state of "readiness", of which I hadn't for three seconds doubted. I mentioned to Harry (with the prospect of whose meeting me in N. Y. I luxuriously revel) that I would briefly diverge before making for your mountain home *if that should seem in advance (as regards the E[mmet]s, for instance,) desirable.* But I have myself but one desire; which will be to get on to Boston with him that day or night, if possible; spending a night, by your leave, in Irving Street, and then renewing my journey. No one is a bit *warranted* in expecting me to do anything else—or to postpone you and W. to anything or anyone. This therefore is what I shall take for granted— and heaven speed the hour I alight at your door. As my ship (Kaiser William II, to repeat once more for safety's sake) leaves Southampton on Wednesday 24th, and is considered abnormally fast, I believe she usually arrives, in such a case, on the Monday, and fairly early in the day: therefore we shall be able, I dare say, to make Boston that night. This will perhaps enable me to be with you at Chocorua *within* a week of embarking here— which is a fond and fantastic thought. You may count on me at any rate, I suppose, by Wednesday 31st—which will also do very well. As for the quantity of your "family life", I shall shrink from no manifestation of it, however monstrous—I know how favourably I shall feel it compare with mine. Therefore I don't suggest your sacrificing so much as a limb, or a finger or toe, of Peggy or Aleck, to make it more shapely. I hope to see and hear it bristle with all the arms and legs and noses and voices of all of you (by which I don't mean any reflection on your nasality.) I have, through my till now unsurmounted skepticism, left everything in the way of preparation still to be done; whereby I was intending to repair to town & the tailor's by a to-morrow evening train, after a day spent in profitable occupation here. But I suddenly received a bolt out of the blue in the form of a telegram from the Paul Bourgets,[56] who have just, apparently, disembarked at Folkestone, and beg me to come over there to lunch with them. Therefore I go, to keep them, cynically speaking, from coming here; and shall proceed thence in the p.m. straight to London, where my errand will be mainly to get some clothes. This abandoned business (as I hate the purchase of clothes more every month I live) will prove to me, better than anything else, that I am really booked. I have had better evidence still, within the last few days, which you will be glad to hear of—in the form of my having quite definitely, though unexpectedly, *let* this house—let it to the two little sisters from Washington, the Miss Horstmanns, whose visit of inquiry, suggested by a London friend of mine, I lately told you of. It appears that one of them is to marry in September, in London, John Boit of Boston, a man much older than herself, and whom I used to know; and this pair greatly desire to spend their first wedded months, with the unmarried sister for company, in just the conditions they will find here. I am letting the house horribly cheap, for scarce more than such a weekly figure as will pay the servants' wages; but that I saw to be necessary, to let it at all, and it will thus be off my hands for six months, with the servants nourished and costing me nothing, and with the place warmed and ventilated and diurnally housemaided. All of which is to the good. I rejoice in your news of W's good season. I continue of course to eat and drink Fletcher—having settled down to it for life; so that I can emulate Wordsworth about his Lucy: "And oh the difference to *me!*" Therefore I rejoice that W isn't passing it by. But I am writing myself to bed. Good-night, with love to all from your ever affectionate

*Henry James*

TLS: Houghton bMS Am 1094 (1661)

*Despite James's earlier protests to Alice that he could not lecture, he has agreed to do a series of lectures to help pay for the expenses of his trip. James's Chicago lecture was a success, and he goes next to speak at Notre Dame. A distant relation, Emily Higginson, is "a pure social & domestic scourge."*

---

56. French writer Paul Bourget (1852–1935) and his wife Minnie (ca. 1868–1932) had long been friends of HJ's. Bourget was a sort of disciple to James, and the Bourgets gave James ideas for several stories.

Letters *here,* please, till Saturday *afternoon* (posted till then.)

Dearest Alice.

I had this a.m. a farewell word from William—by which I see he will have auspiciously sailed on Saturday; & I now feel that we shall rejoice, comfortably, in the sense that he is doing it all—more, that is, than we shld. have rejoiced if we had kept him at home. And those were the only alternatives. So we will lift up our hearts & see nothing but the good of it!———As for me, I am *surviving*—that is the main fact. (And I am surviving the better for having, an hour ago, *got away* from Winnetka & Emily[57] (the *deluvian,* the devastating,) &, by George's exquisite kindness, been invited to enjoy a room here for the rest of my stay; a blissfully greater convenience, (though Winnetka too was most kind & comfortable—& *with* hot water in the bath—except on Mondays—washingday—was *your* day a Monday?) I have lectured twice here with brilliant success (unmistakably,) & the hospitality & importunity of the people touches me, really, brings tears to my eyes by its largeness, frankness &, as ⟨c.r.u.?⟩ would say, sweetness, even while it exhausts & prostrates me. I can't give you either a general picture or details (they must *wait,* alas, for long talks at home;) but the whole thing is funny & fantastic & interesting, & Mary was at my 1*st* lecture & Wilkie's Alice,[58] from Milwaukee at the 2*d* (the image, she, of poor Wilkie now.) I am to lunch with Mary on Wednesday, & tomorrow I go out to Notre Dame, Indiana, to lecture in the afternoon to a Catholic Convent School in the evening & to a Catholic young men's college in the afternoon (sleeping there again that night.) On Thursday I go to Indianapolis, on Sunday to Milwaukee, & on Monday next 20*th* proceed straight hence to Los Angeles, Cal., by the Santa Fe road. George H. is *adorable de bonté* [adorably kind], but what words can render the fell *dreadfulness* of the maddeningly *intarissable* [indefatigable] Emily? She has fine elements, but she seems to me, practically, a pure social & domestic scourge—& another hour of her, I felt today, would have killed me. But we will talk of her. She raves about *you.* I send dear Harry tenderest

---

57. Emily Higginson, wife of George Higginson (1833–1921). George was the brother of WJ's banker and financial consultant Henry Lee Higginson; the Higginsons were distant relations of WJ and HJ, through Jeannette James Barker, their paternal aunt. They lived in Winnetka, Illinois, and entertained HJ during his tour.

58. Alice James (1875–1923) was Garth Wilkinson's (the third youngest James brother) and his wife Carrie's daughter. She later married David Alexander Edgar (b. 1865).

benedictions. May peace abide with you all, these next weeks, & W*m*'s absence have, as the reverse of the medal, an influence for deep repose. I embrace you all & am ever your

*Henry.*

ALS: Houghton bMS Am 1094 (1667)

*James complains of his long train trip from Chicago through "unspeakable alkali deserts" and shares his first impressions of California.*

HOTEL VAN NUYS  LOS ANGELES, CAL.

Dearest Alice. March 24*th* 1905

Here I am, at last, after a weary run, or crawl, from Chicago, beginning Monday night last, & ending late last, Thursday, evening—the trains being many hours late. It was almost all the way through unspeakable alkali deserts, in which, in spite of the Pullman civilization, & its human products, that clattered & chattered along with me, I almost broke down from tension, sickness & weariness. I shall never again attempt a journey of that confined & cooped-up continuity—it was presuming too much of my powers, & of my poor old *back,* whose ancient woes really threatened to wake up again. But I have now (9.45 a.m.) after a night in a clean bed, the sense of being in California, & though it seems as yet less exotic & romantic than I hoped, it is clearly very amusing & different, quite amiably & unexpectedly *gay*—quite another than the eastern note—& even in the large bustling hall of this (very excellent) hotel, where I write, intimations of *climate,* of a highly seductive order, are wafted in upon me. I presently go forth to assist, I trust, at their development, & at that of other pleasing phenomena. The light, in particular, seems most elegant & *soignée* [remarkable]—I scrawled you a word before leaving Chicago (the very last thing,) asking that my letters be ever so kindly forwarded to *Hotel del Monte, Monterey, Cal.*—for which place I shall be making pretty straight, & to stay as many days as possible. I will wire you—no matter what it costs—when to stop, & will write you, abundantly, in between. I hope meanwhile that for you & Harry, in particular, the scene will have been clearing itself, & I especially long for Harry's news, heaven reward & canonise him! Of one thing be sure—of the way all *this* makes me feel that "Europe" was *the* one thing for William—in contradistinction to *these* ordeals. But oh, for the 1*st* news of him—I wish it wasn't so long to come— I mean to *me.* But à la guerre comme à la guerre [one must take things as they come]. I go from here to *Santa Barbara, Hotel Potter;* my only stop before Monterey—I spoke, or didn't speak, of having spent last Sunday at Milwaukee—but hadn't heart to say that the impression of Carry & her children there was far & away the pleasantest I ever had; even poor C. herself being greatly improved by time ( & beautified & refined, with very becoming white hair,) & Cary & Alice so heartbreakingly like Wilkie. Alice a *very* attractive pleasing, civilized little person. But all embraces. Send my scrawls—if you *can*—to W*m*. Ever your

*Henry*

ALS: Houghton bMS Am 1094 (1669)


*HJ greets William, who has just arrived from Europe. He asks Alice to send him his yellow leather portmanteau and gives her explicit directions on opening it.*

[*Typed by HJ*]

36 West 10th Street [New York],

Dearest A. June 6th, 1905.

I am picking out this to you just to take time by the forelock, since I depart on my little three or four days' adventure, as I shall probably be able to snatch no other minute till I get back to this place (if possible by Saturday night; otherwise by Monday.) It is mortally hot, but in for a penny, in for a pound; and I shall probably pull through, though rather seedy and spent, as I have pulled through everything else. This is to bid you embrace William, on his arrival, as effusively as possible—while I rejoice meanwhile to think of him on these summer seas. Since he is coming on the Cedric, I dare say he will arrive Friday—worse luck that I shall so miss him here. Otherwise of course I would hang about the dock from peep of dawn to meet him. It is worse luck too, that, as I think I wrote you, my invaluable Pinker[59] arrives from London, on my affairs, either to-day or tomorrow, and that I shall miss *him,* and shall have in consequence to make it up the first days of next week (I mean make up the threshing-out of an important matter here)—which will, alas, represent delay in my joining you in Cambridge. And I seem to be committed to going to Howells, at Kittery Point on Saturday 17th, for a couple of nights, anyhow: to say nothing of going to the Masons,[60] at Newport for three days, on the 20th. Bear with me, till we meet, and then we will make everything square. Give meanwhile, I repeat, endless welcome for me to W. I am hoping you have

---

59. James Brand Pinker (1863–1922), HJ's trusted literary agent.

60. Probably the family of Alice Mason (1838–1913), an old Boston family that the Jameses had known both in America and abroad since their youth.

been able to come down gently and peacefully from Chocorua, with all your work happily finished there, and that you are finding yourself rested and refreshed, no end, even by the exercise of all your virtue. Don't have a creature in the house at Cambridge, I beseech you, from this time on. Make it the law of your life, and of W's, till you get away altogether. This will leave you the more freedom to think, very kindly, of sending me a small portmanteau, or valise, a Gladstone bag, properly, of yellow leather, which stands empty in my room, and which I should like very much to have here to help get my things together for final departure. Please make sure *it is* empty; the key is not in it, but the clasp, or catch of lock, squeezes together, longitudinally, and the thing holds so, very well, if you make sure, by pressure of the sides of the upper part of the frame, or mouth, toward either end of them, that a sharp little click takes place. I have the key here, by the way, and I think best to enclose it in this—in case the confounded thing should *be locked* with effects in it. A tag on it, by Express, to this address, any time before Sunday next, will greatly oblige. I embrace you all. It is too hot for more detail; but I have decently finished my oration, and shall have made, I think a proper thing of it. Ever yours,

*Henry.*

TLS: Houghton bMS Am 1094 (1677)


*James has had domestic problems since returning to England, announcing the "servant-question* sickens *me." He misses them all.*

Dearest Alice.

I wrote you a poor pale line for the ship—& now a week has passed without my having (to make up for *that* meagreness,) more promptly thanked you for the dear good letter, enclosing notes from William, with which you *have* already so bountifully overtaken me. I have come back to rather high-piled writing *arrears,* & they have much engulfed me. Likewise I've come back, I am sorry to say, to the feared, though not quite expected, disconcertment of a household in decomposition—with Mrs. P.[addington], almost on the threshold, announcing her necessary, her intended, departure. That has probably been averted now, but it cast a chill over my arrival, & I am servantless save for her & Burgess.[61] The 2 other maids were really minxes & goodfornaughts, & my letting the house to the

---

61. Burgess Noakes (1887–1980) was HJ's beloved servant at Lamb House for a number of years.

3 Boits & a poisonous London lady'smaid, proves now to have been a sad mistake. The B.s, I gather, were without tact or discretion in their demands & habits—but it is a tiresome vulgar story, into which I didn't mean to enter—& much of the disaster has occurred since the tenants departed. I allude to it only because, alas, the charm of my sense of security with Mrs. P. is broken—not as to *her* virtue but simply as to her *staying* & having to battle again with possible minxes. They simply abandoned her in the midst of the heavy work & stress (she is 60 years old, it appears,) of seeing the house painting through, & her silence about all sorts of worriments & complications while I was away, to the end, so as not to trouble me, represents a very real sort of consideration. But forgive these sordidries— into which I have thus plunged; it is only because I *have* in fact, & *am,* plunged. I think I can count upon Mrs. P. for a few months more, but she has a cousin, who has made a heritage, wanting her to come & live with *her*—& the spell is broken & the precarious in short introduced. If she *shld.* leave me I feel that I shld. close the house & go & live at an hotel— taking the occasion, probably, for going (for a few—*1st* time for 6 years— months,) abroad. The servant-question *sickens* me—I shld. never be able to face a frequent renewal of its disturbances. If I could only get a proper person to come & really *run* me for a stipend! I wd. rather even come back & "board" in Irving St.! Does *that* put it vividly enough? Otherwise the situation is clearing.——Rye & my four-square little garden better & sweeter than they ever were—George Gammon, blessed youth, has been a perfect trump of fidelity. Vast engagements to work open before me—or rather close me almost formidably in; & no conditions could (again,) be better for meeting all this. Even while I talk of it, however, I read of your formidable heat-wave, in my morning paper, & I find the tears rise to my eyes when I figure its playing about you in the dead Cambridge air. The selfishness of thinking that I had got off in advance of it isn't what possesses me most, but infinite sympathy for you all—& for W*m* most, if his return from Chicago is in the midst of it. All thanks for his letters, & for the news of [dentist] Roberts' *very* moderate charge. Kindly tell R., if you have a chance, that I greatly appreciate this. Are you sure you can conveniently meet it out of my Syracuse incomings?[62] I leave you them all, at any rate, for the present. All love to William—I feel his Chicago visit, from what he says, to have been a big, a great big, success. Robert Herrick[63] has been

62. The family received some income from their Syracuse holdings.

63. Robert Herrick (1868–1938), novelist and professor at the newly created University of Chicago.

here, in the midst of everything, for a night. A sympathetic youth, but a rather foolish Anglophobe. I embrace you all & pray you may be breathing relief (of air,) when this reaches you. Ever your

*Henry*

Lamb House

July 21*st* 1905.

ALS: Houghton bMS Am 1094 (1680)

*Alice needs an easier life, so her family must become doorkeepers to protect her from the countless demands on her time. His servant problems are solved, and he works regularly.*

[*Dictated*]

LAMB HOUSE, RYE, SUSSEX.

Dearest A.                                                    8th September, 1905.

It is I who have been horribly silent since firing-off a couple of melancholy missives at you after my return; and meantime I have had a lovely one myself from Peggy, to whom I should be writing this very night were I not writing thus to you—and have also had a very good one from William, or rather a very bad, since it told me a few days ago of your deplorable little prostration by the most cruel, apparently, of all your attacks. I hope with all my heart that is ancient history now, and I hate to hark back to it at a moment when you may have succeeded a little in forgetting it. Still, I can't help telling you that you have, even if the odious visitation *has* been outlived, my tenderest sympathy in the whole business—for the moral of it is that *you need an Easier Life,* that you need it quite direfully, and that you will perish utterly and leave us blankly bereft if we do not succeed, among us all, in seeing that you absolutely get it. Everything in the lives of all of us ought to be made to render help to your so doing; for you are chronically fatigued and spent by the burden of your fate, and that is what lays you open to these assaults of the fiend. Too many people live upon you—too many strangers and outsiders above all, in addition to your so numerous, so absorbing and devouring family! If William and the children would only make themselves doorkeepers to keep out the crew who have already taken so irreparably much of your power to resist, and not to let them in so that they may rob you within the next year or two of the little that remains, and so leave themselves (i.e. W*m* & the children,) and me, damned and desolate, something might still be done. But it won't be done on the basis of your present life—that is of your life as I, when I was near you, all so apprehensively, yet all so helplessly, saw you leading it. I only weep when I think of you—which isn't at all what I want. But at least I can be more cheerful about myself. I have been back now nearly two months, and, in spite of too much liability to invasion here during this part of the year, I have been able to take up work regularly enough again, and to live back into my little Lamb House habits. (The domestic situation that I found so compromised has cleared up since; Mrs. P[addington] has out-lived her dreams of departure, and I have acquired by patient waiting an apparently excellent young person to take the place, in her single self, of the two wretched little disturbers [his alcoholic servants the Smiths] of Mrs. P.'s peace who had been at the bottom of her alienated state. I breathe much easier with this simplified "establishment"—if I may call it simplify-ing to have raised the little black gnome Burgess to full servant's rank, even though not to full servant's inches, but he is now 18 years old and a very improved little auxiliary.) This, however, is a mere stopgap scrawl. I am truly touched by your effort to write me in the langour of your convales-cence; which is but a proof the more of the extravagance of your burden. Please tell Peggot, with all my love, that she shall have my best written thanks for her generous letter of weeks ago as soon as ever I get a little more settled to the privacy of real autumn. We have had already the summer's end, only too plain, I fear, in cold blustering gales; but there is still rather a buzz of people about my ears: Jonathan Sturges,[64] e.g., has just left after some eleven days, and the J. W. Whites,[65] my so overwhelming Phila-delphia hosts of last winter, arrive to-morrow, in a rage of wind and weather, from Ostend and Nauheim, just as you and William did, at just this date, so few years ago—to such a tune does history repeat itself. But good night, with all thanks to William, please, for his letter on your return to C[hocorua]. I hope he also is purged of the strange poison. But I take you all affectionately in and am yours always and ever

*Henry James*

TLS: Houghton bMS Am 1094 (1681)

*James misses his American family and friends. He works hard on* The American Scene *and plans to spend Christmas in Brighton with the Manton Marbles, who allow him a great deal of privacy.*

64. Jonathan Sturges (1864–1911), journalist, short-story writer, translator, student, and openly gay London-Paris socialite. He and HJ were quite close friends for some time. Sturges was crippled from a childhood attack of polio.

65. Dr. J. William White (1850–1916) was an eminent Philadelphia surgeon with an international reputation.

Dearest Alice. December *15th 1905.*

Will you very kindly give a message to Roberts [his Boston dentist] for me?—which I have only been delaying to send from general superstitious prompting—or scruples rather: the intense aversion to crying out before I am out of the wood—which I find always visited by the retribution of the gods. I should like him to know that now these months have elapsed I appreciate only *more & more* the great merit & apparent perfection of what he has done for me—& what, up to now, has appeared an absolute success. He has created for me a perfect masticating & enunciating mouth—I seem to profit now thoroughly by all my longdrawn elaboration of anguish last winter—& to feel what an impeccable job he & I, between us, made it. So I go on, from day to day, with humble confidence—the confidence even venturing to increase. Please tell him this, from me, with my kind regards—I feel it a definite assurance which is due to him.——And I have put it, dearest Alice, in the forefront of my letter—in order to begin, & start, absolutely, this horribly delayed address to you, the failure of which, so many weeks has made me feel wretchedly cut off from my frequent so sweet circumstances of last winter—those which made the best part of it. I've had a kind of hope (that fruit of perpetual pious *prayer* for you,) that you have been more at peace & ease than for some time before, & I have had a kind of merciful instinct of not laying on you the burden even of a letter. But I wrote the other day to William at some length & you will otherwise have had as much news of me as there has been to give. The autumn has simply melted away here in my grasp, & though we have had endless bad weather the days have dashed past like motorcars. They have been solitudinous, very, & the difference in their tenor & that of my so socially=affluent American time (that of my Irving St. days of sweet family life in especial, alas,) is almost a theme for the philosopher. But I have worked to as good purpose as I am capable of, & the continuity of that partly accounts for the sense of the falling of the ground from under one's feet. I think of all the noble & generous offices you were rendering me *à pareille époque* [at a similar time] of those other months—from the application of poultices to the application of audiences—& I feel dreadfully the sadness of it having all come & gone. It's as if it were only day before yesterday that I sat in this same place planning my American tour & having it all before me—& here I am looking back on it as on an irrecoverable past. Shall I come *again* (without the Roberts abyss, & to give you & William less trouble)? I am afraid that will require much talking about.

What I do yearn to do is to get abroad again for a little—but the house is somehow like a millstone—a blessed millstone, but still a millstone—hanging round my neck. The case seems to be that one is wretched unless one has a house—but that *if* you have a home you can't have anything else. There is no manner of doubt, however, that for me the house is, primarily, the thing to have. The things I *didn't* do in the U. S. meanwhile rise up against me, in the form of reproachful notes & messages finding me out now (a very cutting little one from Emily Cochrane[66] at St. Paul, e. g., the other day—not that *she,* poor thing, matters!) & I realize the hole made in my time & energy by the simple duration & reiteration of the fell Roberts—who none the less, as I have said, is worth every hour & every "loss" he cost me. Only I feel as if I ought to make a visit *without* him. But I am hoping with all my heart that W*m's* & your possibility of Paris for next winter will *renouer* [revive] itself & that I shall see you there & here. I am in deep obscurity about you meanwhile—not knowing où vous en êtes [where you are] with your California pilgrimage, whether it still holds & for *when;* (as I still hope, intensely, for *you,* dearest Alice;) & not knowing, either, what becomes of Peggy—with the apparent *non-sequitur* of her brilliant admission at B. M. [Bryn Mawr] & her not going there. But perhaps she goes (begins,) with the spring term? That will solve everything. I find I do envy you California—to this muggy darkness, a winter, as yet all *harsh* rain & deep mire, that air & light radiantly shine. I shall probably go to spend Xmas at Brighton (with my funny old New York friends the Manton Marbles[67]—it being a very free & independent interior to stay in—life in common not beginning till about 3.30 p.m. & then intermitting again from 5.30 till 8: which gives one lots of time to one's self, & above all a long a.m. for work.) I have spent every Xmas but last at home, since I've been here, & desire to break a certain prescriptive spell. I shall come back here, however, for all January. I am pushing on my American book (it will have to be in 2 separate installments or volumes,) & it is really something of a *tour de force* to do it in this cut=off & purely retrospective way. But I must stay my pen, with a collective embrace of you all. I take the greatest possible comfort in my last winter's vision of all your mass & essence—& wonder how I got on without it before. When you have time

66. Emily Belden Walsh Cochran(e) (1844–1924), daughter of HJ's maternal uncle Alexander Robertson Walsh and HJ's first cousin.

67. Abigail Lambard Marble (d. 1909) and Manton Marble (1834–1917). He was a famous bimetallist and editor of the *World.* HJ met them both in New York in 1874–75.

& strength—& I do intensely hope you are now steady on your pins—tell me (a little) about each of the children & their present phase & status; beginning with Harry & his situation as now constituted. But I do awfully owe *him* a letter, & he shall have it. Isn't Bill painting *you?* He immensely ought & must. *Has Bay E's portrait of Wm come home?—& is it being hung, & where?* Is Peggy successfully going "out," & is it the death of you? All these & so many other things I shld. like so awfully to know. I am haunted with the sense that I didn't before I left, last *4th* July, take proper leave of your mother—though I did see her a day or two before—but without last attentions. Will you tell her, with my love, that I have repined at this ever since?——I think of, these nights—I *see*—Grace Norton's interior gaping wide to the winter winds & the frosty stars, to the whole universe, & it makes me feel as if I could shout a message straight *at* her from here. But I must write to her instead, as soon as I can surmount the sense that having so seen her, poor dear, & her incoherent conditions, & above all, her intellectual inaccessibility, has somehow destroyed in me all the spring of correspondence. I am so glad that my contacts with the opposite house have not done that for yours, dearest Alice, & William's, & all of your, devotissimo

Henry James.

ALS: Houghton bMS Am 1094 (1682)

*William should Fletcherize to end his gout. James responds to Alice's account of Mrs. Piper's séance, where his mother's spirit supposedly appeared and sent a message to him. On the day his mother materialized he had had deep thoughts of her.*

LAMB HOUSE, RYE, SUSSEX.

Dearest Alice. March 14*th* *1906.*

I have just written a long letter to Bill, & one to Ned[68] (both responsive to very good ones—from them—Bill's most beautiful & interesting:) & now I have my go at you & William. Your noble, copious one from your bare & spare little Stanford "home" (*what* a Home!) has been with me these three days & has been as meat & drink to me. I went up to London on Feb. 6*th* for 2 or 3 weeks, then came back here for 10 days & now, in a day or two, return to town for a longer stay—with no doubt two or three little brief relapses here. It is a great blessing, at this time of year, to have

---

68. Ned was Edward Holton James (1873–1954), the youngest James brother Robertson's son.

these little oscillations to & fro so easy & workable. But these are mostly harsh eastwindy times here & there is much virtue in London as a refuge. *Your* refuge, & W*m's,* however, is the one that I have most in mind at present, & when once I have swallowed the vision of the dreadful lone strain of your journey—poor weary untended creature!—I throw myself as with a physical relief to my own nerves into your having got for the time so far away from the fell Irving St—where, as of course you know from those you left behind, measles, introduced by the fatal little child of Adoption, have been raging. Bill tells me about them, but also that they are, or were already then, waning, & I hope the vain vision of them hasn't poisoned your rest. By the time this reaches you they will be, God grant, ancient history. Your acct. of your California conditions, your own personal baggage=handling & all, with the clear, cold Blankness with regard to everything else that was my own *final* impression, recalls all my own last spring's sense of the place, which began, for me, with being so "taking" & grew quickly enough so thin. But may it be thick enough, for you & William, to slide you along in peace & honour to the end of your time. I mourn heartily over W*m's* gout—& it makes me fear he hasn't really come to Fletcherism. You can't have gout if you thoroughly do it—I am more & more witness of this fact. It makes futile little attempts with *me,* gout does, just as lumbago (*very* feebly) does; & I absolutely & immediately chaw & champ them away. Impress this on W; I feel absolutely, that he *needn't* be so caught, & ask myself what is the use or meaning then of his thinking so much of H. F. [Horace Fletcher] (as the latter at least writes me)—very modestly—that he does. He continues, hand & hand with Roberts, to do everything for *me.* All your letter, dearest Alice, is interesting & soothing to me—but I am more touched than I can say by your report of Mrs. Piper's[69] so striking—to me very wonderful—echo of Mother. Her manner of mention of me, & message as it were, to me (dear Mother's own,) makes indeed an immense impression on me, & for a reason of direct & marked *relevancy,* of the most startling kind, than I can scarce, at any rate in *this* poor frustrating way, explain. It comes *in,* extraordinarily, to a

---

69. Lenore (Mrs. William J.) Piper was a Boston medium. Alice James's mother, Mrs. Gibbens, first visited her in 1885 and was amazed at how much the woman revealed about the Gibbens and James families during a trance. William James wrote a report on Mrs. Piper for the British *Proceedings of the Society for Psychical Research* in 1890. Evidently William and Alice had consulted her again, in the hopes of bringing back the spirits of various deceased family members. William frequently investigated extrasensory and psychic phenomena.

situation of "worry" (over a matter known *to no one in the world but myself*—not to you who were there telepathically present—yet one you & Wm needn't *in the least* yourselves wonderingly worry over—it's all an *occult* matter.) Suffice it that I had of late (this last two months or so) quite definitely said to myself: "What wouldn't I give if it were thinkable one might have some outside, all knowing word, some mystic or revealed *guarantee* that 'anxiety' *is* superfluous and that one's premises & hypotheses, in the particular connection, are as right as one wd. have fain think them! What a blessing & aid & *finish,* in such a 'suggestion!' " Whereupon, lo, it's as if the suggestion were exactly what you transmit me—dear Mother's unextinguished consciousness breaking through the interposing vastness of the universe & *pouncing* upon the first occasion helpfully to get *at* me: produced by the collocation of her watch, Mrs. Piper & you. The measure of the value of an instance like this is one's own incommunicable consciousness; & I have been hugely affected & emotionné [moved] by what you tell me. It makes me understand what F. Myers told me of his relation with his mother, & desire immensely to meet Mrs. P., to see her "sit," I mean: so *do* confirm it to me that she is to come out here this summer. Her immediate identification of the ownership of the watch & of K.[atherine] L.[oring]'s relation to it are wonderful enough—but these things you knew & were full of, so to speak. *No living creature knows,* on the other hand, of the question on which, through her, toward me, Mother's still sentient presence in the mystery of things—somewhere & somehow, appears to *me* to have exhaled a conscious, intending, effective, all-beneficent breath! It's very, very wonderful & beautiful! Don't you & Wm think so? And I take it, all rejoicingly, as wholly settling my question! There is a matter, moreover, that, to my mind, adds a still more remarkable element to the thing! Just about at the moment you were present at Mrs. Piper's, that is a little before it, there died in London, on the same day, Mrs. Bancroft, poor lady and that wonderfully gallant and vivid & interesting old woman, Mrs. Sargent, John S.[inger] S.[argent]'s (the painter's) Mother. I wrote to Hester Bancroft about her mother's death, reflecting on the loss of one's mother—but that was not much. At Mrs. B.'s funeral I met, among the very few persons present, Emily Sargent & Mme Ormond, John's two much-stricken sisters, who had come, very much moved, out of kindness, though their own mother lay dead at home—her funeral delayed by their brother hurrying home from the Holy Land, & having, naturally, not yet arrived. I had a few words with Emily S. (a dear, charming person,) & that evening, on reaching home, here, was moved to write to her, very sympathetically, & send a message to John. I had had a great regard for Mrs. Sargent, & have an immense one for J.—& I wrote frankly, that the loss of one's mother *is* a loss that abides with one always, & how, after 25 years, I still feel that of my own, & what the wound was at the time: also that other sorrows in life repeat themselves, only that one—it is the one poor thing to be said for it—that one alone *never.* She wrote me back most responsively, telling me that of all the letters she & her sister had got mine was the only one that bid them not hold their grief off at arm's length &c, but take it home as a friend and added "Do write to John, do write to John." I did so, a day or two later—he was just arriving—& had from him the same grateful reply—(& I went to see Emily a few days after.) I wrote in the same sense to him—& the whole point of my long story is that being interested, much, in these people & their trouble (for they were extraordinarily devoted to their Mother & much overcome,) I did so with particularly frank reference to, & re-experience of, my own abiding acquaintance with a similar bereavement, & a particular *living back,* for the respective hours, into that event of 25 years ago, & into all my then, my subsequent & my actual sense of it. And this concomitantly with that other embarrassment & invocation which I have described to you as so active & urgent at the very moment (about,) before this "sign" that you report to me was to take place. It is as if I had quite insistently pressed some spring (of yearning!) to which the beautiful old maternal consciousness operating still *in respect to me* somewhere in the subtlety of things had, on an opportunity offered, eagerly responded. So at least it all falls together for *me!* But what an interminable (& you may think disproportionate) statement I am writing you about it! I must draw to a close though there seem many things I still wish to say. I have written to Bill that I am longing for his presence here as early in the summer as he can get away, & thereby yearning for the success of his proposition to MacMonnies.[70] Four months of "Europe," even with as big as possible an allowance in it of Lamb House (which improves all the time,) will come in for him very valuably, I am sure. He tells me very good things of Aleck—till poor A.(then convalescent, however,) succumbed to unlucky measles—I mean of the latter's growth in stature, beauty, virtue, &c. How I wish I could do something to testify, to him, to one's gratified sense of this! And of Harry Bill, like yourself, speaks volumes (in a short compass) by the mere brief recital of all he is so valuably doing & being & achieving. I have written him back that H. is

---

70. Sculptor Frederick William Macmonnies (1836–1937) and his artist wife.

probably, after his Parents, the very grandest—noblest—human being that ever lived. I am proud of my relation to him—& can't imagine what you & W*m* must be! I basely forgot in my last to thank you for sending me so considerately at the New Year, the Syracuse cheque for £60. One is always glad of such things at the New Year. And now I suppose I understand, correctly, that this month & April being still again retained by you, my remittances will begin once more with May.——It may interest you to know that I have lately two or three times met, in town, Mrs. Myers,[71] after a very long interval—& found her a greatly improved & more real & serious Mrs. M. *She* is "taking out" her girl (who has prodigious hair,) but on my asking her about Lee has evaded the question, as if he were not satisfactory or she not pleased about him. The other boy is very well placed in some electrical business. She *raffoles* [is mad] about America but above all has wanted pressingly to know, each time, if I "know anything about Hodgson"[72]—that is, I supposed at the time, about the circumstances of his death &c. But your mention of his having "spoken so finely" through Mrs. Piper makes me wonder if what *she* wonders is not whether he may not have given such signs. I can only tell her *that,* if I see her again as I probably shall. Her mother is living on, with black hair & rosy *maquillage* [make-up] to nearly a hundred! Different from *you*—I mean not as to age, but as to hair & complexion!——I hear with great concern that poor Theodora [Sedgwick] has had a "stroke." I go up to town on this coming 16*th,* & on Sunday 18*th* I lunch with William Darwin[73] (considerably broken *he,* I fear,) from whom I learn more about her. But it seems premature & uncanny! Your Cambridge can't have been gay this winter!— But enough & a late good night. Give W*m* for me mille tendresses [much love]! I hope with all my heart his gout is exorcised. *I've* had none since that attack of a year ago at Biltmore!—when my Fletcherizing was all undermined! H. J. wants me [to] spend this May with him in Venice. But I can't—it's impossible! I thank W*m* greatly for his batch of articles—I am getting at them however only now one by one. How I hope you & he will drink deep of your better life! Ever

H. J.
March 15*th*

---

71. Eveleen Tennant Myers, wife of Frederic Myers.

72. Richard Hodgson (d. 1905) was an Australian who became the secretary of the American Society for Psychical Research. After his death Mrs. Piper claimed he was communicating with her through a spirit. WJ evaluated her claims and found them suspicious.

73. William Darwin was the oldest son of Charles Darwin. He married Sara Sedgwick.

P.S. Reading over the foregoing,—finished late last night, I fear you will think I poorly *justify* the impression made on me by Mrs. Piper's message—& find it illegible & incoherent. But there it is! Likewise I see that I have wholly omitted to thank W*m* for *his* good letter from Stanford received some ten days ago & dispatched to me just after his getting there. His impression, of the 1*st* flush, was apparently very favourable—as to general salubrity & "plasticity" of elements. But I found it was somehow the *second* flush of California that one wd. have to live with, apparently, & that gave one to think! Shall you see, later, anything of Berkeley—if you go up to San F. before returning? In that case recall me to that remarkably pleasant Gayle—with Bruce Porter[74] at S. F.—who was my best human recollection of California.

H.J.

ALS: Houghton bMS Am 1094 (1684)

*HJ discusses family finances, William's insomnia, and various relations. His garden has been abundant this summer, and even has a resident chameleon.*

Beloved Alice.                                    LAMB HOUSE, RYE, SUSSEX.

Your beautiful & abundant letter of Aug. 18*th* brings tears of gratitude to my eyes. On hearing from William I radiantly smile—on hearing from *you* I maudlinly weep! A long, long silence has prevailed between us, but I have accepted it as wholly *normal,* in these summer months of storm & stress (I mean of circulation & hospitality, general out-of-doorness & *éparpillement* [going about];) & have felt sure that you & William would be doing the same. In fact I have only rejoiced, in a manner, at your mutism, knowing you have Billy always as food for your pen, & thinking of, & praying for, but one thing—that your summer might be sitting loose on you & make you as effortless as possible. This I gather it *has* done, & I hope the September Chocorua will prove a quiet & comfortable adventure. Touched am I deeply at your snatching the Cambridge hours to give your news so liberally & lucidly. What you tell me, first, about the Syracuse situation, goes to my head through my heart rather than to my heart through my head: that is I see you must, between you (you & William, & your Mother & Harry,) have managed admirably—but I don't quite un-

---

74. Robert Bruce Porter (1865–1961), an art lover and architect whom HJ met in San Francisco during his visit to California the year before. He married Peggy James after HJ's death.

derstand the whole mystery—of the reinvestable moneys &c—which, however, doesn't in the least matter, for I thank you for your so succinct statement, & quite see that anyone but a financial idiot would understand. (It is only that I suppose that when the MacCarthy money, the $26,250 comes in, you mean that *all* that, *plus* the money liberated by the new arrangement from the Sinking fund will be so available, & that they will make together, the two sums, upwards of $36000, for new & careful placing! But it doesn't matter now—you will tell me when the time comes; & meanwhile you will be studying the question, on the spot, in advance, & I will accept your wisdom with my eyes closed!) Everything you tell me of your more or less irresponsible visits, with William, delights me—everything, that is, but his accursed insomnia, over which I all tenderly groan, for the miserable thing it must be. But I trust it may even now be breaking—as it has broken before, & I send him much love. It's charming to hear of your pleasantness with Elly Emmet, & of the felicity of that group—*absit omen!* Bay's solidity is even at this distance, to me, one of the comforts of life, & my privation of a nearer view of it, & of them all, is on the *loss* side of the account of my expatriation. On the other hand the Profit side of that general fact has been wonderfully clearer to me than ever (*never* clearer!) in other ways, this summer; the summer the most continuously beautiful of all my long years in England—quite definitely—& such as has made Lamb House a perfect benediction. I have never so much felt the virtue & charm & sanification of the garden—& still that happy spell goes on. The summer here has indeed been a marvel—three rainless & radiant months, & yet never too hot—& never too cool. I only wish you could have known it—for you can't have been so immune from violence at home. I have had "guests," but not overwhelmingly, & the weather & the garden have made every thing easy. (The kitchen garden has been this year an affluence—even for hedges of sweet peas—a real prize exhibition— nearly 10 feet high & as big as walnuts & as sweet indeed as heaven.) Lily & Louisa Walsh quitted me this a.m.—after a Sunday (from Saturday p.m.) & George Higginson & the redoutable Emily were with me but the other day. So you see I brace myself for efforts. A little of the Walshes (honest & innocent as they are) goes a great way: they are sordid of aspect & platitudinous of chatter. But George H. is always an angel & Emily "improved"—less (a little!) desolating in her flood of discourse, & extraordinarily intelligent & eager & of good taste about Italy & Art &c (they having been the winter in Rome, & now sailed for home.) I yearn for, & over, Bill & enclose you a letter I have just had from him. He has put off his visit to me a little discouragingly late—but is right, of course, as finding elsewhere more than I here can give him. I only fear a little to end by having but a scrap of him. But he is evidently laying in no end of profit. I don't understand his pertinacity to return to Boston this autumn—& have only desired to combat it. If he will only stay the winter in Paris I will go over & see him for a while—more or less instead of taking my time "off" in London. But I must see him to talk about it; though I shall write him, in advance, not to quite burn his ships over there before coming on here. I find it difficult to get *at* him during this addressless tour.——Delightful to me your news of Peg & her worth—of which latter I have always felt so grandly confident. She must have been having a fine, ample, interesting summer—& I think I quite understand her appetite for the noble adventure of Bryn Mawr; on which I give her my affectionate blessing. Tell Aleck with my love that I wish he were here to help to solve the mystery of mysteries in the small garden-annals of L. H.; the abrupt appearance, 5 days since, on the middle of the lawn, of a most interesting & active & inexplicable little *Chameleon* (fruit of the torrid zone,) of whom I am making an exquisite pet, but whose origin & *provenance* it is, after wide inquiry, so impossible either to trace or to imagine, that I am simply accepting him as the gift of God & a 1st=class miracle. He is a most curious & human & tree-climbing little beast (with human hands & feet & arms & legs & eyes & prehensile monkey-tail,) blushing & flushing black & brown, & blanching to pinkish grey &c 10 times a minute, & going up boughs & little posts, placed for him in the warm greenhouse, exactly in the fashion of a sailor "skinning" up a mast & perching, at the top, on the look=out. How glad I should be, did distance permit, to give him to the zoological Aleck! But goodnight, dearest Alice—I renew my love to W*m,* & Harry, & always send it to your Mother. Ever your faithful

*Henry.*
Aug. 27*th* 1906.

ALS: Houghton bMS Am 1094 (1686)


*Brother William's Pragmatism is the ideal philosophy for the artist and the novelist. Spring has arrived, and HJ is hard at work with his scribe, Miss Bosanquet, in the garden-house.*

Dearest Alice. LAMB HOUSE, RYE, SUSSEX.

I have beautiful unacknowledged bounties from you & from William— above all the quite golden gift of the news about the Oxford lecture-course;[75] my failure *sooner* to have "enthused" to you all responsively & devoutly, about that leaves me rueful & ashamed: though there are in general awfully good reasons why, at present—all this winter in short— my letter=writing should have to take an ignominiously back seat. And I think it is since I had the beautiful letter from you, with very interesting & touching mention also of sittings (& with Peggy) chez Mrs. Piper, that I *did* write to blest Aleck & charged him with handsome messages for you. I needn't "tell" you, however, how I rejoice in the prospect of seeing you & of above all for a while possessing you within these walls. It is truly a big thing to look forward to, & it shines ahead of me, through these (at the best) somewhat dusky & shrunken winter days, with a great light. A note from William received since you wrote, throws a shade of doubt upon his feeling sufficiently fit when the time comes—but I shall count him—prefigure him—as fit unless some very special & monstrous unfitness arises, & against that may all the forces of "truth" combine! I have just had from him, & devoured with avidity, his Pragmatic pamphlet of retorts to objections, which penetrating the Enemy at every pore so that it must make him squirm in every fibre, is an indubitable gage of endless fitnesses to come. I find Pragmatism,[76] tell him, *overwhelmingly* the Philosophy for the Artist & the Novelist—if it had been cooked up for *their* direct & particular behoof it couldn't suit me more down to the ground. But the pinkest *nuance* in all the coming rosecolour is your saying that Peg may be fetched out by Harry to spend a month with me here. This is bliss to think of— having them *both!*—& I embrace the prospect (*en attendant* [while awaiting] that I embrace *them*) with rapture. Will you please tell them so, with all manner of yearning love & impatience from me? We'll work out the details later, & meanwhile this is splendid to go on with. That is mainly what I have wanted to say tonight. Straight & smooth & swift melts the winter away here. It really "melts" a little less than usual, being of rather a hard, clear, honest cold, but with lots of sun, & exquisite sunsets & a great general decency. I like always, as with the 1st freshness, my coming down to my breakfast hour here, each day, with the south window straightway opened into the oftener than not sunny garden, where the birds flock to a scattered *régal* [feast or banquet] & George Gammon whistles & puts up,

---

75. In November Oxford University had invited William to give the spring 1908 Hibbert lectures.

76. William James defined pragmatism as a way of thinking that used results as the proper measure of ideas. He thought that consequences, rather than so-called first principles, should be the subject for philosophical inquiry.

with a ringing hammer, new arbours & the master goes in & out, admiring the weather *always,* by rule, & taking the air before turning—as I do regularly now, in these months as much as in summer—into the garden-house to find Miss Bosanquet,[77] my new & *precious* scribe, seated at the piano. (I hadn't *really,* before, put the garden-house to the winter-test—which it beautifully & most conveniently triumphs over—, for the morning hours; an immense discovery.) But goodnight, dearest Alice. I probably shan't go up to London to *stay* any time till about April 1st; where, later on, I shall come to Oxford to *all* the lectures. Please tell Bill I greatly appreciate his delightful letter & Harry that I feel *his* particular attentions unspeakable. I hope your winter has redeeming points. Bill mentioned your Mother's having had a wounding *fall:* please give her my love, & all hopes for good amendment. I rejoice immensely that Bill is painting her. Tell William, with all love, that this is all for *him* too. I have of course directed the Scribners to send you each of the vols. of the Edition[78] as they appear, & hope they began promptly; also that you find them handsome & honourable. If they will only be "taken up!" Ever, dearest Alice, your affectionate

*Henry James*
February *1st* 1908.

ALS: Houghton bMS Am 1094 (1688)


*James takes Alice's son, Aleck, to a performance of HJ's play* The High Bid. *He has stopped Fletcherizing and started walking; as a result, his health is much improved.*


[The Reform Club]

Dearest Alice.                                 Saturday Feb. 20*th* *1909.*

    A beautiful letter from you of Feb. 3*d* deserves as an exquisite thing, a better acknowledgment than this—but please take this as a mere hurried stopgap till I have emerged from the hole (made in time & vital economy) by the particular business & its *sequelae* for which I came the other day up

---

77. Theodora Bosanquet (1880–1961) was HJ's third and last secretary. She later wrote a book about him, *Henry James at Work* (1924), based on diary entries made during her years with him.

78. Scribners was bringing out a twenty-four-volume edition of HJ's novels and tales, selected by him. He wrote prefaces for each volume tracing the origin and development of his texts. The books appeared with Alvin Langdon Coburn's handsome photographs as frontispieces.

to town. The little play, produced (for a series of consecutive matinees) on Thursday last (18*th*) is clearly a charming success—but it isn't as clear unfortunately that the F.R.'s,[79] desperately bent on drawing their fearfully "goody," or, as I believe, platitudinous "Passing of the Third Floor Back"[80] as hard as possible while there is money to be squeezed from it, will *concurrently* repeat my less flagrant thing very often for the present. But I believe it has some admirable future in it & it's moreover rather essentially (for here at least) a matinee play. But the general little acclamation has been all one could wish—& dear little Aleck—wide-eyed & *emerveillé* [filled with wonder]—will report to you of his apparently quite charmed sense of the première—his presence at which was to me the happiest thing about the matter altogether. In regard to *him* be now completely easy. All *present* difficulties are over, & he is at peace—the air blown quite clear of obfuscations for these next months to come. I can't still but think the Smiths[81] tolerably "cavalier"—they are singularly *common* folk, hidebound in their middle=classism, I infer; but Aleck is not a bit impatient or unhappy, & is so *good* that anything, literally, is possible for him or *with* him. So sit easy *about him* as he sits easy—perfectly easy—now himself. And oh, above all, sit easy about *me!* I go down to Brighton an hour or two hence till Monday—& don't return to L. H. till the 27*th*. As soon as I get back from Brighton I shall go to see McKenzie,[82] whose name, as I think I wrote you, Osler had already written me, from Rome, before William so benevolently cabled it. What I then cabled back (about the effect of slowing up on my— practically—about 6 years—5 1/2 quite—of intense Fletcherism) has been each day more vividly brought home to me, & the effect of that & of the greatest possible extension of *movement* that I can give time to has been all these days to make me feel those two things *combined* absolutely curative. I am, pectorally, a different creature than when I came up to town a week ago—as I then was from when I first wrote—& believe that the real prescription for me would be a month's gentle-paced walking—& non-Fletcherizing—tour in a bland country. London, however, *is* bland now—

---

79. Sir Johnston Forbes-Robertson (1853–1937) and his American wife, Gertrude Elliott (1874–1950), after trying out HJ's play *The High Bid,* felt it would not attract audiences, but nonetheless they scheduled five matinee performances in London.

80. Another play by Jerome K. Jerome about a lodging house. The Forbes-Robertsons thought it would make more money than HJ's play.

81. The Smiths, husband and wife, had been his servants for over two decades.

82. Sir James Mackenzie, famous heart specialist. HJ first consulted him in 1909.

& *all* sustained circulation most directly or immediately remedial. The Fletcher side of the matter is deeply strange & unexpected—& there is much more to be said about it than I can now go into—keep it to yourselves *save as* regards H. J. himself if you're "in touch" with him. But evidently—the prolonged unobstructed & unhampered thoroughness & consistency of my application of the process—with the *induced immobility* it more & more established, & which was so unprecedently compatible with the perfect health of everything *but* my heart (& above all with incurious "time for reading") created a non-employment of heart function, circulation or whatever, of which I have had this news. *Motion* instantly did much for me but at the end of some days at Rye, it came over me that I was still doing something unfavourable. What could it be then? The only possible wrong was in Fletcherism itself *where it had after so long brought me?? Could* that be so? I immediately tried, with unmistakably *completing* results & had been doing so three days when I cabled to William. Everything has since confirmed that. I do it (non=fletcherize) & feel righter & righter. I experiment with it again & the bad heart effect is marked. But I'm not without hope that I can get back to it after a *time* of abandonment—if I guard myself against the danger of ever again associating it with immobility. If some one had *only* said to me a year & 1/2 ago (when I was 1*st* symptomatically "thoracic") "move, *move* more—walk, walk more," that would already have begun to counteract what there may be of (so unexpectedly & sadly!) insidious in Fletcherist *excess*. I haven't been to see McKenzie yet, from absolutely absent time for it—combined with the immense help given me by simply *being* here & in motion. But I *have* had to make time for Field, alas (Roberts's dental representative!) and I shall see M*c*K. on the 23*d* or 24*th* & I am sure he will clear up many things. When I've done so—& when *he* has—you shall have a full report. But be meanwhile of high cheer about me. The pleasure of getting back to free walking is of itself almost "worth it." I find myself breaking each day more & more into an unconscious rapid *rewarding pace*—as if my organ had been starved for exercise & was thanking me for every step. The *other* results of non-Fletcherizing may be becoming another affair—but I won't "borrow trouble" & it's too soon to say. Forgive these small tablets—they have the only surface—of this club paper—on which I can easily write. Also forgive the fond egotism of your all-embracing

*Henry*

ALS: Houghton bMS Am 1094 (1690)

*He has collapsed back into bed with high blood pressure and panting.*

21, EAST ELEVENTH STREET

Dearest Alice.                                                                    March 31*st* 1911

Your letter this a.m. (with L. Walsh's &c) is a sad kind of blessing, & I want to write a few words, though I wrote at some length a day or two ago. I am sorry to say I have been having these last days a baddish time— Collins's[83] help as to my blood-pressure & panting proving pretty fallacious, so that I stopped off treatment abruptly yesterday—with his full concurrence. He sent me straight home & to bed instead, & came to see me later in the day. I am up to day, but keeping my room, & not happy— not knowing, above all, what to make of a condition (& *re*-visitation) so anomalous in the midst of a general improvement so marked. I feel that I am holding on to the general improvement—that is that I *can;* & that there must be some definite interfering *cause* that again so subjects me to distress. The thing is to put one's hand upon it—yet that is so mortally hard. At all events, if my present condition doesn't abate I feel that I can't— while that is the case—stay on here, & I shall tumble back on top of you again, as I have so woefully done before—to my profit always, as you have seen. I am afraid Rosina is due with you—& that this may make my return a great complication & embarrassment or inconvenience, & I won't come unless I find this basis of the "false note" of my poor state in such an *entourage* absolutely drives me. I yearn to be among you (& "nearer" to William,) when I am thus down—that feeling, really, when it reaches a grave point, isn't to be resisted. Yet I *may* outweather this sharp little storm—light may, within a day or two, *may* break; & in that case I shall try to stay on. This collapse into bed will have been the *shortest* I shall here have had at any rate—of a few hours only; since I am up today. All the same I do yearn to see you—it terrifies me to find how little long separations do. Ever

*Henry.*

ALS: Houghton bMS Am 1094 (1701)

---

83. Dr. Joseph P. Collins (1866–1950) was a neurologist HJ consulted in New York for depression and related health problems. After HJ's death Collins wrote an account of him in *The Doctor Looks at Biography* (1923).

*James worries over his niece Peggy's bout with depression.*

Salisbury, Conn.

Dearest Alice.                *Saturday a.m.* [May 27, 1911]

Your blest news about Peg's orange-juice &c arrives (with the other kindly-forwarded letters,) this a.m.—& though I was just then writing at some length to Harry I must make you this sign of elation.[84] That the poor dear child's orange=juice shld. *be* such an encouragement brings home to me, however, as nothing else, what a hell of a time she must all this while have been having—yet what a benediction, too, any scrap of diminished distress. I feel most brutally "out of it" here—as if it could help her that I should be uselessly & just hoveringly "in" it! And I have all the while my own battle to fight—though that goes on not losingly—which is all that is strictly required. I mean that my business (of pushing on & up) takes perpetual hard *doing;* but I shall have done it at last.——This place of course is all sweetness & kindness—full of rough charm, really, in itself, too; Elly greatly improved—in reason & temper, Rosina the same old brick &c; & the countryside ever so beautiful. There is evidently plenty of money for the present—Bay's gains oddly inordinate. She & Blanchard[85] are nearly 3 miles off (for the summer)—which is a facilitation. They don't possess their really admirable new place till the autumn. Leslie has just returned from an absence in N. Y. & Grenville arrived today with the new motor from Detroit!—Elly's very own. She insists that I must have one of the same make at Rye—& doesn't see why it isn't perfectly easy. They are exporting them—the Detroit people—to England by the 5000 at a time. Blest Free Trade!—-I am expecting to arrive in Boston on Friday evening next in Theod. Pope's[86] motor; & shall spend Saturday & Sunday in Irving St. if you will let me, & it isn't too hot—or even if it *is;* going on Monday 5*th* to Nahant. All thanks for your hint about the Secrecy of the Harvard Degree.[87] Mr. Lowell said nothing about it to me—but my instinct has

---

84. At this time Peggy James suffered from severe depression, akin to what her aunt Alice James had endured decades ago. Her father had died, her brother Harry was off working, her brother Billy had married and left on his honeymoon, and Aleck was seldom at home. Peggy seemed lost.

85. William Blanchard Rand, Bay Emmet's husband.

86. Theodate Pope Riddle (1868–1946) was a Connecticut architect and a friend of HJ's.

87. HJ received an honorary degree from Harvard that spring.

luckily been silence & I have mentioned it to no soul. Ever your affectionate

Harry.

P. S. I yearn for the time when darling Peg can *take* some fond message.

ALS: Houghton bMS Am 1094 (1713)

*Oxford has offered James an honorary degree, in addition to one Harvard has offered him.*

(Salisbury)

Dearest Alice.           .        *May 27th 1911.*

(A P.S. to what I have just posted.) See how it never rains but it pours—Oxford offers me an Honorary Degree too. I am afraid it must lapse, for this year at least, as I can't be there to accept it—I mean to receive it—in person; in fact, I certainly can't—since Oxford Commencement, or Commemoration, must be (like both the Cambridges') in June; but this is a word to say Please make *sure* the official document spoken of my correspondent (Herbert Warren, President of Magdalen,) is forwarded to me; it hasn't come with his letter, & I only want to avoid it by any chance being overlooked as a *circular.* I must have it to be able to cable properly. I should have accepted, if personal presence had been possible—& I am sure it must depend on that. But I am certain the offer will come up again next year. Oh I only so think—all, *all* the while of William! But of you too! Ever

Henry.

P.S. Kindly return Warren's letter.

Salisbury

P.P.S. *Don't trouble*—for since I wrote the above an hour ago the formal invitation has come from Oxford (through 21 East 11*th* St.,) & I must decline it—for it is (of course) for the end of June & even, oddly enough, for the 28*th,* the same day as Harvard Commencement. So you see it wd. have been impossible even if I *hadn't* shifted my sailing—I wd. probably—or assuredly—have shifted to stay for the Harvard matter—all for William's "sake." They will in all probability renew the Oxford offer next year—& it's better I shldn't. have the 2 the same year. Lovely hot day here—but not too hot; & the beautiful new motor is due in an hour or two with Grenville. But we go out before that—Rosina, Leslie & I—in the old!

How I seem to flaunt these luxuries of landscape & motion at you in your darkened chamber! But wait & see!

H. J.

ALS: Houghton bMS Am 1094 (1714)

*On the one-year anniversary of William's death, James is at Mary Hunter's country estate in Essex. Mrs. Swynnerton is painting a picture of Queen Elizabeth at the Chelsea Town Hall, using Mrs. Hunter as a model. He sends and asks for news of his nephews and niece.*

HILL THEYDON MOUNT EPPING

Dearest Alice! August 27*th* *1911.*

I want to write you while I am here—& it helps me (this putting pen to paper does,) to conjure away the darkness of this black anniversary—just a little. I have been dreading this day—as I have been living through this week, as you & Peg will have done, & Bill not less, under the shadow of all the memories & pangs of a year go; but there is a strange (strange enough!) kind of weak anodyne of association in doing so here, where, thanks to your support & unspeakable charity, utterly & entirely, I got sufficiently better of my own then deadly visitation of misery to struggle with you on to Nauheim. I met here at first, on coming down a week—9 days—ago (quite fleeing from the hot & blighted Rye) the assault of all that miserable & yet in a way helpful vision—but have since been very glad I came; just as I am glad that you *were* here then—in spite of everything. I wrote 3 or 4 days ago to Alice Runnells[88]—in answer to a kind note of hers—& sent such messages to you that you will know of my being here—in response to Mrs. Hunter's[89] immediate & renewed & most persuasive appeal—as soon as I got back. So you will have had a certain amount of small news of me, though I still yearn, unassuaged, for some of the Chocorua house. (I wrote you from Sandy Hook—briefly; & to Harry from Fishguard—to be sent on to you; & then from L. H. as soon as I got there.) But you are not to feel any hustle whatever about writing—I shall send you my little signals entirely independent of that. I am adding day to day here, as you see—

<hr>

88. Alice Runnells James (d. 1957) married Bill James, Alice and William James's second son. Her father was John Summer Runnells, vice president and general counsel for the Pullman Car Company. The Runnellses had a summer home in New Hampshire.

89. Mary Smyth Hunter (1857–1933). She was Dame Ethel Smyth's sister and wife of M.P. Charles Hunter. She entertained many artists and writers informally at her estate, "The Hill," in Essex, just eighteen miles from London.

partly because it helps to tide me over a bad—not *physically* bad—time, & partly because my admirable & more than ever wonderful hostess puts it so as a favour to her that I do, that I can only oblige her in memory of all her great goodness to us—when it *did* make such a difference—of May 1910. So I daresay I shall stay on for ten or twelve days more (I don't want to stir; for one thing, till we have had some relief by *water*. It has now rained in some places, but there has fallen as yet no drop here or hereabouts—& the earth is sickening to behold.) I have my old room—& I have paid a visit to yours—which is empty;—& the house, now more completely filled (& to overflowing) with opulent objects—including a *chef,* whom we didn't have last year—is still more wonderful & luxurious & on the whole agreeable. A great broad pavement of fine old stone slabs has been laid all round—replacing some ancient gravel & some trodden lawn, & has the effect of a complete terrace-walk on every side. Also, within, there are for the present 8 children!—all those of all her 3 daughters, harboured here while the mammas amuse themselves; but with such miraculous art & tact & *management* that, relegated to those great nurseries & schoolrooms that we saw on the top (now all fully developed,) & to an army of nurses & nursemaids & governesses reigning there (I think there must be about 20 different tables served in all the house *per diem,*) that one has no sight or sound or smell or suspicion of them unless one looks them up in the grounds during the morning hours (which I spend till lunch in my room.) They are charming little sweet-voiced natural creatures so far as I *have* seen them—& Mrs. H. rules the whole complex situation with an ease & a serenity, an energy without flush or flutter, that more than ever excites my admiration—& practises all her bounty in the same full-handed way. She is all her year older—but Egypt, last winter, appears to have done her real good, the effort of the journey being nothing to her; & she is to go to Salsomaggiore next month—with a claim that I shall stay here till she *does* go (though as to that I must see—it will depend on her date.) Charles Hunter has been here some days (they have let Wemmergill this autumn—to help a tiny little to make up for the money spent here, I suppose;) & he is a very good & kind & amiable boyish, almost petulantly & harmlessly childish, man—whom one likes the more one sees him. No one else to speak of save brave, sad, lonely little Mrs. Swynnerton, who is doing an historical picture for a decorative competition—the embellishment of the Chelsea Town Hall, I believe: Queen Elizabeth taking refuge (at Chelsea) under an oak during a thunder-storm, & she finds the great oak here & Mrs. H., in a wonderful Tudor dress & headgear & red wig, to be admirably, though too beautifully, the Queen; with the big canvas set up, out of doors, by the tree, where her marvellous model still finds time, on top of everything, to *pose,* hooped & ruffed & decorated, & in a most trying queenly position. Mrs. S. is also doing—finishing—the portrait of me that she pushed on so last year—though under less happy a star than Mrs. H.'s, I fear. That is the thing has a great deal of very able & very lifelike, though slightly ugly & purplish painting; but she hasn't quite "caught the likeness," even by the very tip of its tail. Nevertheless it's a rather "important" piece, I think—& if I weren't obliged this coming year to be too thrifty I would try to buy it of her. (I think she *mainly* wants to exhibit it, though.) Mrs. Hunter appealed to me the very first thing for news of you & the children—full of the desire for all the facts about you, & about *them;* she yearns that all of you shld. "come over" & be harboured here & befriended by her. Well, perhaps that will still come—though as an elegant luxury, thank heavens, not as a necessity! Mrs. Swynnerton always harks back to you, with her stammering little interest, after I have sat to her a little. *Aug. 28th* I had to break off yesterday & the day passed after a fashion. Two or three people came—of no importance; though, tell Aleck that one of them (to tea) was his friend Charley Hotham (a 2-miles-off neighbour) who asked about him with great earnestness & seemed much cheered by hearing that I confidently count on A. soon, to pay me a long visit. But don't let dear A.—tell him with my love—fear that the said Charley is the main inducement I shall have to offer him. I believe the celebrated—or the "notorious"—Lady Warwick motors over from her own place to lunch today. She's a Lady Essex—whom you will remember, on a much greater scale—& has the remains of great beauty. But I must wind up, in spite of my wanting so to try to be *with* you all a little by this poor one-sided talk. I think of you, & of the question of how the rest of the summer has gone, for you, all the time & all the time—of how it is going now, I mean, now that I hope the worst of it is over. There have been no reports of bad American heat-waves in the *Times* since I came back—as there would have been, infallibly, had you had any such—whereby I hope you have been spared & at your ease. Here it has ceased to be *badly* hot—but this new day brings forth again a wickedly rainless sky.——But the great question for me is of the beloved little Peg, over whom her Uncle hangs, tell her, oh so tenderly & fondly. I hope with all my heart she is going on softly & steadily. I owe her [a] decent letter all to herself—just as I owe Bill one; so tell them both to bear up bravely & in patience & they shall be rewarded so far as the poor case allows. But goodbye, dearest Alice, dearest all. I hope your Mother is with you & that Harry has begun to take his holiday—bless him. I bless your Mother too & send her my affectionate love. Goodbye, dearest Alice. Your all-faithful

*Henry.*

P.S. Burgess is of course with me—but *so* bored by these gorgeous vacancies!

ALS: Houghton bMS Am 1094 (1720)

*Staying in Edinburgh makes James miss William even more, but he rejoices at the news of Bill's engagement to Alice Runnells.*

CALEDONIAN HOTEL EDINBURGH

Dearest Alice. SEPT. 24*th* *1911.*

I am spending two nights at this place on the way back from Millden in Forfarshire, where I have just put in a week that I ought to count, I suppose, as wonderful (for weather & for walks,) & whence I wrote a responsive word to Bill. The journey—whole journey at once—is a bit arduous, & I have drawn breath in Edinburgh (I go on tomorrow a.m.) though I don't care if I never see the place—handsome & interesting but unamiable—again. For of my various associations with it, it is that time here with William & you that stand [*sic*] out vividest & saddest—though indeed I find at every turn that *some* association with William, or some reminder of him or some *looking-in* from him, meets me & speaks to me— in a way that costs such pangs! The sense of having dropped him by the way & of going on without him—even to things that he would have so cared for & that would have been good to him & delightful: this is quickened at times by almost everything that happens—though of course you know it & feel it, dearest Alice, far better than I, & it isn't in the least what I meant in this sombre way to say to you. It's only that the old Scotch memory, that of his last so brave effort here, which I was momentarily a troubled witness of myself at that time, has been crowding upon me & bringing back all the old difficulty, the strain & stress & sacrifice, with the old triumph. But I am really turning my face another way now—as one *must,* all the while, & so rightly! Your dear, full letter of the 11*th* came to me just as I was leaving Millden has made me feel still more what I was already feeling—that somehow we are doing something for William, & having him with us a little, by all this beautiful *first happy* thing that we have done since he left us. My letters already will have shown you what joy I take in Bill's engagement—& everything you say makes me feel how right I am &

what a good thing it will be for all of us as well as for dear Bill himself. It is particularly delightful that the good Runnellses are so happily affected— & the great thing is to feel that it will enlarge & beautify the life of all of you at home, darling Peg's & dearest Aleck's not least. My hope is that they *will* be married with no great delay; but even though they be going to live, as I take for granted in Boston, I can't help being glad that Alice is not a Bostonian! The sooner they come out to see *me* the better—& it makes me want to hurry home now to begin to get ready. Indeed I long now intensely to do that—I have quite come to the end of my tether of braving fortune under alien roofs. This postponement of Lamb House—for these last weeks—has been inevitable, &, as they say, indicated: I made a false start there, rather, with those immediate first ten days (with the so amply disconcerting heat, disfigurement & general abnormalism;) but it is the basis to which I must get back. I took more moor & hill walks in Forfarshire that proved to me what I *can*—with patience, slowness & deliberation—do in that way; they were the sort of thing I had yearned for during all our awful American season, & they gave me, I think, a great life, though I still, I am sorry to say, have difficulties & delays. However, getting back to work will, I am sure, greatly help me. The great heat has gone—from Scotland at least; but even yet there has been no rain to speak of—though it made wonderful conditions for my week of the moors. I take great comfort in everything you tell me of the Chocorua life; except perhaps in the thought of your having to pay with your persons so very much in the Shattuck relation—such a heritage of William's humanity! But I hope that has sat on you all as light as it—that is as Shattucks'—could! I have written so to each & all that I seem to have exhausted my voeux [voice]; but I am interested in dear little Robert Allerton's having been with you & in his having been nice to Aleck. I have such a dear little impression of him—& I wince at what he told Aleck of Bay's strange non-writing to him. What gaps & drops of an almost barbarous order, in poor uneducated B! But good-bye, dearest Alice—I am deathly homesick for you all. I think of the beloved Peg with constant & unspeakable tenderness—tell her I hang about her & yearn over her. I gather that Harry will have taken his holiday this year all at C.—& Bill's great stroke will have made that scene very interesting. I hope it won't prevent his *now* putting through the portrait of A. I wish I could, in due time, see photographs of those of Mrs. Farlow & Anne Sherwin. I fondly bless you all. Ever, dearest Alice, your clinging old
Henry.

ALS: Houghton bMS Am 1094 (1721)

*James will rent two small rooms near Miss Bosanquet so that he can work several hours a day. He is looking for family letters to use in his autobiography.*

[The Athenaeum, Pall Mall. S. W.]

Dearest Alice. Nov. 13*th* *1911*.

I must bless you on the spot for your dear letter of the 22*d*—continued on the 31*st*. I clutch so at everything that concerns & emanates from you all, that I kind of pine for the need of it all the while—or at any rate am immensely & positively bettered by every scrap of the dear old Library life that you can manage to waft over to me. I delight in the success of Alice's [Runnells] visit & feel here it must have given a great & beautiful lift to the whole situation—while I fondly congratulate Bill on the pleasure & pride it must be to him to have such a beautiful & distinguished captive to lead in his train & exhibit as his prize. I can well imagine the "success" that Alice must have had—and in especial that they must have had together. But what touches me even more than that is to seem to gather that the beloved Peg came back from the country better than she went—& better above all for her excellent weeks at the Hilltop, for which I am so thankful to the gentle Salters.[90] May the winter begin to "shape" favourably for her—though I wish I could have a hand in the shaping. I find, naturally, that I can think of you all, & mingle with you so, ever so much more vividly than I could of old—through the effect of all those weeks & months of last year—which have had at any rate *that* happy result, that I have the constant image of your days & doings. You must think now very cheerfully & relievedly of mine—because distinctly, yes, dear brave old London is working my cure. The *conditions* here were what I needed all the while that I was so far away from them—I mean because they are the kind materially best addressed to helping me to work my way back to an equilibrium. But I needn't go into the details of this—the process itself works so steadily & smoothly. It isn't an ideal arrangement of course to have Kidd & Burgess & the new cook (excellent woman) withering on the tree of Lamb House; but for this winter, clearly, I must make it do—as they are too tied to me (& valuable) to send away & lose—& by May or June I shall be devoutly thankful for them again (besides going down to them meanwhile for a few days as often as possible;) & by that time I shall have achieved a good long winter's work. In getting back again into that

90. Alice's sister Mary Sherwin Gibbens Salter (1851–1933) and her husband William Mackintire Salter (1853–1931), lecturer in the Society for Ethical Culture and writer on philosophy.

current I feel I should gain so in steady & straight procedure if I could get back to my old way of working—i.e. of dictating to my Remington & to the singularly intelligent & competent Miss Bosanquet; & on my going into this earnestly a very fortunate thing (seemingly) has happened. She & Miss Bradley, settled in Chelsea, in a modest little ground floor flat, proved to have precisely 2 extra little rooms quite independent of theirs but belonging to them (connected with them) which they thriftily wanted to let furnished (to some other young woman,) for a very reasonable little rent indeed—& I have taken them, to go & work at with Miss B. each morning. I think this will be a blessing—as having at all a lady amanuensis was a problem baffled by my present basis of life here—& having a man very uncomfortable (in my room!) & more expensive, & difficult moreover through the rarity of men for just that sort of work. Therefore it is just settled with Bosanquet—the little rooms (entered from a most quiet & most private little court) have been put into "apple-pie" order, & I begin tomorrow. I shall have to take a taxi there every morning: but taxis, even though there has just been a strike, are blessedly cheap here (my fare to far-off Chelsea from here only 1/10—& done (the run) in about 12 minutes.) I shall see how it works—from 10.30 to 1.30 each day—& let you hear more; but it represents the yearning effort really to get, more surely & swiftly now, up to my neck into the book about William & the rest of us.[91] I have written to Harry to ask him for certain of the young, youthful letters (copies of them) which I didn't bring away with me—on the other hand I have found some 6 or 8 very precious ones mixed up with the mass of Father's that I have with me (thrust into Father's envelopes &c). Of Father's alas, very few are useable; they are so intensely domestic, private & personal.

*November 19th* I find with horror dearest Alice that I have inadvertently left this all these days in my portfolio (interrupted where I broke off above,) under the impression that I had finished & posted it! This is dreadful, & I am afraid shows how the beneficent London, for all its beneficence, does interpose, invade & distract, giving one too many things to do & to bear in mind at once. What sickens me is that I have thus kept my letter over a whole wasted week—so far as being in touch with you all is concerned. On the other hand this lapse of time enables me blessedly to confirm, in the light of further experience, whatever of good & hopeful the beginning of

---

91. HJ has started the first volume of his autobiography, which was published in 1913 under the title *A Small Boy and Others*.

the present states to you. In the first place I go on finding myself so much better that I am perillously [*sic*] near finding myself utterly well—& don't hesitate to say that I am not only better than at any time since my illness, but better than at any time also than for 2 years before it—the 2 bad years during which I was consciously & steadily moving toward it & the 1*st* summer of which you & William & Peg were at Lamb House, & you & Peg went to Geneva together—& then joined him in Belgium & Holland, arranging afterwards for Aleck at Oxford. I had sinister previsions & a very poor physical consciousness that summer—while William vaulted gates & seemed so very well. But, not to hark so dismally back, I have had during the past week in particular a supreme sense of my recovery. And in the 2*d* place the two little Chelsea rooms (one but a small separate one for washing my hands, changing my coat &c) are evidently going to work quite blessedly & minister to the straight march of the book &c. I immensely congratulate myself on this arrangement. And the weather being day after day & all day ruthlessly wet—the long & deadly drought of the summer & early autumn made up for by a deluge, I have been devoutly glad not to be prisoned at L. H.—for these London conditions reduce inconvenience to the minimum. In the 3*d* place a most valued letter from Harry has come, accompanying a packet of more of William's letters typed, for which I heartily thank him & promising me some others yet. I am writing to him in a very few days & will then tell him how I am entirely at one with him about the *kind* of use to be made by me of all these early things, the kind of setting they must have, the kind of encompassment that the book, as *my* book, my play of reminiscence & almost of brotherly autobiography & filial autobiography not less, must enshrine them in. The book I see & feel will be difficult & unprecedented & perillous [*sic*]—but if I bring it off it will be exquisite & unique; bring it off as I inwardly project it & oh so devoutly desire it. I greatly regret, only, also, the almost complete absence of letters from [sister] Alice. She clearly destroyed after father's death all the letters she had written to *them*—him & Mother—in absence, & this was natural enough. But it leaves a perfect blank—though there are on the other hand all my own intimate memories. Could you see—ask—if Fanny Morse[92] has kept any?—that is just possible. She wrote after all so little. I marvel that *I* have none—during the Cambridge years. But she was so ill that writing was rare for her—*very* rare. However, I

---

92. Frances Rollins Morse (1850–1928), a Boston friend of Alice James's since their youth. Morse founded the Simmons School of Social Work.

must end this. I hope the Irving St. winter wears a friendly face for you. I think so gratefully & kindly now of the little chintzy parlour—blest refuge. I re-embrace dearest Peg & I do so want some demonstration of what Aleck is doing. It's a pang to hear from you that he "isn't so well physically." What does that sadly mean? I send him all my love & to your Mother. Ever your

Henry.

ALS: Houghton bMS Am 1094 (1722)

*England's coal strike has disrupted life in general. He rejoices to learn that Peggy is in Florida, recuperating from her depression.*

102 PALL MALL, S.W.

Dearest Alice. March 21st 1912.

I have been too horribly silent for a long time both as regards you & as regards Harry (though I did write to Aleck a week or two ago;) & your dear letter of the 5*th*—even this already a week old with me—brings closer home to me my lapse. The reason for this gaping interval has been that there began with me—or began to begin—about the time of Bill's & Alice's arrival (or rather considerably before it,) a rather sharp & dismal fall back from my so extremely improved conditions of body—those that set in particularly on my *really* coming up here for the winter; & though it was less bad than any one—any bad one—of that dismal series of relapses of last year it still disqualified me pretty completely for three weeks (I went down to L. H. & went to bed, heedless of A.'s & B.'s attractions, for a part of the time,) & a good deal ravaged my life, making letters &, too deplorably, work, temporarily quite impossible. I can speak of it now without scruple, because I have emerged from it into a better state even than before it came on, & I only do so to explain that it cast me into such arrears, arrears of every kind, that I have only been slowly & painfully catching up. A very interesting letter from Harry arrived just as the damned thing was coming on—& all your sad & lamentable news about Leigh Gregor & Margaret:[93] which is why I have had to treat these things with wretched dumbness—till now. I deeply desire to write to Margaret—but wanted to recover a better consciousness myself before facing *her* horrible fact. Bill &

---

93. Leigh Gregor was the husband of Margaret Merrill Gibbens (1857–1927), Alice's sister.

Alice will have reported of me—but they really haven't known or under-stood much, & the "cold" they wrote you of was but one feature or symptom of my afflicted 6 or 7 weeks—counting from the time when I began to go really wrong; & was verily but the least part of it. All this simply to elucidate—not a bit to prey on your sympathies, for I have surmounted better than ever before, & by exactly the same physiological logic, & done it wholly myself (not even calling for Skinner when I had to go down twice to Rye & get into bed—once before B. & A. arrived & once after; besides having in the early stage too obligingly gone to pay a week= end visit to Mrs. Julian Sturgis[94] in Surrey, reaching there in so sorry a state that I had to go straight to bed that afternoon & remain there till the Monday a.m., when she kindly sent me back to town in her motor-car. All of which, I repeat, I now tell you for your amusement & to *account for myself.* Let me add that my not sending for Skinner was no phenomenon— I feel so that I know to-day a thousand times more about myself & my whole pathological history than all the Skinners, & even than all the Oslers, in creation. Skinner was good & helpful for *nursing,* & for the cheer &c of his visits; but never really understood or got hold of anything! Basta!)

To speak *1st* about ourselves here, the great fact about us is the black shadow of our colossal Coal Strike, which fills, to a very dismal effect, all our consciousness & in the gloom of which we think of nothing else. It's a daily a more & more [*sic*] grave situation—& the end is not yet, bringing home as never before how coal in this country is not a feature or an accessory, however indispensable, but the underlying motive force of all life & being, the very breath of our existence. The question looms immense & the solution, which everything is ominously shrinking & collapsing— poverty & want, by the arrest of all industries & all employment & rapid failure of supplies already huge—isn't at all visible. The government has proceeded very justly & sanely & ably—the Tories would have landed us in Civil War in a week; but they are very perplexingly & formidably & unprecedently held up, & have up to now the immense pull, if now they have to do something drastic, of not having put themselves in the wrong. It's really an enormous quandary—but we shall come out of it. Meanwhile (though the use of coal is painfully shrinking at this club, & I am writing you tonight in a most frigid Library,) the cellar at L. H. is stocked for some

94. Mary Maud Beresford Sturgis. She was Irish and the wife of writer Julian Russell Sturgis (1848–1904), son of the American banker Russell Sturgis.

weeks to come, & A. & B., I think, have been happily unconscious of my pinch. The great pinch is on the Railways, already cutting down their Services to near the bare bones—& the real pinch for all of us would come if they should—or shall—cease to be able to transport supplies. Then we shall all collapse from simple inanition. But before that comes, or this reaches you, you will probably hear by cable that the tension is somehow relieved—even if by inevitable violence of some sort at last: which last will—or would—only prepare however a worse & merely postponed sequel. "Labour" has got tremendously on its feet & feels itself clutch the key to everything. Tight & dense as everything here, we here feel it connect!

But you will want to know more of other things, though Bill & Alice will probably have told you all the intimate & immediate ones. I hope they write freely—they send me blessedly all your letters, & sent me the other day a most blest of all one from Peggy—a long, delightful, & so reassuring & convincing one they had just had from her in her Florida paradise. It delights & comforts me more than I can say to have this palpable proof of her *enormous* recuperation—which her time in New York had already made me believe in. What an unqualified boon of her having the call to Florida—and in such perfect conditions; & what a pure blessing that you had the confidence to help *her* confidence & send her off. But what cares & anxieties *haven't* you all the while to face, dearest Alice—& what burdens haven't you this winter (as if *I* wasn't enough last!) taken on your hands! But I won't go into that! A spectacle of cheer, all the while, is the apparently perfect felicity of Bill & Alice whom I went down to for a week‗end a little while back. (I shall have to wait, to go again, till the trains are once more possible; 3/4's of them are off & those stop everywhere; besides which I am trying so now to make up lost time at my work.) I think they are absolutely happy—& L. H. is clearly a blessing to them as they are, not less, to *it*. I want them quite intensely to stay to June 1*st* at least—& really quite fondly hope, & even believe, they *will.*

*March 23d.* This was forcibly interrupted day before yesterday, & though I haven't 1/2 said what I want I send it off as it is, so as not to miss today's, Saturday's, American post & wait over till next week. I am writing immediately to Harry, which will be also in a manner to you, & will say to him the other things I wanted particularly to tell you, so that they won't be lost to you. At times, dearest Alice, all these things seem so many! Since beginning this—in fact yesterday a.m.—I had from Alice at Rye your letter to Bill of the 10*th,* the one enclosing Peg's 2*d* letter from Fort Myers

& reproducing Schiller's[95] magnificent dedication to William—which almost breaks me down. (Oh, there is so much to say in all *that* connection!—but I shall presently say much of it to Harry.) I am too enchanted with these helpful experiences of Peg's. What a Paradise she depicts—save for one's sense that it's all somehow so *blank:* just as I remember it at Palm Beach. One feels that when she has told what she has she has told *all*. However, thank God it's so much.——I shall write to Margaret within these next days. I *have* written to James Crafts[96]—what an uncalled for misery *that* extinction! Tell your Mother (I yearn over *her* so!) of all I should like to say to her as well as to Margaret. Of course, I weeks ago had & read Flournoy's exquisite book about William.[97] But this *must* go, & I get off to work. Ever your

*Henry.*

P.S. Tell dear Aleck, who will have had my poor letter, how I rejoice in what you say to Bill, of Benson's injunction to him to exhibit. I shall send him at once a fine photograph of Sargent's admirable charmed head of me—just done (for Mrs. Wharton!)

ALS: Houghton bMS Am 1094 (1724)

---

*James congratulates Alice on Harry's new job as manager of the Rockefeller Institute for Medical Research, and he wishes her a "lotus-eating summer." His sister-in-law Mary sent him a poorly written letter. He relays other news of family and friends.*

Dearest Alice.                                                    LAMB HOUSE, RYE, SUSSEX.

I have received within 3 or 4 days a letter from Alice, one from Bill, one from Aleck; & this a.m. a most blessed one from yourself—without counting the great one from Harry of about a week ago & which I at once & jubilantly answered. I am in unspeakably soothed & gratified possession of all the best of your news, & though yours is the last of these recent letters it must absolutely be the first to be acknowledged. How can I thank you enough for writing me so fully & sanely & bravely about all these things of

---

95. WJ's British humanist-pragmatist friend Frederick Canning Scott Schiller (1864–1937). He was a tutor at Oxford and a professor at the University of Southern California starting in 1929.

96. Mr. and Mrs. James Mason Crafts were Bostonians who lived a good deal in London. James Mason Crafts (1839–1917) was a chemist who later became MIT's president. Mrs. Crafts must have died.

97. Théodore Flournoy (1854–1920) was a Swiss psychologist and friend of WJ's. Flournoy gave a series of lectures in Switzerland in October 1910 that WJ was to have delivered. Flournoy's lectures, *The Philosophy of William James,* were published as a book in 1911.

immediate concern to us? You know by this time what I think of Harry's closing with the Rockefeller proposition,[98] & I do so rejoice that your own view was from the 1st as clear & sharp as mine at once found itself. It seems to me a waste of breath to speak of so much as having *weighed* it, or of any doubt of its being *the* blessed thing as discussable. But all this I expressed to Harry as my overwhelming sense of the matter—& it's a joy that we're all so at one about it. The only pang is that William isn't, by our vision, delightfully & delightedly present at it, such pride & peace as it would have brought to him. But somehow it's all *for* him as much as for the rest of us, & it's through us that his happiness too gets uttered. I feel it, his happiness, in my own blood & pulses, & it enriches & intensifies my own. Harry's removal to New York will enlarge yours & Peg's life—far from impoverishing it; & the "time" you'll in one way & another have with it & from it & over it will leave far in the lurch any other times. What pleasure it must have given your Mother!——I almost shed tears, tell her with all my love, as I think of her noble satisfaction in it. A thousand times, yes, of course, the "big administrative post" his Father so understandingly desired for him was so waiting for him as the one right thing, that everything that has hitherto come & gone has been but the most happy & most subsidiary preparation for it. Only I do hope indeed that he will be able to put in a brave free holiday during the coming weeks. I hope he won't have to be in New York till October 1st. You are taking *your* holiday, dearest Alice, in strenuous fashion, I fear; but everything that any of you do or endure in your monstrous world, as it somehow always looks from here, is of a thrilling interest to me, & I dog these courageous steps of yours through the Cambridge House with as eager an attention as if I were again to be in it. I delight to think of what you are going to do there & see the same practical reason for it—there again Harry's sound vision of all things, *plus* yours & acting *with* it, comes out in its lustre. I could wish you a more lotus-eating summer than the job of sawing planks and breaking bricks that you seem to be in for—& yet after all your lotuses have always been planks & bricks, when it hasn't been the shirt-buttons & the rent socks & the still more inward interests of your children & of all those that are yours. I sicken & falter even here at the breath of your apparently villainous heat, which has largely blown across to us—we have had it bad too, but some-what brokenly (though it seems now to be beginning again;) & the mem-

---

98. Harry had decided to give up his Boston law practice in order to go to New York and manage the Rockefeller Institute for Medical Research.

ory of last summer remains to terrify & haunt me. May the worst not overtake you, & the measure somehow be tempered!——I rejoice with all my heart that Peg is at that high & umbrageous Williamstown of which I gathered that day (I think motoring with Theodate Pope,) so happy an impression. May she develop there to her full compass!——I shall write to her before long, on how much I hope for it. I only got down here to "settle in" about 16 days ago, & I can't tell you the joy it is to feel Lamb House again a normal blessing. I long now for nothing so much as to find myself sticking fast here, all unmolestedly & fruitfully till toward Christmas—I say "toward" because that anniversary itself I find the best reasons for not spending. The fact that Bill & Alice got so much good of the place has endeared it still further to me & added to its wealth of touching associations; though even through that one I still see William up stairs in his distress or sitting a little, a few of the July hours, these very ones, in the garden before we sailed. However, it's quite beautiful now, & the garden as pretty as one can need it, & the lawn fine & tight, & the peas & beans & lettuces blooming & brave (& George a saint alive & Kidd the pearl of her tribe. Joan, the inaudibly monosyllabic & the tearful of one eye, is really a very adequate & "tasty" little cook—Alice having left her ever so much better than she found her.) I have got back to work again after a good many final adversities in London, & I now feel that it, the work, will go on as it hasn't at all yet. There is only *this* sorry circumstance, that the Angel of Devastation (as Howard Sturgis[99] & I unanimously dub her) Mrs. Wharton, who arrived day before yesterday by motor-car from Paris & Folkestone, departed this morning, after 36 most genial hours here, only with the pledge that I will join her at Windsor (Howard S.'s) on Thursday (this is Tuesday) to motor with her up to Wemmergill, the Charles Hunters' Yorkshire place, there to spend 4 or 5 days—motoring again, so far as we can, over that region. This has been in question, Mrs. Hunter much insisting on it, for some time past; & it will be a very beautiful way of seeing a little part of England I don't know at all & perhaps shld. never otherwise see. The pressure on me is great, & I am going & probably shall enjoy it as much as I *can* enjoy with an irritated & distressed sense of interruption & deviation. But I shall keep it down to the shortest possible stint, ten days in all, I hope, at the very most, & I have so few adventures & travels now that I shall endeavour to make this count suggestively &

99. Howard Overing Sturgis (1855–1920), writer and generous host. He lived at Queen's Acre with his partner, William Haynes "The Babe" Smith. HJ met Sturgis in 1877 and was a frequent guest at his home after that.

inspiringly as one. May it be my only absence from home for months to come. Now that I am *really* back here I greatly like it, & it has already done me plenty of good! Bill has enclosed me a quaint little letter from Aleck— it's to you, by the way, & I return it to you in this; all the more that I have one from him by the same post equally quaint (& telling much the same story;) the joy of life exhaled from which it is a blessing to note. He sent me his chalk-drawing of Robt. Allerton, & I am to have it photographed (in London,) for him—clearly they couldn't do that in the wilds of Illinois (Robt.'s chateau & park somehow sound so dreary!) so that you will have a transcript of it. It is very nice & free; & Bill writes me to my exceeding pleasure that the late work of Aleck's that he has seen shows a great forging ahead. Meanwhile I gloat over this so natural & empathetic evidence of the beautiful extent to which he & the ranch & the riding & the grand total are a "combination." What a world of good the whole experience must be, alike physically, spiritually & socially, doing him! I am greatly touched by your mention of your Sister Margie's prospective return to Montreal (which I hadn't somehow taken altogether for granted;) wincing all the more at the vision of it, & of her sore stress, by reason of my utterly helpless dumbness to her—the fruit really of my sick horror of dealing at all with the tragedy of dear Leigh; a simple, selfish, miserable *fear* of it. What an act of courage her return to the grim North—all your Norths, from here, somehow look so grim. The cheerfullest thing you mention—outside of our family existence—is the going of Sally N. & Lily[100] &c to live, for the time, in Mount Vernon St. What a blest break of the spell of the sorry superstition of Shady Hill—it quite refreshes one's interest in them. But on the other hand how sad a story of poor doomed Arthur Cabot—& how much with it will be knocked from under Lilla, & by the same stroke from under Tom.[101] There are times when one *fears* news of people. I had a prim & innocuous little letter from Concord Mary [HJ's brother Robertson's wife] the other day—before the meagreness of whose composition ("mean well" though she may!) one really quite breaks down. But this scrawl, or sprawl, must end—though having for its extent really covered little

100. Sara "Sally" Norton (1864–1922) and Elizabeth Gaskell "Lily" Norton (1866–1958) were both daughters of Charles Eliot Norton. They had visited HJ often in England.

101. Lilla Cabot (Mrs. Thomas) Perry (ca. 1848–1933), painter and poet, and her husband Thomas Sargeant Perry (1845–1928), American writer and educator. Lilla Cabot was the daughter of a Boston surgeon; T. S. Perry had been a friend since he met James in 1858 in Newport, Rhode Island, and remained one until the end of James's life. Arthur Cabot was one of her relatives.

ground. I shall be very glad to have any letter of Wilkie's—the one you speak of enclosing hasn't yet come. Would you mind sending this—in spite of its bulk—on to B. & A. as a stopgap before I get round to them, & even though this will be soon? I should give myself up to the fond vision of them in the garnished & amplified Chocorua house if I hadn't by misfortune had my last sight of the place under the awful blight of that torrid July week of last summer—when I could but wonder how you all remained alive. I can't tell you how I hope, dearest Alice, that you are really this year undergoing no such tests as *that* was! But I pray for you hard all the while & am your affectionate old brother

*Henry James*

July *23: 1912*

ALS: Houghton bMS Am 1094 (1726)

---

*James notes how pleased William would have been at his son's success. He advises Alice on her Cambridge home renovations and tells her he has just been motoring with Edith Wharton.*

LAMB HOUSE, RYE, SUSSEX.

Dearest Alice. August *6th 1912*

This is but a dozen words—I wrote you so lately (from Cliveden on the 31*st*) & so voluminously. But another little letter has come in from you this a.m., enclosing a most heartening one from Peg (to yourself) & accompanied by a blest & delightful one direct to me—the effect of which is to make me want to pass a remark or two back to you at once; especially as you speak of Harry's having just gone on to N. Y.—to take care of the question of his quarters there—& again of what you are doing in Irving St. These things so appeal to me that I can't *not* make you some sign of how longingly I enter into them. I hope Harry will see his way to something really comfortable in N. Y.—by which I mean *positively* pleasant & civilized—& imagine that with his resources he will. The more I have thought of his new outlook the more I have seen in it & rejoiced & believed in it—& the more I have believed & felt too that you & Peg will have been seeing it in the large & noble light that it deserves to be seen in, & which wd. have been so that of William's view. It will be enlarging, & it will be so *interesting,* to & for all of us together—let alone what it will be to H. himself! So let us positively cultivate a fine rich sense of it! This is easy to say to you, indeed, dear Alice, on whom the great difference at home will bear hardest & most directly; but you will probably & characteristic-

91

ally, so project yourself in to his N. Y. situation, in sympathy & intelligence, as to become little by little unaware of how much you are missing him in the flesh. At present, in any case, I can feel how the Irving St. doings beguile & appeal to you—just by reason of the sense of how they appeal to *me;* & oh so much more as I read the word in your today's letter about your & Harry's feeling for our "keeping the house among us." That absolutely must we do—it is so *consecrated* by its history: William is there, always, as he is nowhere else, & to let go of it would be in a manner to lose part of our grasp, or our possession, of him. While I was there last, in my great unwellness, I was to some extent conscious of some of the old (yet after all small) mistakes involved in it; but now & from here I feel nothing but the personal value of the place & give you my blessing on our keeping it as a general stronghold. Besides, you will have so rectified the mistakes & turned the balance the other way. The improved hall that you speak of will be by itself a great thing—& perhaps you are putting a *bath* into the downstairs liberated dressing-room; though on the other hand you may think that a downstairs bath, away from a bedroom, isn't particularly practical—even if it be difficult to have in the U. S., summer or winter, too many baths in a house. I take an interest even in the point you make of a new "ice-box"—though I don't understand it as an (apparently) *constructional* feature. Perhaps it is in some way built into the wall! My blessing at any rate on the whole job! I am glad my letter to Harry on the New York question gave him pleasure—how can any one deserve more that pleasure *should* be given him?——I returned here (from Cliveden straight save for a pause again at Windsor for lunch) on the 2*d:* Edith Wharton (who was to stop over at Howard Sturgis's another day or two,) lending me her admirable car & chauffeur. They brought me all across the so beautiful land hither between 2 p.m. & 6.30—& Cook [E. Wharton's chauffeur] went back (to W.) the same night. The day was lovely, & it is the very poetry & luxury of travel. But now *how* I want to remain untroubled—for weeks & weeks, solid months, to come—in this place. A great wild midsummer gale—the wildest & longest I have ever known at the Season—is blowing here now—& *has* been, more or less, for 3 days; but there has been nothing like it, even in other months, for a long time. I hope you, on your side, aren't grilling or roasting. What a blest berth Aleck's in Montana! Ever dearest Alice, your faithfullest

Henry

P.S. *How* haunted & *sentient,* in its empty fullness, the dear old house must indeed seem to you all alone that way at your evening letters. Even this one is "hauntingly lonely" to me as I sit at eventide (7 p.m. now) through this dreary tempest! All of you have been so blessedly in it—but those last of William's sheltered weeks above all!

ALS: Houghton bMS Am 1094 (1728)

*On the second anniversary of William's death, James imagines Alice alone by the lamp in a haunted room. Rye's summer has been the harshest and cruelest in years. He will not let Ida Tarbell publish some of William's letters in an American periodical but plans instead to have Scribners bring out* Early Letters of William James, with Notes by Henry James.

LAMB HOUSE, RYE, SUSSEX.

August 26*th* p.m. *1912.*

Dearest Alice.

You see I can't help writing as soon as anything blessedly comes from you, & the only way to keep me down will be for you to keep yourself back. Three days ago came your letter of the 12*th* (acknowledging mine from the so incongruous but so fortunately brief Cliveden;) which gave such an image of you all alone by the evening lamp at that tremendous table in that haunted room, where I see you & feel you so that I can't possibly not send you back a sign—above all on this night of all nights, this eve of our black anniversary. What a heroic life you are carrying on—with all your difficult & expensive labour, & so singlehanded & solitary, but to so intensely good & right & desirable an end. Your mention of what it all costs you there on the spot, diurnally, makes my few remaining hairs stand on end, & I think of you *meeting* that with an ineffable desire to contribute. Well, I shall, I think virtually & inevitably—but we will come to that later. You needn't warn me against putting in the electric light here—for there is absolutely none to be had in the place—such is the dense little local benightedness; so that I am powerless even were I wantonly disposed. And I am far from being *that*—having indeed a great dread of the mauling & gouging out, for such a purpose, of this little sensitive & unprepared old structure, which only asks for that tenderest use that consists in being let alone. It's a perfect blessing to me that I think of your admirable mother there beside you as of the essence of your situation in these days; I rejoice that you are there together in your sound, safe, dear, houses respectively, each of which is such interesting & sustaining company to the other. Do *always* give my love to her, & remind her afresh of the comfort I take in her. I feel as if she were a kind of oversheltering mother to *me* too—by her being there with you, & by all she was of so oversheltering to William. And I seem to make

out too that the summer weeks are letting you off easily—you in fact mention it; no news of heat-waves has reached us here since June from your focus of that sort of thing—which reflection is another blessing to me. Here the season is the prey of perfectly devastating cold & wet, I am sorry to say—the harshest & cruellest record for many a year: uninterrupted tempests & deluges & desolations; great gales blowing & torrents descending simply all the while. One suffers from the *confinement* of it— the afternoons made impossible for air & exercise, & the effect of *that* rather dismal. However, one goes on, even though the fury of the elements does too—& it can't be said of me that I don't clutch at *any* rifts & breaks & make the most of them—for indispensable mild circulation even if rather lonely mechanical prowls as they too often seem. ————————
You speak of Miss Tarbell again,[102] & I shall see her in a friendly way, if possible, & if she writes to me—though to go up to town on purpose to see her (for nothing practical) is more than I can now take time & effort for— if that shld. be involved. The whole situation as to what I am doing has cleared up, & there can be no question at all of any use of Miss T. or of the American magazine for it. That periodical is utterly inadequate (with its short newspaper-form snippets &c) & below the argument. The "Family Book," *as a vehicle for William's Early Letters,* has had wholly to break down—after drawing me along into the delusion that I might make the whole thing *one.* It was becoming far too copious & complicated to *be* one, at all; absolutely it will have to be two—but with the Early Letters, as a publication by themselves, the 1st now to be thought of. It has been an immense relief to see the case thus beautifully simplified—for I shall accompany the Letters with as much "Family," all along, as *immediately* concerns them, & with thereby the light so much more completely focussed on William himself. I am in very auspicious treaty with the Scribners for the volume—"Early Letters of William James, with Notes by Henry James," & with the Notes (the simplest & best name for *my* part) I can do *everything* I want. Charles Scribner, who is in England, is keenly interested & eager, & it's pretty clear that I shall be able to make highly advantageous terms. But the book as such, as a whole, will not be serializable—I entirely understand Scribner's view that it is more of a thing, in every way, than a magazine can "carry." (The "American" couldn't either *touch* it—or pay for it.) What he wants is *two* instalments, for Scribner, 2

102. Ida Minerva Tarbell (1857–1944) was a Pennsylvania-born author, lecturer, and editor who wrote an exposé of the Standard Oil Company, as well as a number of other books.

only, of the Letters—the Letters *and* the Notes; as illustrative & annuncia-tory, as it were, before the publication of the book—to be followed *by* the book. This will be very manageable—I shall be perfectly able to lift the 2 instalments, for that use, artfully, out of the mass. And now I see no reason why I shouldn't get on very straight & quite swiftly, to completion. Much of what I had done of the "Family Book" is useable, & being used. But I am wondering if there are, left in Irving St., any Letters (of William's own, only) to which the term Early can still be in a manner applied. Those I have stop at his return from Dresden, Berlin &c, at about 1868—or rather, stay, go on (several to *me*) through the period of 1869–70, of 1872–73–74 (in small numbers) while I was in Europe, 1st alone, & then for a few months with Alice & Aunt Kate. What I want to know is whether there [are] any to me (among those I sent out to Kidd for while in Irving St. & left there on coming away,) that are of 1875 or 76 or 77. I was in Europe from 1875 on, & there may be a few of just those first two or three years. On the other hand the *Early* division comes to an end best—it does—either with his own return from Germany, or with the very 1st beginning of his connection with Harvard—& at that it may easily be left. Let me add to this, in parenthesis, that the Scribners will probably be just as keen for the later letters as they are for these earlier.

*Aug. 27th: 10.30 p.m. I broke* off last night to go to bed, & now *this* bad day will almost have waned for me. It has been unpropitious & difficult—I've been more perversely unwell than I could have wished. But I am better—as my evenings are always better than my days; & the proof of it is that here I sit up late & at my ease to add a little more to this. I thank you more than I can say for your last trouble in the matter of sending me the little book-box from Concord. I shall be very glad to have it when it comes (though really I shall scarcely know when to *place* its contents, where to range & shelve it;) for they are all, I recognised when I saw them at Mary's, things of quite previous old-time (old Newport & old Quincy St. time) association. It will be quite an emotion for me to open the box again—& all the more because you, dearest Alice, have given it this great charitable lift. I shall probably hear of it here more quickly and easily than you hear in Cam-bridge when boxes are sent you from this end. I find myself fairly harrowed by what you tell me of Mary's [Salter] sacrificial state to that dreadful boy & that d—d fool (I can't help calling him so—it relieves me,) of a hus-band. It seems to me a really big case of asininity—& it must indeed be a torment just helplessly to watch it—from so near—and what you say of it, & of poor Mary's unfittedness & blightedness in it, in the heroism of *her* part of it, is so vividly just! It's one of those adjacent things that I think with a kind of relief that William isn't here to have up against him—in the minor way in how it would have been—& yet how one can imagine all the attenuations & excuses that his charity wd. (even while utterly disapprov- ing his course,) have found for [William] Salter!——What a blessing, in a more delightful way, Bill's & Alice's possession of a house, for the winter, by so easy a stroke! Nothing, it seems to me, cld. be better—for helping them to wait for the right thing of their own. Splendid too the young automobile & splendid the source of it—what an extraordinarily munifi- cent Parent! The least Bill can certainly do is to paint him in a valuable way—which I feel certain he *is* doing. But now I must go to bed again. How I hope Harry is having the biggest & longest and rightest kind of a good holiday! When the arrangement with Scribner is clinched I'm going to write him about sending them the drawings for reproduction. But really goodnight. Ever your faithfullest

*Henry.*

ALS: Houghton bMS Am 1094 (1729)

*James's health makes him rely on a bath chair for excursions, and he tells Alice of the chair's "sweet appeal." He recalls a walk with William and Alice in Battersea Park. He praises Woodrow Wilson's recent address and remarks that neither Mildred nor William Dean Howells have "a grain of a sense of comfort."*

[*Dictated*]

21, CARLYLE MANSIONS, CHEYNE WALK. S.W.

Dearest Alice.                                      March 5th., 1913.

An extreme blessing to me is your dear letter from Montreal. I had lately much longed to hear from you—and when do I not?—and had sent you a message to that effect in writing to Harry a week ago. Really to have some of your facts and your current picture straight from yourself is better than anything else. What a benediction your visit to Margaret in her white North must have been to her—what a lift toward better things, I hope, to come. May it all have gone well with you till, and for, and with, the return "south". I think of those Canadian winter conditions somehow as with an unappeased dismay—though I dare say that, like all other formidable things, it is a case with them of "grasping your nettle", that is that they lose much of their dread as you hug them close. If you weren't to be already at home when you get this I should send a particular message to the brave Sister and the ambiguous (I mean as *all* such are ambiguous) Child. It seems to me a great act of devotion and pluck for you to have gone to them. May you by this very time indeed have happily rejoined the family circle. Strange to say, I don't despair of writing to Margaret yet—but of the extent to which so many dire influences since my last leaving America have worked against all correspondence save of the very last urgency I won't attempt any record now.

My letter to Harry, long, only too long, I fear, as well as too considerably dismal, will have told you, alas, of my having had another sharp upset—but also of my now being pretty well out of it and on the way, I devoutly trust, to much better things. It strikes me as having been, as a "pathological" episode, distinctly well-managed; and in spite of its fairly disconcerting connection with a lung-sensibility, I feel day by day more assurance of such good physical assets as I do possess. Besides which the lung-sensibility appears to have been but of the most indirect and superficial and limited order, subject to very prompt rectification, and in the last degree anomalous through the absolutely immune nature of my lifelong lung-consciousness. I have literally never coughed, as one hears people, in our climates, coughing all round one, in all my life; I have had for long years, and in fact absolutely always, an immunity from colds, and from any such liabilities, as has *struck* me, in the midst of such an entourage, and given my total unacquaintance with all the phenomena of influenza and bronchial sensibility, I feel that I have plenty of soundness to draw upon and go on with. This last matter, I also feel, was simply but another, and I devoutly trust a final, exhibition of the horrible poisonous disorder wrought in me by my interminable Herpes, which had its *train* of consequences. So I am going to regard myself as distinctly improvable, with care, caution, intelligence, and oh such treasures of sad experience, unless something *too* overwhelmingly adverse be fastened upon me. What is most overwhelmingly adverse while it lasts is the melancholy blight of work; but what is by the same token a real uplifting, a sense of spreading my wings again, is the least at all renewed and continuous "go" of that faculty. I feel as if I but hang on to it tight enough it will hang on to *me,* and that in fine we shall in one way or another see each other through. But these things I said more or less to Harry so few days since, and he will have let you have the benefit of them.

I write you this in conditions that give me for the hour, this morning-hour, toward noon, such a sense of the possible beneficence of Climate, relenting ethereal mildness, so long and so far as one can at all come by it.

We have been having, as I believe you have, a blessedly mild winter, and the climax at this moment is a kind of all but uncannily premature May-day of softness and beauty. I sit here with my big south window open to the River, open wide, and a sort of healing balm of sunshine flooding the place. Truly I feel I did well for myself in perching—even thus modestly for a "real home"—just on this spot. My beginnings of going out again have consisted, up to to-day, in four successive excursions in a Bath-chair—every command of which resource is installed but a little more than round the corner from me; and the Bath-chair habit or vice is, I fear, only too capable now of marking me for its own. This of course not "really"—my excellent legs are, thank heaven, still too cherished a dependence and resource and remedy to me in the long run, or rather in the long (or even the short) crawl; only, if you've never tried it, the B. C. has a sweet appeal of its own, for contemplative ventilation; and I builded better than I knew when I happened to settle here just where in all London, thanks to the long, long, smooth and really charming and beguiling Thames-side Embankment offers it a quite ideal course for combined publicity (in the sense of variety) and tranquility (in the sense of jostling against nobody and nothing and not having to pick one's steps.) Add to this that just at hand, straight across the River, by the ample and also very quiet Albert Bridge, lies the large, convenient and in its way also very beguiling Battersea Park: which you may but too unspeakably remember our making something of the circuit of with William on that day of the so troubled fortnight in London, after our return from Nauheim, when Theodate Pope called for us in her great car and we came first to just round the corner here, where he and I sat waiting together outside while you and she went into Carlyle's house. Every moment and circumstance of that day has again and again pressed back upon me here—and how, rather suddenly, we had, in the Park, where we went afterwards, to pull up, that is to turn and get back to the sinister little Symonds's as soon as possible. However, I don't know why I should stir that dismal memory. The way the "general location" seems propitious to me ought to succeed in soothing the nerves of association. This last I keep saying—I mean in the sense that, especially on such a morning as this, I quite adore this form of residence (this particular perch I mean) in order to make fully sure of what I have of soothing and reassuring to tell you.

Everything you tell *me* meanwhile, and what I read into Harry's general brave tone, has that blest effect upon myself. How delightful to have so bright and steady a vision of you all together! I didn't know about Bill's blest appointment;[103] and descending upon him straight through the strong magnet of his own merit as it had done, it fills me with joy and pride. Please let him and Alice see this—I have so to economise at present dictational effort, and yet still can *most* economically dictate. Let my blessing perch on that roof-tree of theirs, with covering, quivering wings, for all these next weeks to come. It's a blow to me of course on the other hand to hear that Aleck is *not* to turn up here in June—though I quite see how other proceedings may be during the coming year much more relevant for him. Give him all my love and all my regret, and in particular all my joy in his having such straight work and profit and pleasure cut out for him with Abbott Thayer.[104] May no end of grand results take place in their due order. What a blest good thing that there should be between him and Thayer such a pre-established harmony. Let me add too that till I feel more thoroughly better I shouldn't feel very fit to be a decent provider here for the dear boy's London doings and openings. Others would help—the von Glehns[105] (who are really when you know them a quite golden pair, for sweetness of nature and intelligence of spirit) quite pant and yearn for him; but this wouldn't prevent me from missing rather ruefully, very sadly in fact, the power to tackle his case better—should I *have* to miss it. Lamb House hangs before me from this simplified standpoint here as a rather complicated haze; but I tend, I truly feel, to overdo that view of it—and shan't *settle* to any view at all for another year. It is the more worriment of dragged-out unwellness that makes me see things in wrong dimensions. They right themselves perfectly at better periods. But I mustn't yet discourse too long: I am still under restriction as to uttering too much sound; and I feel how guarding and nursing the vocal resource is beneficial and helpful. I don't speak to you of Harry—there would be too much to say and he must shine upon you even from N. Y. with so big a light of his own. I take him, and I take you all, to have been much moved by Woodrow Wilson's fine, and clearly so sincere, even if so partial and provisional address yesterday. It isn't *he,* but it is the so long and so deeply provincialised and diseducated and, I fear in respect to individual active and

---

103. Bill was hired to teach painting at the Boston Museum School, as the successor to Frank Benson.

104. Abbot Handerson Thayer (1849–1921) was a noted American artist who painted women as madonnas, virgins, and angels. He had a studio in New York from 1879 to 1901 and then at the foot of Mount Monadnock in New Hampshire.

105. Wilfred von Glehn, a painter, and his wife Jane Emmet von Glehn, a cousin of HJ's.

operative, that is administrative value, very below-the-mark "personalities" of the Democratic party, that one is pretty dismally anxious about. An administration that has to "take on" Bryan looks, from the over-here point of view, like the queerest and crudest of all things! But of course I may not know what I'm talking about—save when I thus embrace you all* (*almost principally Peg—and your Mother!!—) again and am your ever affectionate

*Henry James*

P.S. I'm glad you see dear Howells—and I hope that on a nearer view his drifting about, at his age, from pillar to post and relapsing so drearily on a Cambridge boarding-house again, hasn't the same sad aspect that it wears for one so dependent on a home as I am. I can't help feeling that the limp, even though so sweet, Mildred [William Dean Howells's daughter] doesn't imagine or conceive for him in these ways to the extent she might. They have between them, however, it strikes me, not a grain of a sense of comfort—any more now than they ever did have; and surely, "neurasthenic" though she may be, they must have great physical resources to bear up under such strains and strugglings. These same may indeed make for my seeing them here—which I much hope.

TLS: Houghton bMS Am 1094 (1733)

*James welcomes Alice Runnells and Bill James's son, William James III, but regrets his distance from the child. He has seen brother Wilky's daughter, Alice Edgar, who is uninteresting but "not a fool," and her two Chicago friends, "incredible little roaring mice." Nearly 300 English friends gave him special seventieth birthday gifts.*

21 Carlyle Mansions Chelsea S. W.

Dearest Alice.                                                           May 9*th* 1913.

How can I thank you enough for your beautiful letter this a.m. received (of Apr. 27*th,*) telling me about the so many things, the Baby, the Parents, the Runnellses, the Portraits, the Chestnut Street House (if God & Mrs. Runnells grant it,) & ever so many things more? A lovely letter (the loveliest conceivable) from Peg, & a delightful one from Bill, must wait for thanks so owed while I try to get *this* off by tomorrow's post. I am tremendously enlisted on behalf of the Boy, William's grandson, & rejoice intensely in your so beautiful & vivid & competent account of him.[106] I only wish to goodness I could see him with my eyes & study him with my

---

106. William ("Billy") James was born to Alice and Bill James in 1913.

affection. But he will get attention enough, & he really seems to me to have been born into as ideally happy & auspicious conditions as ever surrounded & promoted a young development. Fortunate little being to have nothing but Angels round his cradle—even if *one* Angel has to be so far off. I do hope that Alice proceeds calmly & comfortably—& see her in my mind's eye splendidly on her feet again & making such a vision with her small son in her arms. It strikes me that Bill's "outside" work is in much danger of hampering by this insistence on the part of his family on cropping up as subjects. He will soon be telling you to "quit" it—your irresistible appeal—& let him get on. But a joy to me is your definite & empathetic statement that he has succeeded so with you & Aleck. But oh, & oh, if it were only possible these portraits should be photographed & the photographs sent to poor yearning & privation-suffering *me!* Won't you urge this on Bill? while I write him about the matter too. I take an inexpressible interest in their getting the Boston house, & call down benedictions on the goodness of dear Mrs. Runnells. I see them too most felicitously framed at Chocorua & treating it amply as their own—so that Mr. Runnells seems to me to have even more than a match in their mamma. I shld. have liked to be at your luncheon-party, sole male that I shall have been, just to have been witness of the good it must have done poor little Concord Mary. Apropos of whom I bad good-bye only this afternoon to Alice Edgar, poor dear Wilky's Alice, who has been here some three weeks or so with 2 little chattering snippets of Chicago friends ("mice roaring" as Mrs. Kemble said of the Lenox ladies on the piazza,) & who goes (with them) tomorrow to Paris & thence presently home again. She will have been from thence but 7 or 8 weeks in all—& came out because she was nervously unwell & depressed (for the change,) but I'm afraid won't have found it greatly pay. Her extreme similarity to Wilky rather endears her to me, though she isn't interesting & has a quiet, smiling, uninterruptably & unheeding way of "running on" which leaves the talk all in her hands—& leaves one's self almost out of it save as a patient listener. It is an odd sort of nervous continuity as if to *prevent* one from breaking in any further than she may care to go—as too much on one's own matters. Yet she is very gentle, & in her way graceful, & not a fool—intelligent & interested if she had had but a grain of culture. But the extent to which she *hasn't* had that makes me really pity her. She was most discreet & considerate however, asking nothing of me, but quite affectionately testifying, & coming to luncheon gladly whenever I telephoned her—which I did as often as possible, making her also once bring the incredible little roaring mice. She isn't pretty in any very positive sense—as I rather remembered her being 10 years ago, & her long illness after her marriage (with the operation for appendicitis too) was largely a disturbance of her skin or complexion, on which it has left (not *quite* disfiguring) marks. But to-day I saw her for the first time (at her hotel,) in dinner-dress & without her hat, & she came much nearer to prettiness than before, as her head & hair are very good & becoming, & her "figure" & "dressed" state favourable. Something really pleasing might have been made of her could she have been caught (for real civilization) young. However it's late, & I too am running on. To assist you to appreciate the Birthday pleasantness of a short time since more completely I enclose you my Letter of Thanks issued some days ago—with the addition of some dozen or so belated names—those who didn't know of the affair in time to subscribe, but who have been "let in."[107] I am tempted to add to it, for your further enlightenment, a comment on it in a note just received from Mrs. J. R. Green,[108] the widow of the historian—in return for which I'm afraid I *must,* by a rare exception, dine with her to "meet" Wendell H.,[109] who comes out to stay with her—apparently. (I *never* dine out—that is utterly over & out of the question now, thank the powers. *À quelque chose malheur est bon* [From adversity, we learn]). Your mention of [William Dean] Howells's mention of young (as it were) Minturn's[110] approach to him on the "money" ground in N. Y. makes my flesh creep afresh with the vision of what was so dreadfully started. The silver-gilt porringer & its dish on my mantel-shelf shed meanwhile their harmless benignant glow (daily of a golden tone) & in a few days my sittings to Sargent—very few I hope—will have been arranged.

---

107. In 1913, HJ's English friends formed an informal committee to raise a fund to celebrate his seventieth birthday. Nearly three hundred people subscribed (no one giving more than five pounds). The group bought a Charles II porringer and dish and offered the balance to John Singer Sargent to paint HJ's portrait. Sargent refused the money because of his long friendship with James but still painted the portrait. The money then went to sculptor Derwent Wood to do a bust of James. Just before this an American group of friends (led by Edith Wharton) had tried to raise money for James's birthday, a large purse she proposed giving to him. James's nephew Harry learned of this scheme and cabled his uncle. HJ cabled back that all monies collected by the American group should be returned and the project abandoned.

108. Alice Stopford Green (1847–1929) was the widow of historian J. R. Green and a writer herself. She became a member of the Irish Senate in 1922.

109. Oliver Wendell Holmes Jr. (1841–1935), Supreme Court justice, had known WJ and HJ since he was a young law student at Harvard.

110. This may have been a relation of Bostonian Eliza Theodora ("Bessie") Minturn, a friend of Katherine Peabody Loring and sister Alice James.

But you will note that I have declined possession or ownership of the portrait: the committee must provide for that. This "fixes" me perfectly for any American resentment at my refusing their *Value;* (the value of the porringer being but £50.) And I will tell you more of this—something that will strike you & interest & "affect" you very much (as it has affected *me*) on a future occasion. Let me impress on you again meanwhile that the List is really a very wonderful & significant & touching one—I wish I could comment—for you in detail. Some of the names "stand for" so much more than meets the eye. But I will try & send dearest Peg a *marked* copy! I embrace her & yearn over you all afresh (oh to see some of Aleck's, as well as of Bill's, *production!*) & am yours all affectionately, dearest Alice,

*Henry James.*

P.S. But William is all the while more achingly absent from the Birthday than even all of *you*—& of the 250 others—are present! So much love to your Mother.

ALS: Houghton bMS Am 1094 (1735)

*James and Peggy are doing well at Lamb House: they take long walks daily. Mary Cadwalader Jones visited and Harry will come soon. He has been reading William's typed letters, "treasures of vividness."*

LAMB HOUSE RYE SUSSEX

Dearest Alice. August *5th 1913*.

It's much too long since I have written to you, & the letters to Peg that have come in from you since she has blessedly been with me make me feel as if I had been liberally hearing from you in spite of that. Her appearance in London with Harry 3 weeks ago seemed to begin a new era for me, & I have liked to think that her letters hence to you will have been, & will be for the rest of the time that she is here, almost a like comfort to *you.* You will know when this reaches you everything that has happened, & above all that I began to get better as soon as I got down here of a sharp upset that I had had in town some five days before my departure. I was really *bad* there however but for 24 hours—long enough for the Doctor to send in a nurse before I could turn round; but the nurse remained but for 3 days & 1/2, & as soon as she was gone I rose from my bed & took flight for this retreat with Peg, whom it was then (as it has been every hour since,) a consolation & support to have with me. (The servants, save Burgess had already, when Harry & she arrived, come down here—& then Kidd, whose ability & utility hourly grew, had hurried back to me in London—to depart again once more, rejoining Joan here, on the a.m. of the day when P. & I came down in the afternoon.) I began to mend, I say, the very morrow of our arrival, & am now doing extremely *well,* with work in the a.m. with Miss Bosanquet, & a quiet, delightful, most cheering life with the niece, the chief feature of which has been a long, slowly-taken & extraordinarily beneficial walk (never of less than 2 hours & mostly of 3,) over some of our blest grassy field-paths. They do me much good, & it's an unspeakably fortunate feature of my state that this gentle locomotion (the keeping on my feet for 3 or 4 hours a day) is positively remedial & quasi-"curative" to me. Of course I must be absolutely deliberate, utterly unhurried (the least haste or flurry or agitation I *instantly* pay for;) but on the general basis of *right* circulation, right in kind & in quantity, exercise in the open air is a really blest boon to me. There are walks—the steeper, & hillier ones—I can't take; but we make the most of those we can, & dear Peg's patience with the crawling *routinier* [stick-in-the-mud] old uncle is unspeakably touching & helpful to me. I wish I could only keep her—but I *shall* for a number of weeks more (she will have told you of her having arranged for her sailing home late in September,) & that will have seen me 1/2 through my time down here. The beauty & interest & intelligence & general large nobleness & sweetness of her endear to me more than I can say—we get on ideally together (she reminds me in mind & nature & *tone* intensely of her Father,) & it's a joy to me to think that you feel her to be here, during these dispersed & difficult weeks, happily at her ease & at peace. It seems to me absolutely to suit her to be exactly as she is just now. We are having a summer of the most convenient coolness—in fact of far too much crude cold; & this dear little old refuge, after my 8 months' absence from it, wears a face of irresistible charm. We have just had a visit of 48 hours from Mary Cadwalader (Jones,) which has gone off beautifully & been a test of my improved powers of the most gratifying—as it's the 1*st* "social" visit (to call a social visit) that I have dared to have for many a long day. Mrs. J. & Peg prove an excellent combination, & when it's a question of P.'s paying her next winter in N. Y. the visit of which she has extracted the promise you must back P. up strongly as to really going—I mean see that she doesn't slip out of it, for I am sure that will be a most good *sort* of thing for her. We hear from Harry very happily (you will be receiving the letters transmitted by Peg,) but are now in the act of joyfully thinking that his little tour in the Tyrol will have begun (his mere business, or inquiring & inspecting, movements over, & Vienna & Innsbruck his last postal address;) for that seems to mean that he will get to us here about the 20*th* & stay for 10 good days. I had 4 or 5 days of him in London, though mainly, alas, by my bedside, & I am greatly struck with his big fine development of character & power—his splendid faculty of growth & comprehension, & all in such a genial easy way. The signs of William's example, contact & communication are strong to me both in him & in Peg. Apropos of which I have been reading through the 4 vols. of typed letters of William's that they brought out to me, & have been verily overwhelmed by their beauty, interest & *attraction*—their redolence of intellectual & moral life & of rare genius. They contain treasures of vividness, pages & pages so characteristic that the difficulty among them will be as to what to publish & what to leave. But this difficulty will be eminently soluble with care & judgment. Some of them are to persons one doesn't care about, or at least that *I* don't, but these happily don't, mostly, contain the most valuable parts, though they contain *some*—& everything richly, weightily, or attractively & amusingly, characteristic must be given, no matter whom it's addressed to. The only thing is that all these letters are of the last 20 years or so & less, & I am wondering about the *earlier* ones, those of (about) from '75 to '90. But Harry will tell me about this question when I presently see him. Good night, now, dearest Alice; as usual I am writing late, after a longish snooze following dinner—a snooze very vital now; in fact it's nearly *one* a.m. up here in the little green room which is so haunted for me with memories of your & William's old gathered-in sessions & struggles here (with all your besetting questions & difficulties,) as well as of my own. It endears the whole house to me intensely *more* than it did after all at times serve William & you as a refuge & a haven—& I try to recover the times & remember what they seemed to do for you while they lasted. And oh dearest Alice, how I like to think of you as gathered in on cool shores at this particular season. Your letters from Castine relieve me more than I can say of thinking of you at the torrid Cambridge. I hope you are staying on or "going on" & that you will pass through as many as possible of the *draughty* doors that are open to you. Great to *me* the convenience of such a summer as this here. I think however as trustfully as possible of Bill & Alice at Chocorua & of Aleck in *his* queer places. I bless you all & am ever affectionately

H. J.

ALS: Houghton bMS Am 1094 (1736)

*James continues to miss his grandnephew and wants any sort of photo of him. He congratulates Alice on her restorations at 95 Irving Street. He has finished the second part of his autobiography,* Notes of a Son and Brother, *and has started another novel,* The Ivory Tower. *Katherine Loring found an early self-portrait of William in one of sister Alice's books.*

21 CARLYLE MANSIONS CHEYNE WALK S.W.

Dearest Alice. *Jan. 18th 1914*

How can you undervalue your beautiful & interesting letter today received or speak as if it weren't full of what I want most to know about you? I thank you for it at once, so as to feel more that I am *with* you & in the reconsecrated house, which I delight to think of just *because* it's the commemoration of what William so originally & solidly made. But what a weary labour you must indeed have over it, & how I get the impression that such things are more difficult to do in your conditions than in those that surround me here. I am doing & planning some small enlivations of this small flat—of the most modest little sort; the trail of my predecessor is in some particulars rather painfully over it: that is I have happily "done up" my bedroom, from top-to-toe & have arranged for an expurgation of the diningroom at some near convenient moment, & the excellent little "builder & decorator" whom Emily Sargent put me in relation with when first I came & who has done little things of every sort for me since, is a perfect little angel of facilitation, simplification & promptitude, so that nothing has any terror or any difficulty. But I am comparing absurdly the tiniest jobs with the most spacious—as in vast *95.* And I cherish the image of the more liveable & loveable house. William would indeed so have loved it, & may you now richly rest in it!——I have heard very handsomely from Peggy—& Alice wrote me from Chestnut St. a really charming New Year's letter even though I was then greatly in arrears with her. It's a true blessing to feel that that venture of Bill's was based, for the pair, not upon a mistake, but on a real harmony—for strong is any sense that it won't play them false. I am meanwhile quite grotesquely inconsolable at not having the personal acquaintance of little Walter William [Bill and Alice's young son]—I feel I should "get on" with him so particularly well & that he would "meet such a want" in my life. It's very absurd that a small sub-nephew the less should make such a *lacune* [hole] in the life of a poor old transatlantic great=uncle; but so it is. It comes back to me that I *did* give B. & A. a sofa, & an *old* one, while they were here; but I have so quite forgotten its shape & aspect that I greatly like hearing from you that it plays so good a part. And it can't—at Jarvis's—have been an *upholstered* thing: Alice must have been at costs for all that.——I rejoice much in your telling me that you have been seeing more of poor dear Grace Norton, whom I think of with such affectionate *respect*—for the stiff upper lip she has kept through all dreariness & difficulties—& whom I hope soon to enable to tell you that she has at last heard from me again—as it's a perfect scandal she for so long shouldn't have done. But what a "mysterious providence" the prolongation of poor Theodora [Sedgwick] to such dregs of destruction—what a strange power in her & hapless to herself, of surviving the *fact* of death!——T. S. Perry wrote me lately that he had been to see you & missed you, but he must have been since there with better luck. Very happy his saying that after my book he will be "ready for Long Wharf & Charon's boat"; only to appreciate it you must have known the part played by Newport Long Wharf in our young times. My second Vol.[111] was some time since finished & seen through the Press, & the delay now is all Macmillan's here & the Scribners' in N. Y.—but they promise publication for next month. Àpropos of which I sent Harry some time since a strange & precious little windfall of a small drawing received from Katherine Loring as having unexpectedly fallen out of an old book that had belonged to Alice—& which I at once recognised as a *head of himself* (before a looking glass,) done by William upwards of 50 years ago—that is it must belong, at the latest, to about 1866 (& *may* have been as early as '63.) Harry was to take it to the Scribners to be reproduced as a frontispiece to Notes of a Son and Brother, but I have heard nothing about it since from him, & as you don't mention having a photograph of it from him (or mention it otherwise) I suppose you all know nothing about it. I earnestly hope it will have been found reproducible in N. Y.—it is so interesting & admirable & exhibits so William's "masterly" young sense of drawing. I had it immediately photographed in facsimile & one of my 2 copies hangs, framed, beside my mantel-shelf in this room. The other I am putting up & sending you by the same post as this, on the *chance* that you won't have had any sight of it (& I find it so touching & precious.) I would have sent you this photograph before but for having assumed that Harry would probably have sent the thing *itself* on to you as soon as the Scribners had had it photographed for their "process"—& that this would be a rapid business. Perhaps he has—though I can't help thinking you would in that case have alluded to it. Strange its having lurked 1/2 a century in such an unvisited crevice & been preserved & restored by the rarest of chances. It was evidently most casually done—off hand, on a piece of ruled paper & with

---

111. His second autobiography, *Notes of a Son and Brother*.

another leaf attached to the piece covered with odd old pencil cipherings. The ruled lines have fortunately in the photograph been quite conjured away.——I am writing as usual late—*very* late—in the evening: I am always most slumberous after dinner, but I then wake up. In spite of this second wind I ought to pull up here—but that I want you to know how blest I find again this winter the cheer & support of this retreat—not from the world but rather *toward* it—from too utter solitude. And withal I haven't, with precautions, of which I neglect none, too much of the world here about me—I have for the most part but the sense, without the pressure, of its being there—the pressure I can no longer in the least in any way stand. My power to work, though reduced, is still in strictness sufficient, & I am now getting on with a Novel that I have—or Pinker, for me, has—made better terms with the Scribners for than have ever been made in any such connection of mine. It helps me to get better, this blest ability to work just enough.—— You tell me, interestingly, of Bill's & Aleck's assurance that I shall have photographs of what they are perpetrating, but for heaven's sake let them not wait & wait for something more worthy than what they have *been* perpetrating all the last year etc. *Any* concrete image will do for an illustration of them—though I am very sorry to hear that Aleck is "discouraged." That is exactly the way development comes, but I have no doubt that the temporary inconvenience of it for him comes exactly, as you say, from his having had too Thayerized a summer. It will have made him a little stale—though his native freshness only waits to rebound; & he must do something as different as possible next year—or rather, I mean, *this*. I hug him hard & Peg not less, & am dearest Alice your all-affectionate

Henry James

P.S. I value so what you tell me of your Mother's well-being—please tell her how much!

ALS: Houghton bMS Am 1094 (1743)

*Peggy James stays with her aunt Mary Holton James (brother Bob's wife) in London, with Aleck nearby. James worries about getting his niece and nephew out of England in the "huge blackness" the country endures, but Mary Cadwalader Jones has reached England safely from France. Other war news follows.*

[*Dictated*]

LAMB HOUSE RYE SUSSEX

Dearest Alice. August 20th. [1914]

I should say it seems an age since we were last in direct touch, if everything didn't now seem such an age that one has lost all measure: these last three weeks from the end of July are as if they had laid on us the burden of ten years. I wrote last to Harry, on one of the first days of this month, just a little after Peg and Aleck had joined me here—wrote him in this way, sparely and barely, I'm afraid he may have felt; but after the only fashion I *could* at the moment. Everything is difficult and upsetting; our tension is great, and our general anxieties, with the intensity of our participations and partakings; so that concentration on letters, or on anything else but perhaps the newspapers, doesn't come easy—and one gropes along, as it were, from day to day. All the same you must think of us very quietly and confidently—and I shall be able to tell you better *how* after we know how you yourselves feel since events have so formidably developed. A couple of days since came your letter of the 2nd. to Peg; who is in town now, since yesterday morning, having taken for her Aunt Miss Bosanquet's flat in Chelsea, 10 Lawrence Street, just round the corner from Carlyle Mansions, and blessedly available to them, and being with her Aunt Mary [Robertson James's wife, Mary Holton James] now in it for these days of further uncertainty before news of Salter and Margaret and Rosamund[112] comes. Mary had very urgently to leave Harrow—no place for her *at all,* and Peg, instantly throwing herself into the breach, devised at once this solution— which will last while it can and must. Mary has my deepest sympathy—for if some blest chance had only held her back a day or two longer she probably wouldn't have sailed at all! Your last letter to P. previous to that of Aug. 2nd. mentioned in its earlier installments that you were actively helping her off—and it made us, in possession of all the horrible public history unrolled since, hold our breath with the hope that you would go on later to say that the bad news, that of the Declarations of War, had come, and that she had stayed. But alas we had in fact but to think of her then in mid-ocean and receiving wirelessly the great shock and disconcertment *there.* However, you will know these things by the time this reached you, and perhaps even about Peg's being able thus to be with her, and Aleck's, as happens, having provisionally taken a studio with Demmler,[113] from week to week, just in that quarter too; which puts them most relievingly to-gether—so long as P. and A. are not more inveterately with me here. Peggy

---

112. Margaret Payson was an American school friend of Peggy; James disliked her immensely. Rosamund may have been Mary Salter's daughter.

113. A friend of Aleck James's. HJ also disapproved of him and thought him a very unsuitable companion for his nephew.

*has* been, of course, until now, since the break-up of town—which, however, again, you will already know all about. News has at last—àpropos of that—pierced the complete obscurity from Margaret P.; a telegram getting through two days ago from Houlgate, to the effect that she has all the while been safely and quietly there, and she *has* written. No word but what I mention has nevertheless reached us; but she is in such ways—well, anything you please! She and her friends are now perfectly able (by running of steamers,) to cross to England either from Dieppe or from Havre, to which latter place they are particularly near, with Southampton perfectly accessible, so that if they don't it's because they haven't wanted to—and that indicates on their part comparative tranquility and confidence (as to what is immediately roundabout them.)

What I feel I should say to you almost before anything else is that I hold the two blest Children at your orders, and they so hold themselves, for coming back to you as soon as the rather dislocated ways and means for that purpose seem to promise more regularity and security. There has been no question of their *planning* at all for that hitherto—the congestion in London of every kind of embarrassed American fugitive has been so great, though now, thank goodness, apparently diminishing, that patience and calm, the reasonable waiting attitude, and the due appreciation of our uncommon good fortune in being gathered in *these* comparatively ideal conditions, have imposed themselves absolutely. Moreover the whole prodigious situation has been, in spite of everything, so thrilling and interesting to us all together and alike, that P. and A. have but wanted to cling to the very ground of the scene—and want to still, I think, so long as may appear possible or wise. One can prefigure and forecast nothing—everything is so in the smelting-pot; never did I think to live to be overtaken by such a huge *blackness** (*I think of dear William but to intensely rejoice now—rejoice that he didn't live to know the abyss of this collapse & of this bitterness,) of consciousness! We are all behaving magnificently, and all as one really strong and wise unit; but the earth quakes beneath our feet verily—though at the same time, as we perpetually reflect, the seas groan (in a more practical way,) beneath our Fleet! I only mean, however, that you mustn't in the least extravagantly worry, but think of us with the last confidence and with intense sympathy not only for the depressing and bewildering, but also for the uplifting and enlightening interest. The next letter that comes from you will be enlightening as to your own preferences about the course to be taken by the Children; and it will help me immensely myself so far as it is at all explicit or emphatic. I think I shall much prefer to have them off my mind in the way that their return to you alone can take them off it—this at least unless they violently resist. The case is, at any rate, that the more *days* they at present wait, by every appearance, the more conveniently as to ship and accommodation they will be able to go. There is the very strongest appearance that the great waterway will be absolutely kept more and more free and clear—what is most presumptive, without presumption, being our overwhelming naval strength; and in short on the day you *call* I will answer for their at once coming. (I think they won't be eager to come *without* that—though they *may judge* it best later on.)

There are so many of these dreadful vivid private things to speak to you of, that I can take them in no order, and that in fact speaking of some of them at all is for the moment beyond me. I heard from Peg by a brief word last night that the appearance of a groping inquiry for Mary Salter from Holland, through the blest little Vandyke, our so helpfully-operating Minister there, had reached her; which may mean the beginning of communication with the three lost ones, may amount to a symptom of their having at last got through to Holland, the blessedly neutral, and the as yet not infamously invaded; with the natural effort on their part to learn whether she *had* sailed at so late a moment of the eve, and whether she would thereby be in England. So at least, and so only, without more data we must read it; and if it is a beginning any hour now may add something to it, and any day, promote their arrival by Flushing on these shores. Flushing has been *the* port, alike for English and for American unfortunates in Germany, to strain every nerve to reach, and fortunately the service has been kept going and has been an unspeakable relief. I have thought of your anxieties, and your Mother's, about Margaret and Rosamund, as well as of the poor things themselves, with intensest sympathy; but, believe me, patience and courage and the American representatives' assistance will have ended by seeing them through, and their whole experience have become the greatest feather in their cap for the future. Mary Cadwalader Jones is here with us for a week, or I hope more; she is pretty confident of being able to sail by the Cunard Laconia for Boston some ten days from now. She was held up in Paris, on her way from Aix, for a week, in much stress and anxiety, but got over without any worse trouble than a crammed and jammed and dreadfully longdrawn day: from 4.30 a.m. in Paris to 9 at last in the evening in London. France is evidently most magnificent in the solidity of her behaviour and the working of her consummate organisation. You know, of course, you realise, what has happened up to now and what is all *we* know; that the overwhelming *irruption* scheme of Germany broke down at the very start, through the never-to-be-forgotten stand of the admirable little Belgium, and the time thereby gained by the accumulation of the French along *their* lines, where they are now in tremendous force. Russia is already meanwhile beginning to thunder at G.'s other end. This gain of time will probably make an enormous difference—though, heaven knows, the great thing one fears is to live at all in a fool's paradise. We have accomplished the throwing of upwards of 100,000 English troops into France within the last week or two without the faintest attempt on the part of the German fleet to show itself able to prevent or interfere; and it's impossible not to regard that fact as a sign of *our* ability—so little could one dream in advance that it *would* happen so. But I don't feel as if I could write you another word now. This shall have a rapid sequel as soon as we hear from you again; but I must get it off to-day as it is. I wrote last night to Alice about herself, and our thoughts are now with her—so far as we can spare them!—earnestly and tenderly. You'll of course send this to Harry, and will give all my love and participation to your Mother. Your all affectionate

*Henry James*

TLS: Houghton bMS Am 1094 (1748)


*HJ sends war news: the American ambassador to Belgium Mr. Whitlock's great courage, James's lunch with General Ian Hamilton and dinner with the Winston Churchills, the von Glehns' preparations to go to a hospital in France, and George Prothero's war work. He will hear Émile Boutroux, William's friend, lecture on "Certainty and Truth" at the British Academy. He longs for news of Harry, who is representing the Rockefeller Institute in Belgium.*


[*Dictated*]

21, CARLYLE MANSIONS, CHEYNE WALK, S.W.

Dearest Alice. December 4th. 1914.

I wrote yesterday at considerable length to Peggy, giving her such tidings of my, that is of our, conditions here as seem at all expressible—which only a part, and a very small one, of my whole consciousness just now does; but this morning comes your letter of Nov. 18th., and makes me want to thank you for it on the spot. I have greater comfort in hearing from you than from *any* member of our group, simply; don't ever let yourself forget that when you can at all conveniently remember it. My great circumstance just lately has of course been Harry's appearance, which I have told Peg all I can about; that quantity being so limited by the fact that he had time while here to give me no more than a couple of fractions of hours. But I have related my impression to Peggy, and for the present, in fact for some time, I fear, there will be no news of him. From Belgium, if he is actually there, nothing can reach us—unless indeed (which is very possible) the excellent American Minister there, Mr. Whitlock,[114] can facilitate him: this sturdy man, whom the Germans would greatly like to get rid of as a witness of their infamies, absolutely refuses to budge—he sweetly smiles and smiles, I hear, and says "Not one inch!" You see their theory of the matter is, ferociously, that Belgium is now wholly and entirely German, a simple province of Germany; and that as there is already an American Ambassador at Berlin, what do they want with another? To which this good man replies, "I will move when my Government recalls me, and not a moment before, nor at any request of *your* Government." And as our President of course does nothing of the sort, nor for a minute intends to, there is the good man, as I say, to do everything possible for Harry and his companions.

I don't want to repeat what I said to Peggy; and trying to bethink myself of something else, recover my consciousness of having lunched yesterday with Gen'l Sir Ian Hamilton (the only others his wife and Mary Hunter,) and dined last night with the Lord Chancellor (Haldane) in company with the good Pages,[115] the Winston Churchills, and a couple of others. This is not the pattern of my usual day at our present time; but both of these occasions very interesting to me, as everything is (even with whatever mixture of the dolorous, the dreadful, the scarce-bearable-to-think-of) that steeps one deeper in the huge realities of the really quite immeasurable situation. What most strikes me is that these men close up against the War have on the one hand no illusions, no ignorances, no superficialities, no evasions of the portentous, in short, whatever, and yet they have on the other something that I should call deep confidence if this didn't seem to suggest the form of it to be blatant. Anything less on exhibition or on "tap" than their active relation to what is being done and to do it would be impossible to conceive; which I like to think of in the light of Walter

---

114. Brand Whitlock (1869–1934), American journalist, politician, and diplomat. He gained international fame through his handling of the difficult problems in Belgium.

115. The American ambassador to England, Walter Hines Page (1855–1918) and his wife, Lillian Biddle Page (d. 1935).

Berry's information as to how confidence flaunts itself all over the place, as it were, in Germany. However, the least said about it in either form the better—the issue isn't in any saying, but altogether and exclusively in infinite doing. Infinite, simply—*that* is what hangs prodigiously before us. *Saturday, Dec 5th.*

I had to stop yesterday; and now, an hour or two hence, I risk the long (for me) unprecedented exploit of being motored down to Hill by M. Hunter to stop over from this Saturday p.m. till Monday; my last adventure of the kind having been my visit there with the two "nieces" last June, or whatever it was—it seems so far away and fabulous now—and my next likely to be, if ever, a wholly incalculable time hence. M. H.'s merits shine out strong under all this stress—her energy, activity, generosity and general devotion and ability in the public service are altogether fine and large to behold. She has in her domestic hospital a sort of protégé of mine, a remarkably worthy one, whom she is healing of an obstinate ailment contracted at the front (as well as healing many others of *their* wounds and ills;) and I thus redeem a promise to go down and see my friend. Apropos of which kind of matters, please tell Peggy that just after writing to her I saw Jane and Wilfred [von Glehn], and found them engaged to go off three or four days hence to Ambulance service in France—booked, I mean, for a hospital, an English one, at Le Treport on the Normandy coast: Wilfred, that is, being the regularly enrolled one, and Jane clinging to his side for any charwoman or bottle-washer work that they may consent to let her perform. She is inflamed with the ardour of scrubbing floors, and it's very beautiful to see; especially as yesterday again I called there for a moment and found them both a good bit laid up from the effect of inoculation for typhoid, imposed now on all who go in for such adventures. Wilfrid [*sic*] was really pretty bad—Jane less afflicted; in all of which Peg will take an interest.

I had this morning a letter, which has greatly touched me, from J. B. Warner,[116] enclosing me Charles Eliot's last, and as he pronounces best, declaration on the War; which is the only one that has met my eyes (though I have heard of the others,) and which I agree with him in thinking quite tremendously straight to the purpose. J. B. speaks of it as the most "influential" of these utterances, and I take great comfort in all

---

116. Joseph Bangs Warner (1848–1923) of Cambridge had been sister Alice's and William's lawyer.

the weight it may carry. I have been having just these last days some interesting contacts and hearings—but of a couple of these I have already told you, the principal other point being that I lunched yesterday with the dear Protheros, to meet H. G. Wells (and Lady Cromer and another;) which H. G. W. I find much more interesting now again than he had been for some time before these events, and full of a highly intelligent and ingenious, as well of course as tremendously resolute, relation to all our immediate actualities. At the moment I write this I hear the uplifted voices (in something that must pass for song) of a marching-by section of enrolled Red Cross Service men, who I go to the window to admire in their fresh khaki, but commiserate rather in their want of musical stimulus. Five minutes before, however, an immense long line of Kitchener's Army, backed up, that is, by a multitude of the London Scottish, had passed to the proper inspiring accompaniment, and reminded one of what one hears on all sides and the best authority, that these new recruits, the Kitchener's Army ones and such stuff as the London Scottish, train and develop and get into form with extraordinary rapidity and effect, the like of which has never been seen before. In connection with which don't credit any such echoes as may reach you of an undue slackness of enlistment in any part of the country: the enlightened judgment being, to all appearance, that the Government is getting *all* the men it wants as fast as it can deal with them, equip and arm and train them; which is at the present rate of 30000 a week. Much clearing-up discourse heard I on this point yesterday between H. G. W. and dear George Prothero, who is of an admirable activity of labour and zeal, the very model of the devoted belligerent citizen and worker on the native scene. He has been a bit pessimistic as to produced numbers, Wells on the other hand being, I thought, really illuminating as to our real possibilities in that line if the right ways are taken and the wrong abjured. The rightest way of all is beyond all doubt a really liberal policy of provision for the wives, children, dependent families generally, of the men who go forth—a matter that Government doesn't seem as yet to have had the high wisdom really to face. But they will come to it, and it is impossible not to live here and really observe and consider and *feel* (the truth of things) without being of Wells's declared opinion that there is no reason whatever why we shouldn't raise in time, on the voluntary system absolutely persisted in, the three millions of men that it will probably take to push the War, so far as we are concerned, to the only issue the country can rest content with. This done without conscription will be the biggest feather that ever was in the cap of England; and one must use one's wits of perception and induction here to very little purpose not to be able to think of it as a high feasibility. Ian Hamilton, an ardent partisan of the voluntary system pure and simple, regards the fighting value of the freely enlisted man as three times that of the conscript: that is a scrap recalled from my lunch with him a couple of days since—but only one, and it's a pity I can't give you the others.

I want to tell you that I go on the 11th. to listen to Émile Boutroux,[117] who has come over to deliver a lecture on "Certitude et Verité" [Certainty and Truth] before the British Academy, which Institution has kindly invited me to meet him at tea half an hour or so before the lecture begins. This prospect much rejoices me, as I have never beheld him; it is the prospect of talking with him in practical commemoration of his friendship to William, and that greatly moves me. You shall hear of the occasion further the next time I write. I feel as if there were still other things to tell you; but these, such as they are, must suffice for the present, and my letter, if presently posted, may still catch to-day's American mail. I find the great and peculiar strain of the moment the having to be so without news of Harry, over whom I intensely and *so* admiringly yearn. This blank may, however, at any moment be filled out a bit—so long, that is, as Belgium doesn't for the time engulf him. I mean that a letter from Holland, either to me or to you, ought to be able to turn up any day. I wish I could repeat to you some of the facts in respect to German perpetrations that Walter Berry, before-mentioned, brought back clutched handsful of from Belgium; or rather I am glad I can't—they are too hideous for any but very deliberate and retributive consideration. Good-bye then now and keep up the good-will of others till I pay my debts to them. I am especially thinking of Alice and the grand-little-nephews. Yours, dearest Alice, all affectionately

*Henry James.*

TLS: Houghton bMS Am 1094 (1750)

*James vividly describes nephew Harry's recent travels through war-torn Belgium and France, and he again lauds the American Ambassador to Belgium, Mr. Whitlock.*

---

117. Émile Boutroux (1845–1921) was professor of philosophy at the Sorbonne and president of the French Academy of Moral and Political Sciences. WJ had been an honorary member of that group.

21, CARLYLE MANSIONS CHEYNE WALK. S.W.

Dearest Alice.                                        January 2nd. 1915.

I dispatched to dear Peg a couple of days ago a letter of considerable length, but I last night had exactly an hour and a half (only!) with Harry, who came and dined with me and sat a little—these being the only moments he could give me between his arrival from Rotterdam night before last and his departure for Paris this morning. I promised him that I would at once report of him to you as he seemed not to expect to be able to write you at any length until he has had time to turn round a bit in Paris. I think he did tell me, however, that he had written you at some length from Rotterdam; though about that I am on reflection vague and only more distinctly remember his saying that he had stopped over there (in one of the worst hotels in Europe, though the best in the place) for the purpose of drawing up, during 3 or 4 days, with his two companions, something in the nature of a Report to the Foundation, the very first they had been able to make, on the 25 days they had spent in Belgium. He was much upset by his seasick passage from Holland, and thereby couldn't see me at all his first evening; though he was quite right on the morrow a.m. Only then he began to have pressing business all day, without a moment to spare, so that he only managed here last evening's dinner. This day is beautiful, after a whole month of mostly awful weather; so that I am hoping his passage to Boulogne won't ravage him to speak of. And you mustn't infer from this account of his stress that he feels at all the worse for it; he looks thinner, but assures me that it has only done him good and that the conditions in which they move about as they are putting through their job are of the easiest and the most accommodating. He gave up, for reasons, his idea of going on to Berlin; his fellow-commissioners, parting with him at Rotterdam, went on, while he has preferred this getting straight to France (where, in Paris, he is very impatient to see Carrel and learn without delay something of the French conditions.) His companions are presently to rejoin him there, where they will go into the question of what may be open to them on all that ground, and it is still before them that they probably must manage to get to Serbia. Meanwhile, just after leaving Belgium, they spent 4 days in Northern France, within the German lines; and altogether they have seen, and apparently done, all, or about all, they hoped.

I must say at once that I didn't extract anything very "lurid" from him, because I find that I have mostly to avoid the drawing-out of the lurid, so as to avoid also as much as possible bad pectoral consequences; and he didn't thrust it on me for the same reason—beside the fact that we had so many multifarious things to talk about in our short time, and the fact also that his absolutely exclusive view of the question of their immediate job and business, and how best to do it, confined them intensely to the question of things as they actually are, for the time, and what can best be done about them in this actual shape. They saw all the places, ravaged and unravaged, and above all saw much of the Belgians of the upper sort, of whom, rather surprisingly, a good many remain, and by whom they were inordinately caressed. A great glamour, I gather, has surrounded them, and nothing was too good for them or too expressive of gratitude and appreciation—even to the point of a tremendously heavy banquet offered them by a certain inordinately rich native *industriel* and financier, the Rockefeller, he says, of Belgium, but whose name I forget, and who, oddly enough, was possessed of materials for a banquet. Things are very strange in such hugely abnormal conditions, and it appears that of *articles de luxe* [luxury articles], especially of the comestible sort, there is a great gathered store; those that were on the hands of the big dealers when the War broke out never having been called for or used, and so remaining piled up on their hands. I gather thus that the banquet in question consisted almost wholly of wonderful potted meats, preserved fruits, inordinate confectionery and such like; they found it in bad taste on the part of the old man, in the general conditions, but Mr. Whitlock, the admirable American Minister (H. most highly commends him), instructed them that they couldn't possibly not accept the compliment, as the tradition of such gorgings is the absolute religion of Belgium and it would be an ungraciousness to the great native idea of hospitality not to sit through any amount of the heaviness of it. A certain number of the better sort of people, among those that have remained, they thus saw; such burgomasters and other officials as are working under the German rigour, but whom the Germans left them to make their arrangements for alimentation directly with—so much so that they "saw comparatively little" of the latter. These struck them as doing their business from their own point of view very ably—I am sorry to say!—but when I asked him how he judged the power of resistance of the oppressive horde to expulsion by the Allies, he replied that he was unable to judge of it at all: he had seen too little of the military matter—they hadn't really got near to it. There are a lot of German civil functionaries, of course; and with these they had some contact, treated always with great consideration. The danger of the Germans' diverting relief supplies to their own use he thinks practically very small, by reason of their quite understanding that in that case, once it appeared, the supplies would stop short. On their proceeding from Belgium into the German-occupied France they remained in charge of a German officer, a quite ingenuous and simple and good-humoured person; but who quite broke down at the end of the first day, or rather a few hours, in fact of their reserves of absolute silence on his very instructedly attempting to explain to them why and how his people had come to do this, that and the other ravaging thing, as these unrolled themselves before the motor-car in which they were pretty tightly packed. They kept of course in good relations with him—they *had* to, and he was a good creature; but for the rest of the tournée [journey] he was reduced to the apologetic, as I understand, rather than to the explanatory or defending, and most of all reduced to ignoring altogether many things. It struck Harry rather painfully and disagreeably—but don't state this about freely—that the French of the upper class, all over the region of Valenciennes, Cambrai, Douai, St. Quentin etc., had fled away from their estates and homes in a way that does them no particular credit; leaving all the less well-off sort, those who couldn't "just jump into a motor", to face the invaders without their backing or support. (What the people remaining said to H. was that "everyone that could get into a car did go!") This struck him as considerably less the case in Belgium, where more of the proprietors, the country ones, have stuck on; and he holds very firm views as to the absolute only decency of the return to their places of those who have come away, in order to stand between their people and the Germans. The repatriation of all the Belgians possible he thinks absolutely urgent, and that not to have them away, but to have them there, is the right course for ending the War if the question be looked at in the right and the larger perspective. But I mustn't attempt so much detail of his story—especially as I got it all in so abbreviated a way. He is full of judgments of his own about many things—but you will see him after all at no such long time hence, and have a much better account. The great thing is that he has been having a most rich, so to call it, and edifying experience without being a scrap the worse for it—I mean in body or estate. It's a blessing they can do all things on such ample easy terms. Not less of a blessing, I gathered from him, has been his possession of French and German—under the drawback of the others' not mustering between them a sole non-American word. It's an enormous relief to infer that they may be able to do something in the way of wounded help in France, where the needs are immense, with the vast numbers of *their* stricken, and the supplies and arrangements so scant in proportion—and in comparison with those we continue to make the great muster of here. Don't repeat, for the sake of the Allies, what I said above about the tendency of the "better sort" of French to flee and abandon their homes. It's the absolute reverse of anything conceivable in this country. Goodbye now at any rate. I mustn't attempt to tackle any other aspect. Life is such a perpetual chronic ache, rising at times into almost intolerable acuteness, that it takes all one's virtue to tackle almost anything. Think after that fashion of, and gently allow for yours, dearest Alice, all affectionately

*Henry James*

TLS: Houghton bMS Am 1094 (1739)


*James's last known extant letter to Alice relates architect Theodate Pope's dramatic rescue at sea. He worries over England's ability to recruit enough army volunteers.*

Dearest Alice. 21 CARLYLE MANSIONS CHEYNE WALK S.W.

Your letter of May 10*th,* enclosing one from Harry (to yourself,) has been of an enormous interest & satisfaction to me—above all in speaking of it as more or less definitely settled that you presently take Peggy off to California for 3 months. In this case you will probably even now be starting, & I send you my blessing on your course—rejoicing more than I can say in the turn of your faces away from all this convulsed & over-darkened world, where every sort of horror steadily increases & multiplies. One such has been vividly brought home to me by my now having seen poor ravaged Theodate Pope three or four times—the fourth in fact this afternoon, at the Hyde Park Hotel. She is already less in the depths than the 1*st* time I saw her, on the 21*st,* & will, I think, recover her self in a manner that will speak volumes for her stoutness of heart & of constitution, in spite of whatever "nervous" tendencies. These have of course had much possession of her since those long hours of horror (of only a small amount of which, however, she was *conscious:*) but their effect tends to diminish, & she will soon very considerably emerge. I don't know whether you will have learnt the sense of what happened to her—but don't see *how* you can, inasmuch as I understand her not to have been able to write to any one, a single word—beyond her cabling repeatedly to her Mother. She jumped into the sea in a life-belt (at about 2.45 p.m.) & was picked up for dead—as a floating corpse—by one of the tug-boats, or whatever suchlike, sent out from Queenstown, about 5; but was brought to life, though no sort of consciousness, on that boat, & only became aware again at 11 o'clk. at night, when she found herself lying on the floor of the cabin & being attended to by a Doctor, the boat having just come into harbour. That is the substance of her awful adventure; but she describes herself as having during those 2 hours in the water again & again lost consciousness—& been without it for a long time before the hour at which she afterwards learnt that she had been picked up. She owes her life, she considers, to the exertions of an excellent American lady who had been saved & who, in the rescue-boat, insisted on working upon her, with help, so that she shouldn't succumb. But primarily she owes it to her life-belt, which supported her so long, even after she had utterly collapsed, so that why she didn't sink it, or whatever happened, is a gruesome mystery enough. Her friend & her maid—the former jumped from the deck before her, to show her the way,— were lost, in spite of having the same lifebelt, which the poor man had fastened upon each of them & upon himself. It's a hideous horror enough, but she spoke of it to me only the 1st time with any detail, & doesn't seem inclined to come back to it, which heaven knows I don't want her to, as the mere skeleton facts were about all I could stand. Strange as that may seem, she will little by little get it comparatively behind her—& I seem able to have helped her somewhat.——————— I am afraid this will have to follow after you in rather a dragging fashion if you have started for the Pacific slope, or are starting, during one of these present days; & it will then be quite ancient history. I daresay Peggy will have written me a word when she gets back from New York, & above all that she will by now have got my last letter from her, telling her the many reasons why it seemed to me good & desirable that she shld. *not* fare forth to enter our more & more exasperated war-zone. Whatever reply the foul Enemy will have made, when this reaches you, to the American Note, & whatever consequences may either spring, or fail to spring, from that, vast exasperations are in the air & a tremendously critical period. A great crisis rages *here* even now, as of course you know, coming from the fact of our hitherto "beastly" liberty & of our thereby not in the least yet having become organized for war, as Germany so concentratedly and so prodigiously is, & as France too is, compared with this country. At last that simply won't do, & an enormous change has got to take place in order that we shall go on more—a 100 times more—effectively & powerfully. It *will* take place, but only if this freedom-pampered people submits with a big effort to a discipline it has never known. We have raised more than 2 millions of men by simple volunteering, but have got to raise 2 millions more otherwise, & everything else in proportion. The quality of the Army is sublime, but inordinate quantity has now got to be added to it. It *will* be—it can't *not* be, &

the War will last another year. The prospect appalls, when admirable individual lives are so following each other into the bloody abyss. But I mayn't *talk* nightmare—at this more than belated bedtime hour. Ever, dearest Alice, your affectionate

*H. J.*
May 26*th* 1915.

ALS: Houghton bMS Am 1094 (1742)

*Letters to Mary Cadwalader Jones*
*1883–1915*

## Time Line

1850   Mary Cadwalader Rawle is born.

1870   Minnie Cadwalader Rawle marries Frederic Rhinelander Jones, Edith Wharton's brother.

1883   Minnie Jones meets Henry James in New York.

1902   Minnie Jones and James are reacquainted in England.

1905   James spends time with his friend Minnie during his great American tour.

1911   Minnie and HJ try to help Edith Wharton survive her husband Teddy's mental breakdown.

1916   James dies in London.

1935   Minnie Jones dies in London.

Mary Cadwalader Jones ca. 1895. (Courtesy of the Bar Harbor Historical Society, Bar Harbor, Maine.)

## Introduction

I think ever so tenderly & romantically of my too fleeting Xmas days in Eleventh St. 6 years (wasn't it?) ago; preserved, between you & Trix, in layers of gold paper, but all that period of your protection & hospitality lives in me more & more—is embalmed for me in the fragrantest dried rose-leaves of romance. (27 December 1909, Houghton bMS Am 1094.9 [10])

Mary Cadwalader Rawle Jones's upbringing prepared her for the closeness she and Henry James shared, a closeness his letters demonstrate. Her warm relationship with her father gave her a wider view of the world than most nineteenth-century women and allowed her to view male-female friendships as the most natural, and even desirable, thing in the world.

Mary Cadwalader Rawle was born in Philadelphia in December 1850 to William Henry Rawle and Mary Cadwalader. In her privately printed book, *Lantern Slides,* she said:

I was born the following year, a distinct disappointment to both my parents as my mother had set her heart upon having a son, and my father had already planned to bring him up in the family tradition of the law. But it couldn't be helped, and I seemed determined to live, so after a time my father became reconciled to his loss and a friendship between us began to which I owe much that has made the pleasure of my life.[1]

Minnie's father frequently took her about Philadelphia, introducing her to many prominent people. And he gave her his love of books and poetry. When William Makepeace Thackeray visited America in the winter of 1855–56, he dined at the Cadwalader home, perched her on his broad knee, and drew pictures for her. Later, Mr. Rawle took her to hear Charles Dickens and the wonderful Shakespearean actress Fanny Kemble.

---

1. Mary Cadwalader Jones, *Lantern Slides* (Boston: D. B. Updike, Merrymount Press, 1937), 17.

After twin family tragedies (in 1860 both Minnie's younger brother and mother died), father and daughter became even closer. Later she claimed that her mother's death gave her an early maturity: "Forced to take my mother's place, as best I might, in my father's house and among his friends, I felt more at ease with older people than with boys and girls of my own age, and had no regular 'coming out' because I had never been 'in.'"[2] This enforced maturity made her more open-minded and adventuresome than many Victorian girls, qualities that later endeared her to James.

During the Civil War, Rawle took his lively daughter to the White House to meet Lincoln, and in 1865 she sailed with him to South Carolina, attending a ceremony at Fort Sumter. Of sailing with her father on these naval vessels she said, "I think the crews like a young girl who was frankly interested in whatever they could show her, and I can honestly say that I have never been in better-mannered company."[3] She worked as her father's private secretary, riding with him in the afternoons and sitting up late at night writing out his cases. Minnie realized that this close companionship enabled her to befriend other men:

> Although I do not agree with Freud's pronouncements, and heartily wish he had never been born, I believe that the most natural friendships are those between men and women. Probably my upbringing had something to do with this conviction, but throughout my life my intimate friends, with few exceptions, have been men, and I have found that if they are treated fairly, as decent men treat each other, and not tricked or used, as they so often are by women, they "respond to treatment," as the medical jargon has it, admirably. (113–14)

When she was eighteen her father remarried her mother's cousin. Perhaps lonely at the loss of her father's company, the next year Minnie married Frederic Jones, writer Edith Wharton's brother, and moved to New York. The intimacy she sought in marriage eluded her, however, as the union proved an unhappy one. But even when estranged from her husband, she remained close to her sister-in-law Edith. And in her New York home she held hospitable Sunday afternoon socials, building an elaborate social network that eventually included Henry James. She also became active as a volunteer worker for the New York City Hospital School, later becoming the chairwoman of the advisory board of the Nursing School. By 1892 she was separated from Frederic Jones, just after

2. Jones, *Lantern Slides*, 103.
3. Jones, *Lantern Slides*, 90.

her only daughter Beatrix's tenth birthday, and by 1896 they were divorced.[4]

According to extant James letters, James and Mary Cadwalader Jones met in March 1883, at a dinner party at the home of New York editor Edwin Godkin.[5] Late July that same year, while living in Boston, James visited Mrs. Jones at Mount Desert Island, Maine, afterward thanking her graciously in the first of many lovely letters and sending her a book. In 1886 he told William of his visit to her there: "Mrs. F. Jones alleviated my stay and I remember her very gratefully, even to her Philadelphia accent."[6] In 1895, he again told William that Mrs. Jones, among many others, had been "battering" at his De Vere Gardens door.[7]

While they saw little of one another until the next century, they pursued parallel interests. As James perfected his writing, Minnie too explored the craft. In 1900 she published *European Travel for Women,* a guide for women traveling alone. The book reveals her independence and wit, both qualities James later came to admire. She began by announcing, "Year by year an increasing number of women travel in Europe, often in parties which do not include a man, and there is no reason why they should not, as the pleasure and profit to be gained are far more than worth the trouble which must be taken. . . ."[8] Sound common sense permeates the book. She advised women to adapt to foreign customs cheerfully: "Remember, when you go to a strange country, that its inhabitants have not sent for you; you go among them, presumably, of your own accord, and their manners and customs cannot possibly seem stranger to you than yours do to them" (2). She suggested books to read, reminding readers not to forget to take Mr. James's *Little Tour in France* when visiting the Loire.

Indeed, it was her own willingness to travel that led to a renewal of their friendship. Knowing she would be in England, Mrs. Jones engineered the

4. Jane Brown, *The Gardening Life of Beatrix Jones Farrand, 1872–1959* (New York: Viking, 1995), 10–11.

5. According to James's *Notes of a Son and Brother* (1914; reprint, Princeton: Princeton University Press, 1983), 533–34, his favorite cousin Minny Temple met "Miss Rawle" in the fall of 1869 in New York after she was engaged to Frederic Jones, so there is a possibility that James may have met Minnie before 1883 through his cousin, who thought that Miss Rawle "had a soul" (534).

6. *Henry James Letters,* ed. Leon Edel, vol. 3 (Cambridge: Harvard University Press, 1980), 132.

7. *The Correspondence of William James,* ed. Ignas K. Skrupskelis and Elizabeth M. Berkeley, vol. 2 (Charlottesville: University Press of Virginia, 1993), 366.

8. Mary Cadwalader Jones, *European Travel for Women: Notes and Suggestions* (New York: Macmillan, 1900), vii.

revival of their friendship by sending James copies of Edith Wharton's *Crucial Instances* and *The Touchstone*.[9] James's next known correspondence with her was in 1902 when she visited England; after that their friendship intensified. Every August Minnie and her daughter Beatrix traveled to Millden, Forfarshire, Scotland, where Mrs. Jones was the hostess for her cousin John Cadwalader, a prominent New York lawyer, at his hunting camp. During these trips she frequently saw her Rye friend. James stayed with her at her Eleventh Street, New York, home in 1904 and 1905, and again in 1911 after his brother William's death. Of that last visit, he told Edith Wharton that Mary "Cadwal" was "as tenderest nursing mother" to him.[10]

Millicent Bell studied the manuscript letters from James to Mrs. Jones long ago, as she dealt with Mrs. Jones in *Edith Wharton and Henry James*,[11] discussing her relationship to James and quoting from a number of his letters to her as a way of demonstrating his method of thinking. The letters to her began on a formal note ("Dear Mrs. Cadwalader"), but in later letters he called her "Dearest Benefactress," and "Dear munificent friend." He befriended her daughter Beatrix, later one of America's foremost landscape gardeners; and he and Minnie together shared a love for Edith Wharton. They both feared Edith's husband Teddy would destroy her, and a number of James's letters divulge that fear. In one letter he announced,

> I *did* see Teddy at the Mount—the whole afternoon & evening before I left, he having returned thither, in prime physical condition, from 3 weeks' arduous salmon-fishing in New Brunswick—possessed as he is of full health for all that sort of thing—& for making his renewed & again renewed violent scenes—as to which his capacity constantly grows. He is perfectly sane, for *him* (I mean for his intrinsic childishness of mind;) & it's my absolute conviction that unless they have a personal separation (with an "allowance" from her *to* him) he will absolutely destroy her by a final nervous and cardiac crisis. (17 August 1911, Houghton bMS Am 1094 [775])

Minnie and Henry's struggles with the Whartons brought the two friends even closer. He supported Mrs. Jones emotionally with her own marital and financial difficulties, just as he bolstered his sister-in-law Alice in her family roles. Mrs. Jones announced to William Dean Howells in

---

9. Brown, *Gardening Life*, 82–83.

10. *Henry James Letters*, ed. Leon Edel, vol. 4 (Cambridge: Harvard University Press, 1984), 574.

11. Millicent Bell, *Edith Wharton and Henry James: The Story of a Friendship* (New York: George Braziller, 1965).

1911, "I am so deeply attached to Mr. James, the affection of a life-time" (28 February 1911, Houghton bMS Am 1784 [265]). And her feelings were reciprocated. On 30 August 1911, James told Howard Sturgis that Sturgis and Mary Cadwalader Jones "are my best friends" (Houghton bMS Am 1094 [1284]).

When John Cadwalader died in 1914, James hoped Minnie would be named in the will. Although she received almost nothing from the estate, James wrote to console her:

> I am told that, childless & "unencumbered," he [JC] left a very big fortune—& on this I think back toward the immense mitigations of dreariness, the immense assistances to living & doing, that he went on owing you both. Then the strange show that men so often finally make of themselves overcomes & floors me again, & I fall to howling & gnashing my teeth. (11 April 1914, Houghton bMS Am 1094.9 [32])

When Frederic Jones, Minnie's ex-husband, died in Paris in 1918, neither Minnie nor Edith Wharton mourned his death, although both women had grieved at James's demise two years before. Mrs. Wharton praised Minnie, who had had "a lot of hard knocks lately" but was so brave.[12] Mrs. Jones continued her intellectual interests, translating Mme. Saint-Renée Taillandier's *The Soul of the "C.R.B.": A French View of the Hoover Relief Work* (1919), as well as Raymond Récouley's *Foch, the Winner of the War* (1920). She lived almost two decades beyond her dear friend, dying suddenly in a London hotel in 1935. Edith Wharton made her funeral arrangements, burying her next to writer Mrs. Humphry Ward in Hertfordshire, England, the dried rose-leaves of romance gone forever.

---

12. R. W. B. Lewis, *Edith Wharton: A Biography* (New York: Harper and Row, 1975), 412.

*James's first known extant letter to Mary Cadwalader ("Minnie") Jones thanks her for her hospitality at her Bar Harbor, Maine, home. He sends her a book to read "on some wet Sunday."*

Boston 131 Mount Vernon St.

My dear Mrs. Jones. Aug. 16*th* 1883.

I am living just now at very high pressure, inasmuch as I am attempting to compress into a few hours the most elaborate preparations for a return to Europe for an "indefinite period." But this shall not prevent me from thanking you again, before I go, for the gracious hospitality, the discriminating charities, that you lavished upon us during those fleeting hours a fortnight ago. You squeezed as much hospitality into that brief period as I am endeavouring to squeeze books & clothes into a correspondingly small allowance of luggage. You packed us full of kind things, & the cover of my mind, like the lid of my portmanteau, has a difficulty in shutting down. I open it wide to send you a great many good wishes. Since I left your northern paradise I have been wandering on other shores— Newport, & Cape Cod—& haven't had a quiet moment to pay you my respects. Be assured that you conferred an extraordinary grace upon my impression of Mount Desert,[13] & be prepared to hear (if any preparation is necessary) that, though habitually reserved and even critical, I am heard— at all times & places—to speak of that island with passionate admiration. I met Arthur Rotch yesterday, & embraced him for the sake of your four walls. I hope they contain just now all health & happiness. I send you a little book which you will perhaps read on some wet Sunday unmolested (as you were on that foggy Sabbath of ours,) by desperate Bostonians. If my fellow desperado [William James] were here, he would greet you very cordially. But he is fortunately at Nahant, & I have it all my own way to assure you that I am your particularly grateful & very faithful servant
Henry James.

ALS: Houghton MS Am 1094.9 (4)

*HJ is delighted to hear from Mrs. Jones after so many years, and he invites her and her daughter Beatrix to visit him in Rye, if they can face "the quite austere hospitality of a modest bachelor hermitage."*

---

13. The location of Minnie Jones's summer home near Bar Harbor. This is at least the second time HJ met Minnie Jones; the first presumably was at a dinner party at Edwin Godkin's in New York earlier in the year, although James may have met her even earlier through his cousin, Minny Temple.

Dear Mrs. Fred. Jones. *July 23d 1902*

It is a great pleasure to hear from you & to find one's self so kindly remembered, after more years even than even one likes to count; so that your excellent expressions have *almost* the power of making me wish I were, unnaturally, immersed in the madding & metropolitan crowd. But I am not so immersed and I escape that fate at this season of the year as much as possible; although the success, such as it is, with which I achieve this result is frequently qualified by regrets of the order that your letter produces. I seek refuge from them in this case by wondering, with some intensity, whether I can't still combine absolutely necessary absences from town (too often broken into of late,) with not absolutely losing the chance to see you & Miss Beatrix while in England. You will be doing many, & all interesting, things; but is it conceivable that you could brace yourselves to coming down here for a few hours? The way is long—2½ hours from Charing X, & I am utterly alone with no one but a low & longitudinal Aberdeen terrier to "meet" you; but I should rejoice in your presence; the little place has a small old-time charm & colour, & your welcome wd. be as complete as I can make it. But to this end you wd. have to spend the night—that is arrive to lunch, dine, sleep & depart on the morrow, very conveniently at 9.40, reach town again at 12.20—all this if you can face the extremely homely, the quite austere hospitality of a modest bachelor hermitage (with a little town-garden that Miss Beatrix is *not* to look at it, unless as a grim warning.) I must add that for a reason I will explain on seeing you (if I *have* that pleasure,) I should make free to take time for a full appreciation of your visit after August 1*st*—at any moment during the 1*st* ten days of that month. And if you *can* happily come I will give you all instructions—& drive you in the afternoon over to ancient Winchelsea. There—I have put forth the modest sum of my attractions—& I leave them to ferment. I thank you kindly for John La Farge's[14] message, & too greatly fear I shan't see him. He is one of my oldest friends—from my 17*th* year, but too lost to my sight & hearing. You will have, truly, much else to tell me—& especially of Mrs. Wharton, whose last book [*The Valley of Decision*] I *have* read, so that we can talk *à perte de vue* [interminably]. Please to give my hearty greeting to your daughter. I am very sorry to hear

---

14. John La Farge (1835–1910), famous American painter and stained-glass artist. James met La Farge in Newport in 1858, where they briefly studied painting together in William Hunt's studio. La Farge illustrated *The Turn of the Screw* when it first appeared in *Collier's Weekly*.

she has not been well. We are supposed to "do good" to people at Rye, & I am yours & hers most truly,

Henry James

ALS: Houghton MS Am 1094.9 (5)

*James's lumbago makes him feel as if he were "in the clutches of the vulture of a thousand claws." He thanks her for her advice on his dog Robert, who feels better, eats verdure, and exercises.*

[*Dictated*]

Lamb House, Rye.

Dear heroic and renewedly bountiful Lady.                    Aug 25th, 1902.

Strange and sad to say, deep *already* calleth unto deep, even before Smith-Premier begins to boom responsive to Remington. For I grieve to say that I too am floored and in anguish, blighted and baffled, these many days—since, in fact, I think, the day itself of my last letter—by the fiercest extremity of lumbago. But my commiseration for your own so provokingly mistimed attack almost, by its intensity, lifts off my consciousness every weight but that of the sympathy in question. Please believe in my not only figurative, therefore, but very real and intimate participation. I don't know what's the matter with myself; after long immunity I am, Prometheus-like, in the clutches of the vulture of a thousand claws, more unassuageably, it would seem by the way I resist all my usual agencies, more abjectly than I've ever been. However, I go on hoping, praying, rubbing, sweating (saving your presence) *and* periodically howling. But the domestic Remington is a great blessing. However, it is *you* that matter, for you have much more complex affairs on hand; and I am offering up in *your* name, accordingly, all the choicest burnt-offerings on the sacrificial altar and paying for the biggest candles. How kind of you to communicate while so deeply afflicted, and how inappreciable your instructions, your tips and search-lights—playing all over the subject—in respect to Robert [evidently his dog]. Please believe that no word you utter falls on fruitless or thankless soil. I am only a little scared at the elaborate and special *sound* of the little precautions and regimens. I feel you're certain to be right—authority is enthroned in your word. Happily the animal has been distinctly better since I wrote you, and has had almost no more biscuit; in fact practically none at all. He has had a little meat and a great deal of verdure; also plenty of exercise, in spite of my confinement. Last not least, a box of excellent ointment from a very good vet at S. Leonards, which has precluded paraffin. So there we are. But we shall be further still, under your star. May the latter, however, but operate first, a little more luminously, for yourself. Do really go on feeling better, but don't really do anything wild. Ireland is very well—but only if you are ditto. Stretch out your scheme, and let it include another visit here. You tell me nothing of the young lady, but I hope she bears up. I renew my benedictions, reinforce and try to drive them home. Nothing will give me greater pleasure than to get, at your convenience, better news from you, and meanwhile my imagination presses you hard. Please each of you give the other much love from yours both always

*Henry James*

TLS: Houghton bMS Am 1094 (785)

*He thanks her for the package and inquires about her health, hoping she is in Bar Harbor watching sunsets. He asks whether Mrs. Wharton has chucked them for a dog, claiming he would chuck his dog for Mrs. Wharton.*

[*Dictated*]

Lamb House, Rye, Sussex.

Dear Mrs. Cadwalader.                                                    June 9th, 1903.

You gave me free leave to deal with you by this machinery, and you see how, even in the face of your own so infinitely more poetic, more romantic, more magnanimous and munificent processes, I avail myself, without scruple, of the licence. Let me assure you that you never did a wiser or kinder thing—for I was really born *manchot* [one-armed], that is unhandy *comme personne* [as no one else], whereas I was not born altogether unvocal, unresonant or irresponsive, and yet am obliged more or less to seem so to those of the undiscriminating who will have either the inkpot or nothing. And what inkpot even, either, would really make this present acknowledgement of the last of your beautiful bounties more worthy of the object itself? The object arrived yesterday, in prime condition, and one of my reasons for resorting to mere merciless legibility with you is exactly that I may catch, for thanking you, the very first American post that follows the event. I catch the post thus indeed (which I shouldn't otherwise be able to do;) yet "thanking" is after all in such cases a mean and meagre business. One *doesn't* thank—one is almost ashamed to, so associated is the act with gratitude for things like stamps at the post office, potatoes at dinner, helpings-on with one's overcoat and like limited benefits. The admirable little exotic bowl, with its harmonious adjuncts, that you have been so good as to drop upon me out of the blue—a deeper, diviner blue than bends over us here, from which (here) nothing so good as an unpurchased parcel ever drops—is, in truth, a lovely thing in itself; but what is lovelier still to me is the thought and remembrance, the sign of the generously reverting *mind,* that pushed it forth on its way. These are the things on which I fix my own mind in order not to feel myself almost too splendidly *comblé* [overwhelmed]. I find the cup and cover, in short, admirable (and there's nothing the matter with the saucer either) but if, at this first stage of gaping surprise, I am conscious, as it were, of having done nothing to provoke their arrival, so, already, on the other hand, I throw myself without reserve into the balmy element of accepted *communication.* Let us then communicate as much as possible, cups or no cups, saucers or no saucers; and don't, above all, let me find myself almost fancying that your beautifully-packed little box represents any failure of present power to make other signs. *Some* dim rumour have I heard—did I hear sometime since—that you hadn't, this last winter, been well; but it seemed irresponsible and vague, and I thought best to take it for a mere echo of your indisposition of the autumn. May that really have left no serious sequel—may you have completely recovered each, in particular, of your high characteristic energies. I hope New York has had, during the months, a soft side for you, and I like to suppose that you are even now drinking fresh air, watching sunsets and listening to the sound of waters (not too adulterated with the human voice) at Bar Harbour. I can send you no kinder or more pious wish, can I?—from the point of view of refreshment and relief. I sit here invoking the same benefits for myself after a winter of between four and five months in London, from which I have but lately returned. That was very good, in a sufficient number of ways, while it lasted—but the peace of this little russet hilltop and green garden compete now triumphantly with what seems to me always, at this season, the mere *Danse Macabre* of Babylon. I sit tight here, D. V. [*Deo volente*—God willing], all through summer and autumn, at the least, with a good deal of work to do and a perhaps more than usually (even) offensive determination to do it. I pray the Powers Miss Beatrix be well, and that her year has flourished—increased, multiplied, overflowed. Has Mrs. Wharton migrated to another planet or only returned to Lenox, Newport or wherever? She promised herself to us here many, many weeks ago—I had her signed and sealed word for it. But darkness has, since, to *my* vision, completely engulfed her, and silence to my ears. A wild story has, irresponsibly, reached me that she has chucked us for a little dog, but my mind rejects the horrid legend. I myself have now a beautiful little dog (all my own, not the mere fiduciary one you saw me so haggard about) but I would chuck him in a minute for Mrs. Wharton. Men, however, always were tenderer than women and more finely-discriminating. But the post leaves me no moment more. I call down on you again benedictions, I dedicate to you vows, and I am yours, dear Mrs. Cadwalader, very constantly

*Henry James*

TLS: Houghton bMS Am 1094 (788)

*James thanks her for more grouse. His intellectual life suffers under an onslaught of summer visitors. He recently visited Rudyard Kipling.*

[*Dictated*]

Lamb House, Rye, Sussex.

Dear Mary Cadwalader. Sept. 27th, 1903.

I have too much delayed to resume my now so settled practice of thanking you for something or other—but what has kept me from it is only the continual stress of my situation, my more or less desperate domestic extremity. Pressure—ponderous human pressure—has been constant and insurmountable; though most mercifully lightened, for the fleeting hour, I assure you, by the intervention of your feathered shafts. It has been at moments really very much as if your beautiful fat grouse were sharp winged arrows, piercing the besiegers, from behind shield and tartan, in the form of a brave Highland reinforcement. By which I mean that while eating them—and they are eating them, by my housekeeper's matchless "management", still,—they are almost as quiet and absorbed as if you had positively laid them low. This fact gives you the measure of my gratitude—though even *it* doesn't do much toward giving me time to write you at the length I should like. I am very sorry to miss the pleasure of seeing you—for my coming up to town has not, frankly, been thinkable—not, that is, during these embarrassed days. My "intellectual life"—by which I mean a very pressing job of important work—has gone so to pieces under the assaults of the summer at home that I can't just now take days off, days for the railway, the hansom, the distant social board, without the danger, really, of finding the waters close quite over my head. To go up from here for the day—for the few hours of it that one gets clear—means many hours of train, and, on the other hand, everything is at present against my sleeping out. All of which simply brings home to me the more and more lurid truth that we are all of us together destroying and abolishing margin and leisure, time and space, as hard as ever we can go. The sooner it's over the sooner to sleep! Take that familiar quotation with you to Paris—but let it at least help you both to live hard while you're there. The La Farges have gone, but Mrs. Poultney Bigelow[15] and her daughters are still here in force, as is my American cousin, to whom, while the Mermaid continues to bristle, I am trying to restrict my own "house-party"; and, in addition, the day mostly brings forth its agreeable, its at all events absorbing, surprise. Day before yesterday Harry White[16] motored down from London, for the central hours, with a small party of comrades, and yesterday Rudyard Kipling kindly sent his own snorting Petrolia over from Bateman's to convey us back there—where he is settled, by the way, in a most enchanting and enviable old Jacobean house. In the matter of the Poultneys, to which you interestingly allude, there would be doubtless much to say could one snatch precious moments for it. I only now want to make the little point, however, that you quite misapprehend me in supposing that I ever found a good word for P.—mad, barbarous and impossible in *any* relation as he always seemed to me. Impossible as the merest acquaintance, what *must* he have been as a spouse? But these are trackless deserts, and I must break away from you with my renewed thanks and blessing. I shall communicate with you again before your vanishment, & I am yours very constantly

Henry James

P.S Please express to Miss Beatrix my very cordial joy in her confirmed invigoration. And find also enclosed the amazingly named labels.

TLS: Houghton bMS Am 1094 (793)


*He thanks her for her Christmas gift of red egg caps. He spent the holiday in Rye with Jonathan Sturges, a day complete with "butcherboys, bakerboys, and candlestick-makerboys."*

[*Dictated*]

Lamb House, Rye, Sussex.

Dear munificent Friend.                                          Dec. 31st, 1903.

Your princely cable reached me, in the most graceful manner in the world, exactly when it should—on Christmas morning just as I was about to sit down to tea and toast, enhanced by the company of our gifted little Jonathan [Sturges], who had come down from London a couple of days

---

15. Edith Evelyn Jaffray (Mrs. Poultney) Bigelow (1861–1932), writer and wife of Poultney Bigelow (1855–1954), a writer, journalist, and traveler.

16. Henry White (1850–1927), diplomat and American ambassador to Paris in 1908.

before to spend with me the holy tide, and whom, by a very hard frost, from which in New York we should be protected by stout double windows and universal "pipes,"[17] I am this afternoon to conduct back to town and tuck into his own quarters as warmly as possible, with all due prayerful relief at his not having, in his extreme breakability, come to pieces in my hands. We have tried to pass here, with slender resources, as fine old English a Christmas as infirmity, philosophy and approaching senility permit—and indeed our resources have not at all failed in some directions, that of the cheerful sense of the universal "appeal"—the appeal of waits, bell-ringers, lamp-lighters, town-bandsmen, postmen, dustmen, butcher-boys, bakerboys, candlestickmakerboys, who have enlivened the doorstep by their uninterrupted presence. In the eleemosynary intervals we have talked a good deal about you both, cultivated the flower of reminiscence, regret and hope, and done what we could to keep up, within ourselves, the ideal of grateful friendship. We felt your message, really, as a very effective little benediction, and spirits twain seemed indeed that morning to sit with us at the board. The little red caps of the boiled eggs cocked themselves, of their own motion, quite consciously and *crânement* [gallantly], as from the pride of their connection with you. I hope that meanwhile, in spite of public shame and woe—which I hope, in N. Y., isn't brought too straight home to your fireside—you have been closing in still more warmly and sociably, without any marked gaps in the array of your clients and pensioners.

I mustn't omit to tell you, though you probably by this time know it, that Mrs. Wharton has gone and come—gone, alas, more particularly, fleeing before the dark discipline of the London winter afternoon. I was in town for a day or two during her passage, and I lunched with her, with very great pleasure, and had the opportunity of some talk. This gave me much desire for more—finding her, as I did, *really* conversable (rare characteristic, *par le temps qui court* [these days]!) and sympathetic in every way. I count greatly on her return—as well, I needn't say, as on yours, if yours can only be accompanied, next time, with fewer disconcerting circumstances. But goodbye, with every good wish of the season. I am buried under one of the postal avalanches proper to the same, and make no apology for this blessed reinforcement in the struggle; on which I more and more helplessly and shamelessly (in general) throw myself. It just comes over me that I am destitute of your address—that is oblivious of street and number; of which

17. Central heating, then in little use in England.

I have stupidly kept no record. I shall have therefore to direct this in some groping and tentative manner, trusting to the honour of a Tammany P.O. and hoping with all my heart it won't wholly miscarry. With renewed sympathy, yours always

*Henry James*

TLS: Houghton bMS Am 1094 (794)

---

*James, Howard Sturgis, and Walter Berry are visiting Edith Wharton in Lenox, where the "golden American autumn is a revelation." He commiserates with her on the death of her servant.*

THE MOUNT, LENOX, MASS.

My dear friend & kindest of women.                          Oct: 23*d* 1904.

I won't even *try* to make lucid to you all the overwhelming reasons *why* I have so gracelessly waited & waited to thank you for your so richly benevolent letter of so many weeks ago. By the time it reached me I was already up to my neck in every overwhelming element (even though in the wilds of New Hampshire,) & with you by that time also about to be on the pathless ocean, communication seemed a difficult & hopeless thing to establish. My house in England was let, & *swarming,* if I am not mistaken, with cold aliens. I was in all the trauma & terrors of original initiation over here, & doing my best while in the midst of it to answer 3 letters a day—the number I received during the first 3 weeks I was here. However, I haven't meant to try to explain my silence, or any other aberration committed by me since my arrival—for only those can understand who have been terrified & paralysed absentees restored hither after long years & with every one wanting to see (or to hug) the strawberry marks on different parts of their persons—only such *can* understand! Now, at all events, Mrs. Wharton tells me, that you are in New York & that you have suffered the shock & pain of the sudden death of a very valued old servant & friend. I can feel all the inconvenience of it, in the deepest sense of the word, & I assure you of my liveliest sympathy. The worst is that I don't expect to be able to be in N. Y., long enough to turn round, very immediately—I mean the worst for *me.* Not before *December,* I am afraid—but when I am it will be to stay, I hope some eight or ten weeks. More kind than I can tell you seems to me your offer of hospitality. Kindly suffer me to hesitate a little & scrupulously consider whether any such advantage can be, *should* be, decently taken of you. I always hold that staying with a friend *in town* is an act of indelicacy—so much does one always feel, among the comings & goings inevi-

138

table there, that one is treating their house as an hotel. But there will be time to talk of this—& I wish you meanwhile all recuperation & restoration among your possessions & Penates. The present is but a feverish & provisional signal & stopgap—till we may more commodiously commune. I need scarcely tell you that I am very happy here, surrounded by every loveliness of nature & every luxury of art, & treated with a benevolence that brings tears to my eyes. This golden American autumn is a revelation—*the* revelation to me; & I am learning to see the motor from *within* (the only way,) & proportionally to come round to it. Howard Sturgis is here, & the charming Walter Berry,[18] & we are a very harmonious & happy little party. But I don't like to flaunt these advantages in the face of your mourning. I hope with all my heart that you & Beatrix are both at least well & sound. À bientot [See you soon] or almost—yours & the child's always & ever

*Henry James*

P.S. Forgive this accidentally blank page, which I would fill with important postscriptural matter, if I were only a woman—!

ALS: Houghton bMS Am 1094 (795)

*For the first time in over twenty years James returns to the United States. During his tour, he gives lectures through the Pond bureau to help pay his expenses.*

1810 S. Rittenhouse Sq. Phila.

Dearest Benefactress.             *Monday* [23 January 1905]

This, really, is my 1st *hour* of being able to "turn round" these many days, & it's an infernally short one! I *can't*, alas, be at Parsifal tomorrow,—I mean Wednesday—& you will have guessed as much by my graceless silence. I came from Washington to "lecture" at Bryn Mawr[19] on Thursday last (before *700* people!) spent the night there & then came here to stay 3 days with a kind, overdoing, overwhelming friend, Dr. J. W*m* White, whence I go late today for 4 (formidable—*slightly!*) days with Sarah Wister[20] at Butler Place (Logan Station, Phila.)—retracing *thence* southward

---

18. Walter Van Rensselaer Berry (1859–1927), American lawyer and very close friend of Edith Wharton's.

19. He lectured on "The Lesson of Balzac" on this tour.

20. Sarah Butler Wister (1835–1908), daughter of actress Frances Anne Kemble and mother of novelist Owen Wister. She met HJ in Rome in 1872.

as fast as ever I can. So you see poor Célimare[21] is afloat on a fathomless sea! It is all (including Washington) very worthy & decent & pleasant & chatty & cheerful—but I react against the monotony of monotonous, multitudinous people, vociferating in the void & indistinguishable from each other. But for the love of God, keep this confidence to yourself—the kindliness & friendliness are angelic, only they make me dread, in advance, the celestial choirs. I shall lecture only 3 or 4 times more—I do it only for a fee that is prohibitive to all but a very small no. of associations. And it pays more than my "cab-hire"; it will have paid, I think, all my (future) traveling expenses. Otherwise I would have seen it—further! But "Pond" and his blandishments are murderous & impossible—I will make you a sign whenever I can. Cela me soulage [that soothes] me! Yours & Beatrix's always fondly

Célimare.

ALS: Houghton bMS Am 1094 (745)

*James visits the Vanderbilts' North Carolina Biltmore House. He is in "a vast void of a great lonely glittering ice-house," suffering from painful gout. Next he will visit Charleston, South Carolina, and then Florida.*

[Biltmore House, Biltmore, North Carolina]

Dearest Benefactress. *Monday* [6 February 1905]

Your poor Célimare is in the throes of an attack of gout on this awful ice-boned mountaintop (2,500 feet in the air—& such a place!)—but he reaches painfully out to you in his gratitude, as from a sense of favours perpetually received. I am praying all my gods to be in a state to get away on the 9*th* or 10*th,* Thursday or Friday—away to Charleston & thence to Florida—for, alas, a very few days—a number of days that has shrunken woefully, through inevitable slowness of progression by reason of my having to be in Boston for my great Bugaboo dentist again (& this time really there, without reprieve, by the 24*th*). Between that & Charleston, where I have, for reasons, to spend 2 or 3 days, I must put in my *whole* impression of Florida & *get* north, i.e. to Boston by the 23*d* p.m. Therefore, with but 11 or 12 days for the latter job I shan't be able to take out time to stop over in

---

21. Célimare was Minnie Jones's nickname for him, taken from the name of a character in a play by Eugene Labiche, *Célimare le bien aimé* [Célimare the greatly loved] (1863). The dramatic Célimare had numerous affairs and was beloved by many women.

N.Y. for Parsifal in accordance with your peerless proposal. I mayn't sacrifice *one* Floridian hour, famished as I am for warmth & balm & all but fatally cheated of it; & besides, it wd. be folly for Célimare to show himself in N.Y. for a single occasion before coming back there to stay awhile— would lead to endless notes, invitations, recriminations, & my having to take days to explain that I am not there, but very busy elsewhere.

*Tuesday:* I wrote the foregoing yesterday, but I am better today, but unable to leave the house, the 4*th* day of my incarceration. It is a strange gorgeous colossus, this wasted monstrosity, grotesquely in a vast void of desolation, of unbelievable inconvertible niggerdom. No possible *life* exists for it; to no achievable or conceivable or procurable sociability is it, in its multi-millionaire madness, addressed. And it's "kept up," amazingly—& poor dear G. V. [George Vanderbilt] sits in it as in a great lonely glittering ice-house & takes it seriously. The cold, as I say, is awful; my room is a glacial fantasy, & it is exactly 1/2 a mile's walk (now that I can hop & hobble) to the mile-long library. We measure by leagues & we sit in cathedrals. It's all indescribable, but I must try it for you later; respect meanwhile the strict confidence of my remarks.——I go from Boston straight to Chicago, St. Louis & California. So there I am! There are but 2 other persons here— Mrs. Hunt (*ce louchon de* [that cross-eyed] Mrs. H. as Zola would say— but she is nice) & a very pleasant elderly British soldier-man, General Sir Thomas Fraser, who has lent me a blessed old gout shoe. Mrs. Marble forced on my acceptance a downy Fager bedblanket, and with these mitigations of the royal rigours of Biltmore I am struggling through. I don't know where to tell you to address me, save 95 Irving St. Cambridge Mass. That, in this shifting scene, is my postal anchor. I embrace you, as it were, both & am yours ever-clinging

Célimare.

ALS: Houghton bMS Am 1094 (746)

---

*Minnie is in Scotland, keeping house at her cousin John Cadwalader's hunting camp. He extols Fletcherizing and recommends it for Beatrix. He slanders writer Violet Hunt.*

LAMB HOUSE, RYE, SUSSEX.

Dearest Mary Cadwalader. Aug: 22*d 1905*.

Your Célimare was glad at last to hear from you this a.m., for he had begun to fear a little at last that you might have got lost, beyond recovery, among the multitudinous heather, or gone astray in the wilderness of Northward-faring paraphernalia, gun cases, retrievers, fishing-rods, strapped bathtubs & other insanities of traffic. I still don't quite figure the life you do lead in your bonny Hielands—as I don't suppose you & Beatrix go about barelegged & in "snoods" (whatever snoods may be—the young women in Walter Scott wear 'em.) But you will tell me when we meet, & meanwhile your poor Célimare rejoices that things are no worse with you than they are (that they don't rise above *that* seems to me not quite enough for you to have come all the way from Eleventh St. to deliriate over.) I grieve to learn that Beatrix came back from Carlesbad in disconcerted form—& oh, if I could only get *at* her how I wd. force home to her the golden truth that *her remedy for everything* lies within the covers of the little pale green book I sent you—that is in Fletcherization[22] at any price. Not to Fletcherize, but to live à la Eleventh St. etc. *and* then do the Carlsbads & Aixes &c, & go to the humbugging doctors who tell you to do everything *but* Fletcherize (il s'en gardent bien! [that's the last thing they'd do!])—that is a sight, on the part of an afflicted young lady, that afflicts *me* with even more than her affliction. It—the sole system—takes certainly all the *Doing* it does take & if you are (digestively) "well," or à peu près [almost] I quite understand it shouldn't be folichon [appealing] to you. (You are out of court—the appeal, anymore than the tummy-ache doesn't reach you; & that is *your* case, dear M.C.). *But,* if the tummy &c *are* factors, malefactors, in your darker consciousness, then Fletcher is a thousand times worth *any* trouble, *any* consistency or concentration, he demands. You don't know him till you *do* him, & then you love him like a brother & your whole physical consciousness is transfigured. I mean to go at Beatrix, straight, on this chapter (tell her, please) on the 1st opportunity, for I have lately had an experience that more than ever fixes my faith. While in America my effort to pratiquer [practice] virtually (through social obstacles, &c) went to pieces, & I went to pieces with it—relapsed from the immense good it had done me, & yearned for a return to the normal life (or renounced junketting) & the resumed *practice*. Well, I have now *enjoyed* that for 5 weeks (I began the day, the hour, I landed,) & I am in a condition absolutely transformed. If my sense of the matter needed clinching, it *is* clinched. This to B. and *for* B. *You* are too elegant an ostrich to have a right to be talked to about it, or to be accessible to the pure essence.——All thanks

---

22. Horace Fletcher (1849–1919) was an American nutritionist who popularized the technique of slowly chewing one's food. Although "Fletcherization" was supposedly an aid to digestion, in fact HJ believed that following this technique for six years caused him serious stomach problems. He stopped "fletcherizing" in 1910.

for sending back V. Hunt[23] (poor V.!—she has stupidly & wantonly ruined herself;) *dont à vrai dire, je n'ai que faire* [truth to tell, I don't know what to do about it]. I haven't read her book, & don't want to, & can't; & she doesn't ask it of me, & if she did it wouldn't make any difference. I knew Oswald Crawford[24] and he *was* a blatant bounder! But poor V. isn't the finest flower—! Enfin! [Enough] it's 1 o'clk a.m.[25] & I am very good nightfully your affectionate

Célimare.

P.S. Indeed & indeed I am sticking fast here for weeks & weeks & up to eyes in work, & ready to gobble up grouse (thank'ee kindly) by the brace or by the dozen! Rather!!

ALS: Houghton bMS Am 1094 (753)

---

*James asks Mrs. Jones to entertain H. G. Wells when the writer visits America.*

THE ATHENAEUM, PALL MALL, S.W.

Dear Mrs. Cadwalader Jones.                                      March 25*th* *1906*

I have written to you already on behalf of H.G. Wells[26]—whose significant name I thus find myself no more garnishing than I should that of Charles Dickens. He is more than half known to you already, moreover—by everything he has so potently done, & especially by *Kipps,*[27] the admirable, the rare. But I don't know that I had told you before how much he is my friend & now almost my near country neighbour. He is capable of *seeing,* in New York, & I have said to you in my other note how I shall rejoice in anything you may find it possible kindly to help him to see. You know your New York so beautifully & he will be to you so earnest & so

---

23. English writer Isobel Violet Hunt (1862 or 1866–1942). HJ knew Miss Hunt as a child; she was a frequent guest at Lamb House from 1903 to 1909. In 1909 HJ broke off communication with her temporarily because of the social complications her adulterous love affair with Ford Madox Ford Hueffer caused.

24. He was one of Violet Hunt's lovers.

25. It was HJ's practice to write four or five letters a night, starting around eleven p.m. or midnight. There are over ten thousand of his letters extant, according to Steven H. Jobe.

26. Herbert George Wells (1866–1946), English novelist, historian, and sociologist. James and Wells at first were friends, HJ praising Wells's work. Later, though, they attacked one another in print. Wells wrote *Boon,* in the form of essays by a dead critic, George Boon, including a strong parody of James.

27. A 1905 Wells novel that HJ liked.

grateful an *élève* [student], as Walt Whitman says. Likewise he will carry you the benediction of yours most faithfully

Henry James

ALS: Houghton MS Am 1094.9 (6)

*He thanks her for entertaining H. G. Wells in Washington, and he worries that she may not visit England and Scotland this summer. He sends news of the Whartons, claiming he is glad "that such fantastic wealth and freedom were not his portion."*

[*Dictated*]

LAMB HOUSE, RYE, SUSSEX.

My dear M. C.,                                             18th June, 1906.

Célimare will have been for you, during months, a dreadful and almost incredible Célimare, won't he? But perhaps it's a little just because he is poor exposed and tormented old Célimare that he has had thus to flounder along without catching the right moment for a successful dash at you. He only hurled at your head some weeks ago a jagged missile in the shape of little H. G. W., and scarce even then had the grace to go through the proper forms about it. H. G. W. is back these three or four weeks, I believe, though I haven't yet seen him; but he wrote me from Washington, on the eve of his departure, that you had been divinely kind to him, and I read all sorts of decent charities into that. I thank you for them now ever so sincerely, and will do so again after I have had speech of the ingenious little man—who wasn't really at all, I hope, more of a bore than of a beguilement. I would never have sent him to you if I had thought probable. I believe he has straightway hurled himself upon a Book, a Book of his four or five little bustling weeks, which will be quickly given to the world. But il ne s'agit pas de cela [but it's not about that]! What *has* been a grief to me is that, meeting little Mrs. Whitridge[28] a month ago in London (at luncheon at her Sister's, and on her way to the Spanish marriage,) she spoke of the possibility of your coming out this summer as probably compromised by the fact that Bar Harbour is this year inconveniently on your hands (as I understand it) unless you go and occupy it—and also that you can't, for some reason, have your usual House on the Moor. These lurid newses, combined with the fact of my not hearing from you to the contrary, have made me fear the worst, and poor Célimare seems to be "sort of" dolefully

---

28. Lucy Arnold Whitridge, wife of American lawyer Frederick Wallingford Whitridge (1852–1916).

giving up: which is a dreadful thing for him to have to do. Do write me now at last something a bit cheering or compensatory about it—some hint that if you don't come before, and for these next weeks or months, you *will* come in October, say, for the winter, and in time even to put in three or four little russet autumn days down here. That's the sort of thing I want to hear from you—in fact anything to break the silence. You will by this time perhaps have had a little news of me from our Lady of Lenox [Edith Wharton], who must have got home—though I didn't have very, *very*, VERY many vivid items from her about yourselves (which was probably however but the fault of poor Célimare's morbid discretion, the fruit of his complicated career!) it may be that *you* won't be any more drenched. She didn't tell me, at any rate, that you were, either of you, unduly hampered in health, wealth or spirits: which was so much to the good. They had, the W's. I thought, a rather frustrated, fragmentary merely-motory time to have crossed the dreadful sea for—though it was what seemed to suit them best, and I daresay that after their more successful days in France they reembarked with the sense of a rich adventure. Poor Célimare, always moralising on everything, only rather thanked goodness, as he observed, and during a few days here a little participated in, it, that such fantastic wealth and freedom were not *his* portion—such incoherence, such a nightmare of perpetually renewable choice and decision, such a luxury of bloated alternatives, do they seem to burden life withal! However, I had some very charming and enjoyable, even if half weather-blighted hours with our friends. For the rest, I lately came back here after a longish series of weeks in town (from the end of January) and am settled in plain tranquillity and industry (D. V.) for the summer— only with rather a shadow on it, just yet, as I have hinted, from my being really so much in the dark about you, dear twain. Light me up a little, in charity, tell me really how the case stands. I'm afraid I haven't any *rumeur* of the social situation here to set humming for you, as I am now giving London the widest berth possible and not venturing at all into the whirl-pool. If you [*sic*] twin were there I would go up for a few days and heroically take the plunge, but for no lesser creatures. A seductive sign this morning from Mrs. George Vanderbilt,[29] which leaves me quite uncorrupted. The press to see "the Longworths"[30] (as who should say the Borgias or the

29. HJ stayed with Mr. and Mrs. George Vanderbilt at Biltmore, near Asheville, North Carolina, in February 1905.

30. Probably Nicholas and Alice Roosevelt Longworth. He was a politician and a member of the House of Representatives, and she was the daughter of Theodore Roosevelt. In 1906 they married in the White House.

Bourbons!) appears grotesque—and the Whitelaw Reids[31] blaze in the firmament. "All=seeing heaven, what a world is this!" as somebody says in Shakespeare. But what a letter is this, as you and B. will say! I shall write better, and perhaps less, when you've ticked out for me de votre côté [from your side] something to go by. "Go," you, de votre côté, by the faithful fondness of your constant Célimare & your *affectuosissimo*

Henry James

TLS: Houghton bMS Am 1094 (758)

---

*Minnie has long been silent, so James "racks his aching brain" asking whether he has angered her. His hours at her New York home were "as the most romantic of his life."*

LAMB HOUSE, RYE, SUSSEX.

Dearest Mary Cadwalader. October 2*d* 1906.

I yearn over you, but I yearn in vain; & your long silence really breaks my heart, mystifies, depresses, almost alarms me, to the point even of making me wonder if poor unconscious & doting old Célimare has "done" anything, in some dark somnambulism of spirit, which has—which *may* fantastically have—given you a bad moment, or a wrong impression, or a "colourable pretext," or in short any ghost of a peg on which to hang any false image of his so gentle & devoted nature. He can neither imagine nor conceive it—he racks his aching brain—& then he wonders if you are ill, or blighted in fortune or in spirit, or distraught from any strange cause, or otherwise misguided or bedevilled—& he lies awake at night & bedews his hard pillow (he prefers it hard, you may—as a hostess—remember!) with his tears. However these things may be, he loves you as tenderly as ever; nothing, to the end of time, will ever detach him from you, & he remembers those Eleventh St. matutinal *intimes* [private] hours, those telephonic matinées, as the most romantic of his life—though indeed asking himself why he singles out those when every other moment, of all the many moments, comes back with such a dear value. The great thing, & the blessed, would be for *you* to come back—literally to do that, to return here this autumn, as you talked of doing a year ago. But how can I ask it of you when you seem so little to listen? I wail (for sweetness of remembrance,) over those Brook St. days of last October—even under the

---

31. Whitelaw Reid (1837–1912), editor, journalist, and writer. He hired HJ to be his Paris correspondent in 1875 and then didn't like his articles.

shadow of poor dear Crawford's[32] tragic presence. We have had an incomparable summer—only now at last broken, & this little gardeny corner has been a pure blessing to me. I haven't stirred out of it; & *have* been a little submerged; but it has been (the whole time) a benediction of balmy months. I hope Beatrix hasn't given you, or herself, anxiety—has *that* oppressed you both? God forbid!—& I send her best love. *Tick* me, dearest old friend, a sign of remembrance however scant & believe me your undying

*Célimare.*

ALS: Houghton bMS Am 1094 (759)

*James will find out whether Mrs. Jones can easily bring her dog, Lorna, to England. He asks about the play version of Wharton's* House of Mirth *and also talks about the publication of* The American Scene. *He mourns the death of his dog Max and declares he will never have another.*

Dearest Mary Cadwalader.                    [Lamb House, Rye, Sussex]

Your beautiful & generous & touching letter of now already too many days back (by reason of their having been days of extreme pressure & preoccupation for me) has lifted a black weight from my mind; & you may believe how depressed & anxious I had become about our long intermission when I tell you that even your so interesting & melting tale of woe has been for me on the whole a pleasing substitute for the gloomy void preceding it. You put me into possession of your lively vicissitudes, & I live over them with you, all tenderly & intimately—and I confess with a certain moan of resignation for not having known them at the time—some of them at least, the weariest. Well, it's a dark & depressing, yet in its way a thrilling tale, if only for its record of the *crânerie* [courage], with which, evidently, you conducted yourself. Surely you are having now your reward, you [*sic*] air has cleared, your earth has ceased to quake, & your Vesuvius to erupt—we *all* have a lurking Vesuvius in the landscape of our lives, with our best Bays of Naples more or less at the mercy of it!——Beatrix is, above all, as I understand, on her feet, Lorna Doone [Minnie's dog] is on your lap, & your passages are definitely secured (as I hope & pray,) for January. Your news of this last possibility, which I trust has steadily stiffened into sweet assurances, has filled me with impatient joy, & I do with all

---

32. Popular American novelist Francis Marion Crawford (1854–1909). James and Crawford differed markedly in their views of fiction.

my heart hope you are going to turn up. Give my love to Beatrix please, & tell her my earnest prayers & invocations attend her! Reading over your letters I study afresh the portents, & seem to make out that you speak with a fond confidence. I will write immediately now to Lady Barrington about the conditions, as actually established, for the introduction of little inno-cent angel=hounds,[33]—she will know, I gather, definitely, as she is much concerned with the whole question, & I will then again immediately write *you*. I haven't yet questioned her by letter because I've thought there was a good chance of my being able to see her on some run-up to London, but time for that, through the jealous brevity of my runs, has failed, & I won't wait for it longer. I just hear from Mrs. Wharton of *their* sailing for 18 rue de Varenne for the winter, about January *7th,* & I brace myself—all appreciatively—for the prospect of the pilgrimage to the (to me) formida-ble Paris that this very interesting event opens up. It would still be interest-ing even if as only illustrating further, to my slightly troubled & be-wildered eyes, the wild, the almost incoherent freedoms & restlessness of Wealth, & its wonderful art, when it's combined with Ability, of harmoniz-ing the same with literary Concentration of so positive & productive an order. But I'm getting to quite anarchistically hate, in general, the motor! Àpropos of all of which, how *has* the H. of M. [*House of Mirth*] *play* done? You were to see it in N.Y., when you wrote, & to tell me. The question will much interest me—& I suppose that if it's really having a run the affluence of gain must be great. But *such* a lot of things as I want to ask you. *My* New York of those dear East Eleventh "first=floor-back" hours live again for me as I write, as I touch any matter connected with them; fills me with quite nostalgic yearnings that nothing but your presence in the flesh will assuage. Yes, reading over your letter again does make me feel what a hell of time you must have had—Gouty Foot & all, & with everything "agin" you with such a beautiful consistency. I scan your account of Trix's convalescence, her calisthenic convalescence &c, for every light it can throw on the matter of your sailing "if" she is well enough—I mean for all its possible intima-tion that she was, at your writing, on the way to become so. And by this I earnestly hang. Do tick me out a little more news of the question as soon as you get this. I won't pretend that London is very *folichon* [exciting] in these

---

33. Minnie Jones was concerned about bringing her dog Lorna into England through customs, and Lady Barrington was to advise her. In a second letter James warns Minnie that it will be too difficult to bring the dog and suggests (strongly) that she leave him in New York.

weeks of dark deluge. (We are paying for a summer of extraordinary beauty & dryness, that lasted from June 1st, or earlier, to the end of October without a break: all pure *beauty of climate* too, of this climate that can be desired when the dear humoursome old thing chooses.) But when one is fond of it,—i.e. of London town—as you & Beatrix are, one can always arrange with it, playing all that it has of good against the bad; & by that time the waterspout may have fulfilled its destiny & passed on. Only let me know *à quoi m'en tenir* [where things stand] as soon as you conveniently can. One of my Cambridge nephews is in Paris "painting"—a very charming & earnest youth who was with me here 6 weeks this summer—as *many* persons were with me by the same token—& I am under a sort of gage to go over & see *him* in early February. "The American Scene" down to Florida, is all ready here for publication, but tiresomeness on the Harpers' part, for the N. Y. issue, delays its appearance (which has to be simultaneous in the two countries,) till (probably) January. You shall have, by my direction, the very 1st gift copy. And also you shall now have the "King's English" from Bain, & from me, as fast as it can ever go. I am shy in general of sending to America by the so tariffed & contrabanded bookpost, having learned with disgust on past occasions that my presentees were taxed—mulcted by the Custom House (acting through the P.O.) before being allowed to receive them. I infer, or hope, that this is not now the abominable case. But I must send off my letter, praying it may have a quick transit & find you both altogether on the rebound, & the house let & the berths taken & the little dog wagging his tail. Do you know that poor beautiful Max [HJ's dachshund] is no longer wagging *his?* (unless in the Elysian Fields—where they wag harder than ever—no Elysium, certainly, that doesn't have them.) His extinction a dire little tragedy—about which don't *ask* me. But his absence a simplification of care & an economy of time & he is never, never, never to have a successor. They are too dear (darling) & too overwhelming. But I never the less resemble them in being as fondly as one of *them* could be your absolutely adhesive

*Célimare*
November 18*th* 1906.

ALS: Houghton bMS Am 1094 (760)

*At the midnight hour HJ thanks her for her note and for his recent visit to Scotland. Her home on Eleventh St. was "the great good place."*

Dearest Mary Cadwalader.                    LAMB HOUSE, RYE, SUSSEX.

This little word, a very little word, as befits the midnight hour—in fact the clock has just deeply & reprovingly sounded *one,* like a grave admonishing *Hum!*—is only to acknowledge the sweetness of that precarious pencilling in the train which I was deeply touched to get from you as you fared further away. The day, as I recall, was lovely, & lovely ones have followed it here—till within 48 hours—whereby I have kept hoping that a like peace & plenty (of ethereal mildness) would be running beside you all the way. And now the dear old Empire rooms, with their dimmish "middle distance" enclose you safely, I pray—it's astonishing, it's prodigious, how I find my spirit gratefully haunting them always—or rather, how insidiously turning the tables they, the mystic locality itself, haunt & revisit my own departed identity. Vivid to me still in that December night when, a weary & bewildered pilgrim, I scaled your stoop & invoked your welcome for the first time, & felt on the spot that I had come to the great good place. I don't know what I shld. have done without you *then.* It seems to me too that I didn't know what I shld. have done without you exactly when those 5 recent blessed September days in all that purple sublimity & that exquisite hospitality were vouchsafed me. The value is ineffaceable & every moment of them abides. We *must* renew them next year. I greet you all 3—J. C.[her cousin John Cadwalader] between you twain—ever so tenderly. Always your fondest

Célimare.

Oct: 5. 1907.

ALS: Houghton bMS Am 1094 (767)


*The washcloths she sent him remind him of his nursery days, but he asks her to not send more because they irritate his eczema. He has accompanied Lawrence Godkin to bury his mother, Katherine Sands Godkin, in a remote part of England. The Whartons want James to join them in Paris or Italy, but he has "crossed the absurd Channel for the last time." He finds Edith's latest book,* The Fruit of the Tree, *in some ways superior to the* House of Mirth.


LAMB HOUSE, RYE, SUSSEX.

Dear Mary Cadwalader.                          December 8*th* 1907.

I have groaned beneath the weight of your reiterated bounties—that is groaned with the sore consciousness of my unworthy delay to thank & bless you. Yet at the same time I have had the luxury of feeling that you know, you understand you allow; that no mystery of the busy, inky life is

hidden from you, & that in short there is a heavenly immunity from need to plead with you the cause of the poor man—of any poor man—who doesn't get all his letters written. I get them in *time*—but time I have to take. Everything meanwhile has come from you—from the beautiful little "wash-cloths" (how they remind me of the ancient wash-cloth of my nursery days, with which my whole small upper person used to be conscientiously & soapily excoriated!) to your kind participation in my very tender regret for dear little Katherine Godkin's last suffering ordeal & death. In connection with this I lately had *my* ordeal—which was not a light one—appealed to by Lawrence [Godkin, her son] (by cable) to see him through the dreary business of the extraordinarily inconvenient interment she had desired for herself, by E. L. G. [Edwin Lawrence Godkin], in the remote little Northamptonshire churchyard where he all disconnectedly & incoherently lies, I met him (Lawrence!) the other day (3 weeks ago) on his arrival by the Celtic at Liverpool, & devoted 3 or 4 lugubrious days to doing what I could for him. The last of these—a railway journey of 4 hours across country, in deadly Northern cold, & then a drive of 12 miles of unsurpassable bleakness to the said fantastic little Hazelbeach (with a 6 miles drive back to Market Harborough & a train to London that night)—was an adventure not soon to be forgotten. He sailed immediately home again in the Lusitania (his vow to Katherine really heroically—& in great horror of the whole thing—performed) & perhaps you will have seen him by the time you get this. He will be in possession of quite the latest news of me. But the incident only confirmed me, if confirmation were needed, in my horror of causing posthumous trouble & my determination to be disposed of in the handiest manner conceivable or arrangeable.————
The little face-cloths are of a touching discretion & symmetry, & I am deeply affected by the thought of your having sacrificed so generously & thoughtfully to my faded charms. I value greatly the opportunity to use occasionally my little supply, but I won't have any more, thank you ever so kindly—because why? Well, because I have a tendency to suffer from gouty eczema—not only on certain parts of my "form," but on my poor old forehead & cheeks, &, unless I am very careful, any indiscreet friction (just as any excessive use of *soap,* save on my hands, thank goodness) is rather apt to start it up. I therefore can't rub *much,* & perhaps have even to go a *little* dirty in order not to turn strawberry-colour & itch badly. All the same I'm sure the dear little irritating squares, of which I will take excellent care, will "come in" somehow & some time (I will even return them to you next summer at Millden—where you see I already fondly "fix" you; to say

nothing of myself.) I greatly hope the place is still "redounding" (I never have known quite what "redounding" is) to John Cadwalader's benefit, & I send him my cordial & grateful devotion. Apropos of which has the gentle Newbigging[34] been with you according to the intention he then announced? I am sure you were in this case all kind to him exceedingly, as he deserves; & if his "home" were not such a far cry from here I'd try & get hold of him to hear his news—& yours. I am sticking fast to this little seat of peace, myself—where the weeks rush by with absolutely no "speed limit"—which I wish the magistrates could make effective. I shall stay late—till March at nearest—before making an absence, & then shall next go up to London till May or thereabouts. The Whartons must be at this moment on the windy, wintry sea, & she notifies me that the great Cook[35] has already embarked with the great motor. I foresee *du tirage* [some friction] when she & Teddy really take in that in spite of their tender of the princeliest hospitality it is insurmountably impossible for me to join them either in Paris or in Italy. In fact they must have taken it in already—for I have written it large & bold, & so must leave it. In fact I've told them *all* the rude truth—that it's never to be again,—& that I've really & absolutely crossed the absurd Channel for the last time of my life. It's fantastic, it's grotesque—if you or they will; but nothing can exceed henceforth my aversion to "going abroad." It's dead & done with for me & I've no use for it whatever. The prospect brings with it a peace that passeth understanding. So I shall be here for you whenever you come—which is an immense further beauty of the arrangement. The energy of our friends meanwhile— of Edith's & Teddy's (though I think in him it *must* wane) fills me with a deep & solemn awe. Such an arrangement of my life would be to me the grimmest of nightmares. But my concept of felicity is more & more to crouch behind a Chinese wall; or at least behind a good old English russet brick one. I wish I might hear from you of the "reception"—what it has been—of "The Fruit of the Tree."[36] I have read the book myself with great admiration for the way much of it is done—there is great talent, all along. But it is of a strangely infirm composition & construction—as if she hadn't taken thought for that, & 2 or 3 sane persons here who have read my copy find it a "disappointment" after the H. of M. [*House of Mirth*]. That is not

---

34. Alex Newbigging, who accompanied John Cadwalader on some of his hunting trips to Scotland.

35. Edith Wharton's chauffeur, Charles Cook.

36. Edith Wharton's most recent novel. Here HJ largely approves of it, although other commentators believe he disliked it.

my sense. I find it superior—& think the admirers of the "House" will stultify themselves if they don't at least equally back it up. But I must wipe my pen & take up my candle. It's as usual fantastically late, & all I've got left is questions—which aren't fair asking. How is the brave Beatrix, to whom I send but love? How is poor dear John La Farge (& has he still *près de lui* [near him] gentle dainty Barnes?)[37]—to whom I affectionately commend myself. How above all is my dear Mary Cadwalader, whom I truly cherish & quite unreservedly adore? I hope your winter takes a tolerable form, in spite of the horrible "business crisis" that the papers here are full of & of which I don't understand the least little word. What a strange sad mad country in which everything proceeds by cataclysm & violence & enormity—leaps & bounds from one kind of excess to another kind. I ache with the very action or wince with the very noise of it, & crouch more & more behind my wall. But I hope, fondly, that you are not in the least inconvenienced. Tell Beatrix that I saw Dorothy Ward[38] the other day, & she told me the great maternal progress through "our country" (or whatever portion of it) is fixed for March. So fall into your ranks & tenez-vous bien [hold on tight]! Most of it, I warn, will "come on" Dorothy, & I shall be sorry for that patient maid. But you too will have special opportunities, with the house of Whitridge[39] just under your windows, & you must really let me know all about it. Goodnight—good morning: it's 1.45 a.m., & I am yours all & always

Henry James

ALS: Houghton bMS Am 1094 (768)

*James recalls the Christmas he spent with Mrs. Jones at Eleventh Street six years ago, a time embalmed "in the fragrantest dried rose-leaves of romance." He worries that Teddy Wharton's demented state will affect Edith.*

Dearest Mary Cadwal.                                    LAMB HOUSE, RYE, SUSSEX.

It's a great joy to hear from you, & you were well inspired to make a faithful little sign for poor intensely insulated & sequestrated Célimare. It's a heavy & superfluous moment & one must be dauntless indeed to face—without a melancholy howl—its felicities. We take it, as you know, very harsh here, & "lie low" as one will, the big thick matter-of-course British

37. Grace Edith Barnes was La Farge's personal assistant for many years.
38. Dorothy Ward, oldest child of popular novelist Mary Augusta Ward (1851–1920) and Oxford don and writer Thomas Humphry Ward (1845–1926).
39. Lucy Arnold and Frederick Whitridge, American friends of HJ.

wave breaks upon one & submerges—for the hour. I have been crouching at home this year—after three or four experiments in absence in this latter time; but I scarce know which course is the more desperate & depressing. I have had—& am still having—a lone, lorn, stranded & rather oppressive, though appreciative old friend with me for the stress of it; however, he departs, I believe, tomorrow and the worst is no doubt over. I think ever so tenderly & romantically of my too fleeting Xmas days in Eleventh St. 6 years (wasn't it?) ago; preserved, between you & Trix, in layers of gold paper; but *all* that period of your protection & hospitality lives for me more & more—is embalmed for me in the fragrantest dried rose-leaves of romance.——What you tell me of Teddy W.'s *état d'âme*—& de corps [state of mind and of body]—while among you all consorts with impressions that I can read pretty well into what I hear from Edith—making it out between the lines that he has been playing over-excited & demented in fact not particularly edifying tricks, some of the consequences of which (of a pecuniary—& a *sinister* pecuniary cast, I infer,) he appears to have just sailed *back* again to N. Y.—to repair, I trust, rather than to aggravate. Great worriment, at all events, I seem to divine, has been her portion all these latter months—& I agree with you that there is nothing his further prolonged participation in can be thought of in the light of rendering him indispensable in any relations. (Which round-about phrase might indeed be more vividly compressed!) But such are the conditions of the affluent, the Great & the Parisian; & they more than console me for my indigence, my so moderate size, & my small country-town *milieu.* I wish Edith, for her happiness, could only be *simplified* a good bit; but il lui faut tout de choses—tant & tant [she has to have so many things—so many]; & I seem to view with an appalled & lack-lustre eye the formidable mass they make up. "Il lui faut," [She needs] as I say, Everything but Teddy! I'm anxious as to how the situation may, as regards *his* superfluity, develop. However, I believe, in his power, when it comes to the point, to ride almost any wave.——I was exceedingly sorry—in fact deeply disappointed—to miss Florence La Farge wholly & utterly during an impossible little dash of 7 days that she made at these shores some short time since (as you probably know;) she arranged herself to make it impossible, either I or her desperate little old friend Jonathan Sturges should have a glimpse of her—though she announced herself in advance all intendingly & promisingly. I wanted to *ask* her much—but it was vain, & she must have had a hell of a rush—which she couldn't, either, understand & which was full of elements & abysses that I alone cld. have explained to her! But such are human accidents & frustrations. I rejoice for Trix in *her* big fields & campaigns; & I fold you both in the fond embrace of

Célimare.

Dec: 27: 1909

ALS: Houghton MS Am 1094.9 (10)

*James visits William and Alice James, where William takes the cure and "after cure." When James returns to America with his family he wants to spend part of the winter with her in New York. "Horace Fletcherism" has turned on him, and his health has been very poor. He worries over Edith Wharton: Teddy Wharton is now in a Swiss sanatorium.*

IMSEL HOTEL IM-SEE GRAND HOTEL KONSTANZ

June 24*th* 1910.

Dearest, dearest Mary Cadwal!

Ah, but I yearn to write to you, & your beautiful, unspeakable letter overheaps the measure. It found me yesterday a.m. just as I was leaving Nauheim for this hitherto-by-me-unvisited Constance—through, or by, an extraordinarily beautiful 7 hours' run, the Black Forest of Baden, admirably handsome uninterruptedly all the way. And here we find a remarkably pleasant hotel, in an ancient lakeside monastery (pleasant when parties of 300 compatriotic "mugs," now departed, haven't been violently injected into it, as, at the moment, we too were arriving, last night.) I hope we shall contentedly stay here a week—to help to fill the time of my poor brother's Nauheim "after cure,"[40] & to help me peacefully back to the ways of comparative activity & nerve-tranquillity again. I am getting gradually but steadily better, dearest M.C., & am beginning really to measure my unmistakable progress. But *for* it, in fact, I should never be able to move about with this comparatively normal vigour & success. But for it, in fact, dearest M.C., I think I should really be laid flat on my back again by the heavenly kindness of your letter. Instead of that it gives me—your blest benevolence—a great & blissful lift & touches me ever so deeply without yet making me *too* hysterically blubber. I will come with joy to make you a good visit, & I think with infinite yearning of treading the dear old floors of 21 again. But I go home primarily to be with my brother & sister & their children, in whom I am infinitely interested—1*st* at their "summer home" at Chocorua N. H. & afterwards in Cambridge. That I must more or less

---

40. The curative baths at the spa in Bad Nauheim were debilitating to William James; he required a rest after undergoing this "cure."

· 155

devote the whole autumn to; besides which I must wait upon the successive months, to judge of the rate of my return to intimately normal conditions. You see the state I was in for dismal & dismal weeks was no sudden drop out of the infernal blue, but a perfectly physical visitation prepared these three years by a fell abuse (not measured, though suspected by me at the time) of "Horace Fletcherism" in the whole mode & mystery of eating. For three whole years that system had done me enormous good, been a pure benediction & boon; but it turned upon me at last, obscurely & treacherously, preparing a cataclysm. That I didn't dream of—as to its gravity & damnation at least. Food-loathing overtook me & laid me on my back, & *then*, as strict & connected & involved sequel, the situation took a deplorably & horribly nervous turn. It is from *that* I am struggling up into the light again—after having really been down into hell. My eldest nephew 1*st*, & then my brother & sister came out to me as ministering angels—my brother himself depressingly unwell—& they have rendered me help that I never can repay. I should like at any rate to try some of the midwinter weeks in New York, & if you will take me in, in your abounding charity, I shall thank you both & re-thank you, & thank you yet again—& love you but the better (if that is possible.) I have dreamt of a few weeks of "the South" later on, or some time; but all that must wait upon further developments. I am just these days fighting with the hard effort *completely* to give up anodynes & sedatives & bromides, & the struggle leaves me not a little collapsed. For long they were wholly indispensable, & I have been going, steadily, diminuendo; but the last break of all is hard—so, in my weakness, I shall wind up this with my tenderest blessing. Glad I am you have been with—or near—our wondrous Edith, whose courage & fortitude & *tenue* [bearing] of herself in her fairly grim situation are beyond all praise. Poor dear Teddy—that there should be *enough* of him to create such dire complications! I hope indeed he will stick it out at Kreuzlingen.[41] I don't see her *possibilities* either of quiet or of motion. I wrote her from Nauheim that we were going from there to Munich & the Bavarian Tyrol; but all that collapsed, thank goodness—the dream of a day, & far beyond me. We shall try to stay somehow in Switzerland till it's time to return to England via Geneva—& we have to be there (in E.) 2 or 3 weeks (rather 3 than 2) before sailing on said Aug. 12*th*. But my brother's state makes me anxious (not acutely but *generally*,) & that is not good for me, (*his* nervous condi-

41. Teddy Wharton had volunteered to go to the well-known sanatorium Kuranstalt Bellevue at Kreuzlingen, near Konstanz, Switzerland. After only a week he wanted out, however.

tions good for mine) & yet I cling to him & we are rather a sad trio. So we sit loose, &, as he can't take walks, alas (a great walker, ever, till a year past,) shall make for Lamb House again, with London to follow, if this kind of thing proves too dreary. I am delighted your elegant Aix doesn't, & that it has healed & helped you. I greet Beatrix fondly on her arrival—& oh how I envy you the bonnie moor again! Auf wiedersehen. Always, dearest M.C., your devotedest old *Célimare*.

ALS: Houghton MS Am 1094.9 (11)


*James sends condolences on John La Farge's death, but Minnie can now show him the charity she had bestowed on La Farge. He fears for Edith Wharton, who is alone in France.*

Dearest Mary Cadwal.

I can't let these days pass to the extent of another hour without letting you know how much I've thought of *your* thought, & felt with your feeling, beside poor dear John L. F.'s deathbed, & still more in the midst of his obsequies—for Tom Perry, his brother-in-law, told me today he has had "obsequies" in New York; of which I am extremely glad for him. He would have liked to think that—of course took it for granted. I hope they were really handsome, & am only sorry the Irish side of the C. C. [Catholic Church] here is what on such occasions one feels come uppermost. I think with relief of his sinking to rest after his long overtroubled & confused & even confounded life. A great clearing-up he needed—& what greater could he have than now? But on others labours will now come—& I only hope you won't be caught in the vortex. It would be like you, & your morbid appetite for wanton *bienfaisance* [charity]. You will miss *him* as a receptacle of that. Well, you can make it up a little on Célimare. There will—there must, of course—be an exhibition of a high commemorative kind; for our friend—where a great deal of beauty (& of imperfections—but of very individual beauty none the less,) will come out. I hope I shan't miss it—& believe so the more as I am quite clear about staying on till May or June. This house & its inmates are a great, a precious aid & comfort to me—which I have needed during recent relapses. I had a bad but brief one in N. Y.—at the end; & then again lately another & longer one here—a fortnight during which I was mostly in bed. But I have "come up" again, & really feel at last (unberufen!) as if it might be to stay. (I mean, to stay "up"—not to stay—really stay—"on this side.") My quarters here are excellent, my companions more loveable l'un que l'autre [one as much as the other], the weather wondrous, the walks quite numerous & possible, & the days melt in my grasp. All of which, however, doesn't in the least prevent my wanting to see you—very, very much. That will come—& meanwhile make me some small & easy sign. I wanted just now to make this one—in default of a better—to *you*. And I think anxiously & pretty dismally of Edith. I wonder how Teddy's difficult tour goes on, & what side she hears from J. Morton,[42] devoted & unenviable agent! The waters are out in France again[43] (a dreary prospect,) & Edith yearning for comfort & support & solutions in that glittering iniquitous capital is a figure—so really lonely—that it makes me quake. However, we must all, thank God, go to bed & I do now. All double loves! Ever your revering

Célimare.

Cambridge

Nov: 18: *1910*.

ALS: Houghton MS Am 1094.9 (16)


*James tells Mary Cadwalader of his travel plans. The countryside is still pretty despite the drought.*

95 IRVING STREET CAMBRIDGE MASSACHUSETTS

Dearest Mary Cadwal.                                     May 13*th 1911*.

Again you just make me love & bless you. And I want to tell you I am again handsomely Better—in spite of heat & drought & dust, & the mortal "plainness" of this place—plainer than the plainest woman that ever lived ever paid for the loss of all chances by being. I have come up by the light of my really *heroic* wisdom (which makes doctors babbling infants)—& my wisdom confirms all the reasons of things that I wrote you after I got back here. Hostile fate & accident lays traps—devilishly, baits them poisonously; but I am only temporarily caught & I rise like the phoenix from its ashes! Very interesting again your transcript of dear Edith's last—yet on the whole too rather reassuring, save as indicating that the phases & stages may yet be long. The oracles—my oracles—meanwhile are dumb—that is the Whites are; they have clearly been absorbed in

---

42. Johnson Morton, a minor writer who visited Edith at the Mount. He traveled with Teddy through Europe and America.

43. The "waters" in this sentence may refer to the severe flooding in Paris in January of 1910, which happened just after Edith Wharton moved into her apartment at 53 Rue de Varenne, a flood that coincided with her increasing problems with Teddy. Perhaps James suggests that Mrs. Wharton again experienced personal difficulties.

the Greys—it has made a bad mixture. I can't tell them—if they do break out at last—that I will with this temperature travel 300 miles due south for their beaux yeux [beautiful eyes]. Therefore the question of the amount of "draught through" to be counted on for me from 12*th* St. becomes irrelevant, & I hope you & Lorna are enjoying all there is to be caught on the way—you with the fewest interferences of the drapery sort, & Lorna with whatever is *her* apology for "buff." I feel as if I hadn't left dear old 21 a grain of pretext for further hospitality; she has swept every chord of the lyre for me & now can but hang up the instrument on the 2*d* floor back even as Tara's harp dangled in the banquet hall deserted. We shall next meet—heaven send, & J. C. [John Cadwalader] provide, amid the bonny heather first of all & then afterwards, I hope & pray in Middlesex & eke in Sussex. I don't go to Chocorua for some weeks, I trust—95 Irving St. remains "open" for a good while yet—even if my sister soon goes. Moreover I shall probably be for some time first at Salisbury Conn., & then at Nahant, Mass: I have promised my dear kind old "kinsman" George James[44] to stay with him at the extreme point of that cool promontory as long as I can stand it. So, I have work cut out. I am really writing this part of this not at Cambridge, but during a week=end spent—or to *be* spent, till Tuesday a.m., on this spot [Nashawtuc Road, Concord] with my *smaller* sister-in-law, my poor dear Brother Bob's widow,[45] who has a very pretty commodious house here, in which she dwells all alone & to which I motored down (with Burgess) this afternoon from Irving St. in about 50 minutes. It isn't *folichon* [exciting], but it's high, cool & spacious & the countryside exceedingly pretty & blossomy, in spite of plague & famine—I mean water-famine & tree-disease. Tomorrow I shall see Emersons & things—& shall want to become obscure. But I shall escape in time. Meanwhile I drive my pen in my room by open windows & fresh but windless airs (which don't stir the imprisoned electric light!)—only, though we have retired early, as you can imagine (for there has been no one to "meet" me,) the evening wanes & I am yours, dearest Mary Cadwal, all & always

*Henry James*

ALS: Houghton MS Am 1094.9 (28)

---

44. George Abbott James (b. 1838) had been a law student at Harvard during HJ's brief stay there. They remained life long friends. G. A. James married Elizabeth "Lily" (ca. 1843–1908) Lodge, sister of Senator Henry Cabot Lodge.

45. Mary Lucinda Holton James (b. 1849), wife of Robertson James, Henry's youngest brother. She was from Wisconsin. They separated at one point due to his drinking.

*HJ suffers from Rye's extreme heat. He thinks Edith's decision to sell the Mount (her home in western Massachusetts) and separate from her husband will save her life.*

LAMB HOUSE, RYE, SUSSEX.

Dearest Mary Cadwal. August 10*th* *1911*.

I'm here, yes—but in no very brilliant form, thanks to this long & formidable ordeal of heat, which lasting for weeks, with hideous & inscrutable rage, in the U.S., has awaited me on my arrival in this supposedly temperate zone (after attending me even at sea, too,) & has really much undone me. So I am not good for more than this single fond scratch—to send you all love & hope & thanks. There wd. be so much—there *is* so much—to say. But we will manage it yet—if I am still, through all difficulties, spared! I haven't seen Edith since July 14*th* or so—but I saw Walter Berry at the Belmont the night before I sailed, & he had just been with her at Lenox. Teddy is "well" enough—perfectly sane so far as it suits him, but utterly quarrelsome, abusive & impossible. Definitely, I think, after going through dreadful scenes, E. has decided, *really* decided, to both sell the Mount and separate from him absolutely—making him an allowance but demanding that they live apart. His health, physique, toughness, browness &c, are perfect—& his ill temper perfectly normal. The "family" denounces her—but God grant she carries it through. *It* is the only thing to save her life. Voilà. She will come out again early. Also I will write better. This is all now. Ever your

Célimare.

ALS: Houghton bMS Am 1094 (773)


*James thanks Mary Cadwalader for her gift of grouse and complains of Rye's terrible heat wave.*

Dearest Mary Cadwal! LAMB HOUSE, RYE, SUSSEX.

All thanks for the beautiful children of the moor—& victims of the murderous engine. (Before *I'd* shoot—even if I *could!* But don't repeat this to your gang of assassins—& above all not to its chief. Only thank the last named very gently & kindly for me.) I have a new Scotch cook, who fortunately isn't mawkish, & whom the bonny grouse will on the contrary much appeal to—as a cook. I wrote you the day after getting here—but expression & overflow (save of perspiration) are as yet much hindered for me by the beastly disabling heat & drought—the fire-demon—I fled from in our hell of country only to fall into his arms again here. He lays me flat

& I don't know where I am yet at all—& the sky is still of brass & the earth of tinder (though the nights, in this place, are, even with such days, really convenient enough.) However, I dare say it all suits *your* book thoroughly—as to bonny weather on the brae (whatever the brae *is!*)—though I don't think I envy you the trudge (even equine) to lunch through it all—bonny as it may be. Make me a sign later—I probably want only water as against fire to pick up very well indeed. I probably go away on Friday for 6 or 7 days—that is if there's a change. Edith is too big & complicated a subject for *this* poor art. But we'll talk—in September! Yours & Trix's all &

*Célimare*
Aug: 14: 1911.

ALS: Houghton bMS Am 1094 (774)

*James's worries over Edith Wharton's demented husband Teddy form a continual theme in his letters to Mary Cadwalader.*

LAMB HOUSE, RYE, SUSSEX.

Dearest Mary Cadwal. August 17*th* *1911*

I think I acknowledged, promptly & gratefully, the moorfowl—& I have since been largely occupied in smacking my lips over them. My Scotch Joan is the scotchest, but I think safest, thing in nature. This noon arrives your good word of the 15*th*—as to which this is a fond apology for a response. It's impossible, always, to *write* about Edith—the whole subject is too complex & voluminous, & *viva voce* treatment alone can tackle it in any way. I *did* see Teddy at the Mount—the whole afternoon & evening before I left, he having returned thither, in prime physical condition, from 3 weeks' arduous salmon-fishing in New Brunswick—possessed as he is of full health for all that sort of thing—& for making his renewed & again renewed violent scenes—as to which his capacity constantly grows. He is perfectly sane, for *him* (I mean for his intrinsic childishness of mind;) & it's my absolute conviction that unless they have a personal separation (with an "allowance" from her *to* him) he will absolutely destroy her by a final nervous & cardiac crisis. His power to do so by his worry & folly & his *endless* scene-making habit is indubitable—on the other hand I believe that *with* a separation she would very much come up. But *basta* [enough]—it's all difficult & deadly. Such a *marriage*—originally! But who knows what other she mightn't have made?——The conditions here—the burnt-up land (though the heat has now for the time more or less abated & the nights are cool) & the disfigurement & uglification of everything, cast a blight over my return to England—not diminished by

161

the great looming civil, & it would now appear military, strife. If there could only be some rain I think however I shld. quite bear up—quite pick up.——I'm very glad you're to have George Meyer[46]—I liked him so, & he was so kind to me, on the ship.——Could you meanwhile give me a rough *clandestine* inkling (without asking) as to about what date in Sept. our gallant friend would be likely to make the likes of poor gunless *me* a sign?—saying as how he makes me one at all. The *later* the September date—compatibly with your & his conditions—the better it wd. suit your fond old

Célimare.

P.S. I go *away* on Saturday—strikes allowing—for some eight days; & away for 3 or 4 in the mid-September.

ALS: Houghton bMS Am 1094 (775)

*James's two-day visit to Minnie in Scotland did him much good. His bookseller Bain might propose to her if she weren't already promised to James.*

Dearest Mary Cadwal. [The Athenaeum, Pall Mall, S.W.]

I shan't see you—even if it were possible, with your supreme & sublime high pressure; for I catch my train down to Rye an hour hence. I arrived from Edinburgh only last night—9 p.m., having left the grey Athens of the North at 12. noon—after enjoying the discipline of the Caledonian Hotel from the previous Friday night. My 48 hours there were salutary—I wrote letters & read books & took the measure of the great good Millden had done me. Verily it was a great, & an exquisite week, & I want John Cadwalader to know from me again what a real happy lift it gave me. That last day at the Black Moss is a memory forever—an unspeakable unforgettable thing. I have been talking to the purple (though not fine linen) [James] Bain about you—so fondly! I think he wd. offer you his hand if he didn't fear you were "promised" to *me*. London is charming today—& my heart bleeds for your feeling it so & having to leave it. Things are alas most crookedly arranged. But we will straighten that out yet. I embrace & re-embrace you both & am your fondest faithfullest

Célimare.<br>Sept. 26th 1911.

ALS: Houghton bMS Am 1094 (780)

---

46. George Meyer (1858–1918) was a politician. His career included a stint as the American ambassador to Italy.

*Edith Wharton motors through Italy with Walter Berry, but James is not able to join Edith, as he has not her wealth nor her energy. He is back in London, to the benefit of his physical and mental health.*

Dearest Mary Cadwal.                                105, PALL MALL, S.W.

It's a great joy to hear from you, though your departure affects me as so far off in time that I kind of start on getting a ship letter only now—so far on. But you give me as good news as I suppose a "re-integrated" New Yorker (& especially the particular victim of reaction that *you* are,) can be expected to give—though I am all the same almost as sorry for you as if dear old 21 *hadn't* its mellow charm & its subtle arts. You seem to have had a very literary voyage—"gather you rosebuds while ye may!" Wagner is indeed a blowsy & not very fragrant rose—but rank of bloom & of every colour of the rainbow (or at least of the dyer's hand) at once! Edith's Italian Chronicle I never read—it takes *her* to work such things into a troubled & tinkering, that is a difficult & preoccupied, little life of toil. She is working them in plenty now—doing all Italy (after Salso) in a splendid new 60 h. p. car, with Walter Berry for bon camarade [good company]—which he admirably is. She most kindly appealed to *me* to meet her also at Milan for that purpose (or to join Walter in Paris & come down with him;) but such a feat & flight was not then possible to any of my powers—perhaps least of all my pecuniary. *Her* power to go & to consume & to enjoy—her incomparable restlessness—have me more & more *absourdi* [absolved]. Well, I but feel the poorer & (even with my girth!) leaner creature! I betook myself back to L. H., but it didn't do *at all*—the solitude & smallness & immobilisation (of the darkening, dampening season) threw me back wholly on myself; with the worst physical & mental results. But London, to which I immediately returned on taking stock of the whole truth is a sovereign remedy, *the* remedy—it does me no end of good & I shall never again attempt a live walkless, talkless, appetiteless winter at L. H. I shall put in *all* the present I can here, & am devoutly thankful for this easy & immediate perch. Meanwhile I must look for another regular town one—a small & decent flat, where I may have 2 servants for preference. I want *mobilization*—that, *with full feeding,* was all I wanted in N.Y. The defect there was that I got only the short & scrappy mobilization of the eternal 5*th* Avenue & home again; the rhythm & beat & margin were all scant & inadequate. This vast circular Babylon is exactly now my fit & measure—& I come every day more & more into my "own," as you & the child will be glad to hear. The staying here with 4 servants at home eating their hearts out for

163

me—to say nothing of their heads off—is awkward & not either economic or harmonious, but it's worth any sacrifice to keep on this right &
curative footing—"the *real* right thing" at last. And I shall never again
hibernate in the desert—I too recklessly overdosed myself with it in the
past. I have the friendliest ear for everything that touches you or crops up
about you in the country of East Eleventh St. (bad phrase—it *shld* be E.
11*th* Country:) the prosperity of the dear Pontos is especially delightful to
hear of. I rejoice heartily on little Pontina's performance, & congratulate
her hard—& all concerned. And I respond heartily too to all "inquiring
friends." Keep me in touch particularly with dear Collins till I can lay my
hand straight on him again—I want him to know my physiological
history—to "follow" it (as I do now, with the utmost lucidity, myself:) not
from a foul egotism, but in the luminous cause of science. It's mild &
bright & awfully decent here now, mostly—in short I don't feel it kind,
scarcely, or tactful, to tell you & dear Miss Nimrod how very pleasant &
taking, & all that they should be, Bond St. & its purlieus are to the fond &
faithful old

Célimare.

P.S. I wish I could lend you Kidd & Joanna & even Burgess [his house
servants] for the winter—I afflicted with servants I don't want, for the
hour—& you wanting such as fail you. A perverse world—especially
when I am appealed to from Buckland's to go & see (today) Mrs.
Berdan!—to which I feel like writing *Bedamned!*

Oct: 17*th* 1911.

ALS: Houghton MS Am 1094.9 (30)


*James consoles Mrs. Jones on her husband's poor health. He mentions Edith's motor trip,
as well as mutual friends' marriage problems and divorces. His last book,* The Outcry, *printed from a play, has gone into its fifth edition.*


Dearest Mary Cadwal.                          [The Reform Club]

    I have your 2 brave little letters, both referring to poor Fred's [her ex-
husband Frederic Rhinelander Jones] condition in Paris—or, as I should
more becomingly say, to Trixy's news thence of her Father's stricken state.
You & she must rather have "discounted" it—in the light, or the darkness,
of all these years; but you must be rather haunted, all the same, with the
pitiful & even tragic image & scene. Edith will probably have come back to
Paris (though I haven't yet heard) just in time to have *that* cup of bitterness

too offered to her lips—though Edith's cups are of such mingled mingled strain & the service of them, given her general situation, all incalculable. She has motored far & wide with Walter B. in North Italy & wound up with a week, or whatever, with the Behrensons'—or Berensons![47]—in Florence; or at least with the insidious B. himself, there being a bad split there too, I believe, between husband & wife. *Il n'y a que ça* [there is nothing but that—i.e., looming divorces] here now by the way, & in the most generally edifying circles: the Sydney Waterlows,[48] the Bertie Russells[49] (*she* an American sister of Mrs. Berenson's—though married these 15 years to Hon. Bertram,) have each their tale. But il ne s'agit pas de ça [this isn't about that]. One of your letters contained the report of your Mary's,[50] & "our" Hichens's[51] play—& it all sounds like the most (pecuniarily) expensive "shucks." But you showed me last winter how Shucks succeed in New York—il n'y avait que ça [there was nothing but that]—& I hope dear Mary will be able richly to regild her blason! "The Concert," by the way; which you showed me as an example; has collapsed *here* after 3 or 4 hopeless weeks—for in London there appear to be Shucks *and* Shucks— & that particular bundle at any rate wouldn't do. "The Outcry"[52]—as to which you ask—was written in 1909—the autumn before I was ill; and is simply the *printed* Play—the play I then did for Frohmann's Repertory Theatre of that ill-starred Season, which collapsed even as I collapsed—the

---

47. Mary Logan Whitall Smith Costello Berenson and Bernard Berenson (1865–1959), Lithuanian-born art critic, author and arbiter of taste who specialized in the Italian Renaissance.

48. Alice Pollock Waterlow (1876–1953) and Sir Sydney Phillip Waterlow (1878–1944). She was the daughter of HJ's friends Sir Frederick Pollock and Lady Georgina Defell Pollock. Sydney Waterlow was a British diplomat and scholar. They lived near HJ in Rye and eventually divorced, she marrying Orlando C. Williams in 1912.

49. Alys Russell and Bertrand Russell (1872–1970), British philosopher. In 1902, while working on *Principia Mathematica,* Russell tired of his marriage to Alys. Shortly after this he began an affair with prominent Bloomsbury socialite Ottoline Morrell. He and Alys eventually divorced.

50. Mary Anderson de Navarro (1859–1940) was an American actress. She married Antonio Fernando de Navarro (1860–1932), an Italian-English Papal Privy chamberlain, engineer, and writer.

51. Robert Smyth Hichens (1864–1950), British novelist and playwright.

52. *The Outcry* was HJ's last novel, published in London in 1911 by Methuen. In 1909 American producer Charles Frohmann asked James to write a play for his repertory season. James finished it in 1909 and revised it in 1910; it concerns American millionaires buying European art treasures. It was not produced on stage but was revised and published as a novel.

theatre going to pot under dire failures of Granville Barker,[53] Anthony Hope,[54] Bernard Shaw[55] &c; & my comedy unrehearsable because I was in bed & incapable of giving it the smallest attention. It was therefore not produced, they paid me a forfeit, I recovered my property—& put it away in a drawer. But I took it out again not long since, arranged it as you see it for perusal & publication & now have the amusement (& resulting lucre!) of seeing it the most "successful" thing I have ever put forth. It is going on to its 5*th* Edition, & I have already at the end of 6 or 8 weeks made more money by it than by any "mere book" (non-serialized) that I have ever published. The point is that if *that's* what they want I know intimately well how to do others of the same form—& no one else does in the smallest degree—either in this country or in America; so I may wallow in wealth by my monopoly yet! (So *little*—to me—represents wallowing.) And àpropos of this will you do me another small favour?—in the same connection. This is simply to send or take to the Scribners the address of Edward Sheldon,[56] our young friend of last winter—that they may give you a copy for him—or better still (& this is what I lucidly *mean,* post him one, as from *me*) with the address supplied by you attached. I write to them by this post that you *will* supply it if they will supply the book. I've seen in some American periodical that H. Rhodes[57] has produced another play—but fear it hasn't had a very good fortune: tell me if I am wrong—or even if I ain't. Yes, it's a great blessing to be *racommodé* [reconciled] with London again, dear old thing; & what is still better racommodé *by* it—which is more & more distinctly the case. So if *you* were only here!—but that way madness lies! I greet John Cadwal. very faithfully & think of that last day at the Black Moss as of the fair romance of my life! I have been to see poor brave Kindermann[58]—but failed of him. But he has touchingly written me—& I *shall* see him—! And I mustn't forget my thanks for the word

53. Harley Granville Granville-Barker (1877–1946), English actor, manager, and playwright.

54. Pseudonym of Sir Anthony Hope Hawkins (1863–1933), English novelist and playwright.

55. George Bernard Shaw (1856–1950), British playwright, novelist, critic, and prominent socialist.

56. Edward Sheldon (1886–1946), American playwright. His first successful play was *Salvation Nell* (1908). He was a friend of Minnie's and Edith Wharton's; he later helped adapt some of Wharton's work to stage and screen.

57. Harrison Garfield Rhodes (1871–1929), American writer of novels and plays.

58. HJ met the lame Kindermann at John Cadwalader's hunting party in Scotland in September 1911. He found him "gallant and touching."

about Collins, to whom I shall at once write. Fond love to Trix—& the unutterable to you from your clinging

*Célimare*

Nov. *6th* 1911

ALS: Houghton bMS Am 1094 (782)

*Most of his life James preferred London (or "Babylon") over New York, and here James compares the two cities. He shares concerns on the Whartons' marriage and indicts New York playwrights, especially "little mother's milk Sheldon, the fluid yet undried on his lips."*

LAMB HOUSE, RYE, SUSSEX.

Dearest Mary Cadwal. January *4th 1912.*

A liberal & beautiful letter from you projected its rich ray upon my rather dim path with the approach of the late mirthful Season. My path was dim, I mean, by reason of the thick chiaroscuro of the London midwinter (you really don't know how genial that is, or how rare & romantic it makes the firelight & lamplight at least;) for I am mainly steeped in that medium—I am down here for a few days only, to cock an eye at my small and blameless household. The dear old dusky Babylon, with its past scale & range as a field for circulation, is absolutely my present affinity & has done me more good than anything at all since I was first "took." I am almost forgetting that I have ever been *took,* & my reckoning is that I shall tend to forget it more & more. I have a couple of very modest & sequestered little rooms in the dim depths of Chelsea, which nobody (not even *you,* loved one,) knows the address of, & to which, the blest & cheap & unspeakably efficient London taxi aiding, I hie me each morning by 10.30, to commune with the Muse & my admirable lady-typist till 1:45. Thus I am back at work again, in the straightest, strongest, most savoury way that suits me best, & the sense of being so is an unutterable boon to me. I return to that convenience in three or for [*sic*] days—I can't stand *this* sequestration for any long period. London sins of course always by excess—the *too much* of the social assault &c; but I have it on easier terms than ever before, & its remedial virtues, in my present phase, much surpass its detrimental. If Boston & New York had only been for me a tenth as Babylonian—for the *lack* of monstrous bloody Babylon *was what was the matter with me*—I should have perked up, between you & Beatrix last

167

winter, to a very different tune. But better late than never—& that last walk to the bonnie Black Moss, the climax of my Millden days in September, was what most met my measure by its Babylonian Scale.——Our great Edith has been with us—came & went, with a great flap of her iridescent wings, some three weeks (or so) ago. She seemed very brave & bright & did, in her 10 days, exactly 9000 separate & mutually inconsistent things; but she liked it all, & though she had a rough & evil coming had a very balmy retreat. She has every way great success in England & could easily flourish here—save for gasping, herself, for the right conversational air; not only à la longue [in the long run] but in a very brief span. I have also heard from her since her return to Paris that Teddy had just announced himself for an early date; what has happened I know not, for the rest is silence—but I am holding my breath. She also mentioned (here) that she had lately received a decidedly epoch-making letter from Kinnicutt,[59] saying that the time was up & that she mustn't *think* of trying to make a common ménage with him (I mean have him on hand at all) after this. Which however doesn't *simplify*—the so much greater pressure needs to be made to bear on Teddy himself. It's a weary, wearing, a grim, grey tale. If dear John Cadwal does pass our way—I mean the way of Pall Mall &c, I will hurry to acclaim him all affectionately at the first hint of the same. I should think Egypt would be lovely for him—I could do with it myself. I went (for a Millden memory,) to see poor Kindermann in Golden Square one afternoon & found him in the midst of an extraordinary *mass* of fine old expensive-looking treasures of furniture and bric-à-brac: which made me afresh wonder where that quantity of such strictly limited (in amount) stuff does, everywhere, come from, & where it still more unconceivably avalanches *to*. For another Millden memory I hoped you'd tell me "all about" Tony & Mary & Hichens's play, on the near view, & how the devil those artless powers have operated—but I suppose, in truth, that they operate but by the more abysmal artlessness of their precious public. The dramatization of Bella Donna (Hichen's [*sic*] other product) has been a great success here for Alexander[60] and Mrs. Pat—a very long run, I be-

---

59. Dr. Francis P. Kinnicutt, American physician. He was first the Whartons' family doctor and then Teddy Wharton's personal physician. He thought Teddy's problems were largely mental ones and was never more than slightly hopeful he could be cured. In October 1911 he urged Edith to put him in a sanatorium rather than trying to live with him.

60. Sir George Alexander (1858–1918), the English actor who produced and starred in HJ's failed play *Guy Domville*.

lieve, menaces; so the gentle Hichens must be bathing in the Pactole,[61] though another fellow has in this case made the play—which I am told is beneath criticism. Do you ever see, this winter, little mother's milk Sheldon—I mean with that fluid yet undried on his lips?—or black Harrison Rhodes so the reverse of milky or dewy or rosy? I hope that if the former is again in the arena it's with a better play, and if the latter is it's with a luckier one. On looking back at your letter I see John Cadwal. was sailing on the 20*th* Dec., so he will have had time to be in London without notifying me. As he won't be there (at this season,) when I get back in a few days hence, I shall, to my regret, have missed him. I hang about you and Trix both, I press you to my heart and am all your inexpressible and irrepressible

Célimare

ALS: Houghton bMS Am 1094 (802)

*Although James's health declines, he can work again, and he wants to see her in London, if possible. Edith Wharton's recent visit has been the great event of his summer.*

Dearest Mary Cadwal.                    LAMB HOUSE, RYE, SUSSEX.

Beautiful tribute has come from you, to the enrichment of my carnal consciousness & the simplification of my interviews with my cook. "There's the grouse, you know, sir." "Oh yes, thank God, there's the grouse. That'll do!" And the conference is blissfully shortened—for which I bless & thank you. We make 'em last a long, long time—& they contribute to *my* duration: which I take, dearest, is what you desire. That remarkable phenomenon goes on in spite of some sharp recent worriments of a pectoral, anginal & cardiac kind, over which I triumph, really, each time by (carefully taken) persistences of slow but continuous "exercise"; that is discreet but adequate, & always directly *remedial,* locomotion & circulation (on my own times & in my own way.) So more than ever my agina, *mon agine,* seems of the "false or simulated" order known familiarly to medical science, & indeed to which my Doctor tells me 9 out of 10 cases of the disorder do belong. The heart, in these cases, isn't intimately or directly concerned in them—but other physiological & nervous conditions. This is compatible with their being quite damnable at their worst—but I have had them only 3 or 4 times at their worst; in fact only once at their *real*

---

61. In Greek mythology, the river Pactolus was where Midas bathed to try and rid himself of his golden touch. Figuratively, *un pactole* is a gold mine or a source of great wealth.

worst—when I did think que j'allais passer [that I was going to die]. As I didn't pass, but got quick relief, for the time, from nitro-glycerin, here I am to tell the tale; & I am quite steadily back at work, & in other ways better than for 3 or 4 years. So I mean (D.V.) to get better of this botheration too. Being able to work again is an *enormous* help; especially in the dismalness of the infamous Season, which we seem to hear, however, in these parts, will have been less dreadful & deluvian, less raging & freezing, on your bonnie braesides than in our afflicted zone. If it has been *as* insufferable, heaven pity you & your houseful all. I impart to you all the above intimate facts about myself by reason simply of the love that I believe & hope you bear me; & not at all to worrit you, for there are precious mitigations, rifts of light & reassurance, in my affair. Only please keep all for your exclusive consumption. I do dreadfully yearn to see you—& reflect with woe that when I probably have to spend 2 or 3 days in town between the 11*th* & the 15*th* you won't be there. But we will patch up something for later on—I must absolutely get 48 hours with you. Do give me some idea of your dates & doings. I hope the burden of Millden *isn't* this year greater than the current agreement has mostly kept it from being for you in the past—but such a summer (heaven save the mark,) is capable de tout [of anything]. Edith's prodigious visit will have been the great event of mine—she rode the whirlwind, she played with the storm, she laid waste whatever of the land the other raging elements had spared, she consumed in 15 days what would have served to support an ordinary Christian community (I mean to regale & occupy & excite them) for about ten years. Her powers of devastation are ineffable, her repudiation of repose absolutely tragic, & she was never more brilliant & able & interesting! All *that* for your privatest ear too. Do give a gleam of your news—some morning when the braeside has palled on you & you can take your pen in hand. Is Beatrix again this year the terror of the forest & the scourge of the mountain? I send her my most excellent love. And I am your fondest, faithfullest

Célimare

Sept. 1st 1912.

*James battles shingles, a painful skin disease. He also shares a detailed account of Teddy Wharton's wild exploits on the Continent and fears that Teddy is close to a complete breakdown. Minnie has seen his nephew Harry, who is in New York working for the Rockefeller Institute for Medical Research.*

[*Dictated*]

January 31., 1913.

My dear Mary Cadwal!

I have waited a bit to thank you for your last sign of benevolence (of Jan. 7th.,) in the hope of being able to dispense with this damned (and yet so blest) mechanism—really my greatest aid to life in these days; but the rigours of my state are still such that I am thankful for every kind or degree of easing-off, my crawling out of my deep hole remains so gradual and retarded a matter, even if it be, under a resolute optimism, a more or less obscurely measurable one. You say you have "a feeling that I am not well"; which you may well have had, my dear old friend, any time these last five or six months, and especially these last accurst four; I must have more or less recorded for you at my last communicating (by the machinery) that I was then horribly ridden by virulent Herpes (or as the vulgar say Shingles;[62]) which was an odious and an endless enough history in itself, all October and November, without the still more infernal complications and aggravations that set in on top of it, grafting themselves on all the poor ravaged Herpetic tract, and making the plot thicken to the last tragic intensity. I am still much in the quite indescribably harsh tangle of all that affliction; relatively better, through slow shedding of some of the worst conditions, but much burdened yet with pain and disability—even though absolutely determined and I believe destined, to work little by little out of them: such a snail's pace does it sometimes withal seem! The power of my original dire complaint (and with me it came on top of a previous most trying physical ordeal) to hang on and hold out and keep up its poisonous ravage is a kind of thing one can't "go into", out of the pages of a Pathological Work; especially as its final very damnedest action and resource is to produce a very hell in one's neighbouring stomach and abdominal parts, where it sets up a state of affairs—well, over which I must again drop the veil! The grafting of the most intolerable distension, with all the sore suffering that means, upon so much of the region already made desolate, reduced to a state of chronic laceration, by the long Herpetic rage, has been for me, as you may imagine, a Treat of the first magnitude—and a feast at

---

62. Shingles *(herpes zoster)* is a common viral infection that attacks various nerve trunks and the areas of the skin these nerves supply. The symptoms of shingles tend to be more severe in older people, as was the case with HJ. Even after the skin lesions subside, sufferers can experience many months of pain. HJ refers to this in this letter, when he tells Mary Cadwalader that he has shed some of the worst symptoms but is still in great pain.

which I am still condemned more or less to sit. My days have got gradually better, but my nights from 8 o'clock on, when I have regularly to tear off my clothes, these by that time unbearable, and tumble into bed, continue to be most evil; though less so, no doubt, than during all the weeks and weeks when, getting up by 11, I had to collapse again, under the same scourge, by 4 or 5 or 6 at latest. One grows thankful for small mercies—and let me allow handsomely that I have come in for the comparatively great one of being able to come up to town and settle in these quarters, directly upon the River, in quiet sympathetic Chelsea: where I hope to maintain, for whatever of Life may yet be left in me, a salutary winter home. I have taken a lease of this little place, and was able to flounder in, some three weeks ago, with odds and ends of chairs and tables and beds drawn from the overflow of Lamb House—thanks mainly to the blest efficiency and devotion of my faithful servants. Here I am for the next several months—here even I hope I shall be when you come out, as I still more hope you will, for your great annual exploit. There's one thing you can count on at least in relation to poor dear Célimare, that the future (to say nothing of the present) conditions of his being, if his being is to go on, absolutely preclude any other déplacement than the mere little budge from here to L.H. and from L.H. back here. People write to me from America "If you are not on the Continent"—as if, bless their innocent hearts, there were to be ever more any more question of that than of my being at the north Pole. The Continent has seen me, God grant, for the last time of all my days—and that by itself brings with it a certain peace. It brings with it just now, alas, that our Best Friend in Paris has been these several months much shrouded from my vision—all the more that I have heard very little directly from her; though of course, with all that has been going on, she is in my very acutest thoughts and anxieties. I had but a few days since very straight, and quite intelligent, news of her from the Walter Gays,[63] who have been for a little in London (now gone,) and whose report didn't on the whole still one's solicitude. I mean the mere fact that T. [Edith Wharton's husband Teddy Wharton] is so insanely (for that's what it distinctly comes to) and so invidiously, not to say so odiously, resonant, without her seeing him or being able to get, should she wish, in direct touch with him, acts of course cruelly on her nerves and horridly clouds her life. For he is truly as elatedly, and swaggeringly and extravagantly, mad as he can be—

---

63. Walter Gay (1856–1937) was a Boston-born painter who lived in France. His wife Matilda first knew Edith Wharton in New York when both were young. The Gays helped Wharton with her volunteer work for the military in France during World War I.

whatever duration this particular phase may have. A letter from Monte Carlo, that I got from him but 3 or 4 days ago and sent on to E. (it was fortunately not abusive of her) abundantly proves that he is just noisily and topsyturvily, and alas vulgarly, to say nothing of ruinously in the financial sense, off his poor little head. I had heard from him 2 or 3 times before (he has been in London and elsewhere here save for the Monte Carlo dash,) but I have happily escaped seeing him, and now he talks of sailing for N.Y. on April 4th. Every sound of him is the maddest possible swagger and brag about his exploits and conquests, the first with his prodigious and unique American motor-car—100 miles an hour—in which it is quite open to him to kill himself; the second by his effect on the ladies, especially of the variety-theatres, wherever he goes, and among whom it's equally probably that he will soon find himself, pecuniarily speaking, nu comme un ver [naked as a worm]. The Walter G.s gave me the most extraordinary account of his dashing out to them in the country from Paris (for he *was* in Paris for a few days, unseen of E.) for very calumnious, but above all childishly, or rather crazily, swaggering purposes; during which one of the first things he did was to say: "Have you seen my gold garters?" and then to whisk up his trousers and show them in effect his stockings held up with circles of massive gold! That is the kind of thing—but only grotesque and, as I say, vulgar, and above all self-destructive—if it doesn't pass into a worse phase. My strong impression is that the only phase it *can* pass into is that of both utter pecuniary and personal smash and collapse; in which he will be, besides wholly denuded, completely abject and appealing, completely by way of crying and "making up", till something else happens. To which I may add that the Walter Gs. spoke to me, with emphasis, of his showing, facially, strong marks of "la débauche" [debauchery], vinous and other, and of that terribly and distressfully insane character of his eyes, which he has of recent years, though especially while he was really suffering, it would appear, from great physical pain, always badly shown.[64] The strange thing is (though of course you know it) that the painful condition of his teeth and feet has been completely cured, as to the latter, by the removal of the former, a very wonderful fact; on which he dilated of course at great length to the G.s, wanting above all to know if they found the form of his face unfavourably affected; with other questions not unconnected with a strange personal vanity. But enough of this depressing person and ques-

---

64. Edith Wharton wrote a short story called "The Eyes" (1910) in which the main character's eyes reveal his insanity. It was later in this year (1913) that she initiated divorce proceedings against Teddy.

tion, of which I earnestly hope you may not, in case he does soon return to America, have again too much of a view.

I rejoice that you have seen something of my admirable nephew Harry,[65] on whom I have enjoined to see as much of *you* as he can. Of course his case is that he is up to his neck in onerous work and really great responsibilities, and that I imagine he is feeling extremely the strain of it, at this period of initiation; to which the big social strain and pace of N.Y., compared to the Boston pitch, adds itself very heavily. The more you see of him, at any rate, the higher opinion you will have of him in every way; as to character, ability, judgment, personal charm and everything! But I must pull up—I seem to have emptied my budget. The great thing is that you should think of me with large allowances, for this long last visitation has been, and considerably remains, in the nature of a scourge, which I can hope only gradually to throw off. I am having at last better medical advice, I think, than I have ever had to do with at all; so far, that is, as medical advice is much of a benefit to me at all. Getting out of my hole simply takes all the doing on my *own* part that I can bring to the job—and leaves me with little or no power for any other doing whatever; save, by the blessing of heaven, a pretty regular two hours and a half of work in the forenoon. The recovery of my power for this, so long eclipsed, does me more good than all else put together; and it's an inestimable boon that this strictly sufficient stretch of the morning should happen to be, physically speaking, my best time. I seem to infer that you and Beatrix are not without your best times either—among which I count especially the times you administer to others. I shall absolutely now take means to put a stop to your being drenched with these accurst Round Table notifications. It "kind of comes over me" with horror that I shouldn't have left you so long exposed, and my only excuse is in the long and dire condition which has really caused me to *cultivate* the art of neglecting everything but getting better if I can. Besides I have wished my membership to last for a certain decent period. Now I shall take immediate steps to put an end to it. I embrace you both and am yours all faithfully

Célimare.

TLS: Houghton bMS Am 1094 (809)

---

65. William James's first son Henry (1879–1947) had been a successful lawyer but started a new position as manager for the Rockefeller Institute for Medical Research in New York.

*James thanks her for yet another gift of grouse and for her kindnesses to his niece Peggy. Peggy has just returned from Stratford-on-Avon, where she and the William Dean Howells visited the Shakespeare festival. After motoring about England with his uncle Henry, Harry returns to New York.*

Dearest Mary Cadwal!                                                      August 23 *1913*

Beautiful & bountiful all your doings: I am reported to of a wonderful box of grouse, out of your tragic paucity, & with the rich *secousse* [shock] of this still upon me I listen to Peg's communication of an admirably kind letter from you providing apparently, more or less, for her whole material future. The *trouble* of it, taken by you, is too beautiful—we are all, she & I & Harry, more touched by it than we can say. She will of course acknowledge your goodness with prompt & unlimited effusion. I somehow find her such a natural & congruous subject for rendered kindnesses—she is so dear, & so beautifully & touchingly *undemanding,* & unpreying a thing, & her being with me here so soothed & sustained & rejoiced me these weeks, that I like to see something come to her, even from far Forfarshire, in *return,* as it were. So be thanked most tenderly & all round. I feel, for the bonnie birds, all the grateful appreciation of a thrifty maitre de maison [head of the household] who finds his own provisioning (that looks through my dim glasses a little like *poisoning,* but it isn't) by so much lightened! Peg has just come back from 3 or 4 days of the Stratford-on-Avon Shakespeare month, or whatever it's called, spent with the kind benighted Howellses, who are putting in (*he* at 76) 4 August weeks of twice-a-day at the stuffy theatre & no sitting room at the stuffier & crowdeder hotel—she, Peggy, however much amused & regaled & thrilled. Harry, who has been with me now a number of delightful days, & has liberally motored me for long lovely reaches on several, leaves alas on Friday next & sails for N. Y. on the morrow. Peg pays another small visit or two, but substantially remains through September, bless her. Exceedingly beautiful & bland, though dry to excess, all this recent period here; & I take it that even you children of the mist, if you haven't grouse (save what you part with to me,) have at least weather. I greatly grieve to think of poor John C. so abominably floored—what a ravaged victim of the insatiable demon. I wonder how he bears up, & can so elaborately, expensively chance it, at all. The complicated, the *ponderous,* grievances of the great! I send him the assurance of all my poor vain sympathy & grateful fidelity. I seem alas to have none of that *Birthday* literature *here:* I *must* have some at

Carlyle Mansions—put away—but woefully can't get at it in any delegated way, & am thus ungraciously able to serve you *now.* Stay, I can write to the *Printers*—& I will do so—for 1/2 a dozen copies; & so, with a *little* delay, you shall be served! Voilà. But this has brought me to long past midnight. It is in fact 1:15 a.m. Your ever-fond

Célimare.

ALS: Houghton bMS Am 1094 (812)

*Edith Wharton and widow Bessie Lodge visited James. Edith has begun a new novel* (The Custom of the Country) *and might buy a country home north of London. James laments Lady Hadfield's aging, as it is "the cruellest thing in nature" that beautiful women must age.*

LAMB HOUSE  RYE  SUSSEX

Dearest Mary Cadwal! Sept: 22d *1913.*

Very blest & beautiful your letter. I do greatly feel the loss of the really admirable young Niece, admirable for her soothing interesting presence & the general so happy "combination" & affinity with the aged yet all-appreciative Uncle. But she will come back to L. H. even as piously, with the revolving year, as you & Trix come back to Millden—this at least I trust. I grieve over your own amputation of that fine filial member.[66] But what a magnificently active a member it is—& how she must of course live up to her high destinies. (I believe there's an e too much in that word—but it makes it the more nobly fatal.) To console me for *my* amputations the transcendent Edith arrived yesterday by motor from Le Tourguet (Paris—Plage, near Boulogne—or rather, I believe, an hour, by car, from it,) in company with the beautiful & touching Bessie Lodge,[67] to whom her kindness must be *such* a boon! & after lunching with me, coffeeing & cigaretting in the garden &c—a very lovely day—went on up to London in order to look at Coopersale[68] once more & I imagine this time really decide to acquire it—that is meet the conditions (pecuniary) imposed—which are not heavy ones, given the place. I shall know tomorrow, as they

---

66. HJ refers here to the marriage of her daughter Beatrix to Max Farrand (1869–1945), history professor at Yale and scholar of constitutional history.

67. Matilda Elizabeth Frelinghuysen Davis (Mrs. George "Bay" Cabot) Lodge. Her husband was a son of the Massachusetts Senator Henry Cabot Lodge and a poet. In 1909, at the age of thirty-six, he died.

68. A property near Mary (Mrs. Charles) Hunter's Hill Hall, next to Epping Forest. Edith Wharton thought of buying it and moving to England, but she later abandoned the negotiations.

announced themselves as taking me in again on their return to là-bas [there] via Folkestone. Edith is more wonderful than ever, seemed very well, has just begun a new Novel, of which the idea greatly appeals to her, & has lost her worn & harassed look. Bessie L. is really lovely—& I wonder at her not meeting some fresh espousals—in spite of her being so much children'd & so little financed. But it's a most muddled world!—I rejoice to gather that John C. has had a better time than at first seemed to threaten & that the whole big business has again proved worthwhile— seeing that it's you more than any one thing who has made it so. It's interesting to hear that Lady Hadfield[69] is doing her best to help—a bad best though that rather sounds like, with your vivid descriptions of her pathetic struggle with dilapidation. However, I've always thought it the cruellest thing in nature that beautiful women shld. have to become what they sooner or later do—& I don't wonder that *she* so thinks it. But what a terrifically *losing* battle to feel herself fighting.——The point of *this* mean- while is that I intensely hope you will be able to give me 24 hours, you & your kin. *Do* strain every nerve for it if it's humanly possible. You seem to be cut down to the quick again in respect to London—a really dreadful doom I think it always for you; but you maybe have a margin, mayn't you, if you'd only leave the moor with a certain alertness? However, you will say I talk at my ease! All I want you to feel is that you're an object of great longing to your clinging dear old

*Célimare.*

ALS: Houghton bMS Am 1094 (813)


*James meditates on "the great gobbling mouthfuls of Time."*

Dearest Mary Cadwal.                    LAMB HOUSE   RYE   SUSSEX

  Célimare is indeed disappointed, & this even though he had fairly faint hopes, knowing how very cruelly & unimaginatively your kind kind kins- man *does* scrimp you (heaven deliver us from the benevolent Vampire!) I had a sneaking ghost of a thought that you *might* squeeze in 24 hours; but of course I see the difference Trix's absence makes—to *you;* & how nothing makes any difference—for your benefit, to *him*. What is *most* melancholy is the pretty dismal law under which any "running-up" is now impossible

---

69. She may have been Frances Belt of Philadelphia, who in 1899 married Sir Robert Abbot Hadfield (1858–1940), British metallurgist. They founded a hospital in France soon after the beginning of World War I.

to me; I have to live so very, very gently, & shall have been here from July to December (when I go up to stay, only) without so much as looking at a train. That represents a portentous shrinkage—& these postponements to the "next Junes" (at our ages—*ours*—so to speak!) don't abate the sense of it. Lord, the great gobbling *mouthfuls* of Time—& the board on which so little remains swept clear! But I didn't mean to wail, but only to—well, *waft:* so behold every benediction & form of tenderness sadly & resignedly blown at you; or *resigningly* at least—for there was a difference. May your great courage & all your generous arts carry you comfortably on. I find the months do amazingly melt, more & more—but unfortunately so much melts *with* them. You will have found a word from me awaiting you at Symonds's[70] by now—it was there to kind of lure you on. Alas vain lure! But let us buck up. Edith's image has in a manner become terrific & troublous to me—a figure of entire & unmitigated *agitation;* out of which "literary art" is by way of coming—all in so confounding & upsetting a fashion. How I wouldn't *be* her—for all her possessions! *Do* make me a sign for dear old 21! And do keep hold of Harry—& eke of Peg!—all you can! I pray the Lusitania will *happily* speed you! And that something or other will do the same *back*—to your fond old

Célimare.

Oct: 1st: 1913.

ALS: Houghton bMS Am 1094 (815)

*James advises "Mummy" on coping with her daughter Beatrix's forthcoming marriage to Max Farrand: she can live with him if she feels bereft.*

LAMB HOUSE   RYE   SUSSEX

Dearest Mary Cadwal. October 31st 1913

Trix most kindly wrote me the other day & in answering her, & so earnestly congratulating, I sent you a message—which message can only have been that I would speedily write you. This isn't quite speedily, but it's very, very partakingly—& nothing is in the least speedy with me now. The great point is that I don't think I was even moved to say "what will become of Mummy?"—for the simple reason that nothing *ever* becomes of Mummy but that Mummy throws herself heroically & with the last gener-

---

70. Perhaps a relative of John Addington Symonds (1840–1893), famous Victorian writer and early pioneer of homosexual studies. He and his wife had three daughters, one of whom, Dame Katharine Symonds Furse, served with distinction as a nurse in France during World War I.

osity into the breach; & alas that apart from this graceful habit of hers she's incapable of making for her interest in her daughter the condition that that daughter shall not be a married lady. I see you, dearest Mary, on the contrary, find the child's change of state of the very liveliest interest & feeling that for yourself as well it will be a change of state to a fond *extension* of sympathy & confidence. So I'm not taking any view of the case but that you are seeing it all as gain to yourself of general human "fun" rather than as loss—which is what I all affectionately want you to know. I believe so in the married lady's having a better time of it always & *quand même* [and despite being married] (than the unmarried,) that I can't think of you not, under the same conviction, having your sense of bereavement very much sweetened & even spiced. Furthermore if you feel *very* bereft you'll just come straight over here & live with Célimare—for the condition of an unmarried *gentleman* is sometimes one that, when perfectly hopeless, can't be improved upon. Won't the adventure—I mean Trix's & its *contre-coup* [repercussion] on yourself—somehow give you more *freedom* (which I at the same time indeed recognize that you often perversely don't like nearly so well as some double dose of devoted bondage, if the latter can only swallow you up—or rather be swallowed down by you—unreservedly enough. I make out a dreadful danger of your being handed over now more bound & gagged than ever to genial J.C.—in which event I shall not be an inch the gainer; but my imagination insists on recoiling from that.) Edith was here today—having motored over to tea with me (Percy Lubbock[71] in attendance) from Folkestone (she returns to Paris tomorrow after 10 days in London at Windsor &c: Coopersale is slowly closing round her—slowly but surely, I think; & a jolly good thing too, probably; for it's a wonderful fit to her case & her need;) which is to say that we talked of you all three— the 3 of *you*—most harmoniously, & that she even alluded to the possibility of her coming over to give the child her nuptial blessing: but you will know much more about this. If she does it will be very beautiful & gallant of her, surely. I like it's being so near—& if it only thereby gives the pair of you more obsessionally much to do, "the thrill, the joy of life" will kind of be in that for you too—& perhaps even your coming out to Célimare will be brought proportionally nearer. It greatly makes *him,* alas, wish he weren't so far off. He would tumble in with you, with such zest, to the best of his poor ability—were he only more round the corner. He takes the

---

71. Percy Lubbock (1879–1965), English editor and author. He knew James, Edith Wharton, and other famous writers well. He edited the first two volume edition of James's letters (1920).

liveliest interest in Mr. Max Farrand—what a jolly name!—& only wants to pat him, grandfatherly, on the back. "When the hurly-burly's done" you will perhaps write me a little, philosophically, about it; I don't expect a word before that. I go up to 21 Carlyle Mansions, Cheyne Walk S.W., for the winter, 3 weeks hence; & I am dearest Mary Cadwal, your more than ever fond & faithful old

*Henry James.*

ALS: Houghton bMS Am 1094 (816)

*James thinks Minnie Jones should have benefited from her cousin John Cadwalader's will in return for the years of service she gave him. He wishes she could come to London, even without Trix and without her "Service."*

CARLYLE MANSIONS    CHEYNE WALK    S.W.

Dear old friend! April 11*th* 1914

I didn't write you when I heard of John Cadwalader's death, because I found myself instinctively disposed to await more light on that event or on what might follow it—this in the first place (& I had written you not very long before.) Then too I received at the moment itself a letter from Tony Navarro, inciting me to such almost hysterical grief in the connection, & taking for granted on my part such lamentations & woe, that I think my faculty of expression on the subject had pretty well exhausted itself in replying to *him,* & I wasn't prepared at the time to go further. At present, at all events, I take a certain satisfaction in having stayed my hand—it rather soothes me that I *didn't* write to you as I might have written under the impulse of the hour; & *that* is more particularly what I want to say to you now, though I have a certain difficulty in telling you why. I am moved to this confession of my not regretting my backwardness by the accident of my having a few days ago met Mrs. Berenson here (at tea at her brother's, Logan Pearsall Smith's;[72]) who mentioned to me a fact that I had taken the liberty of wondering about—with a good deal of intensity, though it involved a question that was no absolute or literal business of your poor clinging old Célimare's. No, it was none of my business (in advance at any rate,) whether J. C.'s [John Cadwalader's] testamentary dispositions were, or weren't, likely to betray some practical acknowledgment of your & Trix's long observation of kinship & fidelity of social service to him; & yet my imagination had hovered, insistently, around the possibility—out of the

---

72. Logan Pearsall Smith (1865–1946), literary critic and writer.

incorrigible & indiscreet zeal of my thought on your behalf & my general tenderness of interest in you. Well, the said Mrs. Berenson answered the inquiry I put to her in connection with this by such a statement of the case, according to her belief, as sent a chill to my vitals—&, convinced as I am that her impression was correct, I have kept meddling more & more in the matter, in an intensely sympathetic visionary way, in a deeply resentful & sadly stupefied way, as the few days have gone on. And thus I have had to write to you, & to write to you in this sore sense, & to relieve myself, even to the last crudity, by feeling how right was my instinct to lay no garland on our friend's tomb till I had made sure whether he had done what I expected of him. All this, I needn't say, from the point of view of my own pure intermeddling (of spirit,) & without in the least presuming to impute sentiments or judgments to yourself. I don't impute them to you now in the least, but I do, I freely confess, permit myself, within my own right of fond fancy for you, to be very considerably sickened. I am told that, childless & "unencumbered," he left a very big fortune—& on this I think back toward the immense mitigations of dreariness, the immense as-sistances to living & doing, that he went on owing you both. Then the strange show that men so often finally make of themselves overcomes & floors me again, & I fall to howling & gnashing my teeth. You & Trix, in your decent dignity, will have done nothing of this—so let me have enjoyed the vain luxury off my own bat. The whole circumstance makes me want most consumedly to see you, dearest old friend—& yet perhaps simply overclouds that possibility. I wish you were coming this year at last on your own hook, coming for a little free commerce, such as you hadn't had in all that involved time, with our poor dear old London. And yet without Trix & without your "Service," I somehow think of such a pil-grimage as rather lone & lorn, rather bleak & bare, for you. Oh it's all very dreadful—but a few lines from you might make me feel a little better— though they can't make me, dearest Mary Cadwal, more all-affectionately & tenderly yours,

Henry James

ALS: Houghton MS Am 1094.9 (32)

*A militant suffragette has taken a meat cleaver and slashed John Singer Sargent's portrait of James, which was on display at the Royal Academy. James will soon "be back on my hook," that is, restored and hung again in the gallery. He invites Minnie to play hopscotch with him on the streets of London.*

Dearest Mary Cadwal.

It has been a joy to get your cable with its blest "sailing 23*d*" & its tear of pity for my facial wounds.[73] Let me say at once in respect to the latter that though the foul hag did her damnedest her bloody gashes *can,* it appears, still be made good by the subtlety of the consummate restorer. Such at least is the view, the hope, entertained: I am under masterly treatment & by the time you arrive perhaps, or very shortly after, I shall be back on my hook & in receipt of a great expected affluence of the shillings of the curious—a greater "draw" than ever; for the portrait is so extraordinarily admirable & distinguished that it was already, easily, *the* one gem of the show (little as that by itself is saying:) unless indeed I except Derwent Wood's splendid bust, infinitely applauded & bought by the Chantrey fund, to spend its immortality in our charming Chelsea Tate Gallery. As I neither painted the portrait nor chiselled the marble myself I am free to indulge in these appreciations. But I really appreciate more intensely than anything else the delicious prospect of seeing you at the end of the month, & I rejoice to believe this will still catch you at dear old 21 in time to speed you a little on your enlightened way. I shall be in town till the end of June, & if à quelque chose malheur est bon [something can be learned from adversity] I do earnestly trust that you are going to be free to have for the 1*st* time for so many years a fine free monthful of our beloved metropolis. Don't come simply to tell me that you are "off to Aix," or some other fond invention of the Devil. Come to play with me—on the pavé de Londres [the cobblestones of London]—so far as my aged hamperings permit—& we will do hop-scotch as we haven't been able to do it for so many years. As it will be literally hop-Scotland my figure isn't so much out. I've had so little news of you of any intimate sort during all these months that I don't in the least know on what footing, physical or spiritual, all the occurrences have left you—& fear (from your case at the time of the nuptials,) that cares & things *may* be in question. If so may they indeed be well applied—but may poor old Célimare be a little of a poultice 1*st.* I am doing very decently well myself, considering what I have to do *with.* My niece Peggy & a young

---

73. The portrait of James by John Singer Sargent, painted in oils to commemorate James's seventieth birthday and on display in the Royal Academy in London, was slashed three times with a meat cleaver by a Mrs. Mary Wood in May 1914. Mrs. Wood didn't know James, but she assaulted his portrait because she had learned the painting was worth seven hundred pounds. She told a police court that a woman would not have received that much money for art, and thus the painting was a symbol of female oppression. In the first part of the letter James refers to the subsequent repair of Sargent's work.

Portland, Me., cousin are established for the time in a furnished flat in these mansions, & P. herself is really a great help & interest & a blessing. Of our great Edith I haven't for years had so little news as this all winter. But she soars, swims, she infinitely circles, & will some time alight near us again more vividly than ever. Come & see—yet see above all your fond

Célimare

May 10th. 14.

P.S. I shall write & thank Trix for her so gentle notice of the dispatch to me of a memento of our late friend as soon as I have more news of it. I am greatly touched by his act.

ALS: Houghton MS Am 1094.9 (33)

*Although James's grammar has gone to pieces, his affection for Mrs. Jones has not. Owen Wister has visited him. Mrs. Wharton has returned from Africa and plans to tour France with Walter Berry, but James will crouch unnoticed in Rye.*

LAMB HOUSE   RYE   SUSSEX

Dearest Mary Cadwal. July 16th 1914.

Friday Aug. 14th will do to a charm; especially if followed by as many other days, the very fullest number (as—that! are!) possible. (My grammar has gone to pieces, but what is grammar compared to fond affection?) It's a blessing & a charm to hear from you & to be able to hang again on your vivid particulars. I came down here at last on the 13th, scrambling out of London heat & dust & importunity with unspeakable relief & finding in this dear little nook again all I could ask of it. Today, before lunch arrives Owen Wister,[74] for 2 nights only, thank goodness—speaking gracelessly—he revealed himself to me in London a month ago in so strangely provincialised a form! Peggy, Aleck [Alexander James, son of William and Alice] & M.P. [Margaret Payson] come for 2 or 3 nights a little hence, & then Peg alone to stay continuous & be here when you come. It's funny to see you both contest sweetly for the *grenier* [attic or garret]—but as she is nearer than you to the "vingt uns" [twenties] when one is supposed to y'être "bien" [to feel good] I fear she may carry off the prize. Very interesting your mention of Edith & her high tension—which affects me as of a height so beyond any reach of mine in these old days that I ask myself how I shall be able to keep peace or terms with her at all. She "minds" greatly the absence of a telephone at Stocks—that I had already heard—the

---

74. Owen Wister (1860–1938), American lawyer, musician, and writer. He wrote *The Virginian* (1902) and other books. His grandmother was famous Shakespearean monologist Fanny Kemble. In 1905 Wister gave James a tour of South Carolina.

183

Wards[75] had *kept* it off in order to spare the outside aggression. Walter B. [Berry], in London for a couple of days a short time since, dined with me, & related that, returning to P., he was at once to start with E. on a fresh motor-tour *dans le midi* [in the South of France] &c to fill up the time before she came to "Stocks." And he spoke of it as the most natural violence in the world both for her & for himself: he scarce drawing breath on returning from Asia, & she ditto on returning from Africa. It's very wonderful, but destroys all my sense of proportion! Enfin [Anyway]—à la guerre comme à la guerre [in war as in war]! I *hope* she will crowd the gentle Stocks with the Parisianary—I shall the more securely crouch unnoticed here: which is all in the world I want do. Arrive then to crouch *with* me! But amusez-vous bien [enjoy yourself], as a precaution, meanwhile—Ever your faithfullest old

Célimare.

ALS: Houghton MS Am 1094.9 (35)


*Fearing that his old friend will not be able to leave Paris, James awaits her eagerly on the other side of the Channel.*


LAMB HOUSE   RYE   SUSSEX

Dearest & dearest Mary Cadwal.                        *Aug. 6th 1914.*

I have at last heard from Symonds about you, & it's a cruel shock to learn that you are held up in Paris at such inconvenience & in such possible embarrassment. I haven't reached out at you before because I haven't known where or how to reach till this day, & now that I *am* reaching how do I know at all when you will be touched to awareness of it? I have just written to Edith after learning that White[76] is at Stocks & getting into communication with him about her,—& there's a certain comfort to me in thinking that you are practically together & mutually reassuring. You'll get over [the Channel] with a certain further patience, by some lapse in the density of traffic. Meanwhile I am with you in thought & imagination more affectionately & partakingly than I can say. From day to day (till 2 or 3 ago) have I been expecting to hear from you that you *had* gallantly pushed over. Unutterably dismal to me the whole descent (in a night) of

---

75. Mary Augusta Arnold Ward (1851–1920) and Thomas Humphry Ward (1845–1926). She was a famous Victorian novelist; he was an Oxford don and writer. They lived at Stocks.

76. Probably Henry White, the American diplomat who from 1907 to 1909 had been the ambassador to France. His wife, Margaret Stuyvesant Rutherfurd, had been a good friend of Edith Wharton's in Newport, Rhode Island.

this pall horror—I mean both the size & the suddenness, the *ease,* of our plunge back into barbarism; & through my sickened state with it all I haven't had lucidity of motion. Otherwise I should sooner—3 days ago—have appealed to Symonds. It has taken me 24 hours to get their telegraphic answer—& now when are you going to get this or am *I* to get anything from yourself? Heaven send the hour—if heaven is in the least thinkable in these infamies. As I have just said to Edith, the blackness would be here too dense if this country hadn't so admirably rallied. The Irish tension dropped in one hour, & the attitude on behalf of France & Belgium declared itself, on Germany's last answer, in a *minute.* Those are facts that help—though they don't assist me to see *you* save in the mind's eye. *There,* however, you are all right—brave & serene as I want, for your convenience, to think of you—let alone for mine. But I can't write you more till I have some sign of your possession of the present. *Then* shall you hear more freely. Your room awaits you with an intensity—! Good night, dearest old friend! Oh for a homely fact or two—! for your faithfully fondest old

Célimare.

ALS: Houghton MS Am 1094.9 (36)

*James prays Mrs. Jones has crossed the Channel today, and he gives her explicit directions on taking the train to Rye. The beauty of the English countryside during this time of war is "a monstrous heartless irony of nature."*

LAMB HOUSE    RYE    SUSSEX

Dearest Mary Cadwal.          August (midnight) 13*th* 1914.

Your letter came almost normally to these shores—yet I fear my last to yourself, though 3 or 4 days old at this writing, is still on the way to you. Your freshly admirable one of Tuesday is with me here—by 7.30 this Thursday night—but my own 1*st* of days & days back must have taken at least a week to reach you by Tuesday. I am praying like thunder that you *may* have crossed this day, but the absence of any wire up to this late hour—it is now the evening's end—plunges me, I fear again, but into hope deferred. *Do* turn out to have come by tomorrow, Friday's, facility, & do find, blessedly find, this awaiting you there at the strained Symonds's. We shall press you here to the most heaving bosoms—& lay you upon the steadiest bed. There's an *enormous* margin of room for you, &, even if there wasn't, Aleck is but nominally & vainly here; he spends the whole series of the week-days much more interestedly in town—has now again been away since Monday. There are 2, & only 2, good weekday trains down here—we in general find those quite enough. One leaves Charing Cross at *11. a.m.* & reaches this *1.30;* the second leaves at *4.25* & reaches this at *6* ditto—being thus ½ an hour faster. By both you of course change at Ashford. The Sunday communication is poor, only possible, I fear—we never use it—in the p.m.—I mean so late in the day that if you have to wait *till* then it may be as well to wait to the morrow. But I will go in tomorrow & wire you the facts. I am of course pleading earnestly with fate that the grim creature *do* treat us to the sight of you by one of the Saturday trains. The beauty— though dimmed by long drought—of all this countryside in the mildest of the gathering—& neighbouring abominations has been a thing lately inexpressible—a monstrous heartless irony of nature. You will find England more normal than France—but tremendously abnormal *for* England. I yearn over your advance, I hang upon your telegram, I hug you in anticipation, & I am your uncontrollably impatient & devoted old

*Célimare.*

ALS: Houghton MS Am 1094.9 (38)


*Edith Wharton has reached England safely. He asks Minnie to take Winston Churchill's speech to the American journalist home with her.*

LAMB HOUSE    RYE    SUSSEX

Dearest Mary C. August 30*th 1914.*

This is a very belated little word of thanks for your so interesting letter from Gorhambury—because, alas, I have been so sharply unwell again since your flight hence as to have to be in bed—from a recurrence of that damnable revulsion from food which was the keynote of my dismal illness of 1910–11. Directly I break it I am better—& I have at last succumbed in a manner in breaking it—I have got up this torrid afternoon to scrawl you this poor word, but full of the tenderest intention & affection. The difficulty is that the horrible public situation makes the sense of being down a damnable oppression to pull up against. However, I pull hard. Edith, whom I devoutly hope you are seeing to-day, will have told you of my having been able to greet her here, though in no very brilliant fashion, & have at any rate given you all the facts of her own triumphant little passing of the barriers on Thursday. My relief at her having reached these shores is unspeakable, & I think her own is great; but I am extremely afraid the delay on her younger maid's part & on Walter's & his sister's (*she* dallying at Vichy till the 11*th* hour,) may have imperilled *their* prospects, at the pass things have come to—& as to this I include Cook's & his wife's. But you will know more than I. I am afraid there can be no word from you from the steamer—the blest old Queenstown letter being a light now quenched; but the sight of a Bar Harbour postmark will intensely re-animate. Be a good missionary there of our cause—& take *with* you Winston Churchill's address to the interviewing American journalist; in this a.m.'s Observer— or better in tomorrow's *Times*. Above all enjoy the easiest of voyages & keep the tenderest of memories of your faithfully fondest old

Célimare.

ALS: Houghton MS Am 1094.9 (39)

*James has had heart problems and consequently has been a poor correspondent. He is in London, where he receives better medical care.*

[*Dictated*]

21, CARLYLE MANSIONS, CHEYNE WALK. S.W.

Dearest old Friend. November 8th. 1915

I am in receipt of all your generous newses from the ship and after your landing, but they find me, alas, even a worse correspondent than before we so sadly parted. A darksome light broke upon me immediately after that— which ought to have broken before; the true explanation of all those dismal weeks in the summer was that I was spoiling for a heavy heart-crisis, to which I have been handed over ever since. It has made me, it still makes me, a "rotten" correspondent, and I must now sink in this respect to very small things. I have been getting of course much more into *le vrai* [the real thing] since I invoked the light of Sir James Mackenzie, with that of Dex Voeux,[77] who is now taking the most perfect immediate care of me, superadded; but I have of course been having a stiff struggle—even if now, at present writing, the omens are all for the very best. I went down to Rye, and it was there at once that my poor case became unmistakable—the good Skinner promptly recognising it, and my ability to get back to town and to better advice not being, most fortunately, delayed at L. H. for more than a week. A difficult and complicated week it proved, but I achieved what I had gone for, the place is mercifully lent for the winter, and certain indispensables have come up to town, where they much reinforce my

---

77. HJ's last doctor. Edel lists his name as Des Voeux.

situation. Morton Fullerton[78] has been in London ever since my return; he goes back to Paris tomorrow, and will be able to carry all the essence of my news to E. W. You will have seen Harry well before this reaches you, and have been able to tell him all that it's convenient he should know. I have just written him at better length than this—though length isn't within my compass again yet. My servants have been of the utmost devotion, and Burgess is actually with me, and was with me at Rye—while I am very fondly hoping for news of his discharge. He is of the last indispensability to me now. Forgive this scrappiness and thinness. I enter with you into poor dear Mrs. Schuyler's[79] death—what a long chapter of history seems to wind up with it. I can't expatiate, you see; but am your all affectionate old

*Henry James*

TLS: Houghton MS Am 1094.9 (40)

---

78. William Morton Fullerton (1865–1952), American journalist and intimate friend of both Edith Wharton and HJ. James wrote Fullerton many letters, often giving him advice about his writing and sharing criticism of other writers.

79. Possibly the wife of Montgomery Schuyler (1843–1914), American editor and writer.

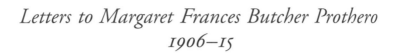

*Letters to Margaret Frances Butcher Prothero*
*1906–15*

TIME LINE

1854    Margaret Frances Butcher is born in Ireland.
1882    "Fanny" Butcher marries George Prothero, English academic.
1894    The Protheros move to Scotland, where he is a history chair at
        the University of Edinburgh.
1906    James's correspondence with Fanny begins. She lives part of the
        year at Dial Cottage, Rye.
1910    Fanny's and Henry's brothers die; both of their brothers were
        scholars and teachers.
1912    Fanny helps James move from Rye to Cheyne Walk, London.
1915    Fanny nurses James during his final illness.
1934    Mary Frances Butcher Prothero dies.

Mary Frances Butcher Prothero, photograph of a portrait by C. W. Furse. (Courtesy of the National Portrait Gallery, London.)

## Introduction

Your admirable note, however, received as I say this noon, makes up for everything by its blest promise of your advent here on Wednesday at 6.30, and its absolutely indestructible implication and predestination of your remaining till Friday. This will give me the most enormous lift, for I am now, I think, just such a lame dog as will be put very much on his way by a leg up over another style. I won't attempt now in the least to touch up for you the picture here, but will leave the whole vivid scene to break at once on your view; only promising you the most delirious greeting, the most enormous attendance of welcome at the station, the most florid fire in your room, and the very best of blankets on your bed. I am already, with the thought of it, almost a-straddle of the stile! I flourish my legs, I wag my tail, I yap for joy with my parched lips, as violently as your keenest appetite for public recognition could require, and I am all gratefully and faithfully yours  —*Henry James* (2 December 1912, Houghton bMS Am 1094.3 [101])

Henry James welcomed Fanny Prothero's frequent visits to Rye. She and her husband, Sir George, owned Dial Cottage on High Street, near his own Lamb House. She was part of his small circle of friends there, and in his declining years she became his nurse and household familiar, his own lares and penates, as he sometimes called her. By 1913 he informed his niece Peggy James that the Protheros, along with a select few, were the "we" of his life.

Margaret Frances Butcher (Fanny) was born 10 April 1854 in Ireland to Mary Leahy Butcher and the Right Honorable and Most Reverend Samuel Butcher, the bishop of Meath. She had five siblings. Sociable and congenial by nature, she and George Prothero (whom she married in 1882) had no children. The academically distinguished Sir George edited the *Quarterly Review,* taught, and wrote, while Fanny ran their households in Bloomsbury and Rye. According to all reports, she engineered the couple's busy social life. Sir William Rothenstein remembers her and her sisters as charming women. "She [Miss Eleanor Butcher] and her sisters, Mrs. Crawley and Mrs. (afterwards Lady) Prothero, were three enchanting ladies, spirited, enlightened and vivacious talkers."[1] But despite her travels and frequent entertaining, Fanny must have been lonely. Some of her prodigious energy and affection she bestowed on Henry James. And he in turn counted on her for "a perfect tangle of intimacy." Theirs was a domestic friendship.

James described Fanny to Grace Norton as "a little Irish lady . . . the minutest scrap of a little delicate black Celt that ever was—full of humour & humanity & curiosity & interrogation—too much interrogation" (10 August 1909, Houghton bMS Am 1094 [1024]). She and James shared (and discussed endlessly) a small group of Rye friends: writer and mystic Alice Dew-Smith (her pen name was "Sarnia"), Captain Dacre and Margaret Vincent (she was the Lucia of E. F. Benson's books), Constance Fletcher (satirizing her was a mainstay of their correspondence), and the unhappily married Sydney Waterlows. He once told her that Constance Fletcher was "a person who has absolutely *Nothing* . . . but her rather large roomy, dressy *needs*" (Houghton bMS Am 1094.3 [17]).

Despite their closeness, only two letters to Fanny (of well over one hundred James wrote her) have been published. She must have loved reading his letters, as no one could gossip as humorously as her friend Henry nor make her feel so wanted. He wrote about parties at Sir George Lewis's, the telepathists currently the rage in London, his reactions to World War I, and health cures. He often addressed her in a mock-romantic voice: she was Juliet and he was Romeo. He shared his pleasure in his new cook Joanna with Fanny, and when he traveled she maintained his household. They both participated actively in war efforts, helping each other survive the traumas it brought to peaceful Rye and to England.

When the Protheros visited the United States in 1909 and 1920 they met James's friends and family. James poured out his grief to her in 1910, the year her brother and his died:

> When I have laid my hand as softly as I am, God knows, moved to (on you & on your Brother's noble image & memory,) I somehow want only thereafter to shrink into the sacredness of silence—until we can *really* talk in our

---

1. Sir William Rothenstein, *Men and Memories* (New York: Tudor, n.d.), 206.

little old russet & green garden-nooks (oh how I *ache* with homesickness for those same!) (30 December 1910, Houghton bMS Am 1094.3 [52])

When he took an apartment in London in Cheyne Walk, Fanny helped him negotiate and plan the move. They communicated constantly during this time, as she advised him on furnishing his flat and dealing with the former tenant.

Occasionally James tired of Fanny's need for affectionate attention and socializing. In October 1913 he complained to Alice James of Dial Cottage's blighting tea-hour. He had previously noted,

> She has a tiresome little Irish habit (it gives at last on one's nerves) of putting *all* her responses (equally,) at first, in the form of interrogative *surprise,* so that one at 1*st* thinks one must repeat & insist on what one has said. But one soon discovers that one needn't in the least *notice* the habit—but go straight on with one's remark or statement or whatever, & the whole annoyance drops. It is her only vice! (9 December 1909, Houghton bMS Am 1094 [1694])

But he was grateful for Fanny's tireless nursing when his health failed. He asked Alice to write and thank her for being "the angel" she was to him. And in 1915 he told his niece Peggy that Fanny was the only old Rye friend he saw.

*This letter sets the tone of James's correspondence with Fanny Prothero. He uses playfully exaggerated rhetoric to lament her absence, creating the persona of a devoted loved one languishing for her company.*

LAMB HOUSE, RYE, SUSSEX.

Dear Mrs. Prothero! [17 September 1906]

This is a word to thank you for your two good notes, to keep you both in heart, to offer *my* shoulder, & eke my collar-bone, to dear Mr. George, for any use they may be to him, & to express the melancholy with which I turned away from little blank=faced Dial House this a.m.—after leaving you there with a shaking faith that you would have arrived last evening. I kind of counted on you, even though you hadn't let me know! I went up to the Steps,[2] accordingly, this wettish afternoon to seek consolation—& Mrs. Dew Smith only chilled me a little more by the exhibition of her post-card. We are ready for you, we hope for you—& yet we understand everything. We deeply participate in every pang of Mr. George's accursed state—& we freely utter on his behalf all the "swear=words" that he is too refined, too patient & too considerate of your *farouche* [shy] sensibility to any undue freedom, to launch upon the air himself. Well, we shall be all here when you do come. We love you more & more, & just fidget about meanwhile, & flatten our noses against Mr. Smith's window=pane, wishing we could do something. The rain has greatly freshened us up, & we are very, very pretty. But above all we are very, very patient and considerate, in our poor way, too, & we control ourselves in deference to what seems to both of you good, even in our yearning. But we watch & listen & are yours both, always & ever,

Henry James<br>Sunday night

ALS: Houghton bMS Am 1094.3 (3)

*James delights in rural life.*

LAMB HOUSE, RYE, SUSSEX.

Dear Mrs. Prothero. Oct: *26th 1906.*

Delightful as it is to hear of you, & from you, anyhow, there is a special joy in knowing, by your own hand, that you pine & suffer & repent—for I

---

2. Home of their mutual Rye friend, writer and psychic Alice Lloyd Murray Dew-Smith (pen name Sarnia). She was alive as late as 1927, when she published *Spiritual Gravitation.*

really don't *want* to stop the wound, & in fact couldn't conscientiously attempt it. Your conjoined folly in not being here is written all over the scene—the golden October scene, a perfect ravishment of weather all the livelong day, with Rye never more amiable & more exquisite. It is in fact *the* scenic moment & I wish you would read the lesson! Therefore I twist the knife in your vitals. Even if I were less interested in your true improvement I shouldn't be *able* to find a shade on the picture or to imagine a fold in one of the slighted roseleaves of Dial Cot. It is just utter dead loss that you suffer, & I wonder that you can bear it. Mrs. Dew & I have lovely times together—we just gloat over everything—rioting among the apples, raving about the sunsets, rushing to & fro (as it were,) from the hill to the valley & back again. I met her yesterday at tea (Fuller Maitland's[3]—think of that & of *them!*) & today I am to be entertained—& I hope entertaining—at the Steps. So now *there!* I see you only less relegated to privation & Error than poor Constance[4] herself—that says all! Can't you make a pretext for sneaking back for a little? If not I shall sneak up to town. But tell Mr. George, please, that I rejoice in his recovered might—I don't go so far as to think that *that's* too good for you. Only I *do* think of the wiser uses you might make of it. However, I *must* off to Mrs. Dew! Ha-ha!

Yours in fondest disapproval
*Henry James*

ALS: Houghton bMS Am 1094.3 (6)

*James gossips about a party at Sir George Lewis's home and another at the Edmund Gosses. He relays the news of Rye and of Constance Fletcher, and he questions the veracity of the Zanzigs, London telepathists and popular dinner party performers.*

Reform Club, S. W.

Dear distant Neighbour! Jan. 1st 1907!

You overwhelm me with subjects for conversation—&, even though blessing the shower, I must take them in their order.

---

3. Florence Henrietta Fisher Maitland (1862–1920) and Frederick W. (Fuller) Maitland (1850–1906). He was a historian and the official biographer of Leslie Stephen. She was a niece of Leslie Stephen's second wife, Julia Prinsep, and the eldest daughter of Herbert Fisher.

4. Julia Constance Fletcher (1858–1938), sentimental novelist and playwright (pseudonym George Fleming), a Rye visitor who lived in Venice with her mother and stepfather, artist Eugene Benson, most of the year. Her most popular novel was *Kismet* (1877). HJ frequently satirizes her in his letters to Fanny Prothero.

1. The Revel at the House of Hanover[5] abounded in everything but particular reasons for its taking place. *You* would have been—for me!—a reason, but it abounded alas only in your absence. It abounded, however, in the presence, of Mrs. Crack.,[6] who abounded, in turn, in white satin, crimson trimmings, silvery hair and liquid eyes, & who sat opposite to me in full panoply of the same, while I was flanked on one side by an empty place & on the other by Countess Feodora Gleiches (she of the Alhambra)—to all of which, or whom, I had resorted after dining at the George Lewis's (with Eliz. Robins,[7] whom I took in, on one side, Lady Lewis on the other, & Marie Tempest well in view.) The Gosses'[8] banquet was a cold, sandwichy, compote of mixed-fruity (mainly *bananine*)—you taste it from here—midnight supper. So you see I had a rich evening—though I had to tear myself from the Lewis's just as the private theatricals (following dinner) began; & the drive from Portland Place through the sloshy sea of the Regents' Park was, though not interminable, sufficient.

2. Your Rye news is thrilling & makes me feel that we are missing—or that *I* am—the great & true emotions by not being there. Mrs. Bracket's death probably "means" a great deal to the town, in one way & another; I don't refer so much to princely bequests as to the general effect of the possible liberation of a good deal of tightly clutched property. Walter Dawes[9] is supposed (—being her intimate *homme de confiance* [confidential clerk]—) to have aspired to be her "residuary legatee"; so perhaps his more immediate bereavement will be softened to him (& perhaps not!) But I'm very sorry to hear of his wife's death—a very excellent, valuable ally to him, a very nice genial woman, of extreme motherly amplitude; & I feel that I must (all sympathizingly,) write! How Rye will be chattering! It's a real pity that, for the deeper pulls & currents, the wider sweep of the lyre of life, we are not there!

3. Mrs. Crack. told me that Stopford Brooke had had a very "sad letter" from Constance, on the subject, I gather, of *their* (her) rather gravely

---

5. A party HJ attended at the home of Sir George Lewis (1833–1911), famous English lawyer who defended Parnell, and his wife Elizabeth Eberstadt Lewis (1844–1931). James knew them socially from the 1880s until 1915.

6. Mrs. Crackanthorpe was probably wife of Hubert Montague Crackanthorpe (1870–1896), English editor and writer. She ran off with another man, and Crackanthorpe later drowned in the Seine.

7. Actress and friend of HJ's.

8. Sir Edmund Wilson Gosse (1849–1928), man of letters, and his wife Ellen Epps Gosse (1850–1929). Both were close friends of HJ's.

9. Walter Dawes, solicitor and town clerk in Rye during HJ's years there.

formidable economic situation.[10] It is sufficiently dreadful to think of & I allude to it all darksomely & helplessly. But Mrs. C. seemed to have received—through Stopford—a rather more acute & definite impression than before.

4. The Zanzig stuff[11] in the newspaper strikes me as, in its cheap crudity, most unfortunately compromising to the theory of the *reality* of their performance (which it appeared to me, under that 1*st* impression, the only one to be held.) But I wish you & Mr. George could go for a *second* impression—I wd. myself if I were remaining. Stuart Cumberland (the old conjurer & trickster) has written somewhere to *declare* it a certain trick—the result of a very wonderfully elaborated code of signalling them (& that he,—an arch-juggler—having seen them, judges this possible, is a little striking.) "Why does he always wear a white coat? Why does she wear "telescopic eyeglasses" of great power?" I confess the sense of her glasses,—watched through an opera-glass,—did a little worry me. Yet their communication by word is almost nil, & in fine, the operation of their code becomes a greater marvel than the idea of their thought transference. Also Stead—John Hare told me last night at the Lewis's—had them at his own house, one upstairs & one down, & with an outsider making the signal (thump on the floor,) when he—the man, above,—had "taken" the article, & another outsider recording in the room below the woman's infallible naming of it. No "code" there if Stead's story be veracious. But I haven't seen it! They had at any rate better, the couple, stop "writing." And so had I! Ever yours

*Henry James*

ALS: Houghton bMS Am 1094.3 (11)

*Constance Fletcher "has positively* Nothing.*"*

LAMB HOUSE, RYE, SUSSEX.

Dearest Mrs. George! Aug. 6th 1907.

Ah no, I haven't forgotten you—but I have nourished my fond memory in silence as celery (isn't it?) is grown to peculiar advantage in the dark. It blooms there, my vigorous plant of fidelity, with increasing & delightful freedom!

---

10. This undoubtedly refers to Constance Fletcher's difficult financial situation in Venice.

11. London telepathists (husband and wife) who allegedly transferred their thoughts to one another, independently of recognized sensory channels. They were quite popular performers at dinner parties during this time.

This very "mixed" news of poor Constance's fresh crisis I have also had from her, & even yesterday disburdened myself of the nearest approach I could achieve to an appropriate letter. I had in truth expected the event any week—since that impression gathered in Venice the other day—& can only believe it to be in an *immediate* way a very great relief & soulagement [relief] to every one concerned—so difficult & desperate had the whole tension become. On the other hand she will terrifically, poor C., *miss* the afflicted & afflicting lady, who was really the only "fond" friend, I imagine, that she had in all the wide world—a great deal of a person every way & occupying a great and near place in her life. She has *nothing* now—she strikes me as a person who has positively *Nothing* (but her rather large roomy, dressy *needs*—with no wherewithal of any kind for them at all;) so that I see absolutely no future for her whatever. Such is my cheerful view— relieved only by a depressed curiosity to see what she does with poor moribund Benson, to whom she will be kind—as kind as she can be with (again) no wherewithal whatever. She can't leave or "chuck" him—he's too ill & too alone & dependent—& will want to come back to London as to a field of action &c—& can't *bring* him: so that I'm very sorry indeed for both of them. And surely one doesn't & wouldn't see her again at the Steps—where the lady at the top of them must have had her once for all. Oh no, not there!—and I pray she make not straight for Rye. She won't indeed probably be able to make "straight" for anything—for even if she shuffles off those fine old shabby quarters in Venice this can't help being, I fear, a tortuous & embarrassed & prolonged business every way. But so let us let her, for the time, rest.——I bade goodbye yesterday to Mrs. D. S., & I grieve having no one left to abuse you to for not being here. You will see her & she will tell you how particularly pretty you are & how Dial Cottage strikes one as quite scandalously wasting its sweetness. But you are com- ing—& I'm sure you'll both find awaiting you here the secret of how much better Mr. George has really been getting. Open the door of the little breakfast room at D. C. & there you will find it serenely seated to await you. You will see. But I want to see too—to come & show yours both so affectionately

*Henry James.*

ALS: Houghton bMS Am 1094.3 (17)

*James stays with Mary Cadwalader Jones in Scotland. Everything is harmonious except the writing paper, which has a "vile surface."*

Dear Mrs. George. Thursday a.m. [18 September 1907]

It has been delightful to hear from you again, even though a little in the minor key. I wrote to you just before leaving home—on this sudden adventure, which I believed I had renounced, but the temptation to which flared up again, under pressure, so that I let myself for *this*—which proves altogether delightful. The weather is so glorious, that I wonder much at your Yorkshire blacknesses or hurricanes or whatever—it is all Scotland in the charmingest possible form; 16000 acres of purple moor & mountain hired by an old American friend of mine from Lord Dalhousie (Brechin Castle & Invermark are at the head of the glen,) & very hospitably & amiably treated, with 4 or 5 sympathetic people in the house. I don't measure, thank heaven, but I walk 20 miles (or upward) a day over the moor & find, thank goodness, that my legs are as good as ever, even though my wind sometimes faileth. Everything is harmonious in short except the writing-paper, which has this vile surface that you see & that aggravates my still viler hand. "The way we live now" is meanwhile interestingly ex-emplified by these wonderful Scotch arrangements & extravagances—especially the way the Bloated live (a little of which indeed—in spite of the noble beauty of this country) will last me for a long time. There's a monstrous kind of a side to it,—& I'm glad that my hands are not imbued nor my "resources" immodest. I return to L. H. on Saturday noon, but dash off again after luncheon, by motor to spend 2 days at Swinford Old Manor again—where my hostess is so surrounded by the unappreciative. It is *their* stupidity—besides, I don't quite see who "they" are; the country-side there is all in the hands of more or less *tarés* [blemished or defective] people; & the most worthy, those of Godinton, quite adore her. But we will talk over these things & many more, sitting against the old flushed fruit-walls in the golden October sun. I hope your hurricane has blown over, & that dear Mr. George is on the rise again. I wish you so heartily an increasing ease. By Tuesday afternoon I expect to be re-seated at L. H. for a long quiet—if heaven will but send it. But let it send *you* twain too, & make me the more constantly yours

*Henry James*

ALS: Houghton bMS Am 1094.3 (19)

*James returns to a rich and mellow Rye after visiting Scotland. He sends news of the Waterlows and the Vincents.*

Dear Mrs. George.

I stretch you out this wild waggle of a mere incoherent hand before I sink beneath the wave of my correspondence! I have 2 charming letters from you, with the good news of George's apparently very handsome amendment (of which the restlessness is a prime sign,) & I manage to uplift even 2 hands above the deluge to clap them together in jubilation. (I can only write on 1 side of a sheet now.) Your moors & your fells seem as if they ministered indeed to a glorious & free life, & the ingenuous young mothers dawdling casual babies in maidens' bowers strike me as a quite harmonious element in such a bright breezy picture. Mrs. Dew writes me (I say *writes,* for in the hurly-burly of life here we have scarce met since her return) that you tell *her* you soon arrive, whereas you tell me you *don't:* whereby I brood over such prevarications & equivocations & seem to make out that you are planning a surreptitious & centrifugal stay. Well, come to deny your door if you will—so as you only come. If you will do the hiding I will do all the finding. I've been away again—for 5 days—but not to the greedy little Posts'—both fleeing & meeting my fate; but thank goodness it seems over for the present, & a robust Miss Bosanquet comes down from town this very day to seat herself formidable before my Remington for the next 4 or 5 months, during which I shall be at High Pressure. Free however, take notice, always from 3.30 to 5.30. Mrs. Dew had planted her muscular relatives at Golf View, & braves the elements & admires the felicity there with them a good deal, I infer; the young Waterlows flap their wings on the hillside, while the maturer Vincents[12] crouch in exile at Winchelsea; people offer to come "over" to see me from Wisterham, from Folkestone, from everywhere & the pulse of life generally beats high. I liked your "visiting" (J.G. &c) reminiscences & anecdotes & am keeping some few of my own to repay them withal. Come & look therefore on the wine while it's red within the cup. This October feeling of Rye is very rich & mellow, & I exchange such public yearning looks with Mrs. Bryan[13] as I pass along the street (she always at her door looking out for you) that it's beginning to be noticed & wondered at. Come therefore & save us, even though I be for

---

12. Captain Dacre Vincent was the secretary of the Rye Golf Course for many years, and his wife Margaret was an accomplished pianist and leader of the town's musical life. She was the model for the fictional character Lucia in E. F. Benson's novels.

13. Mrs. Bryan kept a shop in Rye. She and James frequently discussed the Protheros' comings and goings.

her but the "idol" (& the idolizer!) of others. I bless you both (I don't mean Mrs. B.) & am ever so constantly yours

*Henry James*
Oct: 10*th* *1907.*

ALS: Houghton bMS Am 1094.3 (21)

*This letter constructs an imaginary conversation among James and several Rye friends, who lament Fanny Prothero's prolonged absences from Dial Cottage.*

LAMB HOUSE, RYE, SUSSEX.

Dear Mrs. George! Oct: 18*th* p.m. [1907]

Just as black despair was seizing us—that is 10 minutes ago—the Devotee to the interests of the Idol (though we won't say who the Idol in this case *is*) arrived with an "I hope you don't mind me coming" & a nice little fat=faced boy. I said "Oh dear no, Mrs. Bryan: always so glad to talk with you about them" & then she broke it that she had just had a postcard & that they would be with us tomorrow. You could have knocked me down with a feather—the revulsion was violent. For you see we had, the others of us,[14] met of late in such at last almost deathly tension. It had been, it had *become,* more & more this kind of thing.

""Have you heard—?"

"Oh yes—one 'hears': that's the bitterness of it. She is clearly in-disposed—"

"Indisposed? Don't tell me!"

"Indisposed, I mean"—this very gravely indeed—"to *come.*"

"Oh, *that?* Don't call it indisposed. Call it firmly resolved, call it funda-mentally determined."

"Well—since you go straight to the terrible truth of it—there we are. But she professes—!"

"Oh, she dresses it with ribbons & gardens: you know her enchanting way—!"

"Ah yes, her enchanting way IS the bitterness of it. She *does* deck it out—!"

"As with streamers & a band of music! But all the while—"

"Yes—but don't too awfully *say* it—!"

"I *must*—for we must face the worst! *She has cooled.*"

---

14. "The others" probably included Alice Dew-Smith, Captain Dacre and Margaret Vincent, and Sydney and Alice Pollock Waterlow.

"*Aïe!*"—as of a nerve in anguish. "Not *cooled,* put it—only just a little (in this weather) lowered her temperature."

"Oh, weather me no weather! She has frozen!"

"Let us then *melt* her!"

"We can't—all our tears won't. It's the icy smile."

"Yes, that smile! It maddens, but it means—"

"It means—?" (hanging on one's lips.)

"*That she will never come again.*"

"Aïïee!"—the shriek of ten thousand wincing nerves—a piercing wail, a heavy fall & silence; from my gloomy gaze on the prostrate presence of which imagine the revulsion, as I say, of Mrs. Bryan's breathless approach to yours in ecstasy

Henry James

ALS: Houghton bMS Am 1094.3 (22)

*James compares George Prothero's health cure to Martin Luther's* pecca fortiter *(sin boldly): if George takes a cure, he should cure boldly. James longs for stories of their recent trip to South Africa and hopes to see her on Twelfth Night at Sir George Lewis's home.*

Dear Mrs. George! LAMB HOUSE, RYE, SUSSEX.

Oh how I've had you both in my heart during all this time that the air has been thick with the missives of the closing year, & black not only with *them* but with the despair of delayed & frustrated answers & of unfinished & interrupted & yet most urgent work. By reason of these things I've stayed my hand & waited—waited even while the wondrous worry of your Xmas migration hither was academically discussed. Dear Mrs. Dew was so absolutely competent to the discussion at this end, that I didn't put in my oar—I only maintained an attitude of earnest & ironic observation. I watched the case, as it were, for the Duke of Bedford. Yet I had my feelings. What they mainly were is not to be revealed here, but in the full intimacy & strict privacy of garden-days to come. For there will *be* garden-days, & of the most delicious character—believe *that,* I beseech you, in spite of all temporary hitches & lapses. I've been hearing about the South Africa flight, & selfishly, I confess I kind of yearn for it—that is for the pearls & diamonds of the traveller's tale that your two pair of lips will eventually pour, here, into our laps. We are already smoothing out our laps for the receipt of them, Mrs. Dew & I, & gloating, together, over the brave hours to come. Truly the idea is of the thrillingest, & I say, boldly, to dear Mr.

George, *Try* it! I am only sorry he has to try so many things. I have a horror of Doctors (haven't spoken to one for years,) that, regarding commerce with them more or less as *sin,* I apply to his ease the excellent advice he gave me when I asked his opinion of a *short* chimney (peering above my garden wall,) to my stone=house, rather than a long one. "If you sin, sin boldly!"— whereupon I made my chimney *gross,* & have rejoiced ever since. So if you are *curing,* cure boldly, & go with the utmost possible grossness to S.A., leaving *us* to be refined & desolate & expectant in your absence. Besides, it will, after all, get you *away* from the doctors & the treatments. But I shall very *possibly* see you on 12*th* Night at Hanover Terrace [home of Sir George Lewis]. I shall make every effort to plan at that date a bout of 2 or 3 days that I have imposed on me for town. I have had a tiny little domestic Xmas here, & really expected to eat a baked apple & a biscuit at 7.30 all by myself. In the event I drove across to Winchelsea & partook of indigestibles at the board of the exiled Vincents, in company with Mrs. Dew. The most pressing summons from 58 Rue de Varenne (*She* [Edith Wharton] is again there this winter,) have failed to make me turn a hair. I am working—as constantly & as prosaically as possible. When I want to be poetic, & even a little pathetic, I think of you & Mr. George, & I am very fondly & faithfully yours both, always,

*Henry James*
Dec. 27*th* *1907.*

ALS: Houghton bMS Am 1094.3 (23)


*James and Mrs. Dew made a public scene for the benefit of ten tramps. Constance Fletcher's stepfather, painter Eugene Benson, died in Italy, and now they will "have her always" in England.*

Dearest Mrs. George!                    LAMB HOUSE, RYE, SUSSEX.

Your blest little hand-scrawl throws us into ectsasy [*sic*] & we are lighting bonfires from Dungeness to the tip-top of Winchelsea. (I hope the noble names touch you to tears even amid the ruins of Syracuse.) I rushed up the hill—*our* hill, that is Mrs. Dew's, drat it!—fluttering my Reprieve & met the lady of the Steps half-way, she rushing down with a wild flourish of *hers:* whereupon striking public scene for the benefit of 10 tramps on their way up to our sweet monumental union (the thought of which *will* make you homesick.) Your affirmation of George's betterment of body & mind at Gibraltar (though *what* a Benton he'd be if he didn't feel cock-a-hoop *there!*) is in the highest style of art & promises us rich treats to come. There's an endless virtue of condition in him which the golden air only *yearns* to draw out: so tell him, please, with all our love, just to control his contrary passions & *let* it: whereby the milennium (though I *think* it has 2 l's?) will practically have arrived. I am launching this into space & risking *Poste Restante, Palermo,* on the general theory that sooner or later you *must* get things there. Three days ago came a wire from Constance F: "Mr. Benson dead: tell Protheros." I gave it to Mrs. Dew to forward you, but fear she has lost it. No matter—that was all. It opens up vistas. She is *free,* now, as never before—but she is older, wearier & heavier—of every-thing but cash; of which I *imagine* her at last lightest. She will, of course, however, make for England as soon as she can—& some of their posses-sions there—in Venice—are *assets* (of sorts;) though who knows already how mortgaged? Also, poor woman, how *alone*—! Still, I believe in her emergency & reappearance. *Then* we shall have her for always. How terrific is life! But lead yours, now, *gaily*—as we are trying to do. Mrs. Dew has a company of 3—& Ethel Dilke & her father & the Sidney [*sic*] Waterlows tea'd with me here this day. I go to Manchester on the 16*th* to nurse along my play till the 26*th* at Edinburgh—10 strenuous days. Pray for me *hard.* I embrace you both; Burgess, calling for my post, champs his bit. Give us *addresses* & things.

Your devotissimo
*Henry James*
March 1*st* 1908

ALS: Houghton bMS Am 1094.3 (28)

*James compares himself to Hamlet or Romeo, Mrs. Prothero to Ophelia or Juliet. January's mild weather makes him feel as though he's in the south of Europe. The former local barmaid Chrissie is stiff with age but still sends her love to all in Rye.*

LAMB HOUSE, RYE, SUSSEX.

My dear Fanny Prothero.                                            [12 January 1909]

I have to draw little *tablets* thus from my bosom in these days, even like Hamlet or Romeo in the play; but they have at least the merit that they approximate *you* the more for me to Ophelia & Juliet. Your voice & gesture & roll of eye & flourish of feather & elegant ease of veil are all a-twitter for me in your letter & I cock my old grey cap & slap my dirty brown glasses (*all* the same as when you were here) at you in return, & feel somehow helpless to slip along—for we do slip along, these weeks, amazingly—to something a little less dolefully Platonic. (I brood again as I flap my tablets!) We make no news here in these days—none but the fact of the really exquisite ethereal mildness—thanks to which without fires (only my pipes alight,) I sit here with my window open to the garden, the springing crocuses, the towering wall flowers & the birds, & feel myself in the south of Europe—if I can so much as speak of that world of present nightmare. I like it—I'm having at last my *time,* & I'm taking it all. The young Sidneys—or Alices—have come back & returned to their week end practice of silent loutish youths & of great muddy boot-heaps to tumble over in their Sunday afternoon hall; but otherwise gentle & neighbourly Mrs. Vincent & I meet a little today. We miss Alice Dew many times over—*she* really suffers as from an amputation. But she—Alice—can *never* hibernate there again—so that is in the day's work. Her nephew has returned to the Smith nest, where I have been scandalized to learn that though he is now in his 4*th* month there & being paid for at a fancy figure, he hasn't yet had an hour's tuition from Smith, or from any delegate of Smith, & hasn't either a decent bed to sleep in, but just pigs in as on the cheap, with the rest &c, &c. (*But please repeat this to none*—it will have been threshed out later;— & he—the boy—is behaving with extraordinary virtue & wisdom.) I am very busy indeed—& London seems far off. I shall come up for May & June! The thought of sitting tight till then is inestimable to me. Sidney [*sic*] Waterlow saw "Chrissie" at Hindhead at Xmas (but no other Pollock did;) she has left her barmaid place & seemed stiff & aged & ravaged as to joints & facial surface, but dealt much in Love, to every one all round. I think there must be some for *you.* At any rate I send you & George plenty of that of your

*Henry James*

ALS: Houghton bMS Am 1094.3 (37)

*James's health vacillates, but overall he improves. Dr. Skinner (Rye's doctor) and a six-foot trained nurse are with him. He needs a place in London where he can spend sociable winters and escape Rye's bad weather.*

L[amb]. H[ouse].

Dear ministering Angel Fanny P.!        Feb.  21*st*  [1910]

   You spoil it all when I get from you on this a.m. your little word from "17 Quincy St." (Lawrence Lowells?) speaking of your several priceless mitigations of my misery, from the 1*st* of your arrival, as rigmaroles—they having been truly recurrent benedictions that by transmitting, through their vividness & gaiety & grace, the stale scene about me, helped me on most materially. So if instead of retracting all that you had only wafted me a further whiff of your current experience (having *mine,* of days & days before,) to go to the devil you would have admirably kept up the good work. To have you at last exactly where I have been wanting for you to be, & yet to get no good of it through your exquisite hand—no, this mustn't be, please, again, shall it?—when a scrap of a snatch of a moment once more angelically to minister is able to assert itself. I am getting on through ups & downs—for that is the way my convalescence seems condemned to proceed; being in its nature essentially up-hill work. An advance is followed by a drop-back, pretty infallibly; the only thing being that the drop-back falls far enough short of all the way to have a certain residuum of *gained* ground, on which I go on again. This is why I flounder along slowly—& it seems mortally long. During my good moments & days I am up—very very much up; & during the others I am *not!* But I have to come back from so very far!—I had got so exceedingly bedeviled. I am doing my very damnedest to make the former triumphantly prevail. My general & particular conditions here all these weeks have been exceedingly fortunate—Skinner is excellent as a nurse—& devoted as a friend—supplemented by a 6-foot=high lady of the "trained persuasion," not less benignant & sympathetic & competent in her way, who is still with me. Besides which the house & servants have admirably lent themselves—& in all that manner I have, as they say, "much to be thankful" for. Dear Mrs. Dew has been to see me, most greatly & charmingly, a number of times—& Sydney Waterlow I also saw when I could till he himself was lately taken bad—with "suppressed gastric influenza" (besides which he has been away,) & for 3 weeks I have lacked him—& he is the only man in this dire little social desert. I have been coming round this last winter or two, (& the present horrible season has clinched the matter,) to the sense of a real break-down at last (& after 12 resolute years,) as to the possibility of further fightings-out of it in this place between December & June, & find myself yearning for some regular arrangement by which I can put in 5 or 6 months conveniently in town (more conveniently than by a room at a club, excellent for anything for 6 days & 6 weeks, & disastrous & unworkable in case of illness.) All of which signifies (forgive this vain babble of weakness) that I have conceived a kind of terror of the "social & intellectual void," the absence of human resources, of this familiar scene for the bad half of the year—or, to put it quite abjectly, of its rather deadly lonesomeness. However, why should I thus expound? I wrote you the other day & told you a little of all the joy I take in your wonderful odyssey. Remember that *every*

item is a blessing to me—& every sign & healing hand. So quote shamelessly, you see, I don't spare you or let you off so easily. I am living in the
dire impatience I now feel for my blest nephew Harry's arrival—he is due 6
days hence; & I count the hours & curse the boisterous weather (*such* a
season here!) which *he* however may not be having. He will have seen you
& give me of your news. Mrs. Dew has occasionally shared (I haven't
always been able,) but I always feel an inevitable compassion for her
particular little ever-renewed fight with (I don't mean against) life. I throw
myself fondly on George & am always your

H.J.

ALS: Houghton bMS Am 1094.3 (44)

*James mourns the death of Fanny's brother Henry; he too has just lost a brother. He is
homesick for Rye.*

Cambridge. Mass

Dearest Fanny Prothero.             Dec: 30: 1910

I should have been writing you today at all events, by reason of your so
generous & forgiving & touching little letter of a few days since, written by
your dying Brother's bedside—but this morning I find, by the newspaper,
that the blow has fallen on you—& *that* almost destroys, rather than
reinforces, my power to write. I shall have cabled you a poor faithful word
an hour or two hence—but how shall any poor word, however faithful,
seem to *say* anything—commensurate with what one would like you to
know one feels. Through what lacerations, what renewals of pain & strain
& sorrow, you are condemned endlessly, as it were, to pass, & how the
ashes of bereavement & mourning are piled upon your head! Dark &
dreadful the days must have lately been for you, & cruel & grim, I can't
help fearing, through whatever muffling of his consciousness, for *him*—all
too sad & unspeakable for me to have the courage to turn my face to any of
the hard & dismal facts of. I remember him so charming & gallant, so
delightful & distinguished—with his fine flame of conviction & production & action. And I have only been silent & silent & silent. To write has
been, all along, to have to *report* of myself—& I *couldn't* report of myself. I
can't even now more than to say that I am fighting my battle & dragging
my heavy cart up the interminable hill day by day & step by step, & that
the end is not yet. But I am unmistakably "better" & I do grateful justice to
that. The thing is that I have so very, very far to come back *from*. And I'm
superstitious against the personal statement or any tinge of elation—so

certain is it that whenever I indulge the least bit in these things, some horrid sense of disproof & discouragement seems immediately to pounce on me. Meanwhile I keep clinging to *this* rooftree—& there remain the strangest reasons for my continuing for the present to do so. Alice is magnificent, the others are all dear & delightful, & the time, in spite of everything, passes, the weeks & the months melt away, in a manner that fairly hurries me on to the date for which I am taking my passage homeward, though that is not till the 14*th* June. Everything *but* the immediate interests & attachments & absorptions of this house is unspeakably flat & unprofitable to me here—the whole face of life (or almost,) frankly & confidentially speaking, affects me as repulsive & appalling. I'm afraid I can't say better than that. You may judge therefore of what good reasons I must have for hanging on. I tell you these things in order *not* to talk to you of your own dire sorrow & stress. When I have laid my hand on you as softly as I am, God knows, moved to (on you & on your Brother's noble image & memory,) I somehow want only thereafter to shrink into the sacredness of silence—until we can *really* talk in our little old russet & green garden nooks (Oh how I *ache* with homesickness for those same!) So I go on—*trying* a little to talk even at this hour (about other things, though.) There must come into being some fine *Memorial* of Henry[15]— won't you & J. G. (G. W. P.) be thinking, when you have the heart for it, of *that?* That we all are here much turning over what we long to do for William, & the means & materials (all hanging, however, sadly, on my validity), is one of the links that will keep me these months. Something will come of it—but it's early to say. I had a plan of going on to New York for a longish stay on Jan. 1*st*—but am not really at all fit, & am putting it off till some time in February. Then, I believe, it will really be advisable & salutary. I have *lost,* alas, Constance F.'s address there which you gave me— & have had no word from her & heard, & still less *seen* (though I almost never look at these hideous newspapers) nothing whatever about her. If I had, again her whereabouts— & you have kept any—I would make her some sign. I catch very sympathetic echoes of your & George's beautiful presence here last year[16]—but should do so much more if I had, any "social relations" to speak of with Boston. But I have none such, truly— that human aggregation, such as it is, says nothing to me whatever that is

---

15. Fanny Prothero's brother, Samuel Henry Butcher (1850–1910), scholar and translator.

16. Fanny and George Prothero had visited America the year before and spent time with William James's family during their tour.

worth going through motions for it. The Barrett Wendells[17] are gone on a tour round the world—he a "nervous wreck" & she, it seems to me, pretty awful. I am sorry for *him*—but they are a futile pair surely—& I seem to see few here (save dear Ellen Mason[18] & Fanny Morse) who are not—not even, very much, the good & notoriously non=feeding (their friends) Dan'l Merrimans! Alice will write to you—barely emerging as she is from the immeasurable mountain of correspondence that closed over us like a long & reiterated avalanche with William's death. But she joins with me most tenderly in the word I shall send you this afternoon. Please understand in it—as you *will* have understood—all kind love from me to G. W. P. (without whom I never think of you.) There's a great unwritten letter I still owe *him*. And take all indulgently these poor mixed accents of your all affectionate old

Henry James.

ALS: Houghton bMS Am 1094.3 (52)

*Mrs. Prothero has found a new cook, Joanna, for James. Constance Fletcher is "Gay" and "Huge" and "dentally bankrupt." His health improves and he finds consolation in the company of sister-in-law Alice James and her family. He thanks George Prothero for seeing his play, the* Saloon, *performed.*

95 IRVING STREET   CAMBRIDGE   MASSCHUSETTS<br>Feb. 17th 1911.

Dearest Fanny Prothero:

How noble you have been about the gentle Joanna (has she any other nominal sign?) & how I hug the very image & perfect projection of her! I will *try* & confine myself to the hug intellectual—though there is no knowing what, in the rapturous flush of my re-entrance of L.H., I may not find myself overflowing into—in the happy month of June. Your arrangement is perfect—that if her temporary place *doesn't* suit her & she withdraws from it I will pay her £3. a month for the interval till June 1*st*, during which she may tag with Shakespeare & the musical glasses or any other

---

17. Barrett Wendell (1855–1921) was a Harvard English professor and cofounder of the Harvard *Lampoon*. George Prothero, as an Oxford professor, knew Wendell and his wife. HJ was disappointed in Wendell's book on Shakespeare.

18. Ellen Mason was a Bostonian who taught with Alice James in Miss Ticknor's Society to Encourage Studies at Home, a correspondence school for women.

amusement of a dignified leisure, & at the 1st sign from you that she *is* gracefully upon the town I will instantly remit you the money. I feel great confidence that she will prove every whit as good a cook as I have any right to enjoy. Paddingtonia was purely & densely British, remember—she turned out her culinary toes as little, cut as few culinary capers, as befitted the massive beady, bugly ornament of the Lamb House Pew. I am sure Joanna will be at least as light-footed, or as light-handed. So it's all for the best.——————I wrote to George the other day—since I wrote *you*—& gave him a brief report of my New York interview with the incomparable Constance. That astounder is, I believe, still there—but only from day to day: she has discovered a long lost or bricked-up (in the thickness of the walls!) small Udolpho apartment in their old Venice palace, has secured it for 9d. a year, & returns to take possession of it. Meanwhile her relations with Miss Anghie seem somewhat productively renewed. But one moves with her on such shifting sands & in such mirage horizons. She was Gay!—she was Huge—she has grown another chin & lost another tooth or two—& in spite of chins & teeth & other such items she lolled on a Turkish Divan. Her dental bankruptcy in this dental country is truly tragic! I'm afraid the sale of her stepfather's battered relics, however, haven't made her fortune—have done but very, very little. Also that of his own pictures. These things she had been *strenuously* organizing. However,—she endures—& it's not the end.——————I find the weeks pass like rustling water here, in spite of everything: just as in spite of everything, I distinctly improve. I shall probably in a fortnight or so return again to New York & make a short stay in Washington. But everything is fixed—including the struts &c here; where it freezes & snows only to profusely melt again— with such splendidly sunny vernal thaws & beautiful skies. Alice & Peggy & the Boy are of course consistently admirable, & this company a consola- tion & support beyond what I can say. I drive in tonight to drive with Ellen & Ida Mason, who cherish your memory. But I preach here at home the rupture of this dismal bond (now so motiveless) with this dreary Cam- bridge—& I think in fact hear it crack. Dear Mrs. Gibbens the one last thread by which, for Alice, it holds.——————I thank dear George very kindly for going to see the poor little *Saloon* so badly performed as I feel assured it must be—in my lamentable absence from rehearsal control & supervision. But it's time for me to hurry off & dress. Ever your all-faithful

*Henry James*

ALS: Houghton bMS Am 1094.3 (55)

*The coal strike is over and James visits the Charles Hunters' estate north of London. James is pleased with his new cook, Joanna. He gossips about the Sydney Waterlows' marital problems, predicting both will remarry.*

Dear Fanny Prothero.             Monday Aug. 21*st* [1911]

*This* will tell you a little how things are going on with me—they "went on," on Saturday, to the point of my braving the then apparently spreading Strike by starting for town, with the doughty Burgess's backing, in order to take a motor-car from town on to this place if possible, to which I had even from the American shore promised an early visit. Our progress to Charing Cross took after all only 4 hours & was less unpleasant than I had expected. I obtained a car in town & easily came out—& last night there was rain, & it was continued in very decent measure this a.m.—though even as I write, in my room before breakfast,—or rather luncheon,—the sun glimmers out again rather ominously & hotly. The cessation of the Strike, however, made known to us yesterday by the Sunday papers, will, I feel, help us to bear anything—as its hideous portent, last week, really quite prevented all endurance—or any—whatever. I am convinced that this long horror of heat & drought had had much to say to it—to the outbreak: the conditions had got on everyone's nerves & had made quantities of people vicious & villainous. Great is the *détente,* & may all sorts of good come of it! However, I am not answering your questions about Joanna— which it's so easy to answer. She seems to me absolutely & utterly what I want, & I am profoundly & rejoicingly content with her. She has *more* "ideas," even, clearly, than I can, at my modest pitch, deal with or run through—& during the depressing influences of last week she had even more—or quite as much—conversation. I think with this, that I am not myself repulsive to her—it sounds fatuous, *that*—but there it *is*—& in short every thing is auspicious for happy—I was going to say union—but I confine myself to saying intercourse. I dare say that now I have come here through such agitations I shall stay the week—the place being, perhaps you detect, the Charles Hunters'—& beautifully friendly, kindly, & just now quiet— besides being beautifully beautiful (the huge blight of the water-famine being allowed for.) The huge old William-&-Mary—& older—house is most interesting & fine—& the modern conveniences, to express them mildly—overwhelming. Likewise the proximity to London—with the extraordinary "forest" isolation in spite of it—is, to the brooding visitor, a further note of ease. I left poor dear little Rye cooling off (very pleasantly, fresh breezes & nights,) but at the same time horribly drying up. I hope irrigation has by this time begun. The Pollocks were stewing contently— Fredk. & "Georgie"—& I saw them once for an hour, though seeing them, I confess, isn't easy to me; she being of irritating & stupid sillinesses, for the most part—*burn this straight!*—& he so painfully unendowed for social intercourse. They spoke very frankly & *relievedly* of the Sydney-Alice business—& very kindly as regards *him*—he being as relieved as any of them—& writing most amicably to Alice, who *now* is amicable back & is in their Hillside house making it ready for sale & departure (to spend a year—or the winter—*1st* of all with *them* in London;) while Sydney is editing a "Cambridge Anthology," as to which he writes me from some- where in Surrey (probably his mother's) for leave to include some small old stuff, a poor page or two, of mine. The P.'s told me that the *effect* of the "falseness of position," between Alice & him, has during the previous 2 years become much more salient & active & disturbing—so as to make the whole situation intolerable—& he agreed to their separation with the same sense that everything was at an end—in the way of the survival of a uniting affection—with which she asked for it. And now they have, I think, both to *marry some[one] else*—if they *can;* or at least *she* has! But the time is coming on for *our* at least meeting again—& I am yours & George's both all & always

*Henry James*

P.S. We must pay bigger railway fares—we the public. I'm bound to say I think we ought to. We expect to rush about so much for so little!

ALS: Houghton bMS AM 1094.3 (61)

*While James stays with the Frederick Macmillans (publishers) in Norfolk he wants Mrs. Prothero to straighten out his household finances. He complains of the drought. His nephew Bill is engaged to Alice Runnells, whom James admires.*

MEADOW COTTAGE, OVERSTRAND, NORFOLK.

Dearest Fanny Prothero.                                        Sept. *9th 1911.*

To what unendless & unnatural trouble I have renewedly put you—& gentle Joan scarce less—by my distracted woolgathering ways! *Of course* you sent me a cheque for that residuum—it comes back to me perfectly now, & the beautiful little statement with which you exquisitely accompanied it.[19] Equally of course I mislaid or unconsciously destroyed or forgot the cheque—& I may still find it; though if I don't that will serve me right for my graceless inattention—for I now vividly & gratefully remember the advent of the letter containing it, with your admirable little note, emphasizing it, as to the expenditure of the rest of it. I have instantly written to patient & forsaken Joan, enclosing her the amount belatedly due to her. (I am by custom extremely punctual with my servants—& she shall never wait again—it's a cruelty!) Your letter addressed here awaited me yesterday on my most perspiring advent—London had been dreadful for 3 or 4 days & the journey down here—1.30 to 4.30, from Liverpool St. the objectionable—was quite awful. But a grey sky & a cool—almost a cold—blast have come on in the night, though without a drop of the rain apparently portended as yet. The earth is as blighted here as everywhere & as baked & caked, though this garden testifies to the truly superior art & energy & pecuniosity of my invincible hostess. It's vividly green & exuberantly floral—& as one of the "authors" of the house I keep scratching my head a little. But however handled as a mere genius, I am most kindly treated as a lodger & converser—& I divide the honours here with the American sister & her American sposo [spouse]—the "Charley" Nadols. Also Miss Beresford, Mrs. Julian Sturgis's *so* long-legged & *so* short=bodied & *so* easy & cosy sister I find installed again (as 2 years ago) as "useful" friend or high-born dame de compagnie [ladies' companion]. I am very glad to find her, but it irks me a little [to] find the offshoots of the Kings of Ireland fagging for the bosses of Grub Street. However, that is their affair all round, & Beresfordina is to go with us to tea at Blicking this afternoon—after my host & hostess & I (*minus* the American kin,) have lunched with Lady Battersea.[20]———I have heard again almost *jollily* from Sydney W[aterlow].—who has to me on his side quite the air of drawing a long glad breath of relief.———I also just hear by cable from Chocorua of my dear Nephew Bill's engagement to Alice Runnells of that place (& of Chicago;) in which you may take a gentle interest for his & his mother's sake. A. R. is very tall & goodlooking & gentle & sympathetic & intelligent & well-brought up—& comes of a house full of money. I really don't

---

19. HJ had written Fanny Prothero a letter just before this one asking if there was money left in the funds he had given her for his June housekeeping expenses. She should give any remaining amount to his housekeeper, Joan, he told her.

20. Lady Battersea was Constance de Rothschild Flower (1843–1913), wife of Cyril Flower, Lord Battersea, a Tory M.P. and later member of the House of Lords. She held a political and artistic salon.

see what she lacks, & I think it must give Alice (our Alice) pleasure & comfort: we have been for the last 2 years & more seeing it *come* (on the young woman's part;) & watching for—rather delayed!—symptoms of it on the young man's. But now they are in line! How these things make me want to see you & talk to you. Now that a change of the temperature has come I find the thought of L. H. less formidable than during the ten days I spent there (they were pretty bad) after arriving from America. I hope this blest shift of the pressure has come to you, too. I am not sure you still shan't escape hearing from me of Blicking, Battersea & such—but I am now only yours & George's all & always

*Henry James*

ALS: Houghton bMS Am 1094.3 (63)

*James plans a motor trip with the Ford Madox Fords. Alice Dew-Smith wants him to help her build a bungalow in Camber, so he will have to visit the site.*

THE REFORM CLUB

Dearest Fanny-G! October 21: *1911.*

Your faith hope & charity enormously sustain & reward me—& all the more that *I am,* this afternoon, swerving from the delicious pavement—to the extent, that is, of going down to L.H. an hour hence—to hold on there, if I *can,* to Thursday p.m. The effort is tough—London is *so* right for me; but I shall feel easier than without it, & with the redemption day definite in advance, I daresay I shall escape a "scene." I will bring you every detail—foreseeing that I shall return to you on the widest & wildest wings of relief. The Fords[21] call Sunday afternoon to motor me to their "show-place" & back—& again Monday perhaps even (if *I* will!) to whirl me elsewither—& that will be, though inferior, a sort of stopgap of the pavé [public road]. Also Alice Dew writes me much about her wanting to "build" a bungalow at Camber—for on one's having displayed I fear but a languid interest in the scheme—& indeed a disapproval that went the length of my pronouncing it "squalid"—she has returned to the charge as insistently as if off here *on* the pavé & with "Camber" relegated to the deepest depth of the superfluous, not to say the squalid as beforementioned, one wd. really find her building-plans after all the main actuality. Dreadful things happen there to the dear creature's sense of proportion—

---

21. Ford Madox Ford Hueffer (1873–1939), noted author, and his wife Elsie Martindale Hueffer (1876–1949).

214

to her whole social perspective & in short we must pull her out of it. But I foresee I shall have to go out & judge of the site &c! However it will account for another afternoon—& talking of these momentous matters with Margaret Vincent—with a little more about the Nullifiers spicily thrown in—will perhaps account for a 4*th: ce qui fait mon compte* [that is what makes my account]! I foresee I shall be at you again for a tour of the rabbitwarrens—I so keep toying with the (present) impossible. I shall bespeak you for that adventure at the earliest

*Henry James*

ALS: Houghton bMS Am 1094.3 (65)

*Alice Dew prepares for her houseguests, the Larpents (a cross between varmints and serpents). James complains of Mrs. Dew-Smith's promiscuous albino dog. Although he has been in bed, he begins to walk again with his nephew Bill and Bill's bride Alice.*

LAMB HOUSE, RYE, SUSSEX.

Dearest old friend. Feb: 9*th* 1912

Dumb & graceless have I been—but when that goes *on & on* so blackly you always know, don't you? that there's a reason. I have been in bed with the reason here—after being in bed with it in town *1st;* & if I had been in less intimate & less scandalous relations with it (that is frisking about *without* it) you would before this have had the sign from me. I came down here on Wednesday under final stress of unwellness, & tumbled straight into bed on arrival—having had to tumble for a couple of dreary days in Pall Mall as a preliminary to that. I am up today since 1 p.m.—& now it's 8.30; so that I am better & a little recovering—in fact *much* recovering, you'll say when I tell you that I walked up the hill, in a crawley way, this afternoon, between & supported by Bill & his Bride, & that there we met Alice Dew, who beguiled us in to tea with her, she being here to prepare her house for *Larpents*—who somehow always seem to be such a hocuspocus of a cross between Varmints & Serpents. (She goes—or comes—tomorrow to Margaret Vincent for a few days & was meanwhile all for *pups*—she trotted them, & them only, out!—those, alas, of the awful Albino monster that she still cherishes to whom she permits flirtations, not to say scandals.) She is the same child of Nature & of discourse—& was most kind & most gentle—& pathetic! However, I can't pretend to write much—I only want to do myself a little more credit in your eyes than my long drop of every decent demonstration can have done me. I don't know why quite wholly— but only partly, why: my situation (as to "feelings" & physical equilibrium) took more & more an evil turn, day by day—beginning with a very damnably bad cold (& I haven't had a cold for years!) & eventuating in *this*. But I probably have touched bottom & shall crawl up again now. I shall crawl to 24 as soon as I can crawl *about*. Forgive these weak accents & forms. The Bridal Bills really grace this Scene—& Joan reflects the torchlight of Hymen. I come back the *1st* hour I dare. I embrace you both & am ever your shattered but stubborn old

*Henry James*

ALS: Houghton bMS Am 1094.3 (71)

*James compares Ottoline Morrell's clothing to window-curtains.*

REFORM CLUB, PALL MALL, S.W.

Dearest Fanny P.! May *9th 1912*

On Tuesday, please, let it be—at tea-time (or milk-&-water time;) for we didn't, no—we didn't at all—get at L.H. & your adventures with B. & A. [Bill and Alice James]; all of which I want from your lips. We shall have them then on Tuesday.——Yes, Ottoline[22] is always touching & charming; & yesterday she was very interesting; & also beautiful. But I wish she didn't run so much to the *stale,* but a little more to the fresh, in costume; & wonder if her window-curtainy clothes haven't perhaps a tiny bit to do with the Ducal alienations[23]—as well as her political opinions. However, what a bloated monster he did show for in her picture—a huge gilded idol who can only do with idolaters! We will discuss him—& everything. Yours all

*Henry James.*

ALS: Houghton bMS Am 1094.3 (79)

*HJ, who is in an epistolary tangle of mixed metaphors, finds Alice Dew-Smith "land-ladyish." He is in danger of being whirled away in Edith Wharton's motor car.*

---

22. Lady Ottoline (Mrs. Phillip) Morrell (1873–1938), a notorious socialite who held a literary salon in Bloomsbury. She had an affair with Bertrand Russell, among other men.

23. This may refer to Ottoline's half-brother Arthur Bentinck, sixth duke of Portland. The duke, a staunch conservative, disliked the Morrells' Liberal politics. Phillip Morrell was a Liberal M.P. for a time.

Dearest Fanny P.                                        July 21*st* 1912

What a shame it is that you are not nestling under my wing here at this sharp crisis—instead of our being landed in an epistolary tangle. Which bites so much more than it can chew! Forgive my mixed metaphor—a tangle that bites—& in which one is "landed"!—would scarce satisfy a purist: though *that,* thank God, you are not! A bite that tangles would be more like—though perhaps but a shade better—& without a provision for the "landing" either. No matter; you will seize my point—which is, distinctly, that the deep of Dial Cottage should have been made to call unto the deep of Lamb House before Norway was finally proceeded with—there being always Joan sociably to ply the tuning-fork in case of my fear of a possible congestion of sound—as from a redundancy of remark (which she wouldn't at all encourage.) Here I am alone & there are you ditto, & I take *such* single & solitary afternoon patters; *that* is the melancholy moral. No—it hasn't been well managed & it will be a lesson for the next time. Your echoes of the torrid town & of the reassured (to put it mildly) matrons, (the ex=Barries, ex=Pollocks &c)24 come to me as from far-off, so out of the picture do they, thank goodness, seem to be here. I saw little Carson Barrie once or twice in London, & she looked to me a done=up 75—but they are not cases at the best, that I hang over, broodingly, by the hour. Poor little Alice Dew's case is before me here again a little, of course. I've been at her Garden, which is an almost indecent riot & tumble of Dorothy Perkins, pinkest of her tribe; & Alice was very gentle & genial, & we yearned together for you; & also she was very *letty* and landladyish, after the fashion that tends to make her sex here seem to surround one, too disconcertingly, with an atmosphere of ladyinghouse keepers. She isn't really attuned to so much of it. But I clutch at anything to hang on by—Mrs. Wharton being due in her motor-car 1/2 an hour hence, straight from Paris, which she will have left this a.m. (it's now about 4 p.m.) & designing with a fell intensity, to whirl me away for several days—into the land at large. Nothing could suit me less either for peace or work, health or thrift; but I foresee that I shall have to yield—yield haggling—haggling for the least surrender that will do. Pray for me hard—pray that I may get off with a week at the very most. *She* is in for a "tour"—but even a week utterly appals [*sic*] me (we are to go for three days to Mrs. Ch. Hunter in York-

---

24. Here HJ refers to two recently divorced couples, Sir James Matthew Barrie (1860–1937), author of *Peter Pan,* and his wife, and Alice Pollock Waterlow (1876–1953) and Sir Sydney Waterlow (1878–1944). Alice Waterlow later married Orlando Cyprian Williams.

shire; after 2 here, & 2 with Howard Sturgis at Windsor—and motoring all the time.) Ah our complicated modernity! Yes, pray for me while I am hurried to my doom—while a young typist (temporary substitute for Miss Bosanquet,) eats her head off—she came down for the purpose but a week ago. I shall *crouch* all the rest of the summer & autumn. Arrive therefore & give me your feet, protectingly, to crouch at. I have heard from Alice (the younger) at Chocorua in intense heat, but better & now without any pain at all. She is indeed a valuable & cherishable thing.——*Later.* The Deva-stating Angel [E. Wharton] has arrived—& is reasonable & charming in highest degree. *But* the plot will thicken tomorrow! Your prayers will always be welcome—I mean useful. But don't betray my free talk. And buck up as hard as ever you can yourself till I can gently meander again. George will come back a giant, out of a Saga, even though *I* remain but your very middling normal old human

*Henry James*

ALS: Houghton bMS Am 1094.3 (83)

*Rye shopkeeper Mrs. Bryan's boy wins first prize for his English essay at school. Mrs. Vincent may profit from her dying aunt's will.*

Dearest Fanny.                                    LAMB HOUSE, RYE, SUSSEX.

I have been silent a little because I am *down,* positively, from the force of the blow; likewise because my immediate speech would have been too piercing a wail of anguish—so resounding as to produce almost public scandal. For I had been counting the hours—& it is very hard! However, I dash away the unmanly tear & and am awfully glad—bohoo, bohoo!—that you are going to have your fling in the susceptible North, even though you do sacrifice to it the still more susceptible South. At this rate indeed the North & the South alike are susceptible, it would seem, of scarce anything but drowning. We sit here up to our necks in water, & in your place I shouldn't at all break, as they say in America, for the Moors, but straight, rather, for the Burlington Arcade or for any one, for each in turn, of the blest London resorts that help one through a wet summer. Directly it's like this, dear old London *is* the Arcadia indeed. And this place is a social desert as well as being a watery waste. I positively haunt Mrs. Bryan at her shop door, to talk it all over. She thinks it a shime that you are losing so the beauty of your garden—which has been of late, it appears, more lovely than words can tell. All the same she rather bears up, because her boy, at the Bluecoat school, has got the 1*st* Prize for the English Essay—& him only 14! How delightful for George to think soon he'll be knocking at the door of the Quarterly[25] —whose future is thus more or less assured. Mrs. Vincent's fabulous Aunt is more or less sinking to her end, & I can't be decently calm about it, for hoping that that dear impecunious woman is on the point of profiting substantially by her will. Only she appears not to have told her, decently, that she *is* to—which makes me a little nervous. However, if she *had* told her perhaps she would have lied—& if she doesn't lie it may be the truth! Thus do I desperately chat, or chatter, to hide from you the aching hurt beneath. I am saving up September, to the last minute of the last hour of you, & count upon you then for a perfect tangle of intimacy. I would fain share with you even now the Tottenham Court Road or a stroll up & down in front of Gill & Rugate's window. Still, L. H. rallies to me again, & the Virgin Twain, Joan & Kidd, & I go so far as to suppose Burgess, play up as splendidly as ever. Joan gives more & more the rein to her genius—which at moments seems fairly to bolt with her. So I am helped a little to endure, & from luncheon to dinner &c I hold out. 30 days hath September—though August, alas, hath 31. However, we'll make a September of 40, or so, & I am (àpropos of length of days,) your all=affectionate octogenarian

*Henry James*
Aug: 12: 1912

ALS: Houghton bMS Am 1094.3 (85)

---

*Meeting the Milnes-Gaskells again after twenty-five years was an awful experience, James tells Fanny as she goes to visit them. He and Mrs. Bryan miss her, but he waits like a patient Griseldus.*

LAMB HOUSE, RYE, SUSSEX.

Dearest Fanny. August *16th 1912*

Well, it's a comfort, fairly, in the desolation, to get your little wails of wasted anguish—unto which "deep" the deep of my own tribulation calleth, verily; even while I see history so strangely repeat (& yet diversify) itself, & you haled off to the Milnes-Gaskells'[26] in the flower of your 1st maturity, even as I used to be uncannily concerned with them in the 2*d*

---

25. George Prothero was editor of the *Quarterly Review* from 1899 to 1922. The noted literary and liberal journal was founded in 1809 as a rival to the *Edinburgh Review.*

26. Charles George Milnes Gaskell (1842–1919) and his wife Mary. He lodged below James in Bolton Street in 1878, and HJ frequently visited their houses at Thornes and Wenlock Abbey in Shropshire.

bloom of my far-off youth. I saw them again, this May, in town—*after 25 years:* & it was a pretty awful experience: you will know why when you have wept (to get off it) on this arid bosom. But Wenlock Abbey is a rare old monument & the whole *local* aspect charming. But I say no more—& when you have been there you will know why. We will babble about it as we totter about. Such treasures of tottering—such hoards of babble—as I am laying up for you in myrrh & frankincense. I don't know quite what "myrrh" is, but if I do throw Mrs. Bryan a pinch my store can fairly afford it. I was asked yesterday (by "Doll Lidell") "The Protheros *still* live here, don't they?" To which I replied: "Yes, still: for 5 minutes a year." Such is the bitterness, the gnashing, of my desolation. No Alice Dew, no any one or anything; only the grim voice—garnished with the cold scrap of Mrs. Bryan. And again, again, "Thirty days hath September," but not so August—which has that monstrous 31*st,* which George, by the grim Letter of his Law, will take advantage of—to linger on toying with Lady Cattie (of Wenlock aforesaid.) And I somehow see you at the Crackenthorpes too—& completing the weird picture. The whole thing makes a monument (to human endurance;) on the summit of which see me seated, like Patrina—smiling at Mrs. Bryan. It *is* a shime—but I am all the same your eternal

Griseldus.[27]

ALS: Houghton bMS Am 1094.3 (86)


*HJ thanks Mrs. Prothero for her help choosing curtains and wallpapers for his London flat. He notes that marriage to the recently deceased Richmond Ritchie never brought Lady Anne Thackeray Ritchie happiness.*


[*Dictates*]

LAMB HOUSE, RYE, SUSSEX.

Best of Friends! October 13th., 1912.

Your letter last evening received expresses, like all your letters, that unique mixture of the heroine and the angel. Heroic was it of you indeed to fight your way through that black darkness to Chelsea, and then to peer through it so patiently for my poor sake, plucking this perfect nosegay of information and suggestion out of it all the while and whisking the same so fragrantly under my nose. There's where the angel comes in—if in fact, the

---

27. This is a reference to Chaucer's tale (told by the Clerk) of the patient wife Griselda who submitted to her husband and was eventually rewarded with happiness.

angel, in your behavior, ever so much as went out! It is the most stay-at-home angel (I mean in the way of its going about with you everywhere) that has ever graced this planet. I revel in your green velvet curtains and in the tub of colouring-matter that you further prepare for them; I wrap myself in all the terracotta; I take over, in short, anything that can decently be made to serve the few months' turn. You convince me at a stroke that the various wall-papers *won't* do; and so have cut out for yourself the grand campaign of attending to the others that will. So much for the present, with ten thousand thanks. Do all sorts of selfish pleasant things—that is let others make them pleasant, and try at last a little bit yourself to make them selfish—till you come back to town again and settle to the tubs and the paste-pots. It goes on being lovely here, and I try to go on getting quite right. It appears that one doesn't, that one can't, do that, after this particular kind of visitation, in a decent straightforward way: there are hitches and returns and relapses, as I am finding, and even on a minor scale these are disappointing and time-ravaging. However, I do make gain. There isn't, thank heaven, the smallest scrap of news; that is there isn't here. I see to my sorrow, in this morning's Observer, the death of poor Richmond Ritchie[28]—of the possibility of which I had had a warning a day or two ago in a note from Rhoda Broughton;[29] the latter now again by the way at 99 Cadogan Gardens, where, when you come back, do go charitably to see her. One thinks ever so tenderly of poor dear Anne R.—little as one had ever felt (or at least I had) that her marriage had brought her the full measure of intimate consideration that her exquisite nature seemed to ask for. However, Richmond was a great public servant—and she sits there in abundant honour. I bless and re-bless you and am yours all faithfully

*Henry James.*

TLS: Houghton bMS Am 1094.3 (89)

*James thanks Mrs. Prothero for being his charwoman. Alice Dew-Smith is a wood-nymph wreathed in paradox, Margaret Vincent grows more massive, and Fanny's absence makes him foam at the mouth.*

28. Sir Richmond Thackeray Willoughby Ritchie (1854–1912) was a secretary in the India Office and then permanent undersecretary of state after 1909. He married his second cousin, Anne Thackeray Ritchie (1837–1919), a novelist and the daughter of writer William Makepeace Thackeray.

29. Rhoda Broughton (1840–1920) was a very popular and prolific Victorian novelist. James took little note of her writing after an early review where he noted her "coarseness of sentiment and vacuity of thought," but they became close friends nonetheless.

[*Dictated*]

LAMB HOUSE, RYE, SUSSEX.

Best of Friends! October 17*th.*, 1912.

This isn't a letter—I am trying to do letters, in default of oh such urgent other matters, but it means a desperate brevity for each: it's only a mere hand-waggle, or brush of the keyboard, in acknowledgment of your further bounties; and to tell you that I am just barely floundering on as yet, just sitting with my chin, of the whole poor afflicted extent of me, above the turbid flood. The days are ineffably golden and still (I *like* to twist this invidious knife in your vitals;) Miss Bosanquet is my mainstay, for I manage mainly to "stay" a bit but between breakfast and lunch; and thus somehow the blighted week ebbs—with the further charm upon it of an occasional note from Mrs. Constable.[30] She means well—and this has to cover all disentanglements of exactly *what* she means! We rub along, however, and I feel quite that I shall have inherited no harsh friction, no exchange of tart remarks, even though I possibly *shall* a neat little collection of more palpable monstrosities! (They won't in the least matter—the billing and cooing, especially with yours thrown in, will wash them all down!) For the rest, I dare say I shall be better next week. I kind of languish yet, and I kind of don't eat. So much the better as regards *that,* I can save the money for the green velvet curtains. Alice Dew has been most gently in to see me, wreathed in every paradox even as a wood-nymph in wild poisonous flowers of the forest; Mrs. Vincent also once—more massive each breath she draws; and these are the limits of my excitement. The lease is signed, compliments have been exchanged, but you shall have more the next time. I've raged, simply, roared and raved and foamed at the mouth, with the effect of your absence; but Skinner has at last strapped me down, and now I can only do this—which you see is comparatively mild. To make up for it I wish you with the utmost violence the utmost rueful ease. But the only thing that really does me good is to feel that all the genius of you is really plotting and planning and scrubbing and grubbing, all of it in short charwomanising, every instant of its time, for yours all most confidently

*Henry James.*

TLS: Houghton bMS Am 1094.3 (90)

---

30. The occupant of 21 Carlyle Mansions before HJ. He refers in this letter to the arrangements he is making with her for taking over the flat during the coming winter. They negotiated what, if any, of her furniture would be left there, when he would move in, and so forth.

*While his health deteriorates, he tries to dream of sideboards but can only conjure up bad dreams.*

[*Dictated*]

LAMB HOUSE, RYE, SUSSEX.

Best of Friends!                                                   October 22nd., 1912.

I have always something to thank you for, and the only way is just to put it in when I can, or even when I can't, lest the pile should topple over and submerge us both. I hate to wail at you in return for your generous cheer; but my horrid little case does drag itself out, and there seems thereby less to explain if I just let you know it from time to time and not try to dodge and deceive. Clearly, I take it, the damnable nature of the thing, in its normal course, which is to defy extirpation for just as long as it likes, is all that's the matter with me—though it's enough and to spare! The poorest of days and the blackest of nights seem still the best that can be done for me; to-day, for instance, after really touching bottom, as I hoped, last night, I shall presently seek my couch again as the least of difficulties to face. Whether poor dear Skinner mightn't have, in another Skin, a grain or two more of remedial resource, invention, ingenuity or whatever, is a question I don't so much as presume idly to trifle with. And it isn't at any rate to talk of these things that I just started this momentary ticking. I only want to greet and thank you for the fine spirit and vivid imagery of your last: your adventures and observations soothe the fevered pillow and I prod you on for more at any cost of sitting up to it for a moment as you see. That's all—and now I sit up no longer. I spare myself—but don't, one mite, spare you! I shouldn't forgive myself nevertheless if I looked to you in the least like wanting to harrow you. Analyse it a bit, as I do myself, and you will see that it's all really addressed to the effect of eventually dazzling you, by the turn of a hand, under some sudden final flush of improvement and cheer. *How* I should have liked to potter with you through the big Bath shop! I try and think of sideboards in the watches of the night—but bad dreams, rather more than cakes and pickles (if indeed the latter be not in themselves bad dreams) seem the articles they mainly disgorge: so I end by brushing them by—or curtaining them out with green velvet thrice-dyed. What helps me most as the hours drag is to wonder what dye may still be left in the tub. But good-bye. I wish Mrs. Constable would affably return your visit. Then you could return hers, yet again, or go perhaps, taking your work, and really spend the day with her; which would figure to me, upliftingly, as such a beginning of Possession. Perhaps she *will*—work it if she does, for all it may be worth, and believe me your considerably bruised but not at all beaten old friend

*Henry James.*

TLS: Houghton bMS Am 1094.3 (91)

*Dr. Skinner has given James a morphine injection to help him sleep. The Protheros help James arrange with Mrs. Constable to occupy her London flat after Christmas.*

Dear & Boundless Benefactress!          LAMB HOUSE    RYE    SUSSEX

I am after all not quite up to struggling with the long-distance telephone today—I am only just barely (& literally,) up to scrawling these words: I got out of bed a 1/4 hour ago. Your heavenly offer to come & see me moves me to the depths—but I all tenderly & gratefully deprecate any such heroic action this week. I have been so basely bad again (a brutal & a complete slump after 3 or 4 "better" (save the mark!) days last week)—that I feel precarious & simplifying & wait on events. I am comparatively relieved this a.m., thanks to Skinner's having at last consented (last night) to be for the 1st time "hypodermic": which got me several hours' sleep—after giving me (*at once,* after administration of the even mollified morphia) 2 or 3 of quite imminent, but finally checked, nausea. So of this reprieve I take advantage to wave this feeble hand. I don't understand this *fury* of resistance of my atrocious ill—save on all the evidence that just that, & nothing less, is its hideous & always-observed nature. I may have yet to be carried to 21 [his London winter flat] in an ambulance. But *probably* this present ordeal is the last ditch—even if it be a very deep & broad one. But it has really been the worst.——Yours of last night this minute comes in—& quite "upsets" me (if you can *be* upset when already at your length on the ground) by its goodness. I have *extended* the Flower [Mrs.Constable] because I got a letter from her which shows that any going out *before* Xmas was (naturally enough) not a thing to look to her for, & which asked me pretty earnestly to let her tide over Xmas—as Xmas week is a time at which it is impossible to get anything *done,* & she would pay me "rent" for the week. (Her time, strictly, is up on Xmas day.) I declined of course her rent—*wishing* to be obliging—& saying "all right." It's very true that *I* could do very little more than she in Xmas week, & that if one is to have a little transaction of bargain-&-sale with her (as to the Duds) I shall be better in a position to claim that she shld. "meet" me, from having met *her* on that other point. I have from the 1st thought of proceedings on Xmas week as doubtful, not to say vain—from the moment of feeling sure (as I had come to do,) that she is a person not in a position to sacrifice a day, much less many days, of a roof-over-her-head from simple *gracieuseté* [graciousness]. (And such persons are rare.) So I have been "nice", & now *she* must be. I *wallow* in gratitude & adoration for your visit there tomorrow, & should feel a regular pig of a Shylock (or such like) if I didn't think that George, with his lively response to local colour & vision of the right things & the wrong places &c—if the *whole* place only doesn't seem to him too wrong!—will amuse himself by the way perhaps considerably. I think I must try to ring you up (for a more & part rough sketch) in the *late* afternoon—about 7. I feel prompted to say Don't Damn any Deed, fluid or solid (I call curtains fluid!) that is good enough to save me a little time & shopping, & that isn't, in other words, *sordid*. And now toy with the Flower (Mrs. Constable)!

Your all-grovelling & clinging
*H. J.*
Nov. *5th 1912*

ALS: Houghton bMS Am 1094.3 (93)

*The London skin specialist Dr. Head has helped James's skin problems. James bought some of Mrs. Constable's "old duds" to avoid having to furnish everything in the flat himself.*

[*Dictated*]

LAMB HOUSE   RYE   SUSSEX

Best of Friends! November 21st., 1912.

How can I not feel the tenderness and fidelity of your kind question as to how I am for the great man's [London skin specialist Dr. Head's], as I like to call him for the importance of it, benevolent attention? He was very definitely, and above all *authoritatively,* informing and reassuring. I felt him perfectly master of the whole question, and that he knows entirely what he is talking about. The mere change to a first-rate adviser from just the honest sage of Rye [HJ's Rye doctor, Dr. Skinner]—that by itself was not a little uplifting; besides which Head is a really interesting and agreeable and communicative man; and to his kindness in having come in just the manner he did, and with just the zeal and generosity, I am much indebted. (You are still to have the history, you know, of the now quite far-off *origin* of that possibility, which goes back to some five years ago. But you must patiently wait!) Of course in such a case—the advent of a high specialist—a poor outworn patient conceives hopes, not less high, of almost magical results, a sort of immediate transformation-scene; and those things don't happen, and there can't help being a little reaction and flop. But I *am* better since he was here, and he left me an artful elixir, to take twice during the night, in consequence of which those fell hours have been passing (three times over) very much better. My feeling is that I shall now get on, but that it still won't, alas, move (anything to call) very fast; which impression, for my 8th. week of the damnable thing, isn't, as you may imagine, exhilarating. I must make the best of whatever it is, however, for even if I advance but half a step a day that is something to hold on by. Figure me therefore as holding on and on, and as having even got to the point where locomotion, all the walking and keeping-out I can do (such as it is,) perceptibly helps me and seems rather to show the way. If I can go straight, even at this snail's pace, to a certain point, I shall seriously regard a bold push up to town as perhaps substantially remedial. Head assures me it will be, and I shall do my best, at the earliest possible hour after that, to take my courage in my hands and so try to break the spell. When this prospect comes nearer I shall vividly let you know.

I much appreciate—having reason to!—your little warning about Constabulina! I'm afraid I have flopped into her not very artful or baited little trap (either!) to the extent of a few pounds and a few old duds (bedroom stuff etc.) *more.* I believe I have become possessor even of the famous "red curtains in the 2nd. bedroom"; which casually impressed you as "rep", but which she describes as at least demi-rep, as it were; or in other words as the most meretricious red velvet. If they prove to answer to this description they will do beautifully for the "servants' sitting room", which now, according to our collective scheme, spreads its majestic space in the apartment (or compartment) beyond the kitchen. Don't denounce me for a gobbler-down of trash, for there has been a method in my poor madness— the idea simply of finding certain merely useful objects in the place, the presence of which there will justify itself through shortening, if but by a few hours, the process of my getting in. If they are too base when it comes to a view I shall bestow them in reckless charity! Somebody or other will thus be the gainer, *and I shall meanwhile have got in.* But more the next time. I do so rejoice at your having with you those precious infants. I hope I shall still find them, for a glimpse, when I come up. You see that in spite of everything I am taking that almost brazenly for granted.

Yours both always
*Henry James.*

TLS: Houghton bMS Am 1094.3 (99)

*James is a lame dog, wagging his tail and yapping for joy.*

[*Dictated*]

LAMB HOUSE    RYE    SUSSEX

Best of Friends!                                    December 2nd., 1912.

It is quite awful to learn from you here at 12.30, by the second post, that you were lying in wait at the telephone this a.m. while I was just uninspiredly lying in bed. I had failed of Skinner both morning and evening yesterday—with the consequence that I had added to my still indispensable sleeping-potion such a small independent drop of my own that it made up for a bad early night by a better late one, and that I quite miraculously and unprecedentedly, slept on (after a break at 7 a.m.) to half-past nine. And then I kind of waited myself to be rung up by your convenience—and missed the sweet converse that I had gone to bed looking forward to at as early a moment as possible after our belated winter dawn. Your admirable note, however, received as I say this noon, makes up for everything by its blest promise of your advent here on Wednesday at 6.30, and its absolutely indestructible implication and predestination of your remaining till Friday. This will give me the most enormous lift, for I am now, I think, just such a lame dog as will be put very much on his way by a leg up over another stile. I won't attempt now in the least to touch up for you the picture here, but will leave the whole vivid scene to break at once on your view; only promising you the most delirious greeting, the most enormous attendance of welcome at the station, the most florid fire in your room, and the very best pile of blankets on your bed. I am already, with the thought of it, almost a-straddle of the stile! I flourish my legs, I wag my tail, I yap for joy with my parched lips, as violently as your keenest appetite for public recognition could require, and I am all gratefully and faithfully yours

*Henry James*

TLS: Houghton bMS Am 1094.3 (101)


*James invites Mrs. Prothero to take tea and an opium pill with him. He describes his Chelsea flat.*

[*Dictated*]

LAMB HOUSE    RYE    SUSSEX

Best of Friends!                                    December 11th., 1912.

This is but a tiny wee word to say that I renew my thanks to you for everything; that the omens seem auspicious (if I may presume to risk the remark!) for the great event; that I have really felt, the last 36 hours, as if I were beginning to begin to begin to be better; and that Skinner promises me the possession and free, flourishing use—as almost in the glare of the footlights!—of a mystic pill or potion, to be effectively drawn from my waistcoat pocket on Friday, at the very crisis of the action. All this is sustaining—so that I really feel the prodigious *coup* to be more or less casting its shadow before. I am in the most intimate communication with Grandmamma Garlant, who, like one of the ancient Fates (Atropos, Lachesis—and what was 'tother one's name?) has simply appointed me to Bill's and Alice's apartments; rather riding over the fact that I always romantically cling to any little quarters that may incorporate a bath-room—as I understand the upper set to do. But this will be easily arrange-able, or re-arrangeable, after my agitated advent; in which I shall really expect you to participate to the extent of having tea there, and perhaps another opium pill with me at (say) 4.30. Then there will be such tales to tell!—even though I am fondly hoping *not* such beds to re-enter. My approach appears already to excite in Chelsea the most benevolent flurry; everything clearly prepares for my being up to my neck there before I can turn round. Emily Sargent[31] is of the most excellent practical counsel; and I hear this morning earnestly from Lady Courtney,[32] who gives me much intimate information about my flat. She instructs me that it has two good rooms, but only two—the rest very inferior; and that I shall take one of the good ones for my bedroom and make of one of the bad my dining-room, or in other words my place, more or less, for receiving—well, say you and herself! Atropos and Lachesis are nothing to her; still, I hope to dodge her yet! How funny that one had always been aware of the "unpopularity", based upon a dim want of that graceful backwardness known as tact, which seemed to drape her about in the manner of a mystic veil; and now at last to have the veil shaken straight in one's face! However, I find myself already so fond of Chelsea and so infatuated with it, that even Lady Courtney's fluttering features are destined, clearly, but to grace the scene for me! All thanks for the little paper about the Fulham Road carpets, which it is most kind of you to have sent on. I am afraid I feel rather committed to the Constable treasure by this time; but may be thankful for one or two of the Fulham wonders to cover up other nudities. Let us romantically visit the

31. Emily Sargent (1857–1936) was painter John Singer Sargent's sister.
32. Lady Courtney was probably Kate Webb Courtney, wife of first baron Leonard Courtney (1832–1918), journalist and professor, and sister of Beatrice Webb.

Fulham Bazaar together, and leave no corner of any of its products un-
turned. I shall probably fire off a rocket of some sixpenny sort on Friday
a.m.; but think of me meanwhile as your more brazenly bold as well as your
more fondly faithful

*Henry James.*

TLS: Houghton bMS Am 1094.3 (103)

*James is back in Rye for the summer, where he and Peggy take long walks every
afternoon. Lamb House redecorating, the flower show, and nephew Harry's arrival
occupy him.*

LAMB HOUSE   RYE   SUSSEX

Dearest old Friend. August 12*th* 1913.

How can I express to you the extent to which your dear little letter was
becoming a "felt want"?—I mean in especial as giving me a peg on which
to hang on just to your sweet self! I have really yearned to do this, but
couldn't quite pick the pretext that would serve with you. You ask how we
are, & the simplest account is to say that we're just in a deathly tense state
of long-drawn *waiting*. We are "in waiting" just like the Hon. Derek or the
Hon. Flora White attached to their bloated sovereign. But the days go
while we count them, & every p.m. we check one off with a sigh of relief.
The great thing however, is that I've been ever so much better for coming
down here, & that the dear little old house, with the place generally, has
never worked so beautifully like a friend in need as during these last three
weeks. Reinforced by the dear & delightful niece, it has made a different
creature of the tolerably damaged article who so lately fled from London. It
extremely rejoices me to find L. H. play up once more so handsomely. The
soothing support & blest company that Peg is, is more than I can say, & we
really in truth have as lovely a time together as our great privation allows.
We take every p.m. long grassy strolls—of 2 & 3 hours—to my extreme
benefit & the having the niece to bear me along in them gives them a
double virtue. This will show you by itself how excellently I have come on.
There is "no one" here but Mrs. Bryant—whom I find, as ever, a charming
woman, & philander with, thanks to our common devotion, in a way that
*may* be, for all I know, almost a common scandal to those who pass her
doorstep. Peg & I have likewise had visitors over night, over 3 nights, twice,
& Joan has surpassed herself on these occasions. Bosanquet & Bradley,
established in the late Mrs. Kidd's elderly retreat, have rejuvenated it by

putting off old papers & laying bare grand old oaken anatomies—it's now a charming pale yellow & rich brown interior; & I am having gas laid on for their further convenience. So you see we are least as merry as we know. Today I go with Peg to a kind of Midlothian flowershow (where our George incredibly exhibits,) & tomorrow I am to live through the great tension of allowing Peg to go up to town by herself for the day—to her tailor's & the stores. She insists on the thrill of the adventure, refuses the company of Kidd, & has done the like so in the U. S. that I steel myself against foolish fears. Harry arrives from Germany & Paris, for the rest of the month, a couple of days hence, & will greatly help us over the interval before *you's*. I don't ply you with fond questions, you see, but only make you fond answers.

Ever your faithfullest<br>H. J.

ALS: Houghton bMS Am 1094.3 (108)

*James sends a subscribing cheque for a cause Mrs. Prothero sponsors, claiming that her work will add another row of flowers, stars, or electric lights to her crown.*

21 CARLYLE MANSIONS   CHEYNE WALK S.W.

Dearest old Friend. July *1st 1914*.

    It came over me in a lurid flash during our Anne Ritchie talk last night that the Devil's Dance (in the very temperature of the Devil's own home,) that we have lately been following had quite made me forget to send you my definite little subscribing cheque, which kindly find enclosed.[33] I do think it the very image & definition of the ministering angel that you are, this beautiful little heroism of your shouldering the bothersome burden. It will but add another row of flowers or stars or electric lights, or whatever the ornament is composed of, to your heavenly crown. I am not sure I shall be seeing you *much* before you dazzle upon us at Rye. The way I sweat for that retreat! *This* Pandemonium has left of me only just enough to be devotedly yours

*H.J.*

ALS: Houghton bMS Am 1094.3 (120)

---

33. This probably has to do with Mrs. Prothero's war efforts.

*The war wears James down. Rye appears the same, but life is different and strange.*

LAMB HOUSE   RYE   SUSSEX
Dearest old friends.                                                August 21*st* *1914.*

I feel stricken so dumb that it's difficult to converse—& yet I so like to be face to face with you, as it were, & to so intensely to expect to see you. The unfathomable grimace of nature in presence—well, of the Kaiser, goes on here from day to day—& it's from day to day that one lives, if not from hour to hour. At the same time one *lives into* it to some extent, I think—& I dare say we shall even live through it & out of it; & this whatever it proves. My visitor, "Minnie" Jones, is still with me, & Peggy now at 10 Lawrence St. Chelsea with her castaway Aunt Mary, hanging on news of the latter's husband and sister from Germany. We expect her here for Sunday—but I am afraid she must go back for more consoling & companioning (but Aleck is also at hand there.) "Payson"[34] has at last been heard of by wire as "safe at Houlgate," where she has inscrutably & inarticulately sat from the a.m. of Aug. 2*d.* Rye is also inarticulate—& there are more vague able-bodied young men about than I like to say (though I think they tend to diminish.) There are also golfers—some; & the surface is the sweet & smooth & soft surface we know. *Essentially,* however, it's to my eyes different—strange—unspeakable. I *shall* be able to talk to you—so feel yourself—selves—ardently awaited by your true old
HJ.

ALS: Houghton bMS Am 1094.3 (123)

*The shingles bother James again. He sends news of his family. Burgess has enlisted, and it is rumored that the Russians have infiltrated Belgium.*

[*Dictated*]

LAMB HOUSE   RYE   SUSSEX
Dearest lost—or strayed!—Neighbours.                     September 1st. 1914

I have a most priceless letter from you too long unacknowledged, and too beautiful not to make this form of response a gross affront to it; but necessities, apologies, explanations, are so much of the common stuff of life with us now that to take them at every moment sweepingly for granted is the only thing we can do. The sordid truth has been for me that I have

---

34. Margaret Payson, one of Peggy James's American friends. HJ once called her "aggressive and assertive" and thought her far inferior to Peggy.

had a bad nine days, with the question of letters etc. almost wholly smashed-up: the horrid old virus of my dismal illness of 1910–11 still remains within me sufficiently to give again and again a bad kick on opportunity perceived—and the opportunity offered by the "lowering" influence of the public atmosphere in these days has naturally been seized. It takes the old damnable form of the loss of power to eat, and that kept up awhile, puts one effectually back into the hole—out of which again, however, one has succeeded in scrambling. But by the time all these things have taken place the remarks in letters of some antiquity have become quite uncontemporary things to deal with. I can only bless very devoutly all the charities you pour forth upon me and hug the fond delusion that you may still after all turn up here—even if it *be* but a delusion. It would be inexpressibly good to hear your tap at the door and your fairy feet upon the threshold! Alice Dew looked in yesterday a.m.—greeted me on my first descent from sequestration to sit a bit in the garden with Peg; and she was truly a bit suggestive as to our perhaps not waiting for you in vain. She was more Alice Dew-y than ever—to the tune that without having yet even been out to the Hutch (only having slept her two or three nights at Mrs. Vincent's) she was already expecting a tea-party there in the form of Lady Matthew and Kathleen. She continues in short, as you see, to affect one as having in every connection, like Carlyle's Mirabeau,[35] swallowed all formulas.

Peg, thank the Lord, will now I hope be pretty well able to stick to me for a while—Aleck sails, on the other hand, from Bristol to Montreal on the 7th. next: quite the only thing for him to do. We have just been cabled to that Alice the younger and her Bill had a second son, weighing 9 pounds, born to them at 95 Irving Street—apparently on Sunday. But my little plot of domestic earth shakes up less with that than with the excellent enlistment of my precious little Burgess[36]—which he broke to me his desire for last evening; only of course to receive my unreserved backing and blessing. I felt it in the air for some time back, but wanted it to come *all* of itself, that is not to push or urge him (a responsibility I didn't want to take)—while he had delayed only out of his devoted consideration for myself. Of course I shall inordinately miss him—but that has no practical

35. Portrayed in Thomas Carlyle's book *The French Revolution,* Gabriel Mirabeau was the president of the Constituent Assembly in 1791.

36. After Burgess Noakes was wounded and left deaf while serving in the British army, he returned to work for HJ until the latter's death. Here the historical and the personal converge for HJ, making an already terrible time even worse.

bearing. Save for his short stature he will make a most solid little man-at-arms, and I'm hoping to be able to get him, still, though belated, into the Rye contingent of the Royal Sussex, that went hence to Dover two weeks ago.

That's as near as I shall attempt at this still somewhat invalid moment to address you on the public situation. You and dear George are far more in the thick of it than I, and I can only long to be addressed again by yourselves. I was very glad to have Burgess intimate me that even if he hadn't wanted to go, from the very first, the being an able-bodied youngish man about here and *not* going is a situation becoming too markedly disagreeable to the public eye to be any longer digested. Of course these extraordinary rumours of the infiltration through this country of a big Russian contingent for beyond the Channel during these last days will have assaulted you right and left if they have hummed about poor us in our comparative desert. In spite of ever so many corroborative little indications I had been afraid to risk credence of them till this morning, when my bedside Skinner gave me the reproduced snapshot in to-day's Daily Mail of the so-called disembarkation of "Belgian" troops at Ostend.[37] He told me to scan it closely, and one had to do so for but ten seconds to recognize the living Muscovite in his exact paraphernalia. You may not have had your notice called to it—which is why I do so now. I shouldn't have had mine without the very notice-taking Skinner. Bend your glass upon the reproduced scene and catch in their very truth the Russian faces, caps, overcoats and above all boots. Belgians disembarked moreover from *where?* The thing affects me as such a perfect little gem of evidence that I find it impossible not to believe it will affect you and George in the same way and convince you that we shall now quickly have the sequel. It's inordinately interesting, and if the thing has really been *done,* on the scale implied, it is surely a most brilliant and confidence-giving coup.

However, this is all I can babble to-day. It goes to Bedford Square as the rightest place to catch you. Peggy sits in the garden, which has been the most extraordinarily blest habitation to us, at certain hours—more hours than ever before—all last month; and would osculate, through me, furiously, if she knew I am writing. My old friends, the two Lawrence sisters (of Prince's Gate,) come over from Folkestone to tea with us this

---

37. Ostend is a seaside resort in Belgium that was occupied by the Germans for four years during World War I. Evidently the Belgian troops had gone to try to protect Ostend, but the British believed Russian soldiers had joined them and in fact were secretly in England.

afternoon, by their own proposition, bringing with them Frances Wolseley—of martial association! More at the first possible moment.

Ever your devotedest
*Henry James.*

TLS: Houghton bMS Am 1094.3 (124)

*James's health improves. He sends news of Rye and mutual friends (Elly Hunter, Mary
Cadwalader Jones, the Lowrys) and responds to her news of Constance Fletcher, whose
flesh is like the big round moon.*

[*Dictated*]

21, CARLYLE MANSIONS, CHEYNE WALK S.W.

Dear old Friend. September 20th. 1915

I have this a.m. your letter from Mundesley, and am glad to be able to
tell you that my hope of having really and truly turned an important corner
seems to be confirmed. I had yesterday, for example, a better day, and of a
better *kind* of betterness, than I have had for ever and ever so long; and this
even in the midst of ghosts, fading ghosts, but still ghosts, of old difficulties
that try and hang on from the force of habit, but which I do distinctly feel I
am turning my back upon. It may even be that when I get a little further,
and still a little further, away from them, I shall be better than for—well, I
won't attempt to measure how long. It's a madness, in fine, (a madness of
apparent recuperation) in which there is the most definite method conceivable.

Meanwhile let me thank you for your good office in the question of Elly,
which is probably in the act of taking effect. You will doubtless have
abstained, at my hint, from at all going into that subordinate question I
spoke of—which I am standing off from a little till I am able to see better
where I am. To tell the truth, it does loom a bit formidable—it's a biggish
engagement to take at this hour, but I shall be able to judge of it better after
she has been heard from, and on the spot; by which I mean after I have been
down to L. H. for a short, a very short, time, as I have now taken heart
rather to look forward to early next month. The good Lowrys leave L. H. a
week from to-day and come up to effect their entrance into 73 Cheyne
Walk, S.W. There remains an interval then, brief, I hope, but still an
interval, which I am not yet able to answer for. It depends considerably, not
to say entirely, on the duration of stay in London (before she sails for N.Y.)
made by Mrs. Jones, whom I suppose to return from Paris on Oct. 1st. She

very kindly returns in great part to see me (instead of sailing by a French liner;) and I must make no plan till I know about hers, though I imagine her then stay here to be pretty limited.

My thoughts have turned much to dear little Rye during the beauty of all this last week—I really have found myself thinking of it as probably exquisite; which I take for a good sign and omen of a better intrinsic condition on the part of this fond, though so often deluded, dreamer. Jolly that George is able to stay on.

I wish I could predicate some association of the jolly in respect to your present devoted vigil—before which, alas, one is but hushed to depths of mere wondering and waiting. Do tell her that here is an old friend who never, never forgets her—for all the good that may do her!

What you tell me of C. F. in Venice is on the other hand quite drenched in the jolly; she being like the big round moon, with its lighted quarter mostly glaring woe, no doubt, but with the flesh and the devil always kicking about more or less within its shaded part! The flesh must of course be largely and quite properly concerned in her nursing—though I hope devoutly the devil is kept out of it! At any rate I *will* say for her that though there are kinds of subjection to her, from which one naturally prays to be delivered—though there is in fact no kind but *one* in respect to which one doesn't so pray, I see just that one, the exception, in an almost delightfully, in fact a quite richly, possible light. I *could* bear to be nursed by her, and should back her through it with the greatest confidence. This after all is something of a tribute, and I am yours all faithfully

*Henry James*

TLS: Houghton bMS Am 1094.3 (133)

*Letters to Lady Louisa Erskine Wolseley*
*1882–1913*

## Time Line

1843    Louisa Erskine is born.

1868    "Loo" Erskine marries deputy quartermaster-general Garnet Wolseley.

1882    Henry James writes to Louisa to tell her of his father's death and to congratulate her on General Wolseley's victory over Arabi Pasha at Tel-el-Kebir.

1895    James visits the Wolseleys in Ireland and attends their fancy dress ball at the Royal Hospital.

1898    James moves to Lamb House; Louisa later advises him on decorating it.

1901    General Wolseley retires as commander in chief of the British forces.

1913    James writes to console Lady Wolseley on her husband's death.

1916    James dies.

1920    Estranged from her only daughter, Frances, Lady Wolseley dies.

Lady Louisa Wolseley as a young woman, with her dog, Coffee. (Reprinted by permission of the Hove Reference Library, Sussex, England.)

## Introduction

What I shall choose, of course, will be full uniform: of your kind & various alternatives that is clearly the one marked out for me. If I can't "please myself" in this way I shall simply drape myself in the American flag: dispose it in a few graceful folds. Anything—anything, not to look like a supernumerary Waiter. Please believe I appreciate immensely your giving me this liberal notice. Never shall I have been à pareille fete [at a comparable party]. . . . [A] kind of frenzy is seizing me & I seem to hear already the drums & fifes of your dance. I hear, at any rate, your most generous welcome & am yours, dear Lady Wolseley, more than ever devotedly yours   —*Henry James* (18 February 1895, Hove 35)

Thus Henry James responded to Lady Louisa Wolseley's invitation to her fancy dress ball, to be held in Dublin the next month at the Royal Hospital, where General Wolseley was headquartered as commander in chief of the British forces in Ireland. Lady Wolseley, a partner with her husband in a nineteenth-century joint military career, planned the ball to solidify both her own and her husband's position, and to bolster the British presence in Dublin. It would be a great political, as well as a social, event. Louisa Wolseley asked women to dress as their favorite character from a Gainsborough, Romney, or Reynolds painting; men were to come in uniform, court dress, or hunt evening dress. James, always intrigued by Lady Wolseley's power mongering, mockingly debated what to wear.

James first met Lady Louisa Erskine Wolseley as early as the summer of 1877. In the winter of 1878 he told William that she was "pretty, and has the air, the manners, the toilets and the taste, of an American."[1] By 1882, they

---

1. *Henry James Letters,* ed. Leon Edel, vol. 2 (Cambridge: Harvard University Press, 1975), 151.

were good friends. His first extant letter to her, from 30 December 1882, tells her of his father's death and congratulates her on Wolseley's military triumph over the Egyptian nationalist Arabi Pasha at Tel-el-Kebir, a slaughter engineered by Wolseley and the British cabinet to crush the incipient Egyptian nationalist movement and assure England's access to the Suez Canal. That letter sets the theme for the rest of their correspondence: his delight at her social and political triumphs. While her husband traveled, James provided her with companionship and listened attentively to all her secrets. And as Lady Louisa directed the conquests of the British Empire from behind the scenes, Henry James applauded his friend's maneuvers.

Born to a modest family, Louisa Erskine was intelligent and beautiful, her appearance compared to both the Venus de Milo and the empress Eugenie. Fully aware of her personal charms, in 1884 she sent her husband a picture of herself, with the instructions, "Please slip me out of my frame, and observe the beauty of my arms, which is very remarkable!"[2] She was fluent in French, and she loved clothes (she was known as the best-dressed woman in London), antiques, and books. Wolseley met her in Ireland in 1861 and fell "most dreadfully in love," but they didn't marry until 1868, when his military career was well under way. She promoted that career, entertaining lavishly and consulting with Queen Victoria on military policy. Wolseley himself was the quintessential British officer, satirized in the light opera *The Pirates of Penzance* as "our only General." His rapid promotions were due at least as much to her efforts at home as to his on the battlefield. She cultivated British cabinet officials and their wives, and her correspondence with Wolseley during his frequent absences kept him abreast of important political changes in England. She called herself a "mole," an apt metaphor for such an active conspirator. James enjoyed both Wolseleys, admiring Sir Garnet's military stature and Lady Louisa's beauty and social graces.

When Wolseley was promoted, Henry James wrote witty letters of congratulations to Louisa. He helped her find bookbindings (a hobby she loved), advised her on daughter Frances's social life, and accompanied her on antiquing expeditions. Lady Wolseley in turn helped James find furniture, both for his London apartments and for Lamb House in Rye. Both loved gossiping about their mutual acquaintances, who included the Brit-

---

2. Sir George Arthur, ed., *The Letters of Lord and Lady Wolseley, 1870–1911* (New York: Doubleday, Page, 1922), 140.

ish nobility and other writers. She shared military secrets with James, knowing how he relished her successes and perhaps suspecting that what he learned from her about wielding power eventually found its way into his novels and tales.

James reserved his most provocative rhetoric for his letters to Lady Wolseley. Although he may well have been more attracted to her tall military footmen than to her, flirtatious language permeates their correspondence. Just as she used her beauty to secure her husband's promotion, so James used his familiarity with sexual politics to woo his friend Louisa. In one letter he playfully compares himself to a procurer and Lady Louisa to a prostitute, suggesting that they might be "lighting up the London fog with the twinkle of 3 or 4 sovereigns" (22 September 1885, Hove 12).

When Lord Wolseley died in 1913, James wrote a moving letter of condolence to his widow, restating his admiration for his old friend. Alienated from her daughter Frances, who was by then a successful gardener and businesswoman, this reminder of a decades-old friendship with a delightful and brilliant man must have comforted Louisa Wolseley. Perhaps she too turned once again to the letters she had saved from Henry James, letters that not even a century's passing have faded.

131 Mount Vernon St. Boston, United States.

Dear Lady Wolseley.                                        Dec. 30*th* [1882]

Your gracious & friendly note followed me across the wintry Atlantic, on which I had embarked the day it must have been delivered in Bolton St. I had started at a day's notice, on receipt of the news of the dangerous illness of my father, whom I hoped to see once more in life. My hope, however, was vain, for when I arrived nine days ago, I found that every-thing was over, & I was not even to see him in death. It was a violent shock; in addition to which I was ill for several days after I disembarked; so that it is only now that I am beginning to look round me. One of the first things I see, in this circumspection, is your note waiting for an answer. It shall have one without a day's delay more, but it will not be such an answer as it needs. How glad I should be to talk with you of Parisian things, if it were not to be supposed you have long before this got your information else-where or even dispensed with it altogether & simply charged upon Paris in gallant Tel-el-Kebir fashion.[3] (I don't mean to imply by this, by the way, that Sir Garnet, before Tel-el-Kebir had not taken his *renseignments* [infor-mation].) You are either now in Paris—or you have been there—or you have given it up—or you are receiving a deluge of information from high quarters: in all of which cases my faint illumination of the subject would come too late. If I had not been taking my ship at Southampton at the moment your letter was sent to me, I should have immediately gone to see you, laden with stores of knowledge, for I had already returned to Lon-don—since December 1*st* & was meaning from one day to the other to come & make you my obeisance. I spent the three autumn months in France, but only November in Paris, having been before that wholly *en province* [in the country]. In Paris I was constantly at hotels, but all my friends were in health there, & though they talked a good deal about typhoid, none of them seemed to have picked it up. May you & yours have been at least as fortunate! Truly, you will say, this is the least I can wish you, considering the good wishes I owe you & of which you have so gracefully

---

3. HJ refers to Garnet Wolseley's victory over the Egyptian nationalist leader Arabi Pasha at the battle of Tel-el-Kebir. Recent views of this engagement hold that it was engineered by the British to eliminate Arabi and thus destroy the burgeoning nationalist movement, in order to protect British interests in the Suez Canal.

reminded me. I assure you, it was not from want of interest in your triumphs & honours that I have been holding my peace & staying my hand. I have stood there in the far background—behind the bristling hedge of plumes and coronets—holding my little bouquet. I was only waiting for a little quiet moment to present it—a moment when I might steal up & modestly slip it into your hand. The other floral tributes made such a mountain before you that it was not easy [to] get at you. And yet when I saw with what a kind smile you received the smallest as well as the biggest nosegay, I said to myself, Courage, one congratulation is as good as another, & all are alike good. The truth is, I was not afraid I should forget to congratulate you, or that my good wishes would spoil by keeping. I only wished the big drums to move away a little. I was travelling through old French towns & looking at chateaux and cathedrals when the news of your husband's successive achievements arrived, & with each arrival I saw, through the quiet picture before me, the picture of certain more dreadful & painful things. But that too always changed to quietness again, & to the vision of a pretty drawing-room, somewhere, in which a certain lady stood reading a bulletin. The word "Egypt" ended at last by always evoking you—& always in a proud & happy attitude, as became a conqueror's wife. I congratulate you most heartily on the whole matter—on the thing having been so brilliantly, scientifically, & completely done. I don't wish you any more laurels, because you have enough & because they are plucked in such uncomfortable places; but I wish that those which now mingle so gracefully with your coiffure may never lose their freshness! There is little news, that you will care for, to send you from this big busy, sunny, & for me terribly homesick, side of the world. I find here to-day not another country from England, but another world altogether, & so vast & prosperous a one that it can quite dispense with one's pretending to take a polite interest in it. But a 1000 miles of the new civilization says less to me than five inches of the old. Àpropos of which, how are those two ripe products of an ancient society, the good ladies of Whitehall?[4] How *they* must have congratulated you! You will think a while before conquering another country! Please to give them my very kind remembrances, & if you

---

4. Louisa and Mary Lawrence, sisters of British horticulturalist Trevor Lawrence and close family friends of the Wolseleys. The sisters were devoted to one another and died in the same year. HJ dined with them in March 1878.

would also say something friendly for me to the ⟨?⟩ Mrs. Lecky,[5] I should be greatly obliged. Believe me very cordially & faithfully yours

H. James

ALS: Hove 105[6]

*James empathizes with Lady Wolseley on her husband's departure, but she has mastered "waiting" (as wife of a general) as an occupation. When he last visited her, he suspected that she knew that General Wolseley was on his way to Khartoum to relieve General Gordon.*

Dover, 15 Esplanade

Dear Lady Wolseley. Sept. 3d 1884

I have wished both to congratulate & to condole with you, but I have thought it better to wait till Lord Wolseley has left these shores & the tossed-up waters of your fate had begun to subside. Now (unless you spend all your time in reading *his* missions—though they will hardly, as yet, have begun to pour in)—I suppose you are accessible to a word from an old friend who would like you to know that he appreciates both your glory & your gloom! How clever you were about these mystic elements during that warm episode at the Ralli's! There were moments during that genial walk over the hills when the bout de l'oreille [secret] *might* have cropped out, if it hadn't been such a very cautious, attentive oreille! However, now that we are all in the secrets,[7] I can say that we all *did* suspect it, & can pretend that my discretion (even amid the comparative familiarity of the goose-berry=picking) was almost as great as yours. May your isolation be brief, & sustained by the most felicitous bulletins. I am wondering what other aids you cultivate, during these weeks of waiting. But no one waits so gracefully & genially as you—that is a part of your métier as the wife of a general, that you have thoroughly mastered, & it is an occupation in itself. If you are in Staffordshire, as I suppose, I am afraid (in spite of the occupation just=mentioned) that you have leisure to think about ⟨Crecie?⟩. I *languish*

5. This was Elizabeth Lecky (d. 1912), the baroness van Deden, daughter of the Dutch baron van Deden and wife of the Rt. Hon. William Edward Hartpole Lecky (1838–1903). She had been lady-in-waiting to Queen Sophia of the Netherlands; her husband was an Irish historian, essayist, and politician.

6. All transcriptions from letters marked "Hove" in this edition are used by permission of the Hove Reference Library, Sussex, England, and by permission of Bay James, literary executor of the James papers. "ALS" means "autograph letter signed." "TLS" means "typed letter signed."

7. The "secret" was that Wolseley was going to Khartoum to relieve General Gordon.

for news of her—but it doesn't come. It *must* now, from one day to the other; & then you shall have it all, be it ever so much—which I fear it won't be. I am immersed in unsociable silence & converse only with the winds & waves. We talk often about you, but they tell me less than I should some day, at your convenience, like to hear from a still purer source! Kindly remember this for the benefit of yours, dear Lady Wolseley, very faithfully

Henry James

ALS: Hove 2

---

*James advises Lady Wolseley on Parisian bookbindings. Paul Bourget's book is uninteresting. He extols the marvels of Venice and Florence, wishing he could show her Venice's loveliness himself.*

St. Alban's Cliff Bournemouth

Dear Lady Wolseley.                                     June 6*th* [1885]

There are sure to be interesting bindings at the Bibliothèque Nationale & at the Mazarine, as well as a certain number in the Louvre. The last mentioned ones I have seen in the past (the others I never investigated) but I don't remember in what part of the Musée they are. Any of the gardiens, however, would tell you instantly—& I allow here even for your occasional ill=luck with the "most polite people on earth"—the whereabouts of the "edition de livres rares, de reliures historiques [rare book editions and historic bindings]". The gardiens of the libraries would, I am sure, prostrate themselves before you on the enunciation of your name or presentation of your card, & show you all their treasures. But it occurs to me that if you don't want to escalader [scale] public institutions, a very good place to go for your purpose wd. be *Fontaine's* (the great "fancy" bookseller) in the Passajes des Panoramas[8]—tout au fond [at the very back]. (Or is it perhaps the Passajes des Princes?) I forget which (I confound them) but they are both interesting places to explore—opening out of the Boulevard des Italiens & Montmartre. The said Fontaine is the biggest "swell," as a dealer in books, in Europe, & has *treasures* in the way of antiquities, rare copies, rare bindings &c, & I'm sure that his shop would be worth your visit. I ought to mention that his *prices* are colossal, but for that reason it is *d'usage* [customary] to go & look, to look again & again. Tell him frankly who you are & what you want.——It has been delightful to hear from you & to be

---

8. HJ spells this "Passajes des Panoramas," but there was a Passages des Panoramas opening off the Blvd. Montmarte and Bld. des Italiens, so this is probably what he had in mind.

able to tell you how I have mourned your absence, & how lacerated I was, in particular, by the abruptness of your departure. There was a certain *second* call which I dreamed of paying you, during that momentary perch of yours in London, but when the moment came (ill-fated Thursday) I was howling with an attack of lumbago, which I cursed the more as it prevented me making up for my failure to find you the day or two before. That is over—more or less—I am happy to say, but my life isn't much the gayer, as you may judge from my whereabouts at this festive season. I am evading the mingled pleasures & pains of London altogether; and spending these months in salubrious seclusion. I am not earning thereby, this time, I fear, the dedication of any books, but I shall be the less compromised. I have been considerably so this year, by my dedicating friends. *Cruelle Enigme*[9] is, to my view, wonderfully refined & superior in *form,* but I don't care a straw for the story poor Bourget has undertaken to tell, or for the people of *whom* he tells it. They don't interest me. The idea of your *entertaining* Julia[10] with elegant extracts from *L'Irréparable* [another of Bourget's books] is delicious—irreparable I fear would have been the impression made on that sensitive frank maiden. All this time I don't tell you how much more even than usual I am charmed with you—pardon the freedom of the expression—for being charmed with my Florence. With Venice—that goes without saying: but it isn't every one that appreciates— as you & I do—the adorable little city by the Arno. Some of the happiest moments of my life have been spent there, & the *quality* of the place seems to me quite unspeakable. But I hope, for your happiness, that you are still in Venice: the "dongola"[11] doesn't yield its full enchantment till June yields up its warmth. My imagination lingers about you, wherever you are, just as it hovered vainly in your wake when you went to Cairo & gives me moments—hours—of envy, of sympathy, of curiosity, of ineffectual effort to figure to myself your occupations & interests, & of friendly impatience

---

9. The popular French novel *Cruel Enigma* (1885) by Paul Bourget realistically portrayed corruption in the French upper classes and was the first in a series of successful novels. Bourget admired James, and while James liked him in return, he didn't always admire Bourget's writing.

10. Possibly this is Julia Tollemache (Mrs. Charles) Roundells, a friend of the Wolseleys.

11. The "dongola" probably refers to the Egyptian province of Dongola, where General Wolseley and his troops had been stationed since their unsuccessful attempt to save General Gordon, who had been besieged at Khartoum. In the spring of 1885 Lady Wolseley had met the general in Cairo for three weeks, and James may have been cynically suggesting that Lady Wolseley was better off in Venice than she would have been in Dongola in the summer. The British vanguard finally left Dongola town in June 1885.

for your return. My own life is virtuous (not that I mean to imply that yours isn't,) but slightly grey. I shall scarcely return to London for any part of this detestable Season, & after that my ideas are vague. They would have something to cluster about if I foresaw your return. How I wish I could look at Venice with you—I think I could show you some of its more latent loveliness! But I will meet you by the Arno any day you may in the future be so good as to assignate to yours, dear Lady Wolseley, always most faithfully

*Henry James*

ALS: Hove 6

*James welcomes Lady Wolseley back to England. He is at the circumference of the "gilded throng" greeting her and is "peacefully frightened" by her warriors, so he writes instead. He wants to see the bindings she found in Paris.*

3 Bolton St. W.

Dear Lady Wolseley. July 14*th* [1885]

Welcome back to Old England, qui a du bon [which has some good], after all, in spite of Egyptian improprieties. This is a very friendly line to meet you, & thank you for your Parisian note, more modestly than if I had sought to mingle in the gilded throng yesterday. My place is at the circumference, not at the centre, & among all your warriors I should have been peacefully frightened. Moreover, you had Pandeli,[12] whose sensibility, as I remember, you praised to me highly the last time I had the pleasure of talking with you, and in such a presence (added to Lord Wolseley's) what more could you desire? Though I don't belong to the center I shall close in toward it, now, with rapidity. I am eager for your Parisian anecdotes & reminiscences; as well as for a sight of your bindings; & I shall probably attempt to prove to you that the former are not quite so bad as you suppose, & that the latter are even better. London (I have been back in it but five days) is wanting—at this fag end of the season, in social charm, but you will supply the article, especially to yours very faithful

*Henry James*

ALS: Hove 7

---

12. Pandeli Ralli, one of General Wolseley's aides.

247

*HJ thanks Lady Wolseley for a check but is disappointed not to receive it in person. He hoped they would have a romantic meeting, "lighting up the London fog with the twinkle of 3 or 4 sovereigns." He is in Paris, going to plays and sipping on grenadine.*

29 Rue Cambon

Dear Lady Wolseley.  Sept 22*d* [1885]

The cheque, with its valuable autograph (what a pity I should part with it for so paltry a sum!) lies before me & testifies your excellent business habits. I am much obliged to you for it, but am slightly disappointed, as I sentimentally hoped that we might have a little romantic *personal* transaction, later, on the subject—lighting up the London fog with the twinkle of 3 or 4 sovereigns. I shall only get the check cashed if the inroads of Paris on my modest exchequer reduce me to this extremity: but my extravagances are very moderate, & consist mainly of neckties, croûte au pot [pot pie] & the theatres—after which indeed I generally take a *grenadine glacés* [iced grenadine], with 2 straws. Do you know what that is? I applaud your bookbinding ambitions, & promise you my patronage, although (I ought to say *because*) I am very particular. I don't like books—that people show you sometimes in London—that look as if they had been bound by the shoemaker. Your work, however, will have the trace of fairy-fingers. I should be delighted to know Colonel Grove,[13] & if I have ever have [*sic*] that privilege he will remind me of the little circle of warriors the other day in your heathery park. I can't tell you how my memory glows with all that picture. Paris continues to be as quiet as Angoulême or Levens—but looking very pretty, with a kind of gilded September haze. I have 2 dying friends[14] whom I go to see on alternate days, & that adds to the melancholy impression! It was the same when I was here last—all my spare hours were spent at a deathbed. Do write me about your return to the yellow medium of Hill St; give me back gloom for gloom. Hill St. however, can never be gloomy for your very devoted

*Henry James*

ALS: Hove 12

---

13. Colonel Coleridge Grove was on General Wolseley's staff. He accompanied Lady Wolseley and her daughter Frances to Germany in 1895.

14. One friend was Blanche de Triqueti Childe, wife of Robert E. Lee's nephew Edward Lee Childe. The other was presumably William H. Huntingdon (1820–1885), the *Tribune* correspondent to Paris.

*James discusses Lady Wolseley's Hill Street renovations and suggests her daughter Frances should not marry young. He praises writer Vernon Lee, who lives in Florence. He works on sunny mornings.*

Hotel du Sud. Florence
January 20*th* [1887]

Dear Lady Wolseley.

Your kind & charming letter would have confirmed my worst fears had it not been for the mention of the backstaircase you are having constructed in Hill St. If you are making a back staircase it is because you intend to linger on in that noble mansion—which is all that immediately concerns me. Unless indeed the structure in question is only being called into existence to enable you to steal out of the house—forever—the more effectually! However, I think of the ballroom, & your daughter's debut &c—& I am on the whole reassured. None the less it aggravates me almost as much as if I were in London to hear *you positively flaunt* your contentment in the midwinter Haslemere. I am glad you are happy enough there—but I am very sorry you are more than just exactly that—& I seem to detect something unsocial and defiant in your tone. It bodes ill for the coming years—& I take refuge in hoping that Miss Frances will not marry young—though I hasten to add that even my desire to keep you in town would not make me invoke for her a singleness extending to the period— say—of that of our friends in Whitehall Place.[15] I rejoice that since the backstaircase was to be made you should have chosen this particular winter for it, as it seems to be turning out that I am to spend the full compass of it (I don't mean of the staircase) in Italy. I shall presently have been two months in Florence, & I came hither to stay only three weeks. Rome & Venice remain unvisited & still I linger & procrastinate. Perhaps you will explain it on the theory that I have a passion for Vernon Lee.[16] If it should seem uncivil to that courageous & accomplished girl to repudiate the idea, I am ready to bear the imputation in silence. I am ready even to admit that I see her very often & that I find her one of the very few intelligent persons I have been able to discover in this venerable yet frivolous town—this society commemorated—& worthy to be commemorated—by Ouida.[17] To appreciate her properly one must see her in the setting of her strange, almost sinister domestic circumstances—between her poor paralysed &

---

15. The sisters Louisa and Mary Lawrence lived in Whitehall Place.

16. "Vernon Lee" was the pen name of Violet Paget (1856–1935), prolific British writer. She and James were good friends for a time, but he cooled his friendship with her after 1893.

17. "Ouida" was the pen name of Marie Louise de la Ramée (1839–1908), popular British novelist. She lived in Florence from 1874 and wrote about Italian peasants.

horizontal brother, her fantastic & contorted little mother & her uncanny half-Polish papa. In spite of these drawbacks & others, however, she has something of a salon—in which she herself is easily the cleverest element. I gave her your friendly message—& if she knew I were writing (you see I don't tell her *every* thing!) she could probably charge me with many things. As I want to go to Rome—& I want to go to Venice—& I want to stay in Paris awhile before I return to the city we both adore—& as I shall probably spend three weeks more in Florence—the date of my return to my Kensington perch remains rather vague. To tell the truth, since you, dear lady Wolseley, are perching in the mountains of Sussex (or is it Surrey?) I am not in a particular hurry. Though I adore London, I adore also being out of it; sweet to me is the sense of Italy & of the smaller, easier life one comes in for here. I find it excellent for work—in the sunny mornings. My rooms are flooded with that element, & my windows over-hang the shining Arno. It is inconsistent—but I like it. I shall be en-chanted to do anything for you in Paris & a word to 34 De Vere Gardens will always reach me. Believe me, dear Lady Wolseley, most faithfully & irrevocably yours

*Henry James*

ALS: Hove 14

*James plans to visit Lady Wolseley to escape a boring house party.*

ALDERBROOK, CRANLEIGH, GUILDFORD.

Dear Lady Wolseley.                                     [23 November 1887]

On Friday, please—*do* let me come on Friday. There *is* animation—Lady Cork, Lady D. Nevil, Lord C. & a little girl I don't yet know are all talking at once at my elbow, & at the same time Ralli is reading out a newspaper to them. It is very grim—& you are unspeakably missed. If you were here we might—but let me not dally with the vain thought. I will come on Friday by the first train by which I can escape—& perhaps you will let me go up to town with you on Saturday. Lord Wolseley has given me an account of your enlightened rigidity (in regard to these dangers,) which the rest of my life shall be devoted to emulate. Friday seems far—terribly far, but nothing lasts for ever—not even Lady C. & Lady De N. It is a comfort to feel you are near. Believe me very impatiently yours

*Henry James*
Thursday [deleted] Alas no,
Wednesday a.m.

ALS: Hove 16

*James thanks her for her help buying furniture. He complains of the London fog, and he misses her.*

REFORM CLUB, PALL MALL, S.W.

Dear Lady Wolseley.                    January 15*th 1888*

I feel that I have treated you like a very low brute—never having written to tell you in what good form the famous chairs arrived—the chairs in which you took so humane an interest. They are excellent in every particular, and when their toilette is made, with the aid of your Paddington artist (whom I haven't yet had the right moment to go & see,) I shall feel that I lead a very ornate life, & all by your beneficent care. Will that care give me the advantage of its further attention—some day—any day—when it has nothing better, en passant [in passing], to do, to the extent of mentioning to Mr. Pratt that if he hasn't sold (as he probably has,) the elegant bookcase & écritoire that we admired, I will give him £12, on his sending it to me? I shall take this very kindly of you, if you are not sick of my little wants & delays & omissions. If he *has* sold the object it doesn't matter—this will give me an excellent pretext for coming down again to look for another.— —We have been going through a black tunnel of fog, as I suppose you know, during which I have had mental glimpses of the bright yellow rooms of Oakdene, with the shining weald (or wold?—or whatever it is,) outside & the great logs blazing within, & the armchairs listening to each other say "How handsome & sympathetic we are—though we haven't got a flounce!" (ah, the question of that flounce!) These visions have glowed before me as my retarded hansom has ploughed through the black air to take me to the dinners you don't go to!—or even a little the other day when it conveyed me to the train for Dorking, where (at Burford,) I spent a day with the good sister, the good brother & the good wife. Medical Pagets,[18] Mr. & Mrs. Boehm, Corny Grain (distressing man!) [,] George Meredith[19] & a ten mile walk! We almost walked to Guildford. How, if we had reached it, I would have darted ahead! I hope everything is serene in the golden,

---

18. This probably refers to writer Violet Paget ("Vernon Lee") and her paralyzed half brother Lee-Hamilton. Her mother was also an invalid.

19. George Meredith (1828–1909) was a famous English writer. In a letter to Grace Norton, James said, "He is the wittiest Englishman . . . that I have ever known" (ca. 4 January 1888).

pictorial rooms! I hope the young lady now drills her redcoat.[20] I hope you have either got a footman sufficiently perpendicular, or sufficiently ambitious to become so. I wish *you* were less erect, in your scorn of London— & I am ever your very prostrate, prone & faithful friend

Henry James

ALS: Hove 19

---

*James has decorated the cupboard Lady Wolseley helped him buy, which looks "almost as if you had dressed it." He still misses her.*

34 De Vere Gdns W.

Dear Lady Wolseley. Feb. 8*th* [1888]

I have only waited till I should have lived with the pretty cupboard a little, & be able to speak of it knowingly, to thank you afresh for your generous share in the business of bringing us—me & it—together. It arrived some days ago, blushing & trembling, so that it literally came to pieces on reaching my sky=high little residence. But I found that this was only "a way it had" & that it would all go together again when the flutter was over. I have stood it gently in my dining room (an un-compromising place) & even made it a little toilette of red silk (behind the glass—to cover the nudity of the shelves—brilliant with no Dresden Sêvres;) so that now I think it is quite steady & comfortable. It has a blue & white pot on top of it—a sort of bonnet, to match the red silk *fichu* [headscarf]. It looks almost as if you had dressed it. Some day you must come & see it—& have tea. It smartens me up immensely.——It is very sad to think that as the days lengthen, & the light, & the list of notes, every morning, your advent is not nearer—your share in these pleasures is not what it ought to be. When it really comes over me, a few weeks hence, that you are not here, & that Hill St. mourns its brightest ornament, I shall begin to be haunted with visions of weird pictures upon yellow walls, & shall be bold & presupposing, & find I want another five pounds-worth at Guildford. Till then, & after, I am faithfully & gratefully yours

Henry James

ALS: Hove 21

---

20. Lady Wolseley's daughter Frances had a suitor around this time, Lord Castlemaine. Rumor insinuated that Lady Wolseley discouraged the romance because she resented Frances's attention going to someone else.

3 Bolton St. W.

Dear Lady Wolseley.　　　　　　　　　　　　　　March 20*th* [1888]

I have been immersed, over head & ears, in correspondence, & in writing of other kinds: which is why I didn't answer your charming note (your notes are charming even when they solicit funds) the moment it arrived. You beg so delightfully, so irresistibly, that it is a pity such gifts are wasted on a high position—that you are not in a station in which it might become a career. The sixpences, I am sure, would patter into your extended palm. I assure you I should have taken it very ill if you had applied to the weird sisters without your thought being carried on, by an irresistible association of ideas, to me. I consider that we constitute (we 4) a little fraternity—brotherhood, sisterhood—call it what you will—pervaded & united by the same instincts of charity. You will be prepared doubtless, after this, to learn that I enclose a cheque for at least £100. But I don't, alas; & I can only hope that the very different little document which accompanies this, embodying the poor bachelor's mite, the scribbler's modest dole, will not simply move your scorn. The institution you speak of seems to me worthy of every countenance, & I am glad it is in such good hands as yours.——The idea of your rural beneficence consoles me a little—but only a little—for your absence from our lively *quartier* [neighborhood]— much less lively for me now. The voice of the newsboy, too, is silent; & that is an element of repose. I can well imagine that your refuge should be pleasant to you; I should think a homely peace & plenty, a mild & refreshing stagnation, would rub off from the roof & walls, the sofas and tables impregnated with the spirit of the Roundells.[21] I dined with them the other day, & found them overflowing, as usual, with modest worth. I have also been dining more than once of late (in company) with Mrs. Lang.[22] She is a different type (by which I don't mean that she isn't worthy & modest)—but only that she rather stimulates than soothes. I haven't seen the nymphs of Whitehall for a good while, but now that I am fortified by a letter from you shall probably soon penetrate into their bowers. Listen

---

21. Julia Elizabeth Anne Tollemache and Charles Saville Roundells. HJ met Roundells during an Oxford weekend.

22. Leonora Blanche Alleyne Lang, wife of Andrew Lang (1844–1912), Scottish scholar, writer, and avid collector of fairy tales. They married in 1875 and moved to London. Mrs. Lang did some translating and writing herself.

well, one of these next afternoons, & you will *hear* us, even in the weald (isn't the weald?) of Sussex. I am delighted to hear from yourself that Lord Wolseley's health is all that can be desired—though I knew already that the rumours to the contrary were characteristically false. Don't "take root," as they say in Yankeeland, in the unsocial fields, but remember that the quartier misses you acutely, & none of its inhabitants more intensely than yours, ever faithfully

*Henry James.*

ALS: Hove 22

*HJ is in Italy. He missed seeing her in London, where she must have entertained a brilliant throng.*

Hotel de Londres Verona

Dear Lady Wolseley. June *29th* [1890]

I jump at the opportunity to write you a little note—so long & so cruelly have I languished for a proper occasion to venture to remind you that, though silent, I am far wanting [*sic*], in respect to the intensity of those sentiments that I owe you. Even this splendid Italy of early summer does not console me for having missed the happiness of having mingled obscurely with the brilliant throng that must have pressed through your saloons on the 24*th*. I should (in a quiet way) have enjoyed the occasion only less than you yourself; & I should have enjoyed still more talking it over with you afterwards. I pray the day may not be distant when I may still do that, however. May we not then compare impressions?—mine of the misery of being out of it, with yours of the joy of being in it? Your joy is of course largely your daughter's—& I trust that that is immense & knows not the shade of an intermission. I more than suspect that with her excellent example, you are adoring everything you have hitherto burned. I came to Italy the 1*st* days of May & the end is not yet. I am on my way back to Venice after an absence. In August & September London shall again possess me, & Blackheath shall receive—if Blackheath will or can—yours, dear Lady Wolseley, most indestructibly,

*Henry James*

ALS: Hove 30

*James will visit her in Dublin, where General Wolseley commands the British forces. He hopes she is having a leisurely summer with her two "children" (Wolseley and Frances) gone.*

34 De Vere *Gardens*.W.

Dearest Lady Wolseley. July 26*th* '94

I never "contradicted" you in my life, and I shall certainly not choose this moment to do so—touched as I am to tears by the kindness of your letter & the indulgence of your gentle memory of me—playing so softly out of the grey cloud of what I deeply regret to hear you speak of as invalidism. I hasten to assure you that you may absolutely count upon me for a visit at some moment of the generous period—October to March—that you give me to shake about in! I shall be delighted to settle the date with you later. Meanwhile let me breathe about you all the friendliest sympathy your discomforts, whatever they may be, do unassumingly invite. Somehow, try as I will, I can't see [you] do anything but look extremely well on some pretty *chaise longue* in some delightfully panelled & painted old "Chesterfield" room, as the lady who came to see you at Greenwich wd. have said. (You see how I remember your *moindres anecdotes* [the least of your jokes].) By "looking well" I don't necessarily mean look in the least as if you were a humbug in saying you are *un*well; but you know what I do mean! I am glad you are having an easy, leisurely, irresponsible summer—which I gather to be the case in the absence of your two children[23]—not indeed that they are a source of difficulty. But they are inevitably the world—and when the world rolls off on one of its blessed tangents it leaves—well, it leaves a margin. Kind as you are I don't believe without your margin you would have written to me. All thanks then to margins! I came back from Italy, where I had been since the middle of March, exactly a fortnight ago; & not many days later I bent an eager step to Whitehall place—largely to turn on the tap which the mention of your name causes so happily to flow. It gushed as freely as usual from the punctually alternate fountains—& I lingered long in the more & more decorated bower. The dear ladies [Louisa and Mary Lawrence] are not less remarkable, I think, for quantity than of yore, but the quality strikes me as less strong & heady. They feel, as we mostly do, the pacifications, the resignations of time—& are just perceptibly chastened and subdued. I have seen almost nobody else—& am pretending that I am still abroad, for

---

23. She had only one child, daughter Frances, so here James must refer to Frances and Lord Wolseley.

there are still dinners in the air, & the London dinner on the edge of August is the falsest enjoyment I know. As early as I can next month I go down to Devon & Cornwall till toward the end of September. Then I return to London to stick as tight as a leech save when *you* make me a sign.——Yes, Via Palestro was charming, but I was only a few days in Florence. I spent almost all my weeks in Venice, where I took a little apartment & tried to be comfortable. Too many people wanted to help me to be—that was the only drawback; & it is one of which it is ungracious to complain.——I shall be delighted to see you in the place where you have made the latest chapter of your history—but if one must hurry to do that I shall rejoice in any step nearer that Greenwich will come again. I can't talk reason about Greenwich—j'en suis fou [I'm mad about it]! I mean in a few days to go out and eat bad things at the Trafalgar (or is it the other inn that solely survives?) in order to have a pretext for walking up the little hill and staring homesickly at your closed portals. Roam at your ease in your painted halls, & don't forget, dear Lady Wolseley, that I shall be delighted to join you there. Believe me yours evermore

*Henry James*

ALS: Hove 33

*HJ plans his Irish trip, discussing his costume for her fancy dress ball. If he cannot find full uniform, he will drape himself in the American flag.*

34, DE VERE GARDENS. W.

Dear Lady Wolseley. Feb. 18*th* [1895]

It *is* terrific—especially with Mrs. Jekyll[24] bringing up the rear: but I am bracing myself. What I shall choose, of course, will be full uniform: of your kind & various alternatives that is clearly the one marked out for me. If I can't "please myself" in this way I shall simply drape myself in the American flag: dispose it in a few graceful folds. Anything—anything, not to look like a supernumerary Waiter. Please believe I appreciate immensely your giving me this liberal notice. Never shall I have been à pareille fête [at a comparable party]. I shall rush off to my Tailor, & then it is clear, to Whitehall Place. I wish *they* were coming—say as the Duchess of Devonshire & Lady Hamilton. *Which* Lady H.? I give it up. I saw Edmund Gosse the other evening, & his eloquence made my mouth water. He had evi-

---

24. Herbert Jekyll was Lord Houghton's private secretary. Jekyll lived in a lodge in Phoenix Park in Ireland.

dently passed the golden week of his life. What shall *I* pass? I must find a comparison. At any rate I count the days. As regards Mrs. Jekyll—I fear, however, I must play Doctor Hide. Shall I say to you crudely Keep Her Quiet? No matter—a kind of frenzy is seizing me & I seem to hear already the drums & fifes of your dance. I hear, at any rate, your most generous welcome & am yours, dear Lady Wolseley, more than ever devotedly yours

*Henry James*

ALS: Hove 35

*James is "an obscure & economical black spot" in the middle of all the British military splendor surrounding him in Ireland.*

THE CASTLE, DUBLIN.

Dear Lady Wolseley. [13 March 1895]

Your kind note comforts me unspeakably—& adds fuel to the flame of my impatience for this blessed Saturday next. Will it ever, ever, ever come? I gaze at it through a mournful vista of interposing difficulties & dangers, & it taxes my faith almost as much as the idea of the kingdom of heaven. Tomorrow night, however, that faith will be appreciably fortified—though even tomorrow night is lost in the mists of the far away—the mirage of the desert. How much I shall have to tell you! But it will be all in the plaintive, pathetic key. The sight of all the splendours that surround me here—all the bleu ciel [sky blue] coat-fronts in particular—makes me feel doubly your magnanimity in suffering me to be an obscure & economical black spot on your great picture. I shall have to come "as I am"—but I'm full, dear lady Wolseley, of devotion. That's what "I am." I am full also of sympathy for Miss Frances—please tell her; & also, in general, for you. And—I am bent double with lumbago, which let this clumsily penned note attest. Yours, dear Lady Wolseley, most faithfully

*Henry James*
Wednesday.

ALS: Hove 36

*HJ assures Lady Wolseley of his friendship. The Lawrence ladies go at breakneck speed.*

34, DE VERE GARDENS. W.

Dear Lady Wolseley: April 10*th* 1895.

I have studiously, & from motions of common humanity, spared you the infliction of a letter. I didn't want even to write to you that the idea of an answer can't be entertained. So I have held my hand—with an effort—in order not to hear a pathetic sigh wafted across the tumbled channel & straight to my guilty ears: "Oh, I do wish my friends wouldn't be so oppressively attentive! I wish they would love me in silence—for the burden of my correspondence is simply cruel." Well, I *have* loved you in silence for a fortnight, & if I break that silence at last, it is, really, mainly to tell you that you must do the same by me. Another thing that made me wait was that day after day I have been hoping for a day on which I should be able to make my little pilgrimage to Midhurst, of which I wished to give you news. But that event hasn't yet come off—& now I am finding Easter week unfavourable for it—with all the probabilities of crowds both on the way & at the goal. The quiet cottage is probably bursting with the presence of materfamilias. As soon as materfamilias comes away I shall rush down—that is, I hope, next week; & you shall have the little story of my observations. Meanwhile I have found plenty to do in meeting—adequately—various friends of ours on the common ground of our enthusiasm about you. This has been fruitful in interviews and correspondence. The 1st thing I did was to spend a long & intimate afternoon in Whitehall place. I felt at the end rather exhausted—as if I had taken part in a very long & peculiarly exciting point-to-point race. The dear ladies have a pace, on such occasions—positively breakneck speed. However, I kept up with them fairly—though it was really riding for one's life. In short it was a memorable run. Miss Mary is better, but Miss Louisa is best—& they have discovered a lovely inn in the woods, somewhere in Surrey, where they are going to commemorate their convalescence in seven-league boots. I have been in active correspondence with Lady Arthur Russell about you (she wrote to me for news,) & we are just now discussing the probability of my going, one of these next days, down to Shere to fill up the gaps in my letters. What do you think of it? It is no sinecure, I assure you, to have been to your ball. Lady Reay[25] is voracious, and little rotound Miss Broderick is gushing. (I sat next to the latter on luncheon on Sunday, & she reminded me that we had stayed with you together at the house you once had of Mrs. J-k-ll.) Tall Lady Carew grows taller while she hears about you, & her handsome affected sister grows handsomer & almost natural. So you see I feel as if I were quite staying with you yet, and I get much of the pleasure & you none of the pain. There was very little taste in De Vere Gardens when I got back:

---

25. Lady Reay was the wife of Donald James Mackay, eleventh baron Reay (1839–1921), governor of Bombay from 1885 to 1890. As early as 1878 James knew them both.

it was as if I had been listening—in a dream—to a Wagner opera, and had suddenly been waked up by a street organ—a fall from the clouds. Meanwhile I do what I can to console myself with my reminiscences. They are intensely bright, vivid & affectionate. I forget nothing & no one, & every incident & every figure lives & blooms in my memory. I want to send my love to every one & everything. I hope with all my heart that your burden is lighter & your release sensibly nearer. I shall be in town still when you arrive (London has been quite delightfully quiet & easy,) & shall welcome you with joy. It prolonged my illusion to see Lord Wolseley one of the evenings that he was here. Please assure him of my great attachment. Please give my blessing to Miss Frances. Please remind Captain Smithson of my esteem & Mr. Somerset[26] of my admiration. Above all, dear Lady Wolseley, be convinced of the very great sympathy and devotion of yours very constantly

*Henry James*

ALS: Hove 37


*Lady Wolseley should stay in Germany and avoid London's syrens. He has been ill but has had a number of visitors, including the Daudets and Victor Hugo's grandson.*

34, DE VERE GARDENS. W.

Dear Lady Wolseley.                                                   May 30*th 1895.*

It is delightful to hear from you, though your news is not as robustious as I should like. Still it makes me see you in rustling German woods & beside gushing German waters—& I cherish the thought that these things can't help bringing some degree of healing in their murmurs & plashes. Whatever they are & whatever they do, they are at all events not London, (not Dublin, either,) & they don't kill. *This* is what London is getting itself nicely, smartly, smilingly, infamously ready to do to you as soon as you come back. I speak with feeling—I wave, I frantically brandish, warning, dissuading hands at you from the thick of the fight. I am half dead myself—but I think only of you. I can't put it more strongly than by telling you that if I am at the present moment in the very throes of the gout—with a foot like the dome of St. Paul's—I quite *like* it, because it isn't—for a few precious seconds—the social treadmill, the fatal squash. Don't let *those* syrens allure you back. Stay & play with Undine[27] in the legendary

---

26. He may have been Lord Arthur Somerset of the "Blues."
27. A name for a water nymph.

259

woods. Oh, I've talked it all over with *my* Undines & we have settled exactly, to a turn of your brougham-wheel, how bad it will be for you. I was as unanimous with both as Undine ainée [older] was with Undine *cadette* [younger]. You will ask me why I don't practise what I preach; to which I reply that I am not like you—I haven't had the bliss to escape. If I once *did,* then it is that I would stick fast. It is grotesque & melancholy; but to this hour, ever since I returned from Ireland, I haven't had a single day that I could take to go down & reconnoitre Midhurst. Influenza, gout, arrears of work, plagues of people have paralysed & prostrated me. I was just starting when 7 Daudets arrived—that is 5 Daudets[28] & 2 George Hugos (a grandson of Victor, & his small wife.) They stayed 3 weeks & departed 3 days ago. It proved a serious matter; for they clung to me like a litter of pups to an experienced mamma. They were very amiable, very unin-formed, very bewildered, very observant & perceptive, on the whole, & very overwhelming. To the last day I was unable to make up my mind whether poor Alphonse's infirmity & illness (no legs to speak of) was a relief by what it rendered impossible, or a further complication by what it only rendered difficult. He was, however, poor man, very meridional & charming—every one liked him, warted, morphinised, chloralised though he be. M*me* Alphonse, rotund & romantic—yet a mère de famille avant tout [first and foremost a mother], had very good clothes & golden bronze hair. She was severe on the clothes of London—wanted to know where were the femmes élégantes [elegant women]. I told her at Homburg, Kisseleff Strasse—2 at least. On reading over your letter I see that you put it more definitely (than I at first apprehended) that you are *not* coming back: on which I rejoice with unselfish glee. It rests me, dear Lady Wolse-ley, to know that you are resting. Oh, how I shld. ache to know that you were aching. That knowledge however isn't the only rest I propose to take—I seem to see a tolerably clear avenue for getting away about the 15*th;* in a fortnight. Only then! But I am sure the lumpy bed at Midhurst will, by that time, be pressed by some more fortunate form—fitting into the intervals of the lumps better perhaps, after all, than I. If I *can't* fit in—or get in; for I mean, certainly, to try, I shall content myself with some cocknefied strand. It doesn't matter much where I am, so long as I'm not *here*—& so long as you're not. Be patient—little by little you'll be all right: if Rome wasn't made in a day Dublin can't be unmade. Meanwhile I pray

---

28. Alphonse Daudet (1847–1897), famous French writer; his wife Julie Allard Daudet (1847–1940), French writer; and their three sons Léon, Lucien, and Edmée. Daudet suffered from syphilis contracted during his bohemian youth.

hard for you both. I met my admired Somerset in the street & admire him more than ever. Yours, dear Lady Wolseley, & Miss Frances's evermore

*Henry James*

ALS: Hove 38

*Lord Wolseley has been appointed commander in chief of all the British armed forces. Characteristically, James inquires how her husband's promotion will affect her.*

34, DE VERE GARDENS. W.

Dear Lady Wolseley.                                        Aug. 27*th 1895*

I don't in the least know where this will find you, but find you some-where it must, & say to you for me that I hope with all my heart there is true soothing & sustaining virtue for you in Lord Wolseley's new appoint-ment[29]—an event in which I should venture to take, in my ignorance & incompetency unrestricted satisfaction; were it not for *one* dark cloud that I see resting on it: the cruel accompaniment namely of a deluge of letters on your devoted head. How deeply unhappy you would make me if you were even to *dream* of ever acknowledging this! (To dream, I know, you must first sleep, & I insist on assuming that that boon has now descended on you.) I brazenly write because it's the only way to tell you both what a devoted interest I take in everything that concerns you. If there were any other way of letting you know it I should blush at the thought of adding to the burden you have to carry. But what I am hoping, dear Lady Wolseley, is that you have gained such strength in these last months that you have ceased to stagger under your load—or rather have ceased to suffer from *not* staggering—for, after all, your heroism never permitted you that luxury. Are you in England—or in easier & idler climes? I wish you were at Greenwich—how I shld. spare you *this* infliction by substituting that of a presence as tactful—I don't believe you can read that word: *tactful*—as I should be able to make it! One thing with all my heart I hope—that you're not going to live anywhere but in that sweet suburban home: not in neat apartments at the War Office, or the Horseguards, or the Army & Navy Club, or the Tower. Little by little I shall pick up scraps & crumbs about you, & at one very distant day I hope I may have a chance to hang on your very life. I think I already see the lips *equisser* [outline] a kindly smile as you

---

29. In 1895 Garnet Wolseley was appointed commander in chief of all the British forces, an appointment he held until 1901. Lady Wolseley received as many as fifty-four letters of congratulation in a single day on his appointment.

see that with that yearning for rustication that I confided to you in Ireland & to which you so suggestively responded, I write to you in the month of August from this sultry Babylon. It's a long story—but my country=hunger is as great as ever—Midhurst, I am sorry to say, proved impracticable (for reasons I'll tell you over a cup of tea, when you're next so good as to give me one,) but there were finally—very, very late—alternatives, & I am supposed at the present moment to be staying at Torquay. I return thither next week—till November 1st. I wonder if by that time you'll be accessible, & shall pray hard, in the interval, that such may be the case—I should like to write to Lord Wolseley, but I don't think it fair—I think it barely decent. He must be overwhelmed with manifestations. If you should remember, when you next see him, will you kindly tell him that the pleasure I take (& the intensity of that pleasure) in any event in his career that's a satisfaction to himself, throws a vivid light, to me, on the very tender feeling of friendship for him into which I have recklessly & presumptuously allowed myself to drift! My silence, at this hour, apart from this little word, is simply the last expression of that devotion. Let me repeat, dear Lady Wolseley, how I encourage myself to believe that for you & Miss Frances these are turning into good days. I wish I had something definite to go by—but I'm fond enough of you to be patient. I think of you with a participation that makes me glad I've three grains of imagination; & I am more than ever your affectionate old friend

Henry James

P.S. In my ignorance of how to address this otherwise I send it to Dublin (with a foreign stamp!) Please don't believe I do your spirit the wrong of supposing it will stay there!

ALS: Hove 39

<br>

*HJ and Lady Wolseley visited the home of renowned gardener and stained-glass designer Charles Eamer Kempe, and James enjoyed their trip.*

[*Dictated*]

34, DE VERE GARDENS. W.

Dear Lady Wolseley,                                                           8th March, 1897

I was so deprived, yesterday, for all those beautiful hours, of a word with you away from our host [Kempe] that I felt as if I didn't say to you a tenth of what I wanted; which, however, will make it all the better for our next meeting—when I shall overflow like a river fed by melting snows. Let these few words, therefore, not anticipate the deluge—let them only express to you afresh my grateful sense of the interest and success of our excursion. The whole wonder of it was the greater through my wholly unprepared state, my antecedent inward blank—which blank is now overscored with images and emotions as thick as any page of any of your hospitable house-books ever was with visitors' names. The man himself made the place more wonderful and the place the man. I was greatly affected by his courtesy and charm; and I got afterwards, in the evening, a little of the light that I couldn't snatch from you under his nose. What struck me most about the whole thing was the consummate cleverness: *that* was the note it sounded for me more than any one of the notes more imposing, more deep, that an artistic creation *may* throw out. Don't for the world—and for my ruin—ever breathe to him I have said it; but the whole thing, and his whole taste, are far too Germanic, too Teutonic, a business to make a medium in which I could ever sink down in final peace or take as the domestic and decorative last word. The element of France and Italy are too much out of it—and they, to me, are the real secret of Style. But we will talk of these things—heaven speed the day. Do have a little of France and a great deal of Italy at South Wraxall; but do have also a great deal of the cunning Kempe and of the candid—too candid—companion of your pilgrimage. Don't imagine the companion didn't have a most sweet and glorious day—from which the light, even in the London dusk again, has not wholly faded. I hope your security was complete to the end, and I am, in earnest hope also of a speedy reunion, yours, dear Lady Wolseley, more gratefully, if possible, than ever,

*Henry James*

TLS: Hove 44


*James declines her invitation to dinner but sends a photograph of the garden front at Lamb House.*

LAMB HOUSE, RYE.

Dearest Lady Wolseley. *Friday*

How kind & generous your as yet unacknowledged note! It finds me back at home—but rather tottering from the bed of influenza into which I tumbled on returning here just after seeing you. My attacks are short—but my subsequent aches & pains long. Therefore forgive my delay & my brevity. Your thought of having had me to dinner on Monday (?—Tuesday?) was worthy of your legendary hospitality—but I was, alas, too wet with my cableess walk in the drenching rain to have risked such graces—

though the raspberry soufflé *is*, I feel, an irrecoverable joy. Besides, I was too dirty—& in short it was a kindness to spare me the wrench of having to decline.——I have relapsed into my most congruous corner. It recaptures me each time I come back. Judge yourself by the enclosed little photograph of the "garden front"—the "banquetting-hall," with its porch & steps muffled in greenery, being on the right. You see it's a hall not absolutely like Westminster & the Royal Hospital. But it will swell to *any* pitch of pride the day you cross its threshold—a day I beg heaven to speed. Yours, dear Lady Wolseley, continually *more*—

*Henry James*

ALS: Hove 101

*He discusses the photograph of Lamb House he sent, giving detailed information about his home.*

LAMB HOUSE, RYE.

Dear Lady Wolseley.                                    February 24*th* [1898]

I am so touched by your gentleness about the poor little photograph that I boldly send you 3 bigger & better ones—not, please, to be returned. The only thing is that the one of the *hall* is cruel in its exaggerated white light & staring distinctness: also, in that one, bear gently on the hideous little "gaselier"—a legacy of my barbarous predecessors, which I've lacked time & thought to replace by something right. I'm *looking* for the right—the real good old brass polygonal lantern. The perspective of the oak-parlour is—in the view—! poor & cramped. There is a bedroom (George I's!) just *above* it exactly like it. In the front view, the street—my mansion comes down to the right hand corner *beyond* the door with the arched top (where I'm having the fanlight restored,) to the extent of the space of a largish window. The two windows above—one you don't see—in the annexe—are those of a bedroom, which has a staircase of its own down into the lower-room—which is a sort of a servants' hall. I send you *that* photog. mainly for the view of the façade of the Banqueting Hall! Doesn't it "compare" prettily with the front? These things go in a separate case—apart from this scrawl.——The panelling in the Stationmaster's strange little Pavilion is *excellent* of its kind & considerable in quantity—but I'm afraid I can't get you measurements without delay. It goes to the ceiling in the room—but used as a *high* wainscot (I mean with a couple of feet of "dado" above—the prettiest way to use it,) it could be made to do for a room of smallish "boudoir" size—not for a large room. The pavilion—for *room* purposes—is a small thing, & it exactly *fits* the pavilion, which was made for it. The said P. is smaller for instance than my oak parlour—of which you *see* the size more or less by the measure of the rugs. I'm afraid the Stationmaster is rather bent on a price—though he might take less than £100. I shld. think the pannelling [*sic*] would accord very well with some of the Glynde "Farm House" smaller proportions.

You make me sorry I at last start for the Continent—on Tuesday, at latest, though I'm hoping for Monday. I feel as if you were gradually coming nearer, & that's a thrilling tie. But when I return it will—it shall & must—be real true proximity! Believe me, dear Lady Wolseley, yours very constantly

*Henry James*

ALS: Hove 98

---

*James apologizes for his long silence. He has been in Rome and Venice but is back at Lamb House and applies to see her at Hampton Court.*

LAMB HOUSE, RYE.
Nov. 5. *1899.*

Dearest Lady Wolseley!

I am so exceedingly ashamed of the long silence I have observed toward you that I scarce know how even to break it with any grace, & I feel as if my penalty at your hands—measured by my *own* disgust at my detestable dumbness—might well be grave indeed. On the other hand perhaps you haven't cared a bit & have scarcely heeded, & much less remembered, whether I have been voluble or tongue-tied. I am hoping, rather, for the possibility of that indifference—even though it logically seems to signify that you won't derive the slightest gratification or reassurance from this belated apology. Well, all the same, I *must* feel, for my own poor comfort, that I am again in communication with you—& the comfort will still be a little there even though you avert your head from me & seal your lips. You wrote me a most kind letter early last spring (toward the winter's end,)— giving me therein some admirable advice on no less vital a subject than the arrangement of the chairs in my hall. That letter I had every intention of promptly thanking you for, & should have certainly carried it out, had not my poor little house, before I could turn round, taken fire[30] & made the

---

30. Lamb House caught fire in February 1899, with relatively little damage to the house itself.

confusion of chairs worse confounded. This annoyance disordered, I think, my brain as well as my furniture—though partly, thank heavens, only with the sense of what *might* have happened to me: what did happen being repairable (at cost, alas!) & now happily repaired. At any rate I fled abroad, leaving my house in the hands of workmen, & my *most* odious behavior was in not writing to you from Rome—where I spent 2 or 3 months—or from Venice—where I spent one. I don't know, however, if it's more odious than my miserably awkward submission to successive hindrances & hitches ever since my return. These things are temporary blights (to the guilty one;) strange visitations of gloom & gracelessness beyond his control. I think, moreover, I've been a good deal crushed and quenched, by the cold—chilling—legend of your having, with your irrepressible genius for *dé—&—emménagement*, [HJ's own French slang for disassembling and reassembling a household], spread yourselves through one (I almost forget which) of the royal palaces that had been placed at your disposition. This has seemed to me to make you terribly unneighbourly—to lift you out of my old-friendly & almost familiar ken. And then it's all dim & remote & complicated to me—I confess by my own fault. That makes me only wonder the more when you are to be in residence at H. C. [Hampton Court], & when I may dream of applying there for an audience of you. I don't know if this will find you at Glynde—but I send it you, on the chance, at that humbler & cosier address. Please believe that it carries you the assurance, through all things, of my absolutely uninterrupted affectionate interest. This miserable murderous war (so abject a man of peace am I,) makes me think of you, with deep compassion, as condemned to sit (wherever you are,) sniffing up the smell of gunpowder. Lamb House meanwhile blushes with me, in every old purple brick, for my bad manners & my still worse excuses. This is the sign of our intimate union—Lamb House's & mine. It is the jog-trot of matrimony to which we have settled down—none, I think, will ever put *us* asunder. *You* have flirtations, passions, adventures: *we* are already Darby & Joan.[31] I am sending you another photograph—without chairs. The person at the garden-gate (the little vista is in front of my street-windows—that of the drawingroom ones—) is looking out for your arrival. If I might only hear from you but that it is still arrangeable! If I might only hear from you indeed anyhow—

---

31. A couple in an eighteenth-century sentimental song.

as to anything. I am in this trembling hope, dearest Lady Wolseley, yours most constantly

Henry James.

ALS: Hove 51

James met Lord Wolseley and daughter Frances at Welcombe. He finds Wolseley "the charmer, of all time."

LAMB HOUSE, RYE.

Dearest Lady Wolseley! May 9th 1900

I am writing you only days & days after the deeply interesting occasion, at Easter, that almost put me into direct, & did put me into the most delightful indirect, relation with you. I allude of course to the great joy I had in meeting Lord Wolseley & Miss Frances at Welcombe—an episode that kept putting the pen straight between my fingers—for your benefit, & then (by some still more sociable interruption—in the same general happy connection,) dashing it out again. I came away from brilliant Welcombe, in short, with my endeavour to approach you brilliantly frustrated—& I returned hither to frustrations of a sterner & prosier order. Domestic cares & neglected tasks seemed on my return to swallow me straight up—& I found, among other things, an invalid friend[32] more or less absorbingly housed with me. He is with me still, but I'm happy to say he is better; & nothing, this dreary afternoon, shall deprive me of the consolation of a few words with you. We ought to have had them at Welcombe—that was the place that would have caused our eloquence (at least I can answer for mine!) to flow. I deplored your non-accompaniment of your illustrious relatives for reasons even more far-reaching than ever before. It would have been most interesting to read with you, point by point, the lesson involved in that melancholy monster of a place—which has such a good conscience in its monstrosity. How your companions must have hugged your delicate intime [intimate] Glynde on their return, & how I hugged L. H.! I am hugging it still. That occupation has in fact taken up most of my time.—
————But all this time I haven't expressed my very friendly concern over the consequences of the riding accident to Lord Wolseley, which I heard of (having missed it in the newspapers at the moment,) for the 1st time to-day. I gather, with deep satisfaction, that it was not grave, but I beg to assure him of my most devoted sympathy. I can express to you with more freedom

---

32. This was probably Jonathan Sturges.

than I should—than I *could*—have ventured to do to *them*, the joy I had in being again, for a couple of days, in the company of those two delightful beings. Happy *you*—to live with them! Miss Frances has grown to resemble you in expression, voice, intonation, & a hundred other merits, so much *more* since I last saw her, that I found in her a kind of double admirability. And her Father—well, he's simply *the* charmer, of all time. He is unique. Pardon these irresistible overflows—which have the absurdist air of my offering you news about *les vôtres* [your own]! As if you didn't know better than any one. But I speak in stammering humility & spontaneity.

Above all I want to ask you if I may not come over some day to luncheon & arrange with you & Miss Frances for coming here to the same? When I have made the pilgrimage myself I shall feel firm & happy about indoctrinating you. It would give me such joy to see you here. I hope you are graciously accessible to my appeal—the one I shall make to you on the subject of coming. What we shall like of course is a little *more* summer. As soon as that comes, I shall *begin* with asking your leave to pop up at Glynde—taking a day, &c. I fondly hope the rest may follow. I greet very cordially & faithfully Lord Wolseley & the Daughter & am, dearest Lady Wolseley, your very constant old friend

*Henry James*

ALS: Hove 52

*James waxes eloquent over a gift of figs and sympathizes with Lady Wolseley's servant problems.*

Dear Lady Wolseley.                                        LAMB HOUSE, RYE.

How splendidly kind you are! Your figs are as beautiful as your character—though, alas, less permanent. They have melted lusciously away—though kept as long as I *could* keep them, to be the pride of my breakfast-table. I thank you for them most unreservedly & only cease to wonder how you could magnanimously part with them when I remember with what a store of other triumphs *your* board is graced. It isn't a board to miss half-a-dozen figs. *Mine,* it is true, misses them; but then mine has *had* them. Àpropos of boards, at any rate, I blush—as a man—for your inconceivable butler. I had a sympathetic sense of his perfection—but how little we know! How little, certainly, *he* does! He will learn more, to his cost. It's unimaginable that to be able to be with you & not to *hug* it should be any sane creature's disposition. However, he is evidently *in*sane. Don't, none the less, I beseech you, let him make you so! It's horrid to have your little tour spoiled in advance—or it *would* be—by the thought of returning to such labours, & I wish I could save you them by taking the field myself for you. *I've* a worthy monster who has been with me for 16 years! But it's just this that has deprived me of all practice in the business of finding. When *he* goes *I* must go: I can't find another. I beg you to put your care behind you & live in the happy foreign hour. It will prepare you for anything, for everything. I wave & cheer & urge you on your way. A thousand thanks for the luminous guidance as to gourds. I shan't quite know how to get 40 centimes to the firm, but I shall work it out. Your admirable pot-pourri is a grand success & fills such voids! Also, unlike figs, it abides—even like the gratitude & attachment of yours so constantly

Henry James<br/>Sept. 8: 1900.

ALS: Hove 59

*James supports General Wolseley in his quarrel with Lord Lansdowne. Lady Wolseley should read George Sand's* Histoire de ma vie *[History of My Life]. James socializes nightly in London.*

THE REFORM CLUB

Dearest Lady Wolseley. March *12* 1901[33]

Forgive my delay of 2 or 3 days in acknowledging your beautiful and interesting letter. Pressure, in town, is somehow always upon me, & the desires & purposes of the day are achieved but on the morrow, in the small proportion of cases in which they are achieved at all. My thoughts have been with you both, constantly, throughout the recent episode—I have abounded in sympathy, which I thank you heartily for giving me a chance to express[.] I thought Lord Wolseley's speech so perfect in tone & temper, so *large* & clear and disinterested, that I was, in common with every one I've heard speak of the incident, merely amazed at the line Lord Lansdowne[34] saw fit to take. "Silly" is the mildest term I've heard applied to his speech, & the judgment of the people *I* meet is all that he has done himself no good. I can easily believe that he will prove, a short time hence, to have done himself even still less than yet appears. How I wish I could see you &

---

33. The Hove Central Library lists the date of this letter as 11 March 1912, but the number more closely resembles "12" than "11," given James's handwriting style.

34. Henry Charles Keith Petty-Fitzmaurice, Fifth marquess of Lansdowne (1845–1927). At this time he was foreign secretary; he and Wolseley quarreled over foreign policy.

talk with you of these things. But that will come, with your permission, after the more & more approaching date at which I shall find myself at home again. Please believe that meanwhile I am more than ever firmly & fondly yours. In respect to M*me* Sand's *Histoire de ma vie* (a most delightful book if you haven't read it,) I am going to ask you to be so very good as to take it in at your door one of these next days, without questions asked. You will break my heart if you ask *one,* however small, however superficial,— even however well-intentioned. The Rousseau-Morley, or Morley-Rousseau[35] will either accompany the other work, or be, a day or two after, the subject of a like appeal to your kind, silent, approving, indulgent hospitality. Any absolutely *necessary* explanations given later on—at a personal interview—the very first.——London has been amusing & amazing to my countrified mind, but an amusement that takes the form of dining out every night, leaves very quickly scarce enough of its victim for either joy or surprise to find a nestling place. I am very presently taking flight—to have a feather left in my wings. I'm going to flap them tomorrow to Prince's Gate. How these first shy looks of spring—in the lingering light—must play becomingly over Glynde. I believe I've 3 crocuses & ½ at Lamb House. Yours, dear Lady Wolseley, most devotedly

*Henry James*

ALS: Hove 63

*A siege of gout kept James from writing. Lord Wolseley has gone to war and his brilliant book (a life of Napoleon) should do well. James hopes she and Frances triumph in their quieter arts.*

LAMB HOUSE, RYE, SUSSEX.

Dearest Lady Wolseley. January 15*th* 1904.

Strike, but hear me! Or rather, hear me patiently, & then perhaps you won't strike! I am *not* the irresponsive monster, really, that I must these days have appeared to you; but ever since the receipt of your most kind Xmas note & its accompaniment of the quaint, the really droll little tartan (American tartan!) almanac, I have been, in one way & another, in the fell grip of extreme *unwellness*—that is, mainly, of a prolonged siege from the gout-fiend, (the longest I have ever had,) which has quite shipwrecked my correspondence in general by making it impossible to me to grasp the pen

---

35. James had in his personal library John Morley's *Rousseau* (London: Chapman and Hall, 1873).

or to sit up like a gentleman. I had, in Xmas week, a very incapacitating attack of rheumatism, which I couldn't nevertheless give way to, by reason of two friends spending Xmas with me, one of whom was himself ill & had to be cherished & done for. I went back to town with him to see him safely through, & there I myself collapsed—that is I scrambled home only in time to tumble into bed, where I remained for a week. My rheumatism took the turn of virulent gout, which I have had, for the first time in my life, all at once in my hands & in both feet, though worst in one of the latter. So I have until the last two days been living in one room, & being better, but very lamely crawling about. And I have been able to dictate many notes—but I didn't want to send you a machine-made letter. So I have thus ungraciously & unwishingly waited—though your image, in fevered dreams, has had for me a haunting, & to my bad conscience, a reproachful, obsession. And the worst is that I feel I shall not wave it away (as in strictness, heaven knows, I don't desire to,) by these so retarded explanations—for I had been living under its beautiful mute animadversion (I deeply & deservedly, felt,) for months *before,*—so scant a sign of life must I have seemed to you for a long time to give. Last summer (in the Hampton Court time—when I was down *here,* intensely dodging London, & even here intensely submerged,) & then during the autumn, when freedom to roam again eluded me, I was terribly conscious of the poor show I made, even through the most benevolently rose-coloured field-glasses, from that far-seeing terrace of Glynde. And even now am I much mending the matter? No, I shall not mend it to my own satisfaction until I mount the terrace again myself & there make one prostration at the door. If I were not at this moment lame & blighted, nervous about the gout-fiend, who seems not wholly to have done with me, I would ask your leave to make a pilgrimage of friendship at some early day. But I am a coward about visiting, in wintry months, till I know, with some approach to exactness, where I, physically, *am*—so I project the sweet occasion, with your kind permission, to a not very distant future. It will be a joy to me when all is propitious—including your signified welcome. I go up to town on the 28*th* for 2 months. I shall have then been here 9 months on end, & a certain satiety hangs about me. But I return on one of the first days of April, to stay on again for weeks & weeks, & at that balmier time I shall make you my petition. Perhaps, however, in the interval London won't be quite unmitigatedly deprived of your own presence—in which case I should take a signal of your approach (Reform Club, Pall Mall always quite *intensely* finds me) as an act of high beneficence. One of my 1*st* acts, in town, will be to wait upon the Vocal Sisters [Louisa and Mary Lawrence], who will, in their wild way, make me feel a little nearer to you. They are sure to be possessed of the little biographic facts for which I hanker—&, possessed of them, no mortal power would (even were it to be wished) be able to prevent them from communicating them. I seem to be aware, though I can't cite my authority, that Lord Wolseley has sailed toward the sun—or is otherwise about to indulge in that intensely enviable luxury. I observe with great pleasure how his brilliant book[36] seems to make its way. And I hope you & Frances are triumphing meanwhile on your own lines— in the quiet arts, that is, of health & prosperity. Let me repeat that I think the small plaid pleasantry-book a charmingly magnanimous little demonstration, all things considered, to your too long-eclipsed, yet I trust still unobscured, & always & ever constant old friend

*Henry James*

ALS: Hove 75

*James is a spectacled old nurse who darns a stocking (of friendship) for Lady Wolseley.*

LAMB HOUSE, RYE, SUSSEX.

Dearest Lady Wolseley.                                             August 3*d 1906.*

I have been having, since your kindest of notes arrived, a great complication of life & a great frustration of correspondence, the perpetual bump of the portmanteau (the "friendly" portmanteau,) on my poor old white & green little staircase, & the consequent accumulation of very pressing occupations—arrears of work—which have had to be made up. But I have, during every hour of the time, cherished the fond vision of the right little free moment, at last, for thanking you ever so cordially, so tenderly. Here it is—late, very late in the evening, while the little town sleeps round about Lamb House as a large flourishing nursery of little cribs sleeps round the spectacled old nurse who sits up by the lamp economically darning stockings. I darn *this* stocking for you, dear Lady Wolseley—the good old stocking in which I have hoarded for long years the precious savings of our friendship. It is in capital condition still, thank goodness, & my needle would be capable of making good a much bigger hole than will ever yet be worn in it. The bump of the portmanteau begins again tomorrow on the sage-green drugget which you may flatteringly remember (lately "turned" & even in portions renewed!) but let me meanwhile make it distinct (so far as this wavering "fist" permits,) that I rejoice immensely

---

36. James refers to Wolseley's *Decline and Fall of Napoleon* (1895), a book he annotated.

in the delightful fact you communicate (that of your present stay at Hampton Court,) & revel not less in the prospect of being able to go up sooner or later—certainly on the 1st clear opportunity—& find you there. I don't haunt the automobilized town itself in these dusty weeks a bit more than I can help, but I shall make a pretext, occasion favouring, (& more especially the portmanteau pausing,) & shall then yearningly knock at your door. I have never seen you at all in residence at H.C. [Hampton Court], & the impression for me will be of the most romantic. I like meanwhile, thoroughly, to think of you there, beneath the high old ceilings, in the large, cool, liberal marquis [French for glass porch] (on which even your elaborate & multitudinous "notes" leave space) & with terraces & gardens & vistas & lakes and rivers all about you. Yes, I breathe over you there more freely, I think during the dog=days, than I have sometimes done (over the thought of you) at low=browed—even if adorable—Glynde. I seem to remember your apartment at H.C. as above all high-browed, like a family of clear, candid, serene faces; & I'm sure the faces aren't scowling at anything you have done to them, or even to see you unwontedly settled among them.——I have drawn long breaths here, this admirable summer, in spite of the portmanteaus. The habit of Lamb House has by this time become a second nature to me. The garden is starved & primitive—but if *it* wasn't I should myself be, & its very nudity makes it the better for wandering about in. So I've wandered, at the spare moments, & have even, with the aid of a tottery table or two under the old mulberry tree (more & more aged & yet more & more conducive to jam!) found it favourable to an effect of tea=hospitality. I had a plan or 3 or 4 days with the good sisters [Louisa and Mary Lawrence], our old friends on the North Devon Coast, but they have named, alas, a part of this month when I must stick to my guns here—& remained a little austerely dumb (the 1st time I've ever *known* them dumb!) to my hint that I might be able to come somewhat later. But all is for the best, & I shall be fresher of attention for them the next time I *do* see them. I send—I venture to send *tout carrément* [quite straightforwardly]—my love to Lord Wolseley. How gallantly, even gaily, his step must resound in your echoing courts! I hope Miss Frances is able to be with you, & I wish her a very kind remembrance. Believe me, dear Lady Wolseley, yours always & ever

*Henry James*

ALS: Hove 76

*HJ sends a poetic letter to his friend. The Wolseleys are now in retirement in France.*

Dear Lady Wolseley.

It has been interesting & delightful to hear from you—your letter is like a gust of the warm South bringing with it a sweet sniff as of ripening oranges & a sweet murmur as of blue Mediterranean tides. I snuff up these emanations quite yearningly—then I throw a good stodgy chunk of British oak upon the glowing embers of my coal-fire (the mixture is admirable) &, as I see it flicker up, recognise that to any great distance from that domestic flame I am not likely, for a good while to come, to be able to stray. Your account of your own situation is meanwhile a perfect fairy tale, & it gives me joy to think there are people in the world so perfectly fixed; especially as the people happen to be people I am so exceedingly attached to. What a wondrous benignant star watches over your *installations!* I have seen, thank heaven, many—almost perhaps most, of them; but I haven't seen one that hasn't been a miracle of felicity, & evidently La Tourette thoroughly conforms to the rule. There is always the extra touch of *finish* to the charm—it's the little French lady emerging just from behind the right clump of oleander to play gentle airs to you in the eventide. Happy little wandering minstrel of the female sex and the tasteful race, to have auditors of such high dignity & noble geniality. And then the "comic relief" of your stately pastoral—you've provided even for that in the charming friction of races below stairs—nothing being ever so funny, I think, really, as the bewilderments of English servants confronted with foreign "ways." But I hope all your frictions will be mild. You will feel that I portray a grey life when *I* tell you I have none at all, but am immersed in the dearest British routine of every description—the only variation from which is perhaps that we are having just at this moment days & nights that even Provence can't beat—a vast silver plate of a moon hanging in a bland sky tonight, & almost every rose tree in my garden more or less blooming in the balmy moon today—oh fugitives from rude Sussex! No, I don't compete with the French female minstrel, nor with the polyglot household, & I haven't got a tourette [little tower], & I don't paint in watercolours; but I "guess" Lamb House is about as warm (to the perspiring brow) as your (probably marble) halls. I have pipes (alas—or almost alas!) & my brow often requires attention. You are very vivid & very interesting about dear Mrs. "Charley" [Lawrence] & her late drives in the "wrap" of a pearl necklace. She is a very old friend of mine & I am very fond of her—but the contemplation of her existence, & of Charley's as related (however little) to hers, & hers as related, however expensively & invalidically & anxiously, to his, plunges me in deep depression, from which I don't rally; the reason & the wisdom & the "principle" of it seem to me all so far to seek. They live in panic, but they live in splendour—but the whole thing is incoherent & too little like Darby & Joan, or even like the Field Marshal & his Marichale. But this, already belated, shall catch tonight's post. I am spending here an absolutely solitary Christmas—think of me, & my slice of cold mutton, if your turkey & plum pudding (I'm sure your cordon-bleu [first-rate cook] won't let you off from them,) leaves you power to think. May the New Year let you down ever so gently! I think of you both with tender affection & am yours all & always & ever

Henry James

ALS: Hove 80

*James has returned from almost a year in America, a year of poor health. He hopes to visit the Wolseleys at Hampton Court.*

THE REFORM CLUB   PALL MALL S.W.

Dear Lady Wolseley.        June 3*d* 1912

I saw Mrs. Lawrence yesterday & she told me of your being settled at H. C. & of her having seen you there—& that has extremely quickened *my* desire to enjoy again the great privilege. I have been, I know, for a miserably long time in very dismal eclipse—ill, absent, obstructed & dumb, with a whole year in America (a year of very bad physical conditions for me,) & a return to this country in the autumn (last) only to hear of your having left for the South. But now I am better, ever so much, & present even to myself the appearance of being so (I believe I do that almost ridiculously—or—*grossly*—to others;) I have returned to life & to quiet & refined indulgences, & to taking up again old & cherished threads when my friends are so good as to overlook my long & graceless failure of testimony. There is no thread I so desire to take up as that of seeing you & Lord Wolseley again. Will you let me feel it in my hand? May I come down to tea some afternoon? Would Saturday next suit you, or Sunday or Monday? On a sign from you I would come, & I am yours & Lord Wolseley's ever so faithfully,

Henry James

ALS: Hove 84

*Ill health keeps James in the country, but when he returns to London he will visit her. Her own strength helps her deal with Lord Wolseley's recent death.*

Dear Lady Wolseley.       LAMB HOUSE  RYE  SUSSEX

How very kind & how touching to me your letter—such a proof of faithful patience with me! I had been full of the desire to write you after your return to England, but things in these days are not always well with me in respect to the carrying out of fond purposes or happy thoughts—I have a special physical trouble which causes a certain leak of vitality, or which is at any rate unfavourable to anything like a bustling energy. Luckily intelligent precautions keep it more or less in abeyance, & thanks to these I am very much better then I was a year, & even 6 months, ago. Only I mention it as explaining the too *negative* colour which I fear my poor old appearance & behaviour are apt to present—I more easily & timorously *don't* do things, from day to day, than gracefully, or dashingly, do them! I am, you see, down here for the present—that is for the rest of the summer & as much as possible of the autumn—after which I come back to my small London habitation; a flat at Chelsea pleasantly overhanging the river. Any going to & fro & dealing with the closed little establishment is, I fear, *now* out of order for me, but as soon as I am in town again in anything of a settled way (& then it will be for 6 or 7 months,) I shall make my pilgrimage to see you with great eagerness & all my old sense of privilege. I have wondered much about you in your spacious solitude, but believed you to be living into it & through it as your great memories & resources must help you to do. We only learn what is in us when the great tests come.[37] Please believe at any rate that I greatly long for the opportunity to cross your threshold again, & meet there in my minor fashion all the reminders of the past, which I cherish in thought, & at this regrettable distance, more than I can say. My good little old house here continues to be a blessing to me—now that I utterly abjure it for the melancholy winter; a brave young niece, who is an even greater blessing, kindly gives me her countenance & company for the next couple of months; & I am, thank heaven, though in a reduced way, able to work & to walk. So kindly think of me as still much intending, especially where the kindest old friend is concerned, & as yours, dear Lady Wolseley, all faithfully

*Henry James*

P. S. *Isn't* the dear Ranee[38] a brave apparition & a delightful presence? I am so glad she exists for you!

Aug. 10*th* 1913

ALS: Hove 86

---

37. Lord Wolseley died on 25 March 1913.

38. Lady Margaret Alice Lili de Windt, Ranee of Sarawak (1849–1936), a social friend of HJ's.

# Index

Godkin, Lawrence, 151
Goldsmith, Dr., 38
Goldsmith, Elizabeth C., 14n. 15
Gordon, General, 246n. 11
Gosse, Edmund Wilson, 12–13, 196,
  196n. 8, 256
Gosse, Ellen Epps, 12–13, 196, 196n. 8
Grain, Corney, 251
Granville-Barker, Harley Granville,
  166, 166n. 53
Green, Alice Stopford, 102, 102n. 108
Green, J. R., 102n. 108
Gregor, Leigh, 84, 84n. 93, 90
Gregor, Margaret Gibbens, 84, 84n.
  93, 87, 90, 96–97
Greys, 159
Griselda (literary character), 220n. 27
Grove, Colonel Coleridge, 248, 248n.
  13

Hadfield, Lady, 177, 177n. 69
Hadfield, Sir Robert Abbott, 177n. 69
Haldane, Lord Chancellor, 113
Hamilton, General Ian, 113, 116
Hamilton, Lady (Mrs. Ian), 113
Hamlet (literary character), 204
Hare, John, 197
Harper & Brothers, 38, 38n. 34, 149
*Harper's Weekly*, 33, 48
Harvey, George B. McClellan, 38,
  38n. 34
Hawkins, Sir Anthony Hope, 166,
  166n. 54
Hays, Mrs., 39
Head, Dr., 225, 226
Herrick, Robert, 56–57, 56n. 63
Hichens, Robert Smyth, 165, 165n. 51,
  168–69
Higginson, Emily, 52, 52n. 57, 67
Higginson, George, 52, 52n. 57, 67
Higginson, Henry Lee, 52n. 57
Hill, Georgiana, 14n. 8
Hodgson, Richard, 65, 65n. 72
Holmes, Oliver Wendell, 102, 102n.
  109
Hope, Anthony. *See* Hawkins, Sir
  Anthony Hope
Horstmanns, Miss, 51, 56

Hotham, Charley, 78
Howells, Mildred, 100, 175
Howells, William Dean, 54, 100, 102,
  128–29, 175
Hueffer, Elsie Martindale Ford, 214,
  214n. 21
Hueffer, Ford Madox Ford, 143n. 23,
  214, 214n. 21
Hugo, Mr. and Mrs. George, 259
Hugo, Victor, 259
Hunt, Mrs., 141
Hunt, Violet, 143, 143nn. 23, 24
Hunt, William, 131n. 14
Hunter, Charles, 76n. 89, 77, 89, 211
Hunter, Ellen Temple Emmet (Mrs.
  George) "Elly", 8, 40–41, 40nn. 38,
  40, 42, 67, 74, 234
Hunter, George, 40n. 40
Hunter, Mary (Mrs. Charles), 11, 76–
  78, 76n. 89, 89, 113, 114, 176n. 68,
  211, 217
Huntingdon, William H., 248n. 14

Jalland, Pat, 13–14nn.6, 7, 9, 12
James, Alexander Robertson (Frances
  Tweedy) "Aleck" (son of William
  James): mentioned, 8, 28–29, 50,
  64, 68, 69, 71, 74n. 84, 78, 80, 83,
  84, 87, 90, 92, 101, 103, 105, 109,
  110–11, 183, 185, 231, 232; and painting, 20, 87, 90, 99, 108, 149
James, Alice (daughter of Garth
  Wilkinson James). *See* Edgar, Alice
  James
James, Alice (sister of Henry James):
  and death of, 31; and health, 23, 26,
  29, 30, 36n. 29; and Irish politics,
  25–26; mentioned, 1, 3, 4, 7, 23,
  23n. 3, 25, 29, 30, 31, 31n. 15, 74n.
  84, 83, 83n. 92, 95, 102n. 110, 107,
  114n. 116; and teaching, 3, 209n. 18
James, Alice Howe Gibbens (Mrs.
  William) (sister-in-law of Henry
  James): and her childhood, 17–18;
  and Chocorua, 19, 27, 33, 55, 58,
  66, 76, 80, 91; and education, 18–
  19; and engagement, 18, 22; and
  her father, 17–18; and health, 19,

57–58, 59; and house renovations, 88, 92, 93, 106; and James's texts, 9–10, 20, 26–27; and loss of husband, 20, 76, 79, 88, 91, 92–93, 105, 209; and marriage, 18–19; mentioned, 1–2, 4, 8, 12, 128, 155, 156, 159, 193, 208, 209, 210, 214; and Stanford visit, 60, 61–62, 66; and travel, 18, 30, 31, 37, 40, 42, 46, 60, 96, 120, 121

James, Alice Runnells (Mrs. William, III), 20, 76, 76n. 88, 80, 81, 84–86, 87, 89, 91, 96, 99, 100–101, 105, 106, 112, 116, 213–14, 215–16, 218, 228, 232

James, Bay, 13n. 2, 14n. 11, 23n. 2, 244n. 6

James, Caroline Eames Cary (Mrs. Garth Wilkinson), 34, 34n. 24, 52n. 58, 54

James, Edward Holton (son of Robertson James), 61, 61n. 68

James, Elizabeth Lodge (Mrs. George), 159n. 44

James, Francis Tweedy. *See* James, Alexander Robertson

James, Garth Wilkinson "Wilky" (brother of Henry James), 1, 32n. 19, 34, 34nn. 23, 24, 52, 52n. 58, 54, 91, 101

James, George Abbott, 159, 159n. 44

James, Henry: and aging, 177, 178; and American tour, 50–55, 59, 62, 66, 128, 138–39, 139–41, 150; and bath chair, 98; and the Boer War, 37, 37n. 33; and the chameleon, 4, 68; and children, 5, 7–9, 19, 77; and Christmas, 136–37, 154, 203, 275; and the Civil War, 33; and clothing, 10, 11, 40, 51, 216, 239, 256, 260; and the coal strike, 85–86, 211; and death of, 20; and dental work, 38, 56, 59, 60, 62, 72, 140; and dogs, 131, 132–33, 134–35, 147–48, 148n. 33, 149, 159, 191, 215; and domestic arrangements, 10, 51, 55–56, 58, 60, 61–62, 81, 89, 93, 103–4, 106, 163–64, 169, 172, 187–88,

191, 192, 193, 209–10, 211, 212–13, 217, 219, 222n. 30, 224–25, 228–29, 229–30, 268–69, 276; and drama, 29, 70–71, 165–66, 168–69, 204, 210; and the Dreyfus case, 5, 36, 36n. 28; and education, 3, 9, 40–41; and family, 4, 22, 26, 28–29, 50, 64; and finances, 29–30, 45, 48–49, 56, 56n. 62, 65, 66–67, 247; and Fletcherizing, 51, 62, 65, 71–72, 142, 142n. 22, 156; and food, 10, 26, 135, 143, 160, 161, 169, 264, 268, 275; and friendship, 2–3, 4–5, 10, 11–12, 13, 18, 20, 128, 146, 191, 192, 272; and gardening, 56, 67, 69–70, 89, 217, 273; and gifts, 10, 13, 133–34, 135, 137, 150–51, 160, 161, 169, 175, 268, 270; and the Godkin funeral, 151; and gossip, 11, 240–41; and health, 5, 36n. 29, 43, 47, 53, 65, 73, 73n. 83, 74, 80, 81, 83, 84–85, 95, 97, 99, 103–4, 132, 140, 151, 155, 156–57, 158, 163, 164, 167, 169–70, 171–72, 171n. 62, 174, 186, 187, 192, 193, 199, 206, 207–8, 215–16, 221, 223, 224, 225–26, 227, 231–32, 234, 246, 260, 263, 271, 276; and honorary degrees, 74–75, 74n. 87, 75; and interior decorating, 10, 220–21, 222, 223, 226, 228, 229, 240, 251–52, 263, 264–66; and lecturing, 47–49, 52, 139–40, 139n. 19; and marriage, 5, 6–7, 35, 136, 179, 266; and metaphorical language, 12–13, 217, 272; and portraits, 78, 87, 102–3; and portrait slasher, 182, 182n. 73; and Queen Victoria's Diamond Jubilee, 34, 34n. 25; and Queen Victoria's funeral, 5, 44–45; and séances, 62–63, 62n. 69, 65–66; and seventieth birthday celebration, 102–3, 102n. 107, 175–76, 182n. 73; and sexuality, 4–5, 12, 241; and shopping, 4, 10; and telepathy, 192, 197, 197n. 11; and travel, 27, 29, 31, 34, 74, 79, 89–90, 92, 130, 152, 155, 156, 157, 159, 162, 163, 172, 192, 199, 208,

James, Henry: and travel (*continued*) 209, 210, 217–18, 242, 249–50, 254, 255–56, 262, 265; and weather, 5, 23, 36, 37, 38, 39, 40, 42, 56, 58, 59, 60, 67, 69–70, 77, 78, 80, 83, 88–89, 92, 94, 97–98, 104, 117, 141, 147, 148–49, 150, 158, 159, 160–61, 161–62, 170, 186, 195, 199, 204–5, 207, 210, 211–12, 213, 214, 218, 222, 251; and William's drawing, 107–8; and World War I, 109–12, 113–16, 117–20, 120–22, 184–88, 192, 231, 232–33; and writing, 3–4, 9–10, 13, 25, 25n. 8, 26–27, 37, 48–49, 56, 58, 60, 70, 81–82, 83, 89, 94–95, 97, 104, 105, 107–8, 135, 143n. 25, 149, 167, 174, 200, 203, 212, 222, 250. Works: *Ambassadors, The*, 48; *American Scene, The*, 60, 149; *Golden Bowl, The*, 4, 48; *Guy Domville*, 168n. 60; *High Bid, The*, 71, 71n. 79; *Ivory Tower, The*, 108; *Little Tour in France*, 127; *New York Edition*, 70, 70n. 78; *Notes of a Son and Brother*, 9, 107, 107n. 111; *Outcry, The*, 165, 165n. 52; *Portrait of a Lady*, 4, 10, 24; *Saloon, The*, 210; *Small Boy and Others, A*, 9, 20, 82, 82n. 91, 83; *Spoils of Poynton, The*, 4; *Tragic Muse*, 20, 25, 25n. 8; *Turn of the Screw, The*, 131n. 14; *Wings of the Dove*, 4

James, Henry, Sr. (father of Henry James): and his death, 18, 242; and Swedenborgianism, 3

James, Henry, III, "Harry" (son of William James): and his career, 20, 88, 88n. 98, 91, 99, 174n. 65; mentioned, 9, 17, 17n. 1, 18, 24, 39, 41, 46, 50, 52, 53, 61, 64–65, 66, 68, 69, 70, 74n. 84, 76, 79, 80, 82, 83, 84, 86, 87, 92, 96, 97, 98, 99, 102n. 107, 103, 104–5, 107, 109, 113, 116, 120, 175, 178, 188, 207, 230; and World War I, 117–20

James, John Sumner Runnells (son of William James, III), 116, 232

James, Margaret Mary, "Peggy," "Peggot" (Mrs. Robert Bruce Porter) (daughter of William James): and

depression, 20, 74, 74n. 84, 81, 86; and education, 20, 36, 38–39, 38n. 35, 44, 60, 68; mentioned, 31, 31n. 16, 41, 42, 43, 46, 47, 50, 57, 58, 61, 66n. 74, 68, 69, 75, 76, 78, 80, 83, 87, 88, 89, 91, 100, 103–5, 106, 108, 109–11, 112, 113, 114, 117, 120, 121, 175, 176, 178, 182–83, 191, 193, 210, 229, 230, 231, 231n. 34, 233, 276

James, Mary Lucinda Holton (Mrs. Robertson), 52, 90, 95, 101, 109, 159, 159n. 45

James, Mary Walsh Robertson (mother of Henry James), 3, 22, 24n. 5, 28–29, 62–64, 83

James, Robertson (brother of Henry James), 1, 18, 30, 30n. 14, 47, 61n. 68, 90, 159n. 45

James, Walter William (son of William James, III), 100, 100n. 106, 106, 116

James, William (brother of Henry James): and his career, 3, 18–19, 32–35, 43, 44, 44n. 47, 45–46, 56, 68–69, 69nn. 75, 76, 87, 87n. 97, 116n. 117; and correspondence, 83, 94–95, 105, 127n. 7; and his death, 4, 20, 76, 79, 128, 192, 208–9; and drawing, 107–8; and his health, 12, 19, 20, 30, 36n. 29, 37, 37n. 31, 41–42, 44, 45, 47, 51, 62, 65, 67, 69, 155, 155n. 40, 156–57; and Henry James's texts, 9–10, 20, 23–24, 27; and marriage, 4, 18, 22; mentioned, 1, 4, 8, 18, 19, 22, 23, 24, 25, 25n. 9, 26, 27, 28, 29, 30, 31, 31n. 17, 32n. 19, 34n. 23, 35, 36, 37, 37n. 30, 38, 39, 39nn. 36, 37, 40, 41, 42, 43, 44, 46, 48, 50, 52, 53, 54, 55, 56, 57, 58, 59, 61, 62, 63, 65, 65n. 72, 66, 68, 70, 71, 72, 73, 75, 80, 82, 83, 88, 89, 91, 92, 93, 96, 98, 100, 103, 105, 106, 110, 127, 130, 155, 156, 208, 239; and Shaw monument dedication speech, 19, 32–25; and travel, 18, 30, 40, 42, 46, 52, 54, 56, 60; and writing, 42, 62n. 69, 65, 69

James, William, III, "Billy" (son of

William James): and career, 98–99, 99n. 103, 101, 103, 108; and children, 100–101, 100n. 106, 106, 116, 232; and marriage, 20, 79–80, 81, 84–86, 89, 96, 213–14, 215–16; mentioned, 20, 31, 31n. 17, 35, 36, 47, 61, 64, 66, 67–68, 70, 74n. 84, 76, 78, 79, 87, 90, 91, 105, 228

Jekyll, Herbert, 256n. 24
Jekyll, Mrs. Herbert, 256, 258
Jerome, Jerome K., 71n. 80
Jobe, Steven H., 143n. 25
Jones, Beatrix. *See* Farrand, Beatrix Jones
Jones, Frederick Rhinelander, 4, 126, 127, 129, 164
Jones, Mary Cadwalader Rawle (Mrs. Frederick) "Minnie": and her childhood, 125–26; and daughter's marriage, 176, 176n. 66, 178–79; and her death, 129; and divorce, 2, 126–27; and health, 134, 148; and John Cadwalader's bequest, 129, 180–81; and marriage, 126; mentioned, 2, 3, 4, 9, 10, 12, 104, 231; and Scotland visits, 128, 135, 141–42, 144, 150, 151–52, 157, 159, 160–61, 162, 168, 170, 176, 177, 179; and servant's death, 138; and travel, 127–28, 163, 182, 184, 185, 186, 187, 234–35; and World War I, 111, 184–86; and writing, 127, 129. Works: *European Travel for Women*, 127; *Foch, the Winner of the War* (translation), 129; *Lantern Slides*, 125, 126; *Soul of the "C.R.B.", The* (translation), 129
Juliet (literary character), 192, 204

Kathleen, 232
Kemble, Frances Anne "Fanny," 101, 125, 139n. 20, 183n. 74
Kempe, Charles, 262
Kidd, Mrs. 229
Kidd, Minnie, 81, 89, 95, 103, 164, 219, 230
Kindermann, 166, 166n. 58, 168
Kinnicutt, Dr. Francis, 168, 168n. 59

Kipling, Rudyard, 136

Labiche, Eugene, 140n. 21
Lachesis (mythical figure), 228
*Lady Susan* (novel), 13
La Farge, Florence (Mrs. John), 136, 154
La Farge, John, 131, 131n. 14, 136, 153, 153n. 37, 157
Lang, Andrew, 253n. 22
Lang, Leonora Blanche Alleyne (Mrs. Andrew), 253, 253n. 22
Larpents, 215
Lawrence, Charley, 274
Lawrence, Louisa, 233–34, 243, 243n. 4, 249n. 15, 253, 255, 256, 258, 272, 273
Lawrence, Mary, 233–34, 243, 243n. 4, 249n. 15, 253, 255, 256, 258, 272, 273
Lawrence, Mrs. Charley, 274, 275
Lawrence, Trevor, 243n. 4
Lecky, Elizabeth (Mrs. William), 244, 244n. 5
Lecky, William Edward Hartpole, 244n. 5
Lee, Sir Sidney, 46, 46n. 51
Lee, Vernon (pseud.) *See* Paget, Violet
Lewis, Elizabeth Eberstadt (Mrs. George), 196, 196n. 5, 197
Lewis, R. W. B., 129n. 12
Lewis, Sir George Henry, 192, 196, 196n. 5, 197, 203
Lidell, Doll, 220
Lincoln, Abraham, 126
Lodge, Henry Cabot, 159n. 44
Lodge, Matilda F. Davis (Mrs. George) "Bessie," 176–77, 176n. 67
Longworth, Alice Roosevelt (Mrs. Nicholas), 145, 145n. 30
Longworth, Nicholas, 145, 145n. 30
Loring, Katherine, 4, 23, 23n. 3, 29, 31, 31n. 15, 63, 102n. 110, 107
Lowell, Abbot Lawrence, 47–49, 47n. 54, 74, 205
Lowell, Percy, 38
Lowrys, 234
Lubbock, Percy, 179, 179n. 71

Mackay, Donald James (first baron of Reay), 258n. 25
MacKaye, James Steele Morrison, 39n. 36
MacKaye, Maria Ellery, 39n. 36
MacKaye, Mrs., 39, 39n. 36
MacKaye, Percy, 39n. 36
MacKenzie, Sir James, 71, 71n. 82, 187
Macmillan, Lady Georgiana E. Warrin, 23, 23n. 4
Macmillan, Sir Frederick Orridge, 23, 23n. 4
MacMonnies, Frederick William, 64, 64n. 70
Maitland, Florence Fisher, 195, 195n. 3
Maitland, Frederick W. "Fuller," 195, 195n. 3
Marble, Abigail, 60, 60n. 67
Marble, Manton, 60, 60n. 67
Marble, Mrs., 141
Marriage, Victorian, 5–7
Marshall, Captain Charles H., 24n. 5
Mason, Alice, 54n. 60
Mason, Ellen, 209, 209n. 28, 210
Mason, Ida, 210
Masons, 54, 54n. 60
Matthew, Lady, 232
Maximillian "Max" (dog), 149
McClure, Samuel Sidney, 48–49, 48n. 55
McClure's Magazine, 48n. 55
Merriman, Mr. and Mrs. Daniel, 209
Meredith, George, 251, 251n. 19
Methuen & Co., 48
Meyer, George, 162, 162n. 46
Milnes-Gaskell, Charles George, 219, 219n. 26
Milnes-Gaskell, Mary, 219, 219n. 26
Minturn, 102, 102n. 110
Mirabeau, Gabriel, 232, 232n. 35
Morrell, Ottoline, 165n. 49, 216, 216n. 22
Morrell, Phillip, 216n. 23
Morse, Frances Rollins "Fanny," 83, 83n. 92, 209
Morton, Johnson, 158, 158n. 42
Myers, Eveleen Tennant, 65, 65n. 71

Myers, Frederic, 42, 42n. 43, 43, 44, 63, 65n. 71

Nadol, Mr. and Mrs. Charley, 213
Nation, 26n. 11, 32n. 21
Nevil, Lady D., 250
Newbigging, Alex, 152, 152n. 34
Nimrod, Miss. See Farrand, Beatrix Jones
Noakes, Burgess, 55, 55n. 61, 58, 79, 81, 103, 159, 164, 188, 204, 211, 219, 232–33, 232n. 36
North American Review, 38, 38n. 34, 48–49
Norton, Charles Eliot, 26, 26n. 11, 32n. 20, 35n. 26, 90n. 100
Norton, Elizabeth Gaskell "Lily," 90, 90n. 100
Norton, Grace, 32, 32n. 20, 61, 107, 192
Norton, Sara "Sally," 35, 35n. 26, 90, 90n. 100

Observer, 221
Ophelia (literary character), 204
Ormond, Mme., 63
Osler, Dr., 71, 85
Osmond, Gilbert (fictional character), 9–10, 24
Ouida (pseud.). See Ramée, Marie Louise de la

Paddington, Joan, 55, 56, 58, 89, 104, 161, 164, 192, 209–10, 211, 212–13, 213n. 19, 216, 217, 219, 229
Page, Lillian Biddle (Mrs. Walter), 113, 113n. 115
Page, Walter, 113, 113n. 115
Paget, Violet, 249, 249n. 16, 251n. 18
Pagets, 251, 251n. 18
Parnell, Charles Stewart, 25, 25n. 10
Passing of the Third Floor Back (play), 71, 71n. 80
Payson, Margaret, 109, 109n. 112, 111, 183, 231, 231n. 34
Perry, Lilla Cabot (Mrs. Thomas), 90, 90n. 101

Perry, Thomas Sargent, 90, 90n. 101, 107, 157
Peterson, Jeanne M., 13n. 5, 14nn. 10, 13, 14
Petty-Fitzmaurice, Henry Charles Keith (fifth marquis of Lansdowne), 269, 269n. 34
Pigott, Richard, 25, 25n. 10
Pinker, James, 54, 54n. 59, 108
Piper, Lenore, 62–63, 62n. 69, 65–66, 65n. 72, 69
*Pirates of Penzance* (opera), 240
Pollock, Lady Georgina Defell (Mrs. Frederick), 165n. 48, 212
Pollock, Sir Frederick, 165n. 48, 212
Pond Lecture Bureau, 140
Pontina (performer), 164
Pontos, 164
Pope, Theodate, 74, 74n. 86, 89, 98, 120–21
Porter, Margaret Mary James (Mrs. Robert Bruce Porter). *See* James, Margaret Mary
Porter, Robert Bruce (husband of Peggy James), 66, 66n. 74
Pratt, Mr. (antique dealer), 251
Prothero, Lady Margaret Frances Butcher (Mrs. George): and American visit, 192, 205; and her brother's death, 192, 207–8; and family, 191–92; and Henry James's move to London, 193, 220–21, 222, 223, 224–25, 226, 228–29; and marriage, 191–92; mentioned, 1, 4, 12, 115; and her social circle, 191, 192, 194, 195, 196, 198, 200, 201–2, 203, 204, 205, 212, 214–15, 217, 218–19, 220, 222, 232; and travel, 200, 202
Prothero, Sir George: and career, 191–92, 219n. 25; and health, 194, 195, 198, 199, 200, 202–3; mentioned, 1, 4, 115, 191, 192, 194, 197, 198, 200, 202–3, 204, 205, 207, 208, 208n. 16, 209, 209n. 17, 210, 212, 214, 218, 220, 225, 233, 235

*Quarterly Review,* 191–92, 219, 219n. 25

Ralli, Pandeli, 244, 247, 247n. 12, 250
Ramée, Marie Louise de la, 249, 249n. 17
Rand, Bay Emmet (Mrs. William). *See* Emmet, Bay
Rand, Christopher, 8
Rand, William Blanchard, 8, 74, 74n. 85
Ranee of Sarawak. *See* de Windt, Lady Margaret Alice
Rawle, Mary Cadwalader (Mrs. William), 125–26
Rawle, William Henry, 125–26
Reay, Lady (Mrs. Donald Mackay), 258, 258n. 25
Récouley, Raymond, 129
Reid, Mrs. Whitelaw, 146
Reid, Whitelaw, 146, 146n. 31
Rhodes, Harrison Garfield, 166, 166n. 57, 169
Richards, Annie Ashburner, 31, 31n. 15
Richet, Charles, 37, 37nn. 30, 32
Riddle, Theodate Pope. *See* Pope, Theodate
Ripley, Catharine Walsh Andrews, 24n. 7
Ripley, Helen, 24, 24n. 7
Ripley, Joseph, 24n. 7
Ritchie, Lady Anne Thackeray (Mrs. Richmond), 10–11, 221, 221n. 28, 230
Ritchie, Sir Richmond, 11, 221, 221n. 28
Roberts, Dr., 56, 59, 60, 62, 72
Robins, Elizabeth, 196, 196n. 7
Romeo (literary character), 192, 204
Roosevelt, Eleanor, 36n. 27
Roosevelt, Theodore, 145n. 30
Rosamund, 109, 109n. 112, 111
Rosebery, Lord, 10
Rotch, Arthur, 130
Rothenstein, Sir William, 192, 192n. 1
Roundells, Charles Saville, 253, 253n. 21
Roundells, Julia Elizabeth Anne Tollemache, 253, 253n. 21
Rousseau, Jean Jacques, 270, 270n. 35
Runnells, Alice. *See* James, Alice Runnells

Undine (mythical figure), 259n. 27; 259–60

Vanderbilt, George, 141, 145n. 30
Vanderbilt, Mrs. George, 145, 145n. 30
Venus de Milo, 240
Verver, Maggie (fictional character), 4
Vetch, Fleda (fictional character), 4
Victoria, Queen, 5, 34n. 25, 44–45, 240
Vincent, Captain Dacre, 192, 200, 200n. 12, 201n. 14
Vincent, Margaret (Mrs. Dacre), 192, 200, 200n. 12, 201n. 14, 205, 215, 219, 222, 232
*Virginian, The* (novel), 183n. 74
Von Glehn, Jane Emmet (Mrs. Wilfred), 99, 99n. 105, 114
Von Glehn, Wilfred, 99, 99n. 105, 114

Wagner, Richard, 163, 259
Walsh, Alexander Robertson, 60n. 66
Walsh, Catherine (Aunt Kate), 24–25, 24nn. 5, 6, 25, 36, 95
Walsh, Elizabeth Robertson "Lila," 24–25, 24n. 6, 67, 73
Walsh, Louisa, 67
Ward, Dorothy, 153, 153n. 38
Ward, Mary Augusta Arnold (Mrs. Humphry), 129, 153n. 38, 184, 184n. 75
Ward, Thomas Humphrey, 153n. 38, 184, 184n. 75
Warner, Joseph Bangs, 114, 114n. 116
Warren, Herbert, 75
Warwick, Lady, 78
Waterlow, Alice Pollock (Mrs. Sydney), 165, 165n. 48, 192, 200, 201n. 14, 204, 205, 212, 217, 217n. 24
Waterlow, Sir Sydney, 165, 165n. 48, 192, 200, 201n. 14, 204, 205, 206, 212, 213, 217, 217n. 24
Wells, H. G., 115, 143, 143n. 26, 144; *Kipps,* 143, 143n. 27
Wendell, Mr. and Mrs. Barrett, 209, 209n. 17
Wentworth, Lord, 7
Wharton, Edith: and divorce, 128, 160, 173n. 64; and husband's trou-

bles, 154, 156, 156n. 41, 158, 160, 161, 168, 168n. 59, 172–74; mentioned, 5, 87, 89, 92, 102n. 107, 126, 128, 129, 131, 134–35, 137, 138, 145, 148, 152, 154, 156, 158, 160, 161, 163, 164–65, 166n. 56, 168, 170, 172, 176–77, 178, 179, 179n. 71, 183, 184, 185, 186, 188, 188n. 78, 203, 217, 218; and Walter Berry, 139, 139n. 18. Works: *Crucial Instances,* 128; "Eyes, The," 173n. 64; *Fruit of the Tree, The,* 152–53, 152n. 36; *House of Mirth* (novel), 152–53; *House of Mirth* (play), 148; *Touchstone, The,* 128; *Valley of Decision, The,* 131
Wharton, Edward Robbins "Teddy": and illness, 154, 156, 156n. 41, 158, 160, 161, 168, 168n. 59, 172–74; mentioned, 5, 128, 145, 152
White, Derek, 229
White, Flora, 229
White, Henry "Harry," 136, 136n. 16, 184, 184n. 76
White, J. William, 58, 58n. 65, 139
White, Margaret Stuyvesant Rutherford (Mrs. Henry), 184n. 76
White, Mrs. J. William, 58
Whites, 158–59
Whitlock, Brand, 113, 113n. 114, 118
Whitman, Walt, 144
Whitridge, Frederick, 144n. 28, 153, 153n. 39
Whitridge, Lucy Arnold (Mrs. Frederick), 144, 144n. 28, 153n. 39
Wiess, Miss, 37
Williams, Orlando C., 217n. 24
Wilson, Woodrow, 99
Wister, Owen, 139n. 20, 183, 183n. 74
Wister, Sarah, 139, 139n. 20
Wolseley, Frances: mentioned, 234, 240, 241, 249, 255, 255n. 23, 257, 259, 262, 267–68, 272, 273; and suitors, 249, 252, 252n. 20
Wolseley, General Garnet: and his career, 239, 240, 242, 242n. 3, 244, 246n. 11, 261, 261n. 29, 269, 269n. 34, 272; his death, 241, 276n. 37; *Decline and Fall of Napoleon,*

Wolseley, General Garnet (*continued*)
272, 272n. 36; mentioned, 4, 6,
30, 239, 240, 241, 244, 248, 250,
254–55, 255n. 23, 259, 261, 267,
273, 275

Wolseley, Lady Louisa: and antiques,
240, 251, 252; and her background,
240; and bookbinding, 240, 245,
247; and charity, 253; and domestic
arrangements, 249, 250–52, 265–
66, 268, 272, 273; and entertaining, 239, 240, 254, 256–57; and

husband's career, 240, 241–47, 248,
261, 265, 267, 269; mentioned, 4,
6, 10, 12, 30; and travel, 246–47,
259

Wood, Derwent, 102n. 107, 182
Wood, Mary, 182n. 73
Wordsworth, William, 51

York, Duchess of, 41

Zanzigs, 197, 197n. 11
Zola, Émile, 36n. 28, 141